ALIENS WITHIN
OUR OWN SELVES

BASED ON A TRUE STORY

By

Ruth Ann Friend

I

Aliens Within
Our Own Selves

Based on a True Story
by
Ruth Ann Friend

Library of Congress Registration #1-4292980091

First Edition

All Rights Reserved

ISBN: 978-0-9898255-4-2 Soft Cover
ISBN: 978-0-9898255-5-9   E-Book

Friend Publishing

Ruth Ann Friend
My Web Site
WWW.UniversalConversations.com

Cover Art and Design by Laura Moyar of bookcovermachine.com

BOOKS
By
RUTH ANN FRIEND

ALIENS WITHIN
OUR OWN SELVES
Based on a True Story

A Mother and son's experiences of daily living with
Extraterrestrials, Aliens, and other universal life forms.

THE STORY OF DAVID
Based on a True Story

This is about two people who reincarnated back to Earth because
of their promise and covenant they made to The Creator.
An amazing story of miracles you will remember…

UNDER THE RAINBOW CROSSING
Based on a True Story

The haunting of a heartland home and the
spiritual journey that followed…

ANGELS ON EARTH
GUIDEPOST MAGAZINE
THE END OF THE LINE
Based on a True Story

1998 JULY EDITION

This book I have written is not always in a chronological order although I have done my best to ensure the accuracy of the time frames. Everything written about our experiences is completely true. This is about life and what some of us have chosen to do living on this planet. I have been guided to write our truth as the other side has directed, which is in separate portions for the readers to be able to understand it more clearly, since our worlds are many.

Our story is about living an extremely unusual life on this planet Earth, with choices to travel to unknown realms through multi-dimensional travel with the Extraterrestrials that have schooled my son and me. We both have been supplied with amazing universal information from these Universal Beings on a continuous basis with their messages we are passing to the people on Earth. Are you brave enough to really want to know the experiences some of you may have chosen which holds the truth of our own planet, the vast Universes, and worlds beyond?

Hardships often prepare ordinary people, for an extraordinary destiny.

C. S. Lewis

Those who try to walk the path of others will never follow their own, to believe in our self is a virtue learning to let go and accept that others have their lessons and hardships to grow from and the experiences are theirs and theirs alone. One cannot make another's life as their own, we are all responsible for only ourselves. As we grow the eyes open, and as they open, we begin to see into ourselves and others around us opening the heart and soul which in turn sits us free, for those who believe shall be set free as the meek shall inherit the earth. Let each loved one pass on their journey for each came as to experience life's journey our help can only hinder growth if the growth is interfered with in the hardships, the difficult times, when one tries to change the outcome. As it is sometimes painful and difficult to not pamper and please know when to leave it alone. Know when to let one grow and develop and not be under another's ideas and control for this stunt's the growth just to please ourselves and how we think it should be.

EDGAR MITCHELL
ASTRONAUT

It has occurred to me that human destiny is still very uncertain, that the veneer of civilization is yet exceedingly thin, and our current actions are not sustainable. Dr. Mitchell at age 85 passed away February 4th, 2016, on the eve of the 45th anniversary of his February 5th, 1997 lunar landing.

During their return to Earth, Edgar Mitchell was staring out of the window of Apollo 14 at the Sun, Moon, Earth and Stars. Later in a 2007 documentary "Shadow of the Moon", he said, "Suddenly I realized that the molecules of my body and the molecules of the space craft and the molecules in the bodies of my partners were prototyped and manufactured in some ancient generation of stars. And that was an overwhelming sense of oneness, of connectedness. It wasn't them and us, it was, "That's Me! That's all of it. It's one thing!" And it was accompanied by an ecstasy, a sense of – Oh my god, wow yes! - An insight, an epiphany!

In Edgar Mitchell's 1996 book "The Way of the Explorer" he writes: "Believing as I do that the Universe is an intelligent System, and understanding the absurd and tragic feat that may await us, I have wondered if we are prepared for our own survival, if our own collective consciousness is yet highly enough evolved?"

FORWARD

I want to thank my children and family for their love and support. I know it has not been a completely ordinary life for them with me as their mother. Especially, with their brother and me working together in other Universal realms of existence, but this has never stopped our strong flow of love for us together as a family.

My son David and I have been bestowed with certain gifts from, The Creator/God and the Angels of Ministry since our birth. We were given psychic abilities to see things other people cannot see, and to hear what others cannot hear, which are hidden from them along with the spirits of others who walk among us everywhere. These gifts are not always easy for even us to understand at times; though we know our work here on earth is from the highest Intelligence of love there is, which the Creator of all is. Our spiritual teachers to us are mostly known by others as, The Heavenly Councils, and Christ Light Beings along with the realms of Angels, Archangels, Spiritual Guides and Teachers. Among all of these, there are many other Heavenly Universal Beings of the light we are well acquainted with who are also working together with us called, Extraterrestrials/Aliens, and we reach out to all of them daily with our loving thanks from our heart.

I appreciate those friends and loved ones we have known before in past lives that have returned to earth and are in company with us once more to take this path again together. I thank my beloved son David who crossed over in 2008 to return home to an eternal birth and life.

After my son's last breath, I witnessed him in spirit. He was of pure white light filled with silver sparkling rays; he was more alive than ever beginning his transition. I watched as his beautiful soul passed into a new birth of a deathless life in another glorious place surrounded by our past loved Ones, the Angels, and Great Council of Extraterrestrials of Christ Light Beings all waiting to escort him home. He came onto this earth as a human, but he was much more than that, he is a Radiant Being of Pure White Light among the Stars he came from.

Not many may remember the promise they made before returning to earth but through meditation and prayer they can reawaken the memory of their own revelation. This is one of the Christ Light Beings critical points they are seeking, is to reawaken us to the process of our reunion with the Creator and to help save this earth that man is destroying.

DEDICATIONS

I give my heartfelt dedication to our Divine universal family for giving my son and me the gifts of knowledge, wisdom, strength, and courage with total belief in a higher power who is the Ultimate Intelligence of love who created us all. Through my own earthly experience of incarnations, it is another chance to evolve with what I have chosen with my freewill. This is about the connection with our parents, children, grandchildren, great grandchildren, the mates we each choose, schooling, jobs, and life in general finishing it out with an illusion of death, which is only a transition back to a new birth, a new beginning, and for all my choices I am eternally grateful.

Remember, because we each are different is not what makes the love in a heart it only has to do with the soul within you. The soul is not concerned about color, race, religion, man or woman, gay or straight, it is about what you feed your soul with, and the key is love.

PREFACE

This book is very important to our earth's future and my hope is that you who read it will embrace our remarkable journey. Everything I have written is of the experiences my son David and I have shared while living between this world and the Beyond in an amazing, beautiful unlimited vast universe. The reason I am completely dedicated to writing this book is because of the promise my son and I made to the Supreme Infinite Intelligent of Love, our Creator.

Our story is something I never gave thought to doing many years ago which will produce some very sensitive and important information from certain Universal Beings which can explain and hopefully answer ones many questions. In this way they can bring their superior knowledge to you here on earth to speak their own words to you through this book.

You may hopefully understand how my son and I were learning to handle our lives by living a daily life with the ETs and coexisting between earth and other spheres in the universe. This is how we were being taught to remember what we once knew by the Extraterrestrial Christ Light beings.

This secret life we were living would continue for most of our lives to experience the unseen and unknown realms of existence that mankind does not even realize are there. There would be no conceivable way for us to explain our lives until we were told to. We ourselves have been in a learning school we did not always understand; but through time it became quite clear to us by the experiences we had throughout our lives.

This book has years of sensitive material in it to let others know there are other universal beings that have existed since the beginning of Creation, and many of these beings are waiting to help humankind here on earth. You will not only read of how we managed our lives as normal, but at the same time sharing our lives between dimensions into other universal galaxies and other beings, which was like a science fiction movie to us!

The episodes which have been written are not only based on true experiences but are also to reveal unheard of information coming forth from other universal beings of a superior intelligence. These beings have taken our world under their care as much as they can and agreed on doing this but, time is getting away from us here on Earth, and they want to help us before our world is destroyed by mankind.

Through this book universal information will be revealed so people may learn "Love is not only alive in our earth world; it is everywhere, and in everything that has ever been created". Many of the universal benevolent Extraterrestrial beings are standing by waiting for us here on earth to *"wake up!"*

INTRODUCTION

One doesn't always know what is real in our World

As the Bible tells us: *"In the beginning: God created the heavens and the earth"* which is what some of us humans have been taught and believe in, and that an amazing infinite supreme intelligence of love, who we call Lord, created our race and all other matter and life. We are humans, breathing, and living on this planet who can have thoughts of our earthly experiences, and feel that there is more in our universe besides us. The universe is very large, perhaps limitless, without ever ending, and the earth is actually a very small part of it. Surely, there must be more?

Millions of people believe that there is much more in the way of life that exists in the universe than just us here on planet earth. I don't ask anyone to believe the same as I do, and since there are no records of the very beginning, and of course there could not have been, we came from somewhere and are living on this planet sharing an earthly experience.

Our earth is sitting in a universal *never-ending space* where numerous other planets, solar systems and worlds exist and perhaps there are more beings in it. Most may have no positive idea, but through our experiences we know there are! This idea is becoming better known because of strange events happening to others that occur on a regular basis. Such as, unexplained lights, strange mutilated animals found in fields with certain parts removed by precise surgical procedures, unknown anomalies, and unexplained sightings of objects in the skies called UFO's the world over. With all of this, we don't want to forget the amazing Crop Circles, reported abductions, lost or gained time by those who report contact from beyond' and more. People sense we are not alone, and no one person has the answers which can't be identified in our world.

Several scientific researchers along with the millions of people have concluded that *"we weren't the only beings created."* I can only vouch for my son and I since we have plenty of evidence that points to other beings in a never-ending space beyond because of our years with Extraterrestrial experiences and the proof we kept in secret.

Many of today's well-known scientists, archaeologist, military, NASA, reported abductees, researchers of science, and many other investigators, including typical citizens of earth which includes your ordinary housewife, are only a few from all walks of life that are searching for answers about the *"unknown and UFO's"*.

There are many unanswered questions over the world such as, *"Where do the Crop Circles come from?* England alone has the most crop circles found in farmers' fields and sometimes more than one, two or three appear in a day! What are these unknown objects in our skies that move with superior speed and agility to our aircraft some pilots and people report? Why do they come here, and how do they move through the universes? The questions go on and on and no one really has the answers except perhaps those who have had contact from beyond, and videos of the UFO objects thousands of people have taken.

Even with these, there are many other kinds of amazing proof presented such as the ancient unexplainable findings that directly point to another type of beings. This points to an Intelligence who was once here, you must question, what else is there? The people over the world who decide to come forward and tell of an experience must be stressed to the point of exhaustion at times with the teasing they probably get. The experts work very hard to bring ancient findings to the public with their years of hard work, what more does it take to get the truth across?

There is much more evidence today than ever before that has been found and verified proving that much of history is wrong! There are many videos and pictures that are taken of UFOs by individuals over the world classified as *"unknown objects"* which continues to take modern science into new uncharted territories for years with the question, *"what and who is in our skies?"*

Because so many millions of people are asking these important questions they are having on this subject, I am writing this very personal story my son and I have experienced throughout our lives but have kept in secret. What happened to both of us over the years regarding the subject of UFO'S and abductions has been more than real, it happened! And now, the time has come to share these true experiences with others to let you know that many universal beings do exist, perhaps in the Trillions.

We ourselves believe without a doubt that *"not only were we humans created but so were other Beings"* this is because we have lived it! We are not alone in deciding that our rare stories needed to be shared and this is where the ETs and Universal Councils have led us to share their messages and information to the public, which may possibly lead to answers and help for others, and those who have had their own abductions or contact, and UFO experiences.

We have been chosen to be the ETs voices to bring their messages and words they have provided us. One important point that I would like the reader to know is; the messages from the universal beings to share with the world have not been changed in any way I have written them exactly as the ET beings and heavenly beings gave to us. We have not changed the wording to make the messages more grammatically correct or to fix spelling errors. In the beginning it may have been hard to read what was written by them, but we tried our best to ensure accuracy. These messages are in their own words and thoughts they have learned from humans over the centuries from when they first visited this planet and helped create history on Earth.

My son David passed over several years ago, but I am here to tell our story and continue our work. It has been difficult without him to share this life's work, knowing many will never understand. But those seeking the truth will and this is all that matters.

We were taught how to communicate mentally and physically with different species of alien beings most of our lives. These beings are from other dimensions; star, solar systems, and other planets beyond with most never heard of. The information I am writing of is how we interacted with them for certain reasons, and our travel together since we both were children.

The extraordinary happenings we have had put us onto a new road in life and nothing of what we have endured surfaced while under hypnosis to bring out our experiences and their information. Our experiences with our family of ETs have been firsthand. I am an absolute true believer that hypnosis is an extremely important tool to access ones hidden problems leading to one's memories and healing. I understand this because I also practice hypnosis, but it sometimes can be difficult. I believe negative or positive experiences people have had with UFO's and other universal beings may many times be brought out, which can provide help to release the fear a person might have. It is sometimes very possible to bring out one's past lives finding answers to who one was in another time and place. These past lives may be carried over causing problems in today's world; I can't say enough of how much hypnosis can help people in distress, with habits, and loss of memory. Each person is different, our minds are like a great storehouse, a library of all recorded information each person holds, which at times can be assessable to finding answers.

My son and I met one of the greatest hypnosis teachers in our history years ago who was amazing, and her name is Delores Cannon who is very well known around the world. Delores helped many people and held her own UFO Conference in Eureka Springs, Arkansas each year, for many years, which was attended with people from all over the world and she will never be forgotten. Delores is not with us anymore, but she was a dedicated amazing teacher making new breakthroughs in her own work to help others. And her beloved devoted family has kept her UFO Conference going since.

Our Journey Together

The accounts my son and I have had are written in detail and I have taken great care to use the exact information from the time contact was made with other Beings from in the universe. I have kept journals and recordings of our strange involvement living between earth and a phenomenal place we know as the Universe, and most of what we experienced in our world is never supposed to happen! Nevertheless, we found ourselves in our blessed agreement and this journey was something we never expected to experience in a million years in our human part of the mind! We weren't even who we thought we were as a regular human being, so I believe you will be taken by surprise, even hard pressed to find a similar true story with the same experiences we have had! Through all we have endured, our lives changed dramatically, we came to realize our mind had to have a great defensive barrier built into it that only recognized what we have been taught to believe in and have been conditioned to. In other words, we had been living in a man-made existence called

Earth which is our home, but in our case our life had been a much larger part of several worlds!

One day it was suddenly time for me to completely remember the entire agreement in place of only knowing parts of it; this is when suddenly the bottom fell out of everything, I thought was real in this part of my world. It was as if a light switch had been turned on pushing back the darkness and clearly, I heard the words: *"Let There Be Light!"* This was a special light, a different light, for us to investigate other worlds beyond man-kinds, just like that! What I am talking about now is *"sharing an amazing life between worlds"* so please read on and you will see what I mean.

Our story cannot be told in a few words or pages with what I must tell you, our lives had been going on mostly in an *"illusion of a world"* we chose, called earth. Although the veil is becoming thinner, we had been living mostly in several different dimensions! At first, I lost sleep over what was happening on a regular basis, it was unbelievably intense to accept this enormous information plus leaving my imagination in suspense. Not knowing then what the future would be for us there would be no turning back, since our lives would never be the same! This was something that could not be changed, it just WAS...

Our Beginning

Before I go any further, I want to introduce our universal families that are known by many others as *"Extraterrestrials"*, but we call them *"ETs"* for short. There are many, *probably millions if not trillions* throughout the entire unending worlds and universes. Those that we work together with are of the benevolent spiritual nature and have our complete devotion who are called *Christ Light beings.*

My son David and I continued to be educated from these very intelligent universal beings that come from other places in our universe! Nothing terrifying has ever happened to us such as abductions by any force, and we have never felt that we were a victim. Everything happening was agreed on beforehand, and by beforehand, I mean in another time and space with the deep connection we have together that was happening to us right on schedule. This part of our lives was something we were going to be doing with them on this planet, which is very important, something so phenomenal it seemed as if I was living through someone else's make believe life.

As you may have guessed we did not dare speak of this to anyone if so, who would have believed it anyway? We were busy in universal school with our heavenly teachers, and ET's of The Christ Light, which may throw you off balance, but you will understand later. Some days I felt quite isolated with this part of our chosen life and I thanked the Creator often that my son and I were sharing the same experiences together. And even though he was terminally ill we were uplifted with our exciting travels of learning and schooling, and many times the ET's worked on my son and helped him with his illness. This is how his miracles of healing came to him through these Extraterrestrial/ Christ Light Beings of love.

We lived the days as anyone does doing ordinary things but spending our time mostly at doctors' offices and in hospitals for years. Sometimes my son was at the hospital three times a week. Unless we were with our family, the ET's came often to take us with them; so many of our nights were very busy with them in travel. They came to us even when I stayed beside my son at the hospitals which I will explain as we go along. This was a life we led in secret even from our loved ones.

Our normal part of life was with our immediate family which is quite large so we were together every chance we could have, and our spirits were high with so much love. I went through my household duties and all the typical things one does, but I never felt I belonged to my earth side, especially as more time passed. My son knew why we committed ourselves before birth to our promise we made with the Creator, but I had to figure it out by pulling out my memories that were beginning to flood into my mind. It was the love with our family here that mattered greatly to my son and me knowing we had returned to Earth to be together as in past times to do this work, but we did not mention this to our loved ones yet, one day we would...

Moving Back in Time

Moving back in time to the day I discovered David had been having similar experiences as myself was long before he became ill and living in another state. On that day we were talking by phone

XV

and he shared an experience he had about a UFO! From then on, we shared our experiences together finding out we were the same.

In my story you will discover apparently there are those of us who have *chosen* to go with other beings through our free will. When you are a small child your memory is mostly taken away, one is not to remember because it is not the right time, but the memories are stored in the mind for when they are to be brought out. More than likely one may think in the beginning, these were only dreams of contact with something else until it becomes real for the chosen ones. In time, we both regained our memories and were learning why the timing for us had to be right, nothing happens before it should, if we believe this or not.

Our story begins when the ET's first arrived to re-introduce themselves to us in order to gain our trust by bringing out our stored memories. After this, we felt perfectly *"normal"* with them and the other spiritual beings who had always been our heavenly teachers. We went with them to travel each time they wanted us for *class* without any force or fear, and of our own free will.

At first, it was a total shock to find out we had chosen certain lessons and promises we ourselves had made before we entered our earth cycle! It has been surprising to find out nothing enters our life until it is the right time for each soul's development, and that everything we choose is agreed on before with The Great Council of Beings from the Christ Light. This is not about man-made religion this is about spiritual beings that live in our universe who are of a supreme intelligence of love our Creator also created.

By finding out what we really are a part of a little at a time was all we could handle, this is when our *learning portions* came to us, with an incredible journey ahead which blew my mind. I would find out everything happening had nothing to do with imagination. Things I did not remember before began to come to me in visions and from the universal beings we had contact with. On occasion I was *reprogrammed* to remember the past, and that's why I was having the experiences I was! I needed more time to understand why we were only given so much information in these portions and my thoughts were heard immediately. We were told they were preparing us with small portions, for reasons that made sense when it was explained. The ET's told us: *"The human mind is conditioned to a human way we would have to be patient the human mind cannot process quickly*". Neither of us was ever rushed when we were taken into the Universal School where we received only kindness and gratitude thanking us as their honorable students! This was a complete surprise to be called this, especially many times throughout the years we were known by different universal names.

I have been able to discover an enormous awakening; given to me through *powerful* universal information which has proved the mind is like a huge, vast, and limitless library we call the *Akashi* records. I have always known about the records; we both have gone into that dimension when needed so this description made perfect sense to us. This is where all information of every being is stored.

This is the only way I know as an introduction to describe the starting of our phenomenal journey and reunion to our other family in detail, which my late son David and I have been a part of throughout our entire lives. This was a lost remembrance for my mind at first, but the evidence has since been made clear to me, and I would never deny we had made this plan together before this lifetime! By coming into this earth, we had been empowered with psychic gifts as in past lives before, but still our reunion with the ETs and the other universal worlds swept me off my feet! We were waking up to another amazing commitment on a higher level of our own existence of consciousness. My son and I loved our ties with the ETs we were from, and once everything settled down in our minds, we were ready to advance to learning what we once knew.

I need to comment that those of us who are working together in the universal worlds are working to help achieve a great earthly change, so those who are in power acknowledge that when they lift the curtain to the truth. Then people on earth may learn to not judge so fast and leave the killing on our planet behind. Then the door of opportunity has opened to pass into a new way of living and to grow to a new spiritual level. Many people for many years have been working towards a higher level to help earth, so keep on seeking and keep your mind open to new possibilities of a new world in the future.

In today's world Scientists, Explorers, Astronauts, and many other experts are proving *we have kept our eyes closed.* Look at ancient history, the discoveries of ancient finds many thousands of years old no one knew of until man's breakthrough. The two most important discoveries are done with DNA and Carbon dating. These alone has proven what we thought we knew all along was mostly *inaccurate!* For some time, courageous people have written and shared their discoveries revealing the truths found in our world proven by carbon dating and DNA, and these do not lie! Some minds are set to find things you thought you knew is not even close to being correct, and this is hard for many people to ever accept so much in the old ways were wrong. Will history books be changed from old information to the new proven facts my opinion is, "I doubt it!" That would tell people worldwide everything many people thought we knew was wrong! In this case, I am specifically speaking of not only earth, but of the existence of other life forms, other beings, planets, universes, star and solar systems, and worlds, it is endless!

This is where organized religion steps in for some people not wanting to think there are others in space who are divine workers created with love. Many holds to their beliefs of the old ways we have been taught and known of for generations, and this is what people have known to be true! It is time to move forward with the truth for unbelievers.

God our Creator is the Infinite Supreme Intelligence of Love and Jesus is absolutely without a doubt the loving Christ who had made his choices on Earth which most believe. The reason I bring this up is that there are other Universal beings of the Christ Light who are also the Creators workers, along with the Angels/Archangels and others. But there are those here on Earth who does not want to believe there are other universal beings that have also been created. And my question is, why not? I feel it is because many of the teachings in the past have been taught this way by those who are afraid of what they do not know and cannot understand, and those who are in power to control others. Most people have been taught *"we here on earth are the only life that has been created"*, what a waste that would be in a never-ending beautifully created universe! Thinking there is only this one small planet with life called Earth!

The universal beings who work beside of us we know as *"Christ Light beings!"* They are more than the names many give them as Extraterrestrials or Aliens furthermore the beings who come to work with us are loving and precious, and if they were not, we would not have anything to do with them! We may see them in different bodies along with other universal beings called by other names, but they are all under God's protection, the same as the ones we know as Angels therefore, I repeat, *"We were all created at the same time"*.

The positive ETs fight evil the same as the Angels and Archangels and the rest of God's creations of his love. The negative and evil exist in the universes and other worlds; the balance of the universe is of positive and negative.

The Seeker Continued

To be a *seeker* means the door is opened for those of us who are ready to venture out and explore the unthinkable. There are millions of people who naturally assume we here are the only beings that exist because... this is what we have been taught all our life. This alone creates fear of the *unknown* and an enormous *disbelief* since this is not something taught in our schools, churches, or anyplace else. But others and I have evidence to prove other beings do exist as I mentioned in the above paragraph. I say this, because of the experiences myself, my son, and the thousand/millions of others around the world are having that are true. And others who have the evidence brought out through hypnosis or direct contact of some way. A person doesn't lie under hypnosis unless they already are a habitual liar in the first place and knowing this, most stories are extremely accurate! What do I mean by evidence? These items are evidence, pictures, video tapes, missing time, gaining time, finding oneself in a strange location without memory of how you got there, why you are experiencing this, memory of being on a Craft, being taken in contact, time travel, and seeing other beings are only a few. Why society has made us so fearful seems clear to me, there are those in power who still deny other beings exist for their own benefit which is another story.

What fear can do?

I remember I was a true loner growing up and felt I didn't fit in anywhere. I was able to see and hear many things others couldn't and at sleep overs while growing up I begged my little girl friends to stay awake until I went to sleep first. So much of what I experienced I didn't understand yet and later when my life began to change to another level was sometime after I married and bought the home I live in today. I remember at times strange thoughts and memories would suddenly come to me that I didn't understand. This was happening to me coming from an Intelligence I did not remember that was connecting me with memories I had known before. Therefore, I felt different than seemingly normal people since I was a young child.

I guess you could say I was *extremely sensitive,* I never felt I fit in anyplace I was oddly different than my friends and those I met... I was comfortable by staying in the background and strange as it was at the same time, I wanted to be included by others I wanted to fit in, but how, what was wrong with me? All of this often brought me down to a low opinion of myself and feeling misplaced. I recall getting in trouble when I was small, telling my mother *"I wasn't a part of the family, I didn't even look like them!"* I didn't do this again because I would recall my spanking from then on, but I knew something wasn't right. I had odd dreams of floating around up high and later float back down into my bed. I don't know all the in-between memory, but I loved the feeling of my strange dream, because *I was so free and happy with whomever and wherever I went. I loved going on these trips.*

In later years when drifting off to sleep I would catch myself thinking *"they are coming tonight I would journey tonight, but with who, journey where?"* I was curious but not afraid; I only felt a kindness, an attachment of some kind to something. I knew that if I told anyone about my feelings people would think I was crazy, but something always led me to keep searching forward to find the answers. I felt drawn to whatever this was with a strange kind of immense love and my strong connection to this unseen puzzle.

I knew at times to put everything away I thought about there was nothing I could do, and I should try to forget those silly dreams I had. As I became older the dreams came for a while and at other times they didn't, or I didn't recall them going on with my everyday life. I don't recall ever being afraid except for a few times as a child of not understanding any of this; since the fear factor wasn't something that could hold me hostage. I didn't know it was also the spirit and paranormal world that sometimes frightened me as a small child with the other things I was also experiencing. When I was grown, I remember a dream state when a voice told me: *"The human mind can only accept so much at a time so after I had digested each lesson, I would be given more"*.

This kind of information continued steadily on with a slow 100 percent change in me. I didn't know I was getting reacquainted with other worlds on the other side I had forgotten! I was being prepared then for my adult life and a lot was going on in my mind, I didn't know I was redeveloping my senses to a higher level. As I looked back much later, this was plain to see…

These things were to help me with my life on earth to learn there is much more than just earth I had someplace else to go, places unknown. I was taught with more words I could hear at times *"we humans are all a part of the whole, a part of everything and everyone, as a circle is with no beginning and no ending."* Circles seemed to be very important I would see them often. What an important statement this would turn out to be! I knew somehow in my future there would be amazing world events to come tied to all of this. It was at this time in my life I suddenly became extremely open through my spiritual life more than ever, and when the time came years later to teach others I taught *"universal truths"* along with Reiki energy techniques to the many I met.

Universal Teachings from the ETs to Us

The many gifts my son David and I received went *"hand in hand"* with the universal spiritual beings who have been assigned to us together with our past over loved ones who minister to us on our journey. We were taught that when a person can keep the mind open and practice positive thinking with their love there is nothing impossible, because the universe responds to our needs. This works with how one thinks so be careful with the thoughts you send out to the universe in how you think. Most of us realize negative thoughts and needless worry can bring you down into a negative level so your life stays the same or even worse. This is a main lesson; to not let others push your buttons and put you down you are a *powerful* being more than you can know.

Using grace to those in your life will improve bringing what you may need, even to those who are negative, and then move on. This doesn't mean one has to connect with them personally but to treat anyone deliberately cruel is never the way to go. Using grace is a great gift and will improve bringing what you need to learn for creating your own life. We know there are the devastating times, the steppingstones we must fight to keep going but do not let them block the way of your path. To grow we need never give up, this is a very hard part for anyone, but no matter the pain keep going, this is the most important time for growth. Try and remember to keep on moving forward for it is more important than the end results, these were some truths we were being taught by our universal family.

Our story will explain what we have learned of value and love with respect, knowing each one of us as a human has an *unseen help* standing by to help us who loves us unconditionally waiting to be recognized. This superior help we have is through different spiritual beings that have existed since creation from our beginning *eons ago.* They have a supreme intelligence beyond any human being; some are called *Aliens, Extraterrestrials, Angels, Heavenly beings, Christ Light beings, Archangels, Teachers and Guides.* But on the other hand there are negative beings so be aware, these beings have taken others from this planet by force, and those many people are called *"abductees"* who have endured excruciating things by these species who are a negative source of a *warring nature* from outer space...

Would you be surprised to know there are many battles going on in the universe between good and evil? We have been told of this battle ground by the space beings, and those on earth have no idea it is ever occurring! This again brings me to the main point of where we are at this time in history with the many thousands of UFO sightings people reported. For many years people have been reporting them with frequency; thousands can't be lying, can they? Why would anyone want to put their character on the line, their credibility, and everything dear to them to come forward to tell of a UFO experience if what they experienced was not their own personal truth? No one wants to seem like a person who imagines things, but each person has their own personal truth to experience with the right to share it. So, try to be open you can continue to learn something you may not expect, and find the answers you have been looking for. If one doesn't learn something in life my own feeling is *"if you feel in your lifetime you did not learn anything this time, welcome back, to learn again".*

I have been directly informed by the benevolent *Beings and Extraterrestrials* in our partnership that they will forever watch over and protect us, and will come when we need them to intervene in a bad situations, I found all we needed do was *call them* with our own thoughts called *telepathy*. These are things I want to say to you up front, I hope this book opens a new doorway of understanding for you the reader, and gives you time to explore a possibility that we here on earth are not alone, and the only beings created.

My feelings are to tell you, at least pay attention to the ET phenomenon that has been recognized throughout the world by *millions of people* from government to ordinary citizens for many years.

Now, onto a hidden secret life my son David and I have which came to be so *extraordinary* some days it was almost too much for us. There were times I felt I had to be dreaming it up into a fantasy land, but this would have been the easy way out! I eventually came to fully believe I could not deny what we both are a part of. Eventually, I dared asked myself *"what is the real world, is it here, or out in space somewhere?"* The way I made sense of what was happening was the connection we had with our sources, the heavenly spiritual teachers and guides, dream states of visions, and most of all our many visits in travel with the positive ET universal beings!

It wasn't often I seemed to get off track, but help was waiting for me when I did, we always knew we had help and guidance from these heavenly loving beings. Let's begin when the ETs knew to restart the old hidden memories that I had forgotten along with the personal experiences beyond anything I could ever have imagined.

What was about to happen I would deal with, so I began to set aside a part of my life into motion that had been waiting. Early on, I was stunned at what was happening in my worlds as you or anyone else may have been and eventually I couldn't rationalize so much happening with the experiences any longer. You would think after this much time I would not have my moments, but I am also a Being living in this human world. I finally gave into it all by letting myself be completely submersed to the startling occurrences that sometimes overwhelmed me. It was time for us to begin our work with a new reminder from the other side advising us, we were to continue a familiar life here, which was changing my son and me into a more curious, seeking, evolving person with many questions. We were trying to understand what our human and alien part would be like in the far future, which made us who we are and in our own struggle to understand our part living in different worlds.

I will explain how our forgotten memories were given to us a little at a time along with the true discovery of ourselves, and then years later I was told by the Beings to write their story! The whole concept is, we wanted to serve as a *vehicle* on our mission to help others who may be having similar experiences to help and teach them what is real. When you read of our unlimited connections to other universes and worlds beyond hopefully you will understand more of our strange lives. Each one of us needs understanding and a positive belief system and we were fortunate to have had one another through lifetimes to experience the many experiences we have had!

Our lives have been unique especially as mother and son working together with the ET's. You may be quite shocked when you join in our life journey with our universal family. You may call them ET's, Extraterrestrials, Christ Light Beings of Light, or Aliens, which ever fit for you and believe it or not, I guarantee you *THEY* are here, and *THEY* are real! There is no *denying* it as far as we and millions of others are concerned.

Table of Contents

CHAPTER 1

THE HOUSE OF SECRETS

After getting up one sunny morning I went into the bathroom to get ready for work, it was that first glance looking into the mirror that shocked me. It was then I noticed I was *fully dressed* in the same clothes I had worn the day before! I was totally confused and began talking to myself, *"where are my pajamas"*? I stood paralyzed, motionless; my clothes were on *backwards* and turned *inside out*! I tried to make sense out of this while looking at where my clothes had been hung up the night before and where they should be now! But they were on me in the way I have just described them. I was frozen; I couldn't quit looking back and forth from the clothes hanger to the mirror I didn't know what to do!

When I could get some control of myself, I checked out my body since I had at times noticed unfamiliar red spots or bruises on me, and at other times I felt different emotions with low or high energy levels which was unusual. I had been having strange phenomenal experiences for most of my life being a psychic clairvoyant, but this was different. I was deep into my *paranormal, spiritual* work and *communication* within the spirit world so why was I so surprised by this adding up to something else! All I knew was this happened and confirming to me of what I needed to face from long ago. This was no dream; this was real and discoveries such as this that more was going on in my life than I could understand at this time.

This was part of a turning point in my life that something else was occurring which made me more than eager to search for answers to what had happened when I was a child, and now it was back! I knew how to get answers through my spiritual teachers and guides and made up my mind to seek their insight and help. I wanted extra confirmations even though I knew I had hidden answers inside of myself that were yet to be released at some time.

The Early Years of Growing Up

Going to grade school I was quite a loner and my feelings told me I was not like the others who were around me. I was different and extremely shy, and I wasn't sure what I was or how I felt, and the feelings never left. When I became older, I was at times withdrawn and lonely I sometimes felt I was watching a movie of myself storing strange new information which I was constantly receiving with profound experiences (I would be shown this later). My attitude was *"I wonder what's wrong with me, why don't I interact with others?"* Looking back now I understand my real memories were starting to be returned to me *little by little,* so my mind could comprehend the information I received, and this is the way it would be for me through the coming years. This happened because a deep influence, a high intelligence, was connecting me with something familiar I knew before. Therefore, I felt different than seemingly normal people; I was very shy wanting everything to be at peace, even shouting would disturb me, or those who called other people and races by mean names. I guess you could say I was *extremely sensitive,* and I never felt I fit in anyplace I was oddly different than my friends and those I met.

I was comfortable by staying in the background and strange as it was at the same time I wanted to be included by others. I wanted to fit in, but how what was wrong with me? All of this brought me down to a low opinion of myself and feeling misplaced. I recall getting in trouble when I was small by telling my mother I wasn't a part of the family I didn't even look like them! I didn't do this again I would recall my spanking from then on, but I knew something wasn't right. I had odd dreams of floating around up high, and later I would float back down into my bed. I didn't understand the in-between memory, but I loved the feeling of my strange *"dream"* which made me feel free and happy!

Beginning to Understand

When I became an adult, everything became intertwined all together with a daily knowledge given to me by the *"Great Council, my Spiritual teachers and guides,"* who would come to me from other Universal realms. It was quite common for me to do *astral* traveling in my spirit work with the other side, but something else had been going on I needed to find out about. I felt a *prodding pressure* going on in my mind, so I began to dissect some odd dreams I had been having. But first, let me explain about what *astral travel* means to make this clearer to you. *"When we sleep at night or are in a resting state, sometimes the spirit may leave our body traveling to distant locations, it may move about the earth going to others, even to loved ones who live miles away and/or who may even be thinking of the astral traveler at the same time or even to people we know that are sick"*. When one is in astral travel distance doesn't matter and all kinds of amazing experiences can happen. These experiences vary with each person and unfortunately most people think their experience was only a dream, yet it seemed so real.

When astral travel happens to some of these people, they may know the person they traveled to, and those people may also remember seeing the astral traveler in their room so they know it was NOT just a dream when they talk to the other person later to discuss it. We sometimes visit our loved ones who are on the other side during our astral travel and often one may hear, *"I saw Mom and Dad in my dreams, or I saw my old dog I loved so much!"* The stories go on, and many people do not have a *clue* they were really experiencing this which is a normal thing everyone does at times.

In my later years when drifting off to sleep I would catch myself thinking, *"they are coming tonight I would journey tonight, but with who, journey where?"* I was curious but not afraid; I only felt a kindness, an attachment of some kind to something. I knew that if I told anyone about my feelings people would think I was crazy, and something always led me to continue to search forward. I felt pulled to whatever this was with a strange kind of love and my strong connection to an unseen puzzle.

I knew to just file everything away there was nothing I could really do when I was a young child growing up, so I tried to forget those silly dreams. Becoming older the dreams came for a while and at other times they didn't, or I didn't recall them going on with my everyday life. I don't recall ever being afraid of not understanding any of this; the fear factor wasn't something that held me hostage. When I was grown, I remember one dream state when a voice told me, *"the human mind can only accept so much at a time so after I had digested each lesson I would be given more."* This information continued steadily on with a slow 100 percent change in me, I didn't know at first, I was getting *"reacquainted"* with another world on the other side I had forgotten. I was being prepared for my adult life and much was waiting for me. I didn't know I was redeveloping my senses to a higher level and as I looked back much later this was plain to see…

This was my life on earth to learn *"there is much more than just earth I had someplace else to go to"*. I was being taught with words I could hear, *"we humans are all a part of the whole, a part of everything and everyone as a circle is with no beginning and no ending."* What an important statement this would turn out to be, I knew in my future, somehow there would be amazing world events to come. It was at this time in my life I became extremely open through my spiritual life more than ever, and years later when the time came to teach others I taught more *"universal truths"* along with the ancient way of Reiki energy to the many I met, but with them not knowing they were also receiving certain truths to live by.

Now, getting back to my strange life, I am a person who wants to know answers which means, I do not live in *fear* of what happens because so much has happened in my life with hard to explain circumstances. I go after answers, reasons, and anything else that I can to enrich what I feel inside of me in my search of truth. The human mind has been thoroughly conditioned since birth with man-made ideas which makes things difficult, at least for me. I will guess that most people grow up to think a certain way with this old motto *"seeing is believing"* and it does seem most must see things to believe them. In this old way, one can *rationalize* almost anything that happens, or they want to believe. But there comes a time when one can't do this anymore because we run out of answers to rationalize the experience, and I believe this is when this becomes one's *acceptance of reality.*

It is the Time

The ETs who come to us are *benevolent spiritual teachers* and have told my son and me, *"the time is ready now to write about them with what they want earth people to know"*. They are not trying to frighten anyone they are only trying to warn earth, which until our planet changes to a friendlier place for them to appear; they will NOT come to the public masses because of what has happened to some of them in the past and when we are more ready. They have good reasons for this since they DO NOT trust our government enough, since many of them have died when the beings tried to trust us. Many secrets have been hidden from the earth people and fear has been put into many people about Aliens. My son David and I have known since we have existed that we were not exactly a part of this Earth planet at least not completely; there was always something very different about our part humanness. When my son was born, he nearly died as a young baby, I knew he was fighting to *go back* to what he knew on the other side, but he had made a promise. Life here was going to be extremely difficult to blend back into and it would be a giant struggle. I felt strongly his life would be as mine being hard to adjust to with life's struggles, but the best part is the beauty of being reunited with our loved ones. All of this is arranged in certain cycles of time, I first by being the mother and the children born in the order as they were.

The promise my son and I made to one another is deeply with-in our souls and this is the reason we feel so strongly with our emotions and feelings combined with super-sensitivity knowing of events to come. Words would be difficult to come by to describe our genetic makeup, we have been told, *it can't be.*

As a teenager David had a difficult time, he knew what others were thinking at school and because he was gentle and compassionate, he protected those who were not able to protect themselves by taking them under his *"wing"* with his concern and friendship. He came into this world knowing why he returned here, who he was, and he would fulfill his commitment to the Creator to the best he could. In our minds we had some hidden left-over memories after we each arrived in this world. Most were taken away until later with many of mine being held back until the time was right for me to remember, while David's stayed mostly intact for other reasons. Yet together we had a mission to accomplish and he knew my memories would progress and surface a little at a time as needed in the way of *"portions"*.

Your Introduction to Our Alien Family

I am going to introduce you, to our *Extraterrestrial* families and hopefully, this will be the basis to understand our dedicated work and help the pieces fall into place as our story unfolds.

I needed more time for my mind to grow and understand to a certain degree from in my beginning. I clearly remember we were told by the universal Beings, *"we would not be given too much information at once for the human mind is fragile, and we had to learn to accept small amounts in order to learn."* These were the portions they often mentioned we would be receiving more of.

One night I was taken by the Supreme Christ Light, then told, *"to keep everything written down with their messages and other information, I was going to be like a secretary!"* Although, I couldn't comprehend this amazing information at the time, I would do exactly as I was told by the Christ Light Being of Supreme Intelligence; I was humbled and proud to be a worker of the Light. Later, I was silently laughing to myself at the humor of the word *secretary*, but it had a great and divine meaning! This is how I discovered I was to keep; ledgers, messages, notebooks, pictures, and video for years of everything that came from the universal beings. This I would uphold and keep safe for future books I was to write. I kept notebooks beside my bed on a nightstand which made two notebooks near to me to write their messages in the night. This was not going to ever be easy I thought; how would I ever get people to understand all of this? Quickly my answer came to me, *"Do not concern yourselves, our information will go to who it is supposed to, everything will be fine. You both are our honorable students."* I was happy and *excited* to hear this response; it was something unbelievable happening but true!

When anything is different some people naturally find it's too out of their norm and hard to deal with like the UFO subject, and this life we had been given was extremely different! These are the subjects so many people make fun of, little green men, twilight zone, UFOs, abductions, stories of terror and fear. Everything with UFOs is bad and horrible it seems because of Hollywood, disbelievers, and the way they have become such a BIG joke. The main reason is, *"We have been taught to be afraid of the unknown"* which seems to be normal for some people on earth and it starts early with old manmade ways!

Sharing It Together

Going back to the day I first began to share my own UFO experiences with my son he was in the military in a distant state. I told him what had been happening to me and he wasn't surprised at all! I was in for a treat to say the least when I learned that David had been experiencing these same things since he was a boy and had been waiting for me to get to this point to open and share mine. The Universal Beings told him, *"He was not to tell me until the right timing came for him to let me know."* Immediately, I felt so much better, in fact; I was overjoyed, because now we could share our experiences together! I was not alone anymore with my phenomenal secret life his information had relieved my mind at once! This is how I knew his struggle to survive as a baby when he nearly died, he had his memories of why he was here, and this planet would be hard getting through it. We began to talk of our journeys by sharing together and *"not telling a soul"* about the ETs until we were told it was time. I would learn more about this *holding pattern* we committed to later in the future, we would remain faithful to the ET beings who schooled us for life. I was much stronger than ever now that I had my son to share experiences with. We accepted and learned from them as they taught us the universal differences in our humanness and alien-self which has made this quite a journey!

My son knew all along we could not speak of this and we didn't and thank God we had one another in this venture, one day we would understand the entire life plan we had made to be here. With our combined experiences I found my mind to be a unique and wonderful part of my human growth and how I handled the concepts of *"who I really am!"* This seemed to be sinking right into my brain and it was amazing, I was beginning to accept that my mind was complete being prepared by a great universal force! We would be relearning our forgotten memories in portions, of undiscovered, magnificent knowledge, and even though our lives were extremely different I knew who I was. I was eager to understand more about our Universal Teachers for together we had developed deep and beautiful commitments together by working in the paranormal and spiritual worlds. My son and I also intermingled with heavenly beings who help us in our spiritual and healing work coming from other dimensions, and when doing readings, this was now our life! (More of this is in my second book "The Story of David"). We knew that everything created is *intertwined together,* like a basket is woven in a beautiful way, and within everything there is purpose and we are all woven into perfect patterns. The Creator had a purpose for us as it is with everyone created.

My heart and soul work perfectly with my mind this alone have let me know that certain universal beings and humans have always been a part of each other since the beginning of Creation. Life comes from the most *Supreme Infinite Loving Superior Knowledge which can't be described called Creator.* The ETs we are acquainted with are not to be *feared,* for if the Beings had wanted to do anything to us or to Earth it would have been done long ago! The ETs who work with my son and I are highly evolved Spiritual Beings of the Christ Light, and if not, why would they wait to do harm here when their technology is superior from the beginning, and much more advanced than ours will ever be.

We are but a speck in a vast universe not to mention the fact that our technology as the ETs have said, *"they consider Earth to be like the Flintstones to them."* They say this is NOT to sound superior but because they have learned much of our *humor,* they use it often to put us at ease. They want me to explain something here which is of great importance and this is in their exact words, *"This is certainly not meant to be a put down to humankind, our planet Earth is very important to them and it is vitally important to keep Earth safe, this is a main goal of the ETs, yet they can't do everything alone; man must wake up and clean up our precious Earth and time is getting shorter for this to be accomplished and it is vital for us humans to listen to what they are saying!"* Does this sound like they want to kill us and destroy our planet, of course not! But many people who watch the skies do believe this with great fear because this is the way we have been taught. I am not saying the warring negative Species will be nice, they aren't!

Here are answers to what the ETs have just said, *"you see, if anything happens to our planet Earth our ET family clearly explained to us how this would create a complete catastrophe in the universe! Try to understand* this information in earthly terms such as *"when a bowling ball hits the pins and they scatter in all directions with everything in chaos."* If something happened to planet Earth this would upset everything within the universes, worlds, planets, stars, solar systems, dimensions, and so on! This would create an unbalancing of everything, a terrible thing to have happen, yet we ourselves have everything to do with this ever happening or not happening! Man's own greed for power has brought things to this point and this is something the ETs *DO NOT* want to happen! Man has *destroyed* much of our own planet, we here on earth need to change our ways or this will slowly make the earth *extinct* forever as we know it! Can this be stopped or is it already too late? We must make haste to take care of our beautiful world while there is still time if not, the *EARTH SHIFT* will. The good part is a shift would renew our Earth for us to start over in a clean new world which will be a wonderful loving one, but this will take time, many years to rebuild it. Who knows how much time is left, we don't, the *Earth cleansing* will be what the final answer is, and I am not alone by not wanting the universe destroyed…? So, you see this is a very serious situation and vital to begin working on change, my question is: who will listen and start this enormous task?

The missions David and I agreed to will hopefully give you a new perspective about the ETs we work with, and I can't stress enough about their caring and love so please read on to see what I mean. I am sure you may question, *"are there others in our vast universe and worlds that are destructive, you bet there are!"* Those are the ones called *"Warring Species"* you are going to learn more about along with the positive who are *"High Council Christ Light Beings who come from the Christ Light"*.

Back to what happened that morning with my clothes on backwards, from then on, I knew I would need to adjust to my life, so I began to set another part of my life aside. I was stunned with what was happening as you or anyone else may have been, but I couldn't rationalize my experiences any longer. You would think after this much time I would not have my moments, but I am living in a human world. I gave in letting myself be completely submersed to the ongoing occurrences that sometimes overwhelmed me. These new reminders meant we were to continue a familiar life, changing my son and me into a more curious, seeking, evolving individuals trying to figure out what our human and alien part would be like in the far future which made us who we were.

I can't help but wonder how hard it will be for some others to understand how this all plays together with our connections to the Christ Light ET Beings, and Spiritual Heavenly Beings throughout the other worlds. With what I have been told to write by the ETs to my knowledge their truth has never been known of like this in any way possible other than hypnosis and sightings, but not on *a one to one, basis* with the information they have given to us. They said, *"this is to educate the earthlings about some of the technical advances, who they really are, and how they think!"* They feel they may never get this chance in this way and we can help them, or they would not have chosen us, so we each have a large purpose to accomplish. The ETs are not like a robot they have feelings, love and humor, and their own highest intelligence of truth. With having interaction together since before our birth why would they pretend to be of the Christ Light if this was not true? They call my son and I *"Pioneers"* to come here to teach others of them, so maybe they are to be *"the leap for man-kind!"*

Are the Grays Getting a Bad Rap?

And what about the *Grays* (sometimes spelled Greys) these beings seem to be known by many as "evil" by having a bad *reputation* as provided in books, papers, abductions, and stories. But our contact with them has been the complete opposite! I want to explain our contact with the *species* of Grays we know of, which a whole different story is! I think we sort of *"blew the whistle"* on common theories about them, at least how we have experienced them in only a good way. I won't go so far as to speak for all of them since I have *no idea* if other Beings are different by their universal locations or by their motives. I only know of those who have been with us and around us, who seem to feel and know emotions. I have never met one yet who was harmful, and love is the most powerful force of all!

The ETs began to urge me to think about the book and our connection with them and other Beings, but I was not to start it until they told me it was the right time to begin. From our beginning my son and I have had countless *visits* with them in this world and with other species. Although, my son David has passed over I am still in contact with him thank God, we made our covenant to stay together forever in order to finish out any chosen work because we will never part. The ETs we are acquainted with know everything about us which makes complete sense, we belong to them. They have always known us they are our universal family; we are a part of everything they are. They have been present as we work in all areas, such as being led to others through Hypnosis, healing energy techniques, teaching Reiki in college classes, workshops, and doing readings from past over loved ones, and mainly as spiritual teachers. They monitor us since we both are connected to the spirit world, all our lives we pass messages from loved ones in spirit back to their families here on earth to give them peace and to pass on their love. The ET beings were very concerned to not *over tax us* in our eagerness to accomplish too much at a time. There were several times we reached exhaustion then the High Council who is the Ultimate Universal Beings of all humanity who guards us closely helps us to regain our strength. In our work with the Angels ministering to those who call for help and are in their own misery with sadness sometimes their deep religious convictions stand in their way to have the faith they need. When we explain to someone who has suffered from a loved one passed over *"that it is possible to talk to their loved one after their death our religion may tell us this is impossible, even though this is in the Bible."* Those who believe are leaving behind old practices of total fear onto a higher road towards a higher level of goodness and truth.

Sometime in earlier years on one occasion the ETs had written in my notebook about three future book titles for me to use! They wanted me to choose one out of the three for this future book to come. I was to write about their Species with their information and through our connection. Included under the titles they had printed *"CHOOSE ONE!"* I was thrilled they did this; and I am more than happy with what they do for us. Although, sometimes we joked about their writing, it was hard at first to read their printing and writing, I am proud of them! They work with symbols and thought transference and accommodate us as needed, my son and I felt honored they wanted us to choose one of the titles they gave us. I waited a short time mulling this over until finally we chose this one from the three that were given. I was thinking I still had plenty of time to get started and the years rolled by when the day came, I was fondly reminded *"it was time to begin the book"* so I did.

Even though time has passed we are truly in awe of them and their loving benevolence! Try to imagine finding their messages which seemed not only unbelievable but one of the most amazing things to ever experience, and then the book title!

I truly understand why the Spiritual Beings and ETs want the world to learn and understand them better by their teachings, instead of people living in *fear* of them, thinking all species in the universe are the *bad guys* waiting to hurt us! These highly evolved spiritual teachers and guides have watched over us all our lives and before. Perhaps this book will help people to understand them and be better prepared when they make themselves known to Earth someday. This would eventually unite all people perhaps then humankind may begin to remember they are *"already spiritual beings having an earthly experience instead of humans having an occasional spiritual one"*. Our universal family taught David and I the main key in every life is *love, simple huh, love to all; love is the key to everything in this world!* This is all it takes to live a good life and just one person can change many lives!

An ET description is an intelligent life form from outer space. There are many different species reported who are of the highest source of goodness and light, and a few species are of a very negative source with a warring nature. They have divisions in the universes the same as we on earth of good and evil. Have you ever wondered how many humans who live on Earth were designed with their connection to the Extraterrestrial family? The truth of the ETs has been hidden for many eons of time the same as other intelligent Beings of long ago. Centuries ago the ETs easily disassembled and reassembled atoms to travel or to move thousands of pounds by their thoughts to help build many finds such as the Pyramids, Mayan temples, and other structures over the world. Studies for years written by world leading archaeologist shows our ancient history books are mostly wrong.

CHAPTER 2

The Stranger

One day I happen to have extra time and decided to check out a newly opened bookstore. As I was searching through the many available books, a woman who I had never seen before caught my attention by approaching me on my right. It was easy to tell she was nervous and anxious, and I couldn't help but noticing the *fear* in her eyes as she blurted out, *"Do you know where the books on UFOs are?"* I told her I didn't, and as soon as I answered she began to blurt out some astounding, even terrifying experiences her sister was having in Alaska where she resides. The woman was talking extremely fast but enough for me to understand her saying, *"her sister's husband was in the service where they had been stationed and they lived on base"*, then not hesitating she said, *"Her sister had confided in her about having several Alien abductions and UFO sightings she had been having over time!"* This woman didn't take a breath while mentioning her sister had went to different doctors who put her on medications telling her *"this was all in her mind."* The woman told me she lived in a small town close to where I live here, and was looking for books on UFOs to send to her sister who had wanted her to mail any books or articles she could find on others experiences with this sort of thing.

I felt badly for her with fear escalating in her voice this poor woman was a *nervous wreck.* I explained to her that I didn't know the section she was looking for, and I was sorry I couldn't help her with any of this. The last thing she told me as she was leaving was good news about her sister who had recently met a high-ranking military officer who had come to be stationed at their base as a new doctor she could see. This doctor was different; he truly listened to her at long last! He let her talk to him at length then explained *"that he himself had had some experiences as a Pilot".* He described once experiencing strange oval-round silver shaped objects in a formation of sorts that he couldn't ID what *they* were, but he had a good idea they were not from this earth. He knew this woman told him the truth of her bewildering life and he understood! The woman said, *her sister felt a great relief because she finally had a friend of a high intelligence and this officer not only believed her but had other similar experiences himself!* Then she turned leaving the store, I was left wondering *who was this woman and where did she come from?*

I don't know whatever happened to the woman I met that day because I never saw her again, but I feel she was absolutely a *direct* link to me somehow in my future to come. Over the years I thought of her often because since then I *know* she was a direct connection to me on that long-ago day… I felt this strange meeting was somehow an early preparation for me which was how it turned out. I had no idea this happened to let me know the ETs would soon be coming back into my life. Throughout the years this strange meeting with the woman in the bookstore that day would come into my thoughts. I realized this experience with her was important and meant to be, she was a direct link to help me bring back memories from my other worlds and it took me a while to figure this out.

Some nights after going to bed I was finding myself in another place floating about I didn't feel any fear at all. I was confident knowing I was completely safe, and only remembered having a pleasant wonderful feeling about being able to do this. I didn't tell anyone about these experiences I thought perhaps everyone did this, and for me it felt normal. It would be years later after the bookshop incident I would be able to connect my past experiences with the ETs. And later, I remembered my earlier experiences of when I was re-taught how to communicate telepathically and physically with the universal beings in other dimensions, galaxies, and worlds beyond.

There were selected times to be with the beings in order to gain more insight, so I decided to seek answers from our spiritual teachers who I often called on for advice. I knew my guides and teachers related to the ET Beings as we did, so the information I was seeking would be the same from either one. The ETs would tell me what I needed to know unless I was to complete another lesson first than I used the gift of patience. My universal teachers confirmed my years of visits with them beginning when I was very small and how we used thoughts to communicate as we were accustomed to doing. And for me to remember *"to trust them, no harm would ever come to me."* After all, I had been with them long before this life and at the right time I would have all my memories back, and then my life would become more than I could ever imagine!

14

The Art of Hypnosis

I have not been regressed or hypnotized to recall any *encounters* I have had but I would be agreeable to do this. I know without doubt hypnosis is an asset to finding answers and to heal within one I am positive about this subject since I have been trained to do this technique. I have found this to be a valuable tool to use for many issues as people who may have a fear of height, death, smoking, abductions, hunger, stage fright, flying, and many other problems which hold one hostage in this life. Hypnosis can also bring forth hidden answers we each have that lie deep and hidden within our layers of subconsciousness. The results are endless, and I have at times used hypnosis to explore past lives along with other habits one may have had in a past life they have carried over into this current one, such as drugs, alcohol, frequent partners, anger, and so on they may be burdened with. An important thing is; one doesn't lie under hypnosis unless they are already a habitual liar and it is completely safe to have it done, even though some movies and people have sometimes given hypnosis a negative name. What happened to my son and me regarding our universal travel and accounts with the ETs were experienced *without ever being in a hypnotic state, this was on a one to one basis with our universal family...*

The Four Beings beside my bed

The Universal beings came to me at different times of the day and night for my teachings to awaken my mind and unlock memories, to know what is real, who I am, and where I came from. I remembered long after I had children, I was awoken out of what I thought was a dream and looking to my left standing beside my bed were four Beings looking directly at me with huge black eyes. They stood no taller than a young child with small spindly bodies, with unusually thin legs and long thin arms with strange shaped long skinny fingers, not like ours though! The fingers did not have the same digits as we have, and their feet were not in my view to describe them at the time but when I could see them, their feet were shaped differently without the ordinary five toes we have! I felt as if I knew them, did I? I felt we were somehow bonded together I had feelings of being relaxed,

15

and happy like seeing old friends after a long time! Then they began to communicate with me with their thoughts *"do not be afraid we are only observing you."* I can't explain my feelings and emotions, but the feelings coming from them were positive and good. I felt very excited to see them again and later put their visit in my notebook. This was another wake-up call, my new beginning from earlier years of the visits from them, I knew something extraordinary was happening I couldn't explain, but it felt like a family event I couldn't shake off.

Agreements

The little *Grays* began to visit me often and I welcomed them, they reminded me of how connected my son and I were to them and to know *"that only when the mind can absorb certain memories, they would let me remember a little more about them, in order to not rush me the same as our other heavenly spiritual teachers and guides had done."* I knew my son and I were both in this together, but I wasn't saying anything first then talk with him.

The Extraterrestrials have always been very gentle with us and they first ask for permission to accept whatever the lessons are about, and my universal travel must be agreed on before I go with them. They made it very clear they will do nothing to me without permission. The way I understand some information told about aliens in stories I have read, some people are being taken by abduction and having terrible experiments done on them which does not add up to my own experiences. This immediately told me there are apparently many species of Aliens negative and positive.

The ETs informed me that there are those of us earthlings who offered to do these visits at some point in our lifetime with our permission before coming to earth to be born. Along with this promise each one made they would not remember it until the right time. Their point in doing this is to *monitor* each of us, and the peaceful *abductions* are to follow our progress on earth. I can't imagine how abductees may feel after reading this, if they have experienced a *hurtful abduction* and been taken by force! These are two completely different types of species I am talking of, the positive and the negative. I have seen some species that are evil who are very angry, cruel and mean, but I have been fortunate enough to know what to do. In an instance such as this when bad beings come to cause harm, we have been taught how to get rid of them with the Archangels at our side!

The main reason some of us return to earth is because we agreed or volunteered to become an EXPERIMENT to help the positive alien beings connect again, to learn more of our emotions and feelings. They come to *school us* back to what we will be teaching about them which hopefully will reconnect others to not be afraid of them. This is meant to bring each person back to realizing how important earth and everything beyond is, not to mention love for one another. This transformation can begin changing our world to a newer more loving one together with the ETs help. They are also learning from us as human emotions and how we live in this world, even though they have a *superior intelligence* far beyond ours, and together one day they will merge with us in love. There is so much to explain and why the tests they do with us are important to them and this planet, along with new cures for many things.

I agree whole heartedly with those who have had a *terrifying* experience that this may sound crazy to them. All they know and remember is the fear, dreading, and thoughts of when the Aliens will return for them, and in those cases the waiting would be horrible! They cannot sleep, and never a place to hide, they can be found easily by monitoring them. This only happens with species that are negative, the warring ones I have mentioned who are extremely mean and cruel! Unfortunately, the positive species of beings are judged in the same way by those who have terrible experiences, they expect the worst from any of them not knowing there are different species. Most earth people are afraid of all Aliens mentioned because we have been conditioned to believe this way. It's the same as people living here, some are good, and some are evil! The time may come when some of the people will begin to understand and remember their agreement, and hopefully realize they had their bad encounters with very *negative* beings of another species who took them with nothing agreed to! I will explain later of the few negative encounters my son and I have been told of and very few we experienced ourselves. There are many different species in the universes and worlds, who knows what is *"out there"* some of them are the worst of the worst, who create havoc everywhere they go.

17

The ETs explained to David and me with their descriptions of two specific species that are very negative and harmful and how to be aware of them. Later, I will describe those beings as the ETs have described them to my son and me. We experienced negative Beings soon after that information was given to us, and we were ready for them, if a person can ever be ready and we were. The warring species battle throughout the other worlds continuously.

We have had countless interactions and experiences with the little Gray Beings that get a large blame for people's bad experiences, which so far, I have not found with our species to be true whatsoever. In our case of being with the Grays we are acquainted with are for various reasons and there again are countless little Grays and many types of Beings in the many galaxies. I really don't spend time wondering what all I agreed to do with them, and some information has been temporarily erased from my mind. I strongly feel it will be made clear to me when the time is right. I have found it satisfying to awaken to a new way of living and learning in my everyday life, with my extraordinary existence here on earth. We here living as human beings are all unique, precious, and learning, each one is on a different mission and some we are sharing together.

A Brief on Reiki Information

My life was led to become a Reiki Master/ Practitioner/ Teacher, the name Reiki means, "universal life force energy" and to teach this ancient art of healing the original way it was found, we had dedicated our life to this. For many years I have experienced and witnessed a large spiritual part of my life working with Reiki experiencing many wonderful results that makes my heart and soul thrive as they resonate together. Reiki has been an extremely rewarding part of life by using it and teaching my students. This keeps the original Reiki energy healing going on into the future, so it is never lost again, it is a very important part of our work.

My son and I both became Reiki Masters well over two decades ago when we were taught by the first passed over ancient spirit teachers of Reiki healing, and an Earthly Reiki Master/Teacher which I explained in my other book. Everything is made of energy and can be used as healing to help the spiritual, physical, mental, and emotional part for the wellbeing of a person, and in achieving this result our body becomes a clear channel to good health. I was led to teach this technique to others by my eastern teacher and later, I was welcomed to teach the Reiki method in college classes, and work with AIDS clients at Heartland services, in my workshops, seminars, and to many people who were divinely guided to want and learn Reiki. This amazing energy cannot be used for negative purposes, if someone tries to send Reiki in a negative way it will bounce back to the sender, because it is divinely sent. I'm very proud and honored that I chose this mission long ago with my son; together we can assure others and ourselves that Reiki will go on and on forever.

This energy has been around long as our universe has been, and this energy is directed to those of us who work in Reiki by our highest power, the Universal Creator source. Some may call Reiki healing techniques *lying of hands* and that's what a Reiki practitioner is doing in a sense but there is much more. David and I have witnessed extraordinary results with people and my son in his terminal illness, it can help in all walks of life. Reiki complements medical practice it goes *"hand in hand"* working together. A practitioner is not trying to be as a doctor, it is forbidden to prescribe or even suggest over-the-counter medications. We must obtain a client's free will and permission before a practitioner can ever start to work with them.

There are people everywhere in this world who are of different cultures and different names for their highest power we know as our Creator/God, and each system of learning that each one is on currently is where we are to be. We all go through many, levels of learning and growing, we are like little children learning throughout our lives, and we are never too old to learn. There is a reason to tell this because our ET family has worked with us for our sojourn on earth by teaching us universal subjects and ancient techniques, and how energy is used by them so we would know to use it in this way too. In this book I will discuss some of what the ETs want told about universal energy and how it is used by them.

CHAPTER 3

The Solid and Unseen Are All

Integrated into One

I found myself lying on a table with bright lights shining over me. Looking overhead I could see what appeared to be *wires or tubes* hanging down not far from my face with what looked like glass attached to the wires, almost like regular *eyeglasses* of some sort. I clearly remember briefly looking around seeing all kind of equipment on the other side of me but nothing I could identify. Not knowing what was going on I was startled, but I was not afraid. I seemed to know this was necessary to be done and then I went blank, this is all I remembered of that night with the ETs. I had felt no pain nor was I hurt in any way and was in no discomfort, I knew somehow this was something very important they were doing and that it was ok to do.

This happened on the same date as my mother's birthday which seemed *strange* to me although I had felt a strong connection with her presence being close to me in this experience. Ok, I thought *"I know Mom is somehow connected with this ET experience, but how, and in her life, we had never spoken of Aliens of any sort"*. I guess with this being her earth birthday I was more than curious, and my question was, why was she here with me? I was happy to see her no matter the answers, but this was uncanny. When I came out of this experience, I woke up back in my bed, and then made notes of what had happened.

Soon my son and I were debriefed once more by the ETs about Earth school and told us, *"it is the most important learning school universally"* which led us to know as we thought, our missions with them were combined with our paranormal/spiritual work and in everything we do. They were very serious with us about completing our lessons and to teach others, *"From ones past mistakes each soul on earth can lift themselves up to higher vibrations and levels. In this way one can evolve closer to our Creator so one may be able to choose to not come back anymore! This is how to make things right within ourselves so we here can grow to the higher levels and not return unless we chose to with free will. Now is a good time to let others know there are many, many other universal places one can choose to go in a next life to keep learning in." This was very interesting for others to know.*

I was continually assured by the other side and ET Beings that David's health would continue to improve each moment of each day, even if things didn't seem to be that way now. But to remain patient that we had been tested over time and to always keep our belief and faith. We were reminded everything happening to us was for others around us to witness and grow from it. Our faith would continue to grow even stronger along our way; and that any leftover manmade fear had been washed away from us forever. We were reminded again and again, to not let the negative ones drag us down or put any negative emotions back into us while we were here.

Honored Within Our Own Reality

One day when my son and I arrived home I opened the front door to come in the house and what a surprise, six sofa pillows had been taken off the sofa and lying in a circle in the middle of the living room floor! With this strange formation of pillows, we found information written on a script of paper left for us beside the pillows! The Heavenly Beings of the Christ Light composed of the ETs and combined with the High Council let it be known to us, *"to be ready at a certain time that night as there would be a joyous celebration of us throughout the entire Universe. This celebration was for the son to name the mother and the mother shall name thy son, then we would be known throughout the universes by our universal names forever! We were to sit facing the east and would not have the memory of this afterward until they chose to let us. We would only remember this experience happened, and our names."* Wow! We both exclaimed at the same time when we could think clearly. We were so excited; this was unbelievable to both of us! We wasted no time and went to each one's private place in the house to select our names without telling the other one what we had chosen! That night exactly as we were told we went to our rooms as usual to go to sleep. Everything went as the Beings and High Council told us it would without our ever remembering anything. All we knew was that after this grand celebration was over, we would both be known with our

21

Universal given names. We were ecstatic, honored, and humbled now we could tell one another the name we each had chosen. Since that night we both are known by our Universal names throughout everywhere! This celebration was more important than we knew it was a very important one and we were completely awestruck! This was extraordinary to us we felt completely in a state of shock and questioned ourselves, what did this mean, was it our new work through the Universal Creator?

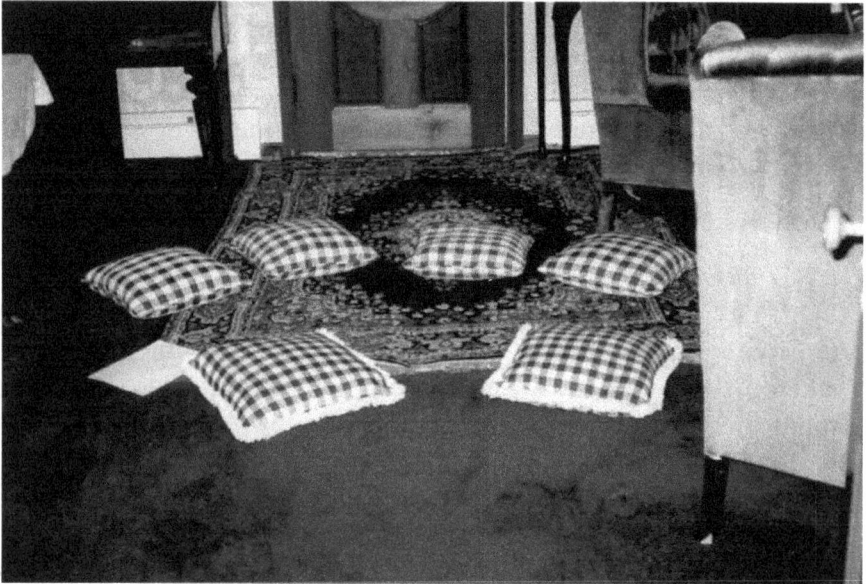

This is how we found the pillows when returning to the house. They were informing us the Beings of the High Council were preparing a celebration where both of us would be known by our Universal Given Names, a great honor.

I took pictures the next day of the setting they had chosen for us within the circle, nothing had been moved or was out of place. This was important because I wanted to do this for my records. The two pillows, one for each of us had been placed facing east, which is our main direction out of the four directions. The four other cushions faced to the west, so the High Council Beings of Light faced us. The script of paper was still in its place beside the cushions as they left it which had a message to us of the celebration that evening and to name one another…

Soon it happened again we were honored once more with a wonderful celebration when the beings began calling us their *"Universal Soldiers"* and with this honor they told us, *"we are known throughout the Universes by all Beings forever"!* We were absolutely overwhelmed as we had been when the Great Council had each of us name the other one, so we would be known throughout the universal realms, and now we will be known as their *"Universal Soldiers!"* We didn't exactly know what was taking place but even so, this *more than validated* to us that we were doing what we came here to do. The Beings told me, *"to keep using the energy healing on my son for he would heal, and be well for his time to be here, and to stay patient as I have been"*. Other messages such as this one made me feel much more positive and my faith was strong for my son, David.

The ETs expressed to us through the next several days, *"you both have received information and will remember more in time you will see us again soon"* then the ETs replied: *"Happy Birthday to Mother!"* I really smiled with their birthday greetings to my late earth mother! Then things hit me like a ton of bricks my mother had to be a large part of our experiences we were having since our universal lives were blended together no matter where we may be! I questioned myself, *"is what we were experiencing absolutely integrated together?"* With this thought I received my answer I felt a wonderful warm rush of peace wash over me with her love which let me know in my heart she was here in spirit. Everything is integrated, mom, dad, the other worlds, Christ Light ET beings, Heavenly Beings, and all that exists! I didn't need to question this any further anymore… I felt I had it down pretty good now!

Every day I had much to think about I had said good-by long ago to my last few left over *old beliefs* which were fading away forever, and I never looked back! We had living proof of how things really are, and we both were living our truth!

The timing had been set for me before I was born to let me know when this story was to be written it would be after my first two books. The last book I had written was about my *beloved son* who had returned home to the universal heavens where we all come from after a long terminal illness. This is still extremely hard to go over and think about as his devoted mother, but I had to be strong and separate my human feelings to be happy for him to never have to suffer again, 19 years was more than enough for him to fight and never once complain!

When a loved one is suffering in pain needing to leave us, we need to think of how they have stayed for us prolonging and enduring extra pain to hold on longer. No matter how hard it is; *please,* let them know it's ok, that you will be alright, and you understand. This gives them your *permission* they need to hear, so they can release. *Please* don't beg them to stay; the one who suffers will try to hold on because they love you and will suffer FOR YOU even longer.

When I begin to write each book I am told from Beyond to do this in order to share our stories and explain how it is to live in different worlds, universal realms, and Heavenly Beings of Light which is our ET beings as well. The information of our experiences over many years fills many storage tubs and, in the beginning, I couldn't imagine how to do this or where to start, so I needed the beings to help guide my work. They came to me and said, *"To write the stories in the books in Portions"* as I mentioned earlier which helped me tremendously, everything is in portions in life.

It was the beginning of 2016; those of the *Christ Light* told me: *"this is the time for the book to be written now and to continue the work."* I wondered if I would be able to do this a thousand times over after my son left, I am sure many of you have experienced how it is when a loved one goes home to the other side. My life stopped for what seemed like an eternity before I could continue. My son David in spirit has helped me to become stronger to go on with our family and to tell of our story of existence in the worlds beyond... He has never left me.

Edgar Cayce our beloved friend
and Teacher

One evening after falling asleep I was *transported* to a different place which looked like a waiting room on a UFO ship. I quickly noticed a man sitting across from me who was smiling as if he knew me. He began asking me, *"If I knew of Edgar Cayce?"* *"Oh yes! I called out!"* I became excited when he asked me because of Edgar being one of our beloved spiritual teachers who has taught my son and I throughout our lives I have written about before. I could deeply feel the man's essence of love radiating from him he had for Edgar's work. I eagerly replied, *"Edgar Cayce was the most wonderful healer with extraordinary gifts, and such a good and faithful man when he was on earth!"* This man, this *"Being of Light"* I should say, whom I was talking with had appeared to me as a man; but I knew he was much more than human, and I strongly felt we had a very important reason to meet on this occasion, and this was why I was there. I went on to speak to this stranger about *Jesus Christ* who I mentioned was the *greatest* healer of all on Earth and in the Heavens. After this, I only remember I was back at home in bed feeling wonderful and loved. I knew I would never forget this meeting it was very important for me to have this experience; I was at peace! I believe this divine being in disguise was an *ET High Christ Light Being* and it may even be possible he was *Jesus Christ* as a human man! I say this in all honesty because of my strong intuition and the feelings I was getting. I will leave it there that whoever it was I felt very loved, energized, and full of joy! This was a special time in my work, and I will never forget this experience. I have been told more than a few times by the Great Council: *"not to worry what anyone thinks about my work no matter about any negative comments, just keep believing and tell the world the truth"*. This is the way I feel too; I made this chosen path.

A few days later at a good friend's home Edgar Cayce's name came up again it was good to share what an amazing couple he and his wife Gertrude were. I held back about Edgar being a teacher to my son and me because I knew this person wasn't open and ready to understand this; how could they, since they were still in the old ways of believing, and I understood this…

One night, I was out in the Universe in *astral travel*. This is when one is asleep and leaves the physical body in their spirit. While I am in this state, I recognize spirits on the other side in many ways, some by their certain colors of light, or in their transparent forms appearing in these ways. We converse together with telepathically *"mind to mind"* but I know exactly who it is by their light and energy. These beings are very beautiful in this way and at other times I see spirits as solid as you and me.

One important experience was when I suddenly noticed one of my daughters with me in the universal galaxies of beauty. I quickly realized we were with others and in our colors of light, which wrapped around us as if we were incased within them giving us the feeling of BLISS! Our light bodies felt like a warm blanket of tremendous love! As I looked over at my daughter then down at myself, I could see our colors were even more extraordinarily bright and beautiful we were in our *Etheric* bodies! We were layered *within* our colors which were shaped around us like an Egyptian *sarcophagus*! I fully realized we were traveling in this experience with other Beings of light, and how wonderful it was to be in such beauty with it all around us, this must be hard for one to imagine! There are no human words to describe this phenomenal experience in any way! I have met an assortment of different Beings of Light from other places in universes, planets, worlds, star and solar systems, and galaxies, finding out there are a *zillion* magnificent places in space which is endless!

The Universal ETs once told David and me, *"that we were in training for many things to come"*, and whatever that entailed we felt honored! Thinking back to *past lives* my son and I have had was our strong connections to Egyptian culture from those past lifetimes in Egypt, perhaps I was finding out my daughter was also connected deeply with the Egyptian culture as well. I am sure my whole family has experienced life in that time period; at least it wouldn't surprise me since we stay together each time in some way as many others choose to do, this is done by one's Free will.

I don't usually ask questions on my journey since I know the information will be supplied to me when I am to receive it. But on this journey that night it was important to know. In our Egyptian lives my son David was a figure of higher standing, an important healer, and when I saw him, he was dressed in a long beautiful green Egyptian robe carrying a golden staff. I watched him walking across a *golden bridge* with other healers following along behind him as I stood in the distance down below. I was being shown this past life together in Egypt long ago and his connection once more as a gifted healer and I was told, *"This golden bridge he crossed was our symbol meaning from our world into the world of past lives to view, to remember this, that there would be many more of these visions*

26

and lessons to come." I was very proud of my son watching him, he has always helped others as he did in this lifetime and those before. What a beautiful and mystic life we shared.

Among the ET travels we had taken together there were times we would meet with other people who didn't seem to know they were on a craft (UFO), and then there were others who would refuse to go when they were being picked up. They would never think this was more than a dream when they woke up the next day. I was filled in from the ETs, if a person is not yet ready to go with them it's no problem, they do not take them; it's only with their *free will* when they do. Many people who refused were simply not remembering what they consented to a long time ago. You may think WHO in their right mind would consent to that! Keep reading, I will explain the best I can about why one must give permission first to go with the ETs, although they may never remember this was arranged by themselves before their birth!

I remember one woman I know very well who was going with us on a UFO, I was already there on board with my son to help her feel more comfortable as she walked up to the ship to be picked up. I knew her neighborhood and where she lived which was not far from my family member's home. I had been waiting inside the doorway of the UFO for her to ease her mind but the closer she got I could see *sheer fear* growing in her face. It was when the ETs went to help her that she became frightened and stopped, then turning she ran as fast as she could back to her home, and it was ok. The ETs understand these outbursts and were those who work with us I have mentioned who are highly spiritually evolved. They want no harm done to anyone even though she had given her permission at some time, they will not let anyone go with them without the person's permission. It is not unusual at all for people to not remember anything or very little when they give permission or not give it, because after one does the person goes into a *trance* like state and the ETs simply block the entire event from their mind. The person may possibly remember a very small part of what happened the next day thinking it was only a dream other than that thought they usually never think any more about it.

The other species that are negative don't care who they hurt they take people without permission and usually do it in very forceful ways then may do horrific things to them. They have no feelings for anything, even one another. I am not sure why those species do these horrible things to humans they take, except just to hurt them. Perhaps they program some negative people to do deceitful things for them on earth! Most people remember their frightful abductions and become so fearful of the evil Aliens they are never the same! The evil ones do not erase the abductees' memories, they love to instill fear in them for the rest of their lives!

When my son and I are with the ETs they tell us, *"to just relax, sit back, and let it all come into you both enjoy the ride."* They like using *our language* since they have always known it and are used to the human way of speech, especially the *slang* we use, in this way they can communicate when they are on earth in disguise as a human. The ETs many times walk among us and you will never know it and in some instances, people are helped by them in certain situations, accidents, or in a miracle they experience. They may also take on the appearance of an angel in a vision or as a regular person to not frighten someone here on earth. Some know us by working with them and they are known to help us. Those who look human may choose to work in a high-up position learning those ways to blend in with us to learn more about humankind. There are many here on this earth as a human trying to help us.

Several years ago, the Beings of Light/the ETs, expressed that they would come through to us on my *electrical* machine as they calmly called *my old word processer* and later my *computer*, this was their term they used for them at the time. My son and I had a good laugh about some of the names they used, and they reminded us, *"You will soon see what we mean"* and we did! I didn't know at the time what this statement meant but soon know, I confess I had never put a screen saver on my computer myself because of not knowing how. But the other side, the ETs, loved ones in spirit, and different Beings of the Light began to leave extraordinary messages at various times in the day and nights on my computer! The messages would stay on for a few hours, a day, or week; some were on for over a month we never knew how long they would get to stay. This is when I was able to get a video camera, I kept handy to video and take pictures of the messages they left for us. For some reason I knew I was to have *proof* of everything they did along with dates and time.

The ETs seemed to be even busier around special events such as birthdays, Christmas, Easter, 4th of July, the passing over of a loved one, anniversaries, holidays, and in times of needed healing and support in my son's illness and hospital stays. They gave him their help with his healing, and both of us uplifting messages of love. Even the computer screen had become a *bulletin* board of sorts; each day was exciting waking up to see what they had done! We were geared up each day hoping to find a message going across the screen written in beautiful font and color with uplifting words to us we could understand.

Most of the time the ETs didn't leave us in suspense long they would let us know when another message from them would be coming, and they were very good in sending us their information often. I confess in those years I did well to answer e-mail and I rather enjoyed them continuing to surprise us by leaving their messages to find, which were amazing! What was so great about this was my Mother and Dad were a huge part of the messages that were being left, and the funny part as I said, they didn't know what a computer was when they were living on Earth! In their lifetime there were no computers around for the average person, but now they both knew how to use this technology, leaving messages with different backgrounds of colors and pictures sometimes even with added music! How advanced my parents were now that they were on the other side, we were overjoyed to have our constant contact with them! When my dad was living, he was fearful of so much, even to drive in or out of town, and now they seem to easily make these extraordinary things happen, it just blew our minds! They were more alive than ever, and we felt even more connected to them in this way than when they were on earth! I felt all the bases were covered so if they couldn't get through to us in one way, I was sure they could in another, what an amazing life we had! I wanted to shout out to the world, *"There is no doubt of another life after we pass from this one!"* This world is only temporary to learn in and achieve our wanted goals.

Many times, the ETs left important messages on the computer about worldly or future world events to come. Sometimes I would find answers we were seeking to know they would help us in certain work, and they were good about using our humor many times to catch us off guard.

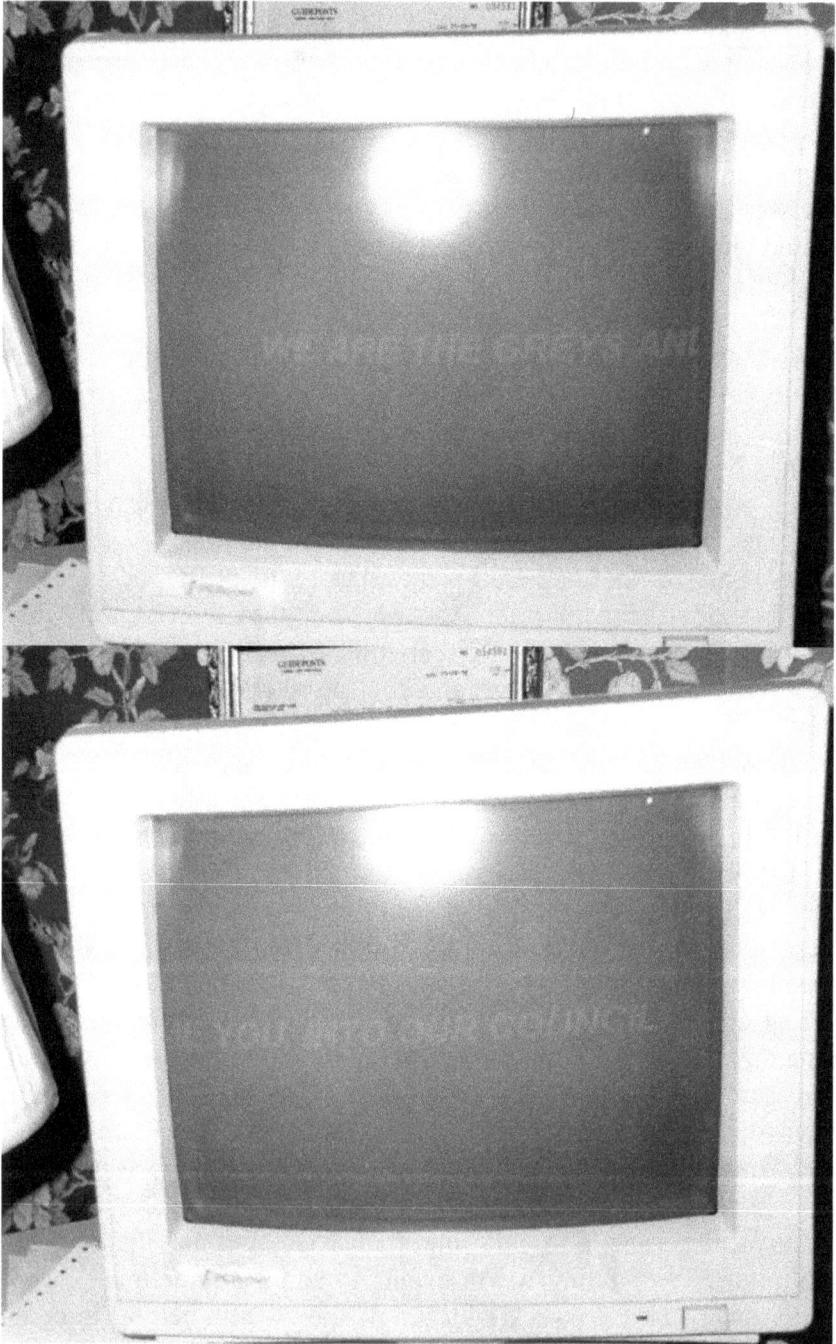

The above message says, "We are the Grays and we welcome you into our Council."

The prior page is an example of the many messages we received from the ETs on the computer screen.

Our Guides, and Why this Book
Is Written in Portions

For those of you who are asking *"what is a guide"?* Every single person has a guide who is assigned to each one of us throughout our lives from birth. They are souls like us who have lived life on earth before, perhaps many times. They may be a passed over loved one or one you have no knowledge of, and who you have never known that is helping you through your life cycle. Some people have more than one guide they may have several depending on their journey. One does well to listen to their guide so pay attention to your *intuition* and you may get to know them by learning to quiet your mind and learning to meditate. This can help you connect with your guide so keep your patience and see what happens. Listen for that *still small voice* inside of you where your intuition is, and where your guide is guiding you from to help you. Your one main guide stays with you all your life and some beyond even that. If you desire to return for another lifetime to help loved ones you may choose to be one. Some of us have more than one guide and I hope you remember, *"No one ever dies alone"* no matter where they may be. Contrary to what some think there are always spiritual beings and passed over loved ones ready to assist us.

The Divine Beings had begun leaving more messages on my screen saver and in my notebooks! We never knew when they would change to a new one unless we were told, *"a new one was coming".* It was always a wonderful surprise to walk into the house, get up in the morning and go into the family room and there a new one was! I love it when they put a message on the computer right in front of us which happened one day to my Aunt Evie! When this happened, she screamed and laughed at the same time! The message said, *"Why hello Evie so glad to see you*! *Thank you for the flowers."* She nearly *flipped* out, even though I had shared with her what was happening daily with our world of companions. But for her to see this happen

31

right in front of her, wow! Evie is my dad's sister and only he called her Evie as a pet name for Evelyn. To top it off, we had just come from the cemetery where we had put flowers on my mother, dad and Aunt Evelyn's husband (my uncle) grave sites just a short time before! I told my aunt while laughing; *"there is nothing the other side doesn't seem to be aware of or can't do if they want to!"* I knew my aunt would never forget this greeting to her!

Now you may see why we understood our Universal connection that existed between us and the ETs, High Council, Angel/Archangel Heavenly, Paranormal /Spirit worlds. They are all working together in some amazing unique way, so everything is connected! We are all living and breathing beings in an enormous array of worlds. I had many questions in my mind for the other side to answer but I knew to remain patient until they thought I was ready for them. David was ahead of me in our training, he came into this world remembering as a very young child but could not reveal my answers to me because I had to remember this part of my past lives on my own. Then after I would remember more advanced information, I was gaining! It was as if I was given *time out* to have my babies and be a mom!

Back to the computer, the messages came even more often now, and, on many occasions, we would know about certain things that were going to happen ahead in the future. Through our intuition and straight-line connection to the beings that sent them; it was like having a direct private telephone line. At times I would look over to see the glimpse of a new message in a vision clearly and later it would be on the computer, sort of a *preview* to come! There were times the Beings would show me certain things in a dream state ahead of time to write down. It is not always comfortable to know the future of things they wanted us to know, but it was for very important reasons to come and we both understood this. Therefore, these *premonitions* were becoming common for us we had been given the gifts to do this. There were stories in newspapers that I would sometimes come across with similar connections to ours, which helped to know that others someplace else are also having extraordinary experiences. We were not the only ones although *living a daily life with the ETs* was not among the stories!

I recall reading of a mother who found a message from her young son who had just passed over that came on her computer. I was *so happy* she was getting her son's messages in this way which was familiar to how we received all kind of messages. It made me content to find other people have extraordinary events that happen to them also, but I don't know of others getting messages from the ETs on the computer and in person. This doesn't mean it doesn't happen I just haven't read of it but perhaps others do? While reading back through my old notebooks many future events had been given to us years ago and the new people we would meet. Upon finding these exact facts I sometimes am overwhelmed but happy with the information.

I know hypnosis can bring deep memories to the surface, but what I am writing about is a different thing and both are very important. We are in *direct* contact with the other side not only directly, but with divine interaction and guidance from many universal teachers, guides, and beings from the other side. I treasure the variety of their amazing help interacting together with us in our lessons, regardless, of how this is done they are also teaching us about the many levels of love and humbleness!

On occasion, an ET from the High Council called *"The Great Traveler"* would come to us which was an honor to have his presence I will acquaint you with later in this book. I might add never have any messages been negative to us in any way. They are only positive, helpful, and loving ones with some having certain information we are never to reveal, the higher Beings of the Christ Light will not let us print or save those messages. They clearly tell us, "THIS IS FOR YOUR EYES ONLY!!" We humbly respect their wish; and have never shared them and never will! On the other hand, many of the subjects from them are funny, even hilarious; yes, they have a good way of joking around with us sometimes catching us off guard. This way of thinking about aliens and heavenly beings must seem silly, but it is true as you will later find out. They keep learning our way of humor and say to us, *"we want to learn your ways to know you better as you live on earth, how humans think, how human's emotions are meaningful so we can learn and understand better."*

At times messages they send to us are specifically to comfort us in times of difficulty; as an example, I may be shown when to move on from a situation with a job, a friend, or relationship. Because in my work I need to release this person so they can also move on in their life, even though we may share a bond then we can both move forward. We are on life's journey and each have times we call the seasons, these seasons in life bring us together at times to spend a certain amount of time with specific people for definite reasons, this occurs for us to learn selected lessons from one another. Sometimes this can reunite a friendship, and then we may move on so both people can do what they each chose to with their own mission. Everything is for a reason, the good part and the hard part if we understand it or not.

We are taught never to *divorce* but this is a myth, an idea. Even in divorce I believe this happens for a positive reason, the Supreme Creator wants no one soul to be beaten, mistreated, hurt, or abused in any way. And I believe if one person meets another person for only a five-minute connection it is meant to be, we are all teachers in some way learning from one another all through life, in that respect we are all teachers. Much of life may not seem be a positive to one but it is what we each learn from our experiences that counts so much.

In the ET world it is too difficult even now to explain our part in it and it doesn't matter, except if the one you want to be with doesn't understand. Try to understand, this it is not an ordinary life we chose by any means and we wouldn't change the reality of it for anything. Our mission here is made with our dedication and love for the universal source, the Supreme Creator who steers David and I onward. The other side wants us to be happy within our own-selves, we are meant to be happy, they say to us, *"enjoy life and every beautiful day you are here to do as best you can for life on earth is very short"*. I listen closely to what the Universal Beings tell us; to me this is a blessed way to live to do the best one can, and not be afraid. Relax, be a child again in your heart, enjoy all you can and look at the hardest times in your life as steppingstones to keep raising yourself to a higher level of learning. This is all that is required, it's not an easy assignment for most of us, this life here is tough just don't give up. There are no short cuts in Earth school, and it is the way we handle our problems more than the outcome. It is normal to get as we say *down* at times, these I call are our tests in life. This is the school *of hard knocks* but keep going, it to shall pass.

More about Our Relationship with Edgar Cayce and ETs

The ETs have more to do with our world than most people can ever imagine! When we realized with our memories intact the beings were also working with our other spiritual teachers such as Edgar Cayce this was exciting! My son and I had been receiving messages from him earlier on when he first made himself known to us in various ways. I didn't know anything about Edgar in the early beginning so to fill you in, I began to see this person in *visions* and the initials EC, drawn in my bedroom carpet, some of his clues were typed on my old *word processor*! I only had the old *word processor* back then and I didn't know much about it. The processor sat on my desk at the time when Cayce began his typed communication to us. And later, he led me (through my intuition) to the library and a first book about his life which I also did not know of titled *"There is a River"*. This was a more formal way for him to re-introduce himself to ma and slowly bring back memories of our connection.

I read this book of his life story; he led a very humble and poor life I cried while I read it because I felt I had known this man and his wife Gertrude forever. Right then, I felt positive we had a strong connection to one another perhaps as family that worked together in past times with other events that had happened. I didn't know why I felt as strongly as I did but while reading his story, I discovered all kinds of *similar* things from my own past lifetimes of experiences to other places. A huge surprise was finding his book had familiar names and parts of names that related to me and my family I felt connected to his! It was uncanny what we call a coincidence, but there are NO coincidences.

I did not realize at first and for some time it was both Edgar and our ancient eastern spiritual teacher *"Han Tia Chen Su"* that led David and I to research the Edgar Cayce A.R.E. which means *"Area of Research and Enlightenment"* based in Virginia Beach, VA. Cayce had made himself known to us at the perfect time, so it was easy to figure he had been waiting for us with the clues he gave us. He was very instrumental leading us into our work of Reiki as the Angel and Han Tai Chen Su had also been. Throughout everything happening the ETs were monitoring and pre-programming us both.

35

You will understand more as you read along our story explains everything happening proves we are all truly *integrated together with everything.* Edgar soon showed me a vision of the time we worked together in Atlantis! In this vision, I could see the three of us together in what I will call a *laboratory*; there was a huge crystal which stood in the middle of the floor providing the power to run everything and to everywhere. There were others with the authority to increase the power of this powerful energy who became greedy to rule everything. This is what brought about the destruction of Atlantis, which had been a large thriving city extremely advanced into the future to come. It was those in high positions who had even higher aspirations to rule everything and everyone to its destruction! The powerful crystal rays were used for most things in Atlantis and across the waters, the rays were so strong they could travel any distance. In my mind's eye I could see the greedy continued to push the energy power of it more and more, we could not stop them, it became so strong it *exploded* leading to *mass destruction!* We were among remaining survivors who made our way to other lands and places to start over, which brought forth the different races and cultures of people. We and other survivors began a new way of living with little to nothing left, it was hard, but we made our way to settling in Egypt where our new lives began... Over centuries we evolved going on at times with different paths yet staying close to one another in spirit.

In This Century We Met Again

The past lives of Edgar, Gertrude, David & I continued sharing our lives and times together since the beginning, we made plans to return in this life again to be re-united as we promised. This was in the heavenly *"contract"* we made when the times came in this century and in correct earth years, we would meet again with them both as our spirit teachers. When he first re-entered our lives to know him was with his gentle approach. Another first time was when I noticed my son's favorite small book he kept beside his bed *"Think on These Things"* I was so curiously drawn to it I asked David about this man Edgar Cayce. I knew my son loved him for the work he had done helping others all his life this led me to want to know more about him! I know now what David knew then, Edgar was coming into our lives as a teacher to us both, he knew we had connected over lifetimes, but he was not to reveal this yet. Edgar was leading me, and I briefly recall after quickly looking through his book I wanted to read it as soon as possible. This is when Edgar led me to find his first book at the library *"There Is a River"*. This is when he began appearing in separate ways with me by hearing his words, finding his messages on the word processor, his initials in my bedroom carpet and accompanying ET beings. There was nothing left to doubt these things were done to help me draw out my old memories to remember our promise together for in this lifetime. In the heavenly contract made before we came here, we each had chosen this part of the journey, and now it was the time to start remembering our work. This phase was very important and would be done through Edgar, the two of us, the ETs, our Heavenly spiritual teachers, guides, and other universal beings. To get back to Edgar in this time period we are in today, this explains how he began working with us once more and still does...he said, *"we have always worked together and always will."*

What Edgar did was to draw attention with finding his messages in the assorted places and using the carpet as a black board of sorts. He later changed our way of communicating after my young son-in-law Charley passed over, it was then I inherited his computer, so Charley knew just what to do *once* he was on the other side. After this, Edgar also used the computer to connect with us I would think of how he once knew no such thing as a computer in his life just like my parents. One reason this story and my other books were to be written was to tell the real universal truth of how important all lives are. Those who mostly live life with man-made *untruths* taught to them can sometimes break one's spirit from a young child. David knew why Edgar did these things he had kept his memory for reasons to help me along, but I had to discover mine in time, my early path was a mother so the ETs could learn these emotions...

Entering my room one day Edgar had arranged my bed pillow on the floor as a kneeing alter in a church, it was in front of my dresser which has a Holy box on top of it. This Holy box belonged to my son who purchased it at a flea market sale, he was becoming sick at that time and we both wondered how could such a precious piece end up in a flea market? Afterwards, we felt sure the precious box had been waiting for a special reason, we needed it in our work and had no idea how much it would come to mean to us in that way. The small wooden box contained the original healing prayer complete with two candles still wrapped in paper. Old time Ministers use to carry a Holy box like this one on horseback and in their buggies to those who were too sick to travel or to those who were dying.

I was shocked to find this *precious alter* that day like an alter yet I knew it to be a *Holy* message about *healing*s and our work. On the floor next to my dresser I found the familiar large initials E.C. drawn in the carpet as if they had been put there by hand where it stayed for days! After this, Edgar began making his appearances in transparent and at times a solid body, hearing his voice and seeing him visions. He also came to me in my *dream states,* there was no doubt he was our teacher helping to steer us into our future healing, and with his help we became his students as well as our eastern teacher Han Tai Chen Su. Looking back, it is easy to see how we were all connected with The High Council of the highest heavenly order. After my extraordinary awakening Edgar and the rest of the higher beings opened the doorway to my mind, and old memories flooded in, not only of working together in the past but also as best friends in Atlantis which I wrote about earlier. With this information we were excited, Edgar was spurring us on as his students bringing his knowledge to us from those lifetimes. I have also written about this in my second book "The Story of David".

As mentioned above are Edgar Cayce's initials in the carpeting.

One special night a beautiful Angel appeared after I had sat down on my bed, I was not of aware it until I heard its beautiful voice asking me, *"What does thou seek most?"* I called out in less than a heartbeat, *"TO HELP OTHERS!"* then quickly the Angel vanished! With this question answered I knew we would begin a new healing journey. The next morning the Angel appeared once more to tell me, *"I would be going in a southerly direction to teach healing and that I would be led into a ministry of healing".* It wasn't long after this I found a sign of the four arrows drawn in the carpet which meant the four directions. More information followed and our wait was short, the following day the Angel appeared again and told me, *"We would soon be going south to help the souls there and to go and stand in front of the mirror, to hold my hands out with the palms up and look into the mirror." Looking into my reflection I could see beautiful emerald green light coming from my eyes, nose, mouth, heart, and the palms of my hands then I was told once more, "I would be going into a healing ministry". The Angel read my next thoughts, I was thinking "who me I'm just a housewife with children, immediately the Angel said, "why not you!" Then it was gone!* This mirror I was looking in had mysteriously appeared one day I found it hanging on the bedroom wall, NO one knew where it came from! It still hangs there today; we are positive it was brought here for us as a portal opening where I see constant spirit traffic day and night moving in and out!

Soon after this experience, I would be learning the ancient art of healing, it was as if I was in a deep trance after those amazing experiences, I couldn't believe what was happening!! In time after my Reiki energy studies when my son was able, I took him to my Reiki teacher I was led to. He also studied under him to review the healing work we had known before. This ancient way of energy healing was not known about much at all in our state and in other places back then, so it wasn't going to be easy for some time to even mention the word meanwhile, we used it on who we could. I worked several times a day on David as the heavenly beings told me to do, he was improving! We both worked with Reiki energy through the next many years' together to gain all levels of energy by working on others and after many years we became Reiki Masters, Practitioners and Teachers... We had achieved the highest levels and now we could teach others.

Many times, my son and I wished there was an Edgar Cayce A.R.E. (Area of Research & Enlightenment) meeting close to us. Surprisingly, this was being set into motion by our spiritual teachers and sure enough we were led to a new meeting about to begin some 40 miles south of us. Cayce had heard us and *"the door opened",* *we would be going south* exactly as the arrows drawn in the carpet had pointed. They had been a confirmation for us, and we were prepared! With our gifts of clairvoyance, we were soon going southward to work with others just as we were told we would be doing. We felt happy and excited many of the people would be *"liked minds"* our dreams were coming true... This was a good experience for us and those we met, and things went great for some time however, we knew our mission would soon come to an end at the meetings and we would be sent to another place. In the beginning both of us sensed our time there may be short but it was very important to be there while we were, we knew Cayce would move us onto other things and other positive people. I was next drawn once more to the sign of the four directions to a college to introduce the energy work and teach students of all ages the gift of the Ancient Art of Reiki Energy to help themselves and to use on other people. I was extremely proud to be the first Reiki master to teach classes especially because, *the original ancient techniques would never be lost!* It was a wonderful time period in our lives, with exciting results on some of the students and people who wanted to experience it I will mention later. Even two dogs were brought in with severe problems both of us and the students worked on them and they recovered from dying! I will explain the name Reiki; the name means "Universal Spiritually Guided Life Force Energy."

I am proud of the souls in my class who came to learn Reiki; this sacred healing is for the physical, mental, emotional, and spiritual body. Reiki goes *hand in hand* with medical healing and sometimes with amazing results in healing when others have given up! Nothing can stop our time to pass over, but Reiki can ease pain, promote faster healing, and relax the body, mind, and spirit which can make a person's transition of passing much easier and smoother. Reiki always helps in some way; it is a *spiritually* guided energy always working to help whatever one needs until it is our time to leave here. Reiki is not a *religion* and is for anyone who desires to learn it to help others; this is all that is needed. This energy can only be used in a good positive way and NEVER in a negative way, if a person tries to send this energy in a negative way to someone it will return to the sender.

Before and throughout my son's long illness Cayce has been with us guiding and reinforcing our work together. When we were doing readings for others he continued to reinforce to David and me *"that my son would be healed one day"*. His messages are always full of love for us and I was aware that my son's healing could mean in two different ways, either to help David go on longer in his life here, or to make his passing easier into the other side one day where we are perfect again. I knew this meant he would continue to have miracles and healings so he could go on with his teachings to others which was a revelation! We had 100% faith in Edgar's guidance, and he has have never proven to us to be wrong, he is a *magnificent* teacher and healer. He with his wife Gertrude and son Hugh Lynn who are all in spirit know we love them very much. Not only was David and I led into healing by them but also Han Tai Chen Su, our *celestial* teachers and angels of healing, and the ETs who escorted us home

41

on the long drive from school at night. From the beginning of Creation, they have been with us in some way assisting and teaching us in our work together. We were to meet again in this time from our past and it has been a grand reunion. The one amazing thing Edgar planned to do was to teach us both his *Trance states* which he did, and how very honored we were!!

The Pyramids

One night while in a vision I was looking at a *Pyramid* and in one blink I was inside of it! There were painted pictures of birds, Egyptian people, chariots, burials, and beautiful symbols in Egyptian script on long tablets which all looked very familiar to me. The long tablets told of their culture, Kings, Queens, and their families from thousands of years ago. Instantly I focused on one picture of what appeared to be two Egyptians who were kneeling, one across from the other so they faced, and each one had the head of a Jackal! It was then my memories flooded in, I had done this, I was called *Anubis* with the head of a Jackal and a human body! There was more, suddenly I understood *this represented a coming funeral* to me! I would remember this experience from then on, only a few hours later one of my family called me from a hospital her young husband had suddenly died! What a shock, although I had seen this illness inside of him only two days before while visiting at their home. I could see inside of his stomach area and something burst, this was terrible for me to know ahead knowing I could not change his path I felt so helpless! I hoped he would be saved somehow although I knew different, his time was up! He was a brilliant young man who worked in medicine only 30 years old, but he suffered from pancreatic disease. It's horrible to know things ahead at times but they are for a reason, and then I understood why the vision came in two ways. Seeing myself in this Egyptian life being *Anubis* I prepared kings, queens and high authorities funerals in that time; this was also showing me a passing would be coming to a loved one. I took this was to prepare me for a *family death,* by viewing my Egyptian afterlife as *Anubis* when I prepared royal funerals. I am shown my own symbols and understand them in visions and dreams, and I existed during that *Egyptian* time period. Perhaps our family member who passed had been of Egyptian blood in a past life. He was a Pharmacist in this life helping others, a healer.

In another of my Egyptian lives I hid treasures that were extremely valuable and sacred; that may never be found, and among these were some of the sacred records from Atlantis. Those sacred items and others are still buried there today in a special place inside the Great pyramid. When I hid these relics, I knew my son and I would gladly be giving our life for their safety to keep them hidden. We were hurrying down the ancient steps inside of the Pyramid with barely enough time to accomplish this with only seconds left to complete our mission! Only moments later we were overtaken by the guards and our own death was imminent we had gladly sacrificed our lives to do this important work. The precious items have never been found and may never be.

The work we both chose was not going to be easy on this earth; especially now with our family loss, but our loved one's time was up he was home free. My son and I knew we were sent to help those who were still here with life to live and experience theirs, and those grieving, and to send thy Creators healing to all we could through Reiki. I would be reminded by the Angels of healing who came to me saying, *"Let not those who are on a negative level tear you down to their level of thinking for the nonbelievers will believe when they face the truth! There are many levels of learning and each one of us is on our own level."* We would keep this message inside our heart and soul knowing these words have the power to get us through any negative ones who come along the path we have taken. Through time, much of the negatives have been cleared out of our way from the other side but more will come. When I had a down period all I needed to do is remember what I have been told.

After this I encountered a heavenly Angel Being one evening who came to help me and told me something I shall never forget bringing tears to my eyes, *"that my son had come to earth to take on his suffering and illness so others would see his belief, faith, and determination to fight so they too may learn from him and that we would always work together to help others."* My heart silently cried in sorrow I was in awe when the Angel gave me the message. I watched David suffer silently for many years giving his young life up without ever complaining, and in his years of suffering he was given many *miracles* even when all hope had been given up by doctors. He survived each time for others to see and inspire them to fight for life, to not give up, as he continued to live and completed his work with others.

He once said, *"that he had been BLESSED with his illness to come here to earth to do this work."* Can you imagine anyone saying this? This was before I understood our promise long ago more clearly, so his statement shocked me at first then I understood and so proud of him! I had never heard anyone say *"they felt blessed"* to have a *terminal diagnosis* so young or old, but I knew he was an *old soul*; he knew he came to suffer and teach; this was his mission on earth. He had always known when he would leave here *"when his mission was finished"* he knew this at FIVE years of age when he told us he would die young! I was realizing in those early days he was a *teacher* not only for others but also for me, his sisters, family and many others. In the early years he was helping me to *remember* our healing work together in past lifetimes without him *saying anything;* I had to grasp the memories myself as each door opened since I was working on other things. The ETs who work with us are highly spiritual beings who help us both, we have surly been blessed to have this chosen life...

The Angel said, *"David came here to suffer so we could do our work together and through his suffering others would be given hope, faith, and strength along with courage to not give up until it is time to."* By now you may be wondering what this means and how it will end, and it has everything to do with Aliens/ETs in the overall picture, hopefully our story will explain our phenomenal connection to them. I somehow always felt everything is different but somehow combined in one huge magnificent Evolution, which was only the beginning hopefully our story can help to prove it! We were dealing with so much trying to fit in the different pieces, it was like putting a puzzle together and sometimes it's hard to find the pieces.

Rolling down the Car Window, "I sure
Can tell the ETs will be coming
Tonight."

Our ET visits had been going on for quite some time, in fact for so long I am not quite sure of when they started exactly but as I have said, since a small child. I can't remember much in those early years except I would suddenly wake up as if I knew it was time to go somewhere or that someone was in my room. I was afraid of the dark back then but not for long soon my attention was caught off guard because I would be looking into someone's big black eyes that was looking right back into mine! Amazingly, I was not afraid just the opposite I felt comforted, nothing bothered me about this happening. I knew the *"little ones were my friends"* with their small child like size they had. Sometimes they would appear to be floating in front or above me or sometimes just standing beside my bed looking at me like a small crowd gathered around wondering what made me tick. They made me feel good, and I quickly found we could talk to one another without our mouth moving. It's called telepathically *"mind to mind"* this was like a game learning to talk with our thoughts. Even when I was a mother with nearly grown children, the Grays would still assure me each time they came, *"to not be afraid that they were only observing."* At some point it seemed like a long time before I had this experience with them again. I knew when they appeared, they were not there to hurt or harm me in any way and this is what takes me to my story of the Grays who began returning.

These little people are known as the *Gray's* or *Grey's* and can be spelled either way by others in today's world, it was those little guys who have always assured me I was safe every time we met. Later, I would find signs to me in their own different ways to let me know ahead of their arrival, sort of like their own official announcement. I loved our visits and they were kind to me, so I enjoyed seeing them!

When my own children were raised and gone the Grays began to come back even more it was on one of those visits I was honored to meet one of the higher up ETs who came to see me, or I may have traveled to him; I'm not sure which it was. I only know I had not remembered meeting with this one before, but I would find out at another time I knew him well, I just hadn't remembered yet or they hadn't let me recall him. You see, until one is ready to remember things, they can keep it repressed... the timing needs to be right for all things to happen and this is a lesson I have lived with.

There was so much stored in our memories from them and until we could handle certain information those memories would not be released. Everything that happens is in certain timing they taught us this, and that our subconscious mind is like a large warehouse full of secrets of our whole existence. The ET I strongly felt I knew and was very comfortable with I felt love coming from his eyes, which is the same as how love feels for a child of your own. This ET being was known to be a *highly evolved spiritual being* who had communication with me, and this quickly made sense as to why I felt tremendous love for him, sort of like he was a mentor to me. I felt he was someone I have always known, and I would find out I wasn't far off from my thoughts.

I kept noticing the tallness of him, he was very different, nothing like the *little Grays*. I do not recall his features except that he was human looking, I knew he was highly intelligent and a high up leader, an important one. It was in his eyes that I knew I was safe and protected I knew somehow, we had a strong connection, a bond, to one another which had me puzzled. I clearly remember asking him, *"where are you from"?* This was among one of my first questions when he returned one evening standing beside my bed. I thought I was still in my home but I am not so sure now, he answered me with a bit of human humor, *"that is like asking you where the "Wizard of Oz" is from you would not be able to understand if I told you but I will call it "The North Quad"*. I was more than satisfied because I understood this was as much as he could explain to me in a human way. The *"North Quad"* he referred to was somewhere out in space in some unknown Galaxy who knows where? It surely must cover many universes and galaxies beyond human understanding, the *"North Quad"* might be a zillion light years away in some Universe we have no knowledge of and perhaps never will. I could see he was trying to explain to me in the only way he could, at least it gave me something to go by in my mind. I felt good knowing that much, he had given me an answer with his learned humor...

Soon some funny things began to happen in the house to alert us so we would know when they were coming back, to be ready to travel with them, reminding us this travel would only happen with our given permission. Permission was really a big deal with them!

One day as a surprise my son decided to buy me a necklace as a gift for my birthday, it was unique and beautiful with a small illuminating full moon. I really liked it; my birth sign in astrology is the moon, therefore he wanted me to have it. Looking back, I am sure he knew it would be used by the ETs as well. About this same time, I bought myself a pretty scarf with fringe around it and after I did, I was puzzled as to why I did this! I never wore them since they were long out of style but for some reason, I was strongly attracted to it and finally put the scarf away in my room. All of this adds up to pointing out more of the ETs humor because when I went into my bedroom to get something on my birthday, I was startled to see what the ETs had done that caught my attention! Hanging from my ceiling fan was my *moon necklace* with my *new scarf* both had been placed perfectly around the ceiling fan blades! I also noticed both items faced the northerly direction! It didn't take me long to understand their message remembering they are from the *"North Quad"* like the ET had told me and it was a full moon that night! It would be later that I would find out the significance of the scarf draped so cleverly on the fan blades with my new moon necklace!

I called to my son David who was downstairs, *"Come up and see what the ETs have done!"* I was laughing so hard I couldn't quit, I was barely able to say, *"You won't believe it"* I couldn't get over their humor and wit! Entering the room, he had an astonished look on his face then he burst out laughing finally saying, *"He liked what they had done to announce their arrival that evening".* I want to point out something you may have noticed or not, the ETs didn't always come in the night, they made different visits at different times of the day or night! I believe when they appear at night it is easier to move us out of our physical bodies into energy so we will not be missed out of bed by family. In this way, we appear to still be sleeping even though we are gone in our break down of energy. This was just the beginning of many Alien visitors letting us know in advance of their coming visits. I would be lying if I said; we didn't check the room each day and night for their signs. We were never afraid thinking the worst of our strange connection to them it seemed perfectly normal to us, like waiting for company.

*The ETs notice of arrival by leaving my scarf hanging
from the ceiling fan facing North with its white label which says
Dimensions.*

I was awakened the next night after the recent episode with the scarf and necklace by a loud crashing sound as if my bedroom window had been hit very hard by a terrific force! My head came up off the pillow fast and even though I was groggy and half asleep I remained very still to listen, not moving, waiting to see what would happen next. I was thinking, what could that noise be at the window at this time of night? As fast as I had those thoughts a huge loud sound of the wind hit this same side of the house fiercely shaking the windows once more! I had never experienced anything like this in the years I have lived here, and then nothing, it was so quiet you could not hear a sound except my breathing. This happened on a night without a breeze let alone a wind which was very strange. Before I went back to sleep that night, I thought of my dad he had passed away a few years before and even though I often communicated with him it was not unnatural for me to send out my thoughts to him. That's about the last thing I remembered until I saw a bright light coming to me beginning to take shape. I strained to focus my eyes watching the light as it formed into my father holding out his arms to hug me!! I was so happy and calling out to him, dad! I had hoped something would happen on this night because it was his birthday and our loved ones are always around going back and forth especially on special occasions. I wish there was a simpler way other could understand, or that I knew to explain about the spirit world being able to connect with others here.

When I awoke the next morning, I went straight to the window remembering how strong the wind was or whatever had happened that hit the window so hard in the night. I wanted to explore what it could have been other than my dad announcing his arrival to wake me, I knew better I was thinking with my human thoughts then. At first look I thought I would see damage from a tree limb or something but there was nothing, human thinking again! What surprised me the most was the stained-glass window I had hanging in front of the regular window was blown off the nails that held it in place! The curtains were the only thing that kept it from falling on the floor and breaking. I knew this was another one of those impossible things to happen because the regular window was NOT raised up to let any wind in, and the stained-glass window had been secured very well! All I knew was that a very powerful force of some kind came through here which I believe was Dad's energy coming through with the ETs! I would have to wait to see if I could find out from them, so I reminded myself; just let that thought go because of the bliss I was feeling remembering the visit from my Dad. So many beautiful things were happening I dared not share with anyone but my son, since we both were a large part of a phenomenal existence we were living, and who could understand any of this if we couldn't always.

I would be reaching to turn my table lamp on, but it turned on before I reached it! Other electrical lights did the same thing right before I touched the switch. I didn't know what was happening with my energy and vibrations they were sure changing and one of the things I noticed my *energy* changing to a higher level in some way.

I had a little alarm clock I kept beside my bed on a table; this is also described in my first book *"Under the Rainbow Crossing"*. One early morning I heard a loud crash and quickly sat up; I saw the small clock used to wake me lying on the floor several feet away from the table where it normally was! Once more the back was completely off with its batteries spilled out scattered onto the floor, I was stunned! It couldn't have done it by itself, but it had and as I picked it up, I heard *TICKING!* I put the clock up to my ear and believe it or not, it was ticking away without a battery!! This little clock ran perfectly *WITHOUT* batteries for over three months! Then one day as I walked past the table, I accidentally did knock it off and it never ran again!

When I lived in my late son's home years later after he crossed over my dad's old wall clock also ran without batteries for some time, how do you explain something like that? My take is, the spirits are energy like us, so it is probably easy for them to do. I have no doubts the other side can do anything, and I have my ideas on how the other side arranges things we would never think possible! That day when my dad's clock did this (with no batteries in it) I was astounded wondering, *"Who would ever believe this; on second thought will I ever tell anyone about this?"* When I wrote my first and second books, I did tell this and it was one of the few times I didn't get to take pictures of an unusual occurrence I wish now I had videoed it. Perhaps because so much was going on out of the ordinary day and night and my attention was only on my son who had recently passed over at this time, I was completely distraught! I am sure David and his grandfather did this together to give me a smile. They were very close in life and the things I am writing about happened in my home and my late parent's old home when David lived there. After David passed, he was busy appearing to me with his words of comfort and doing things to let me know he was with me. I lived there for some time after he passed and each day amazing things took place in the house and no matter where I went! My son and I had lived in the other worlds and dimensions at the same time since we each were very small. I recalled David said, *"He felt the same way as I did about everything we experienced as lessons of our universal learning"*.

CHAPTER 4

Who Are They Really?

When life is busy like David's and mine one certainly doesn't get to sleep like most normal human beings, and as strange as this may sound to you I would not change a thing in my life because I'm re-learning and the more I learn the more I seek to learn, through our experiences. David and I were the alike with the same mind set and gifts, and I may not have felt so strongly if we couldn't have shared our experiences together, but we had one another to share our unusual life as planned. The other side told us, *"to live life here on Earth first and foremost enjoying loved ones and all the gifts that we have every day are right here under our nose on this beautiful earth by appreciating the beauty of what is nature."* I truly believe this!

The experiences we were reliving were very important for many reasons; our searching minds are being filled with information that we need to know about in our work. Some of the information given to us we will never be able to speak about or to reveal, only the information we are free to give will be in the books I write for the world to read. These are the instructions I have been given by the High Council of ETs, and Universal Spiritual Christ Light Beings that work with both of us. Now you may understand with universal information supplied to us daily why my son and I would know when the ETs were coming to us throughout our life span. They were also learning from us, such as our emotions we use here, and we were building an old bond we could share. The humor they had begun to show us the first time was by moving my *moon* necklace and *scarf* around to the top of the chandelier and on a fan light as I described and soon it was gone, completely missing! I searched around for it quite a while then I happened to look out of the 2nd story window where it was fluttering in the breeze attached to the weathervane on the garage roof! They seemed to be breaking us in little by little, they had mastered our earth humor to kid us back! We thought this was really a class-act they did with my scarf on the weathervane keeping us busy with their jokes at all hours. Humans may never think of Aliens as being funny, but these can be!

51

Everything they taught us we shared together, and their lessons were important! The ETs wanted what they said, written about them.

One day I decided to meditate on my *moon* necklace and *my scarf* the ETs had been moving from place to place. Realize things they sometimes did could happen in daytime, which made no difference to them. I stopped my meditation after a short while deciding to do my normal things to see what they would do. I left to get something and when I came back, I found my moon necklace and scarf that had been hanging from my fan/light gone again and in another place!

This is where we found the scarf later the same day hanging on the chandelier in the tower area off the bedroom, after earlier finding it hanging on the ceiling fan.

The ETs began to move my scarf around the house onto lamps in other rooms, hiding it in my closet, and once one of my collector dolls had my scarf around its shoulders like a shawl! On some day's items would be moved up to three different times! We laughed so much about their learned humor and loved the telepathic messages to us letting us know when they were coming. Soon I would say, *"I know the ETs are coming in tonight, David would laugh, I know!"*

At certain times traveling in my car on the highway the ETs would make contact telepathically telling me to *"look!"*. I would pull over and park where I could watch them with their blinking lights darting *erratically* back and forth, up and down, as if they were having fun entertaining us along our way. When David and I were in the car I would ask him, if anything was going on? He could *sense* them but could not clearly see them his sight was not as good so I would stop and describe what they were doing. Then we would laugh knowing they were entertaining us and tracking us.

This is the scarf we found on top of the weathervane. This determined they were coming from the north.

Every chance we rolled down the windows and enjoyed what they were doing; it was like our own private *ET* air show, our own *Space Angels*. The ETs told us, *"They can put up a shield anytime they needed to, and no one can see them,"* we knew that made perfect sense or there would be a *massive* pile up of cars on the roads and in front of our house! Many times, I would remark, *"the ETs would be coming in tonight."* We looked forward to them every time it was so exciting to be re-learning from them...

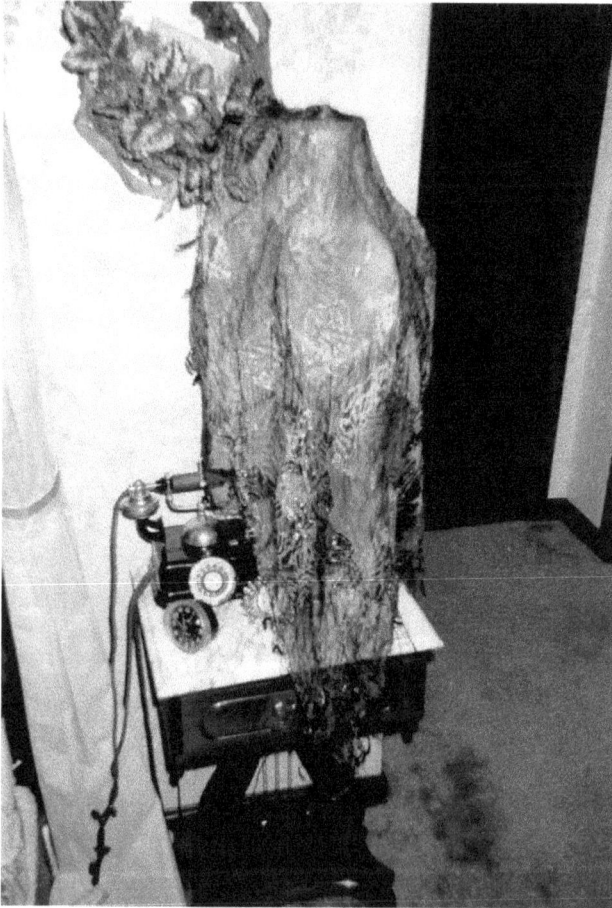

The ETs were trying to tell us something about light by putting my scarf over my bedside lamp and to the right is a face in the carpet.

I have to say our excitement was escalating with our familiar connection to them and we were learning many things. I recalled the ETs saying, *"we only give you so much at a time then we let you digest that information because the human mind can only take in so much at a time or as you humans say, it would blow the mind!"* When it came to our working in the spirit side with loved one's past, different entities, or families of ETs, we were receiving all kind of incoming information to figure out who and what we really are a part of functioning as we did day by day, in what is called a normal way.

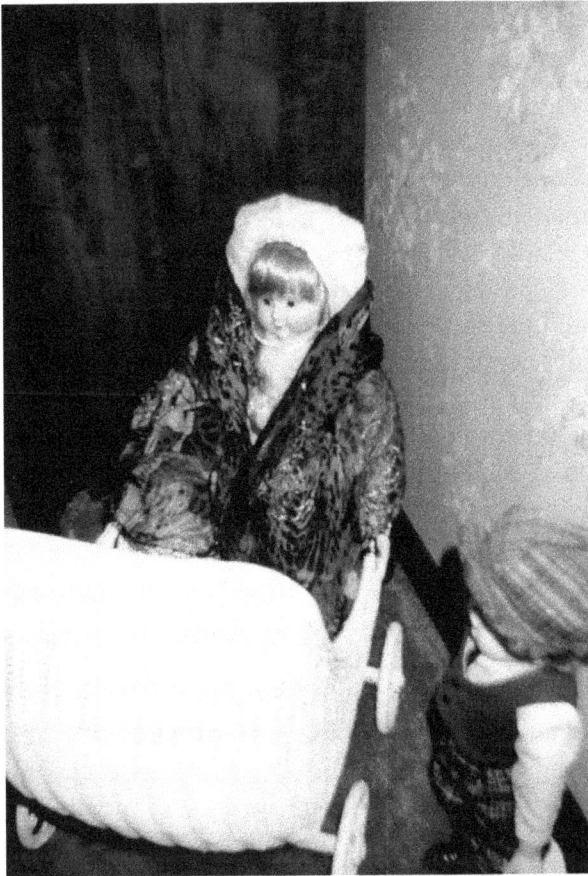

How we found the Traveling scarf draped like a shawl over the doll.

After learning various special information in those many years of experiences we were told to *"begin teaching others how we are ALL*

55

COMBINED TOGETHER". With everything happening I knew we had to have very strong minds and had to be more than just the word *strong,* we had been designed! I found I cannot find a word in our language to describe how our minds could hold so much information. I do know neither of us would have changed one thing and no matter how hard everything may get, it's more than worth the trip! After years of working beside many Beings who are not human, I believe everyone no matter how different has been created by the same Infinite Supreme Intelligence of Creation of a loving source! I also wonder how some humans became so fearful in their thinking that the universe has no other Beings except man this just astounds me, but times are clearly changing now through more UFO experiences others are having over the world which is wonderful!

In times of serious sickness, death, or whatever was going on in our own family of an emotional experience I would begin meditating to get guidance because of the nature of the problem. In times of *sorrow* I would experience what I perceived and know to be a beautiful *Angel Being* who would speak to me knowing I was troubled telling me, *"Now, I will sweeten your path".* Those words meant things would get better, they knew we became overwhelmed at times and their magnificent words came when we needed them the most! The beautiful Beings who assisted us gave us the strength we desperately needed at that time. We were elated to experience those who came to comfort us reinforcing our feelings we needed so badly. It was as if I needed to pinch myself to make sure I was awake to know without a doubt this Earth plane is only a *dream world, an Earth school, an illusion* we live in to grow and learn.

The other side is our real place of existence and home, *"to sweeten your path"* told me I was on track to know things would get better and *this too shall pass.* I thought long and hard of how we each chose our missions in life and the experiences happening to each person are to learn by in their own way, and this is often never understood. I believe it was around this time I thought about being in the car accident years ago when I died for many long minutes and during this amazing time, I had a remarkable DOA experience, a miracle! When I passed out of my body, I went to the Christ Light to pure infinite love and told many things past, present, future, and then I was sent back although, I wasn't thinking of coming back! I was so loved and not thinking of returning. I had been told my journey, my future loving family with children, and what I was to do and teach. Many things I was to complete but could not reveal. When I was older, I understood more of this experience about my *planned future mission* in life. I have never felt such complete love as when I passed, and it can't be described how it is in this heavenly realm. I knew I was a part of everything there is and ever created, we all are! Not only did I feel an amazing completeness which is unexplainable but a total undescribed love that I cannot begin to understand myself, and with this was humor, a rapture of joy combined in my death experience. This was something I did not expect, I was brought up to think God, Jesus, and Heaven was all very serious, scary, and very quiet, and if bad one could go to a hell! When I returned into my body; I had no idea of how much I agreed to do in my creation to fulfill in my lifetime, I had made a contract, a promise, to the Creator of all I wanted to accomplish in my life.

My healing took close to a year or more from the accident and I felt strangely different from then on, in time I would understand as I grew into an adult. I am thankful and extremely grateful for the gift of dying in the accident to experience what I needed to know, and I gladly left the man-made fears behind I had grown up with. The ET Christ Light beings are my teachers as they always have been, who continue watching over me along with other heavenly beings to assure me I am growing in my mission as planned. Those were the baby steps in my training years, and I continue to find myself changing according to my blessed work.

I was unknowingly turning on and off electrical things without touching them at times and driving my car at night I noticed after I passed under streetlights looking back through the car mirror, they would pop off one by one. In a short time as I drove further down the road they popped back on, this happened frequently even parking under a streetlight was usually the same way. I don't know if I was exceeding my regular energy balance in my system or something the ETs were adjusting but I continue at times to have this happen. When my son and I were in Oklahoma years ago we were walking down a toy aisle in a store and the toys began coming on by themselves making noise and moving we had not touched them! This was before toys were made to do this as in today's world. This type of thing still occasionally happens as I go here and there with lights. There are questions I don't have answers for that still happen and they may never be answered here, then it won't matter...

One day I had my little granddaughter over and as I walked by the TV it came on by itself! Being so young, she was amazed, *"do it again"* so I would go back and forth, the television continued to turn on and off with her laughing "you do it" I said, and amazingly it happened with her going back and forth over and over! Whoever orchestrated this event must have been laughing, she has always remembered this.

The ETs Had a New Plan for My Sight

One of the new physical things that began to happen was the way I began to see things my vision changed, yes changed. The ETs were working on both of our bodies and sight at times, and when I woke up one day trying to focus my eyes, they were not wanting to wake up! I heard one of my ET teachers from the other side speak to me, *"From this day on you will be seeing things differently when you are meant to"*. I immediately knew for whatever the reason this was about to happen my eyes, they would be more like a camera I would be able to focus both close and far away! It didn't take long to find out what my teacher meant with this new information, I began seeing more *entities* in solid form and some formed in amazing beautiful colors, different shapes and textures. Some figures were woven together with the look of *gold threads;* it's very hard to explain. I will never forget when my dad appeared to me one night formed in beautiful gold threads of light and his 3rd eye a brilliant cobalt blue, which is located a little higher above the bridge in the middle of the forehead! This was the most beautiful experience one I can't really explain how it looked to give it justice! Then later, I was shown in a book by Barbara Ann Brennan how this looks when a spirit is in gold *threads of Light,* just like my dad had been! I understood it more now, I only wished I had a picture of him in this way! Did this startle me with this change in my eyes, you can't imagine how amazing this was! It was something I had never experienced before and one more thing with my eyes that occurred at another time was when I was woken up by an ET of High Levels. I was startled when he told me, *"my sight would be as a camera, a telescope, which can zoom in and out"!* When I looked across my bedroom to where my eyes *focused,* they *zoomed in* to a certain object lying on a table and it was as if I was looking through a *telescope* or *binoculars!* This happened so quickly it scared me, and the new way of *focusing* was extremely fast, it was *instant, different,* and I wondered in silence, *"is this going to happen all the time?"* These were another of the amazing changes that occurred to me by the ETs, and it isn't all the time, I have NO control when this does happen.

I want to share some experiences when certain teachers or guides would come to work with both of us from the other side. At times when the teachers and guides are present, I would hear what can only be described as a *tiny bell* or *buzzing* that sounds as if it's beside my ear, then they have my complete attention to listen as I anxiously await their words. The ETs also made a sound at times like a *cricket or a clicking sound* on a summer night when they came, we became very familiar with it. I have not asked why it occurs since it is not every time, we heard this often and sometimes use this sound outside, our hearing and sight are extra sensitive now.

If you know it or not each person has a spiritual teacher or teachers, and a guide or guides who work with each one of us in various ways. One of the guides is with you from the day we each are born throughout our entire life span, often nudging us to pay attention, trying to steer and guide us to keep us on track if only we will listen. This is what is called your *intuition,* use it and you will stay *on track* more than *off track,* but we as humans tend to *override* intuition in our life for things we want. In those times of what we want we don't always listen to *that little voice,* but being a human is not perfect by any means. If a person will take a few minutes a day learning to be quiet, listen, and meditate, much can be *revealed* to you in this way, to communicate with you, and perhaps eventually you will learn to know your guide/teacher. A guide is a spirit who has lived on earth before such as a loved one, they are helping us from the other side and every single person has an assigned guide. Some people perhaps have more than the one guide who help them throughout their lives. The assigned guide is with you from birth and may come back with you in the next lifetime again if you so choose to return. You may have several guides in your lifetime but never be afraid to replace one if the guide does not have your best interest at heart. You have the right to get rid of one and ask for another in detail as to what you want and need to help you in a positive way.

It's all about free will and sometimes a new guide will step in to help with a certain experience in my life with needed expertise and join up with a main guide, but the main one is always with you. I have several guides and teachers to help me in various ways with where I am in my life, and with the kind of experience I am going through. I was being prepared in many ways through my life and even though the ETs had everything to do with the messages I was receiving I also received some from others such as Edgar Cayce and passed over ones. For instance, one morning about 10 am I felt the presence of one of my teachers and he began to speak to me with one short sentence, *"you are on the threshold of sorrow"* I understood I was being prepared ahead of time for *heartbreak,* and even though I was upset I was grateful to be warned. I would never forget what my teacher said, *"a sorrowful tragedy was coming and would be difficult for everyone when it happened, because so many people loved this person and would miss him when he passed."* His name was Charley a loved one who I mentioned before, and he has been busy appearing to some of us from the very day he passed. He comforts in various ways with what he can do from the other side. For those who would be frightened when he makes a visit, he comes in their dreams. I believe at some point after he crossed over, he made a *"turnaround"* this is, with his choice to return in a new baby, he wanted to be with his loved ones again to be held and loved. This is done with a soul's choice and called reincarnation.

The ETs programmed us in their schools

In the night I was shown symbols by the ETs and other Alien Beings of light they told me, *"This next experience was important to them for me to study which was in front of me. I was told to watch them and learn from them".* This had to do with universal language written in universal script, I knew some of the languages were Egyptian hieroglyphics, Greek, with other familiar looking symbols they wanted us to relearn in their languages. Most of what I looked at was made with these symbols and designs, and at the time I had no idea of what those meanings were. If I had known at one time and I strongly suspected I did, they had been erased from my part human mind. I figured in time I would come to know them again. My *schooling* usually happened after I went to sleep at night and then suddenly, I was wide-awake sitting in front of a screen sort of like a large television screen. Telepathically I was being told, *"I was being programmed and at other times re-programmed to things I had done in another time and with languages I had known before '.* This information would fly by rapidly on the screen and I would find myself saying out loud, *"slow down, slow down"* I was excited to learn about everything I was being taught in order to communicate better. They already knew my thoughts and what was inside my mind and I knew everything they were doing was for a later time when I would need it.

I can only describe myself to be like a tape recorder, a memory bank of sorts relearning the old knowledge we had forgotten and needed. I guess I could call this a *refresher course* for past secrets and information that were set aside. As I watched information fly by it was nothing but a blur going faster and never slowing down! In no time they had another new way to communicate and surprised us. We began to find messages from them in more detail on my old computer! As I mentioned the universal messages were only for us and some of them said, *"We could not save them, they were for our eyes only"* and we couldn't, they would be gone in no time! We valued the ETs as our teachers and family and their words of wisdom along with their instructions, we gladly did as they asked. The screen savers we could save with the messages and I used my video camera for those, but it was hard to take pictures with the words running across the screen. We knew nothing about computers I was sure there was a way to slow the words and pictures down and thinking back, all we had to do was ask the ETs for help to do this and the computer would have been slowed down. They don't want to do everything for us but were very helpful anytime we asked.

One day I was up much earlier than usual because I heard soft sounds of music coming from downstairs where the computer was, so I called for David who was in his room. This was absolutely the *ultimate surprise* for us so far showing us the humor they have with a two-way joke because...the music they had playing on the computer was from *STAR WARS!!* Oh! How funny! We absolutely LOVED what they had done it was brilliant and hilarious, they knew we would love the surprise! The screen saver was full of spaceships, stars, planets, worm holes, galaxies, even an Astronaut in a space suit drifting through space with a pack on his back and tubes going to his face, mask, and helmet!! All kinds of things were moving along in space, even the UFOs were in amazing shapes we had never seen before! We both bet we were being shown the future since we were not familiar with several things on this display, they left for us, especially the astronaut floating in space which happened in the future. I was able to save this unique space setting before it disappeared from the screen with my video camera. By this time, I had been using my camera for everything I could, and how we *loved* the *"Star Wars"*. We knew we were being shown this because one day in the future our own Astronauts would be able to move around outside the shuttles in space! Can you imagine how happy we felt knowing this was the future, of course we dared not tell anyone, we couldn't anyway with our promise.

Later that same evening after going to bed I woke up to my son's voice calling out I hurried into his room and he was grinning ear to ear and very excited! He was laughing and talking at the same time he said, *"he couldn't sleep thinking of the "Star Wars "episode!"* I couldn't imagine what to think still laughing myself, there had been so many things the ETs were showing us! I could only hope all I had recorded would still be there one day so I could use it. Well, this is that day I am in that future time to be writing about our life with them. We were witness to some of the new discoveries of this generation they told us of back then with more occurring today!

The next time we traveled we were *transported* to what looked to be a *jungle* setting. This was not unfamiliar to me because this had happened to us many times before. I was aware of going through foliage (I don't think I was walking it was more like floating) the plants alongside us looked like huge fern leaves in various sizes and shapes and were thick everywhere I looked I could not see much else. Even though I opened my eyes once thinking I was back at home in my bed, I saw I wasn't, so I closed my eyes again for a moment then opened them again, I was still in this *jungle*! I think this was the ETs way to make me feel more comfortable disguising where I was at first or maybe my journey with them was in between worlds and not completed when I thought I was at home in my bed, so I was seeing both places, my thoughts is my reality...

Then there were a kind of spirals and circles we had experienced before associated with our frequent travels and later I made a connection to the big plants as what I seen as ferns, designs, and spirals we saw. They were likely *Vortexes or Crop Circles'* we were experiencing with the ETs when they use symbols and designs in Crop Circles over our world. It could be either, and we wondered why this had become a frequent experience of ours with them since we had seen many of the same plant forms and spirals over the years with them. I never thought to ask that question in all of that time, was it time for us to possibly remember being with them while they created some of the *"Crop Circles"* was this the ETs way trying to warn earth of future things to come, which needed to be aware of to help earth? We certainly believe so; these designs were very important communication from them to humankind with whatever the answers were. We had many questions with unknown answers and the ETs were going slow in teaching and reminding us of what we had known before about this. Later, I met others at conferences who were researchers of Crop Circles for years and some most of their lives, with our great interest in them maybe this had been our preview of something we had known before?

It was the beginning of a New Year on that morning I was using the video camera aiming it into the family room because often I would capture *impossible* events and spirits on film which were not of this world! My mind couldn't process fast enough because I couldn't believe what happening, my find of an old antique sofa and chair I had purchased began *glittering* with tiny lights as they quickly made their way around the outline of the sofa and matching chair just like a border! I had bought the old furniture finding it on the top floor of an old empty building one day in Kentucky. I thought it must have brought along a spirit or two with a story to tell! The tiny lights were like small miniature white Christmas lights, I couldn't believe it! I captured this extraordinary experience on video and later had pictures made from it I felt those spirit/spirits from the other side were *orchestrating* this event instead of the ETs, but maybe it was worked out between them. This was unbelievable to watch and experience but there it was in front of my own eyes and since it was into the New Year I wondered if this amazing happening was linked to the holiday, this could be a New Year celebration! After the magical lights ended a new message came to me almost at the same time from one of my spiritual teachers: *"for me to smile and bow before the light"*. This seemed to us the Christ light let us know they are always around us, we are protected, loved, and to be happy in our spiritual work with a New Year!

There were times in *out of body* travel we would be helping people in spirit to cross over and guide them to the other side. I remember telling two males in our care, *"not to be afraid to walk into the light, just walk into the light and don't be afraid"*. We felt this was what the above message *"smile and bow"* meant for us which made sense. I can't tell you how strange and beautiful it is to be with a person who has just passed into spirit, to guide them across universal planes in this way. Sometimes the same day later or the next one after we would see their obituary in a newspaper, TV news, or get a phone call that this person who we helped had passed. And even though you helped them the moment they died it hits you with *awe* to know it was real! This often happens even with those who live miles away or those we do not know personally or have ever met we were able to help, by escorting their soul/spirit into the other dimensions of an everlasting life!

Let me define soul and spirit, the definition of the soul is: best known as I, our personality, our memories, and our uniqueness of being, I myself. The definition of the spirit is: the essence of the Creator which is ever present and uplifting forever.

Our assistance of the spirits continues, we know we can trust our thoughts *"we do help certain souls 'crossover!'"* Sometimes souls were mostly unknown to us, but it did not matter, and I have no answer to how this entire transformation works except this was what we agreed to in our *contract*. We see the spirits so well and know when one is stuck or too afraid to advance, or whatever the reason is. When people die some are too afraid to move forward or do not know they have died and wander around in their home as a *"ghost"* and to places they loved to spend time in when living. It could be for numerous reasons but thank God we can help deliver those we have to the other side. They are usually those who lived in fear of dying, afraid of a scary punishment they were taught about who stay and some for other reasons of not knowing they have passed.

There would be times we were given news from the other side of a new scientific discovery coming to help people on earth. This information would be given to a scientist thinking it was their own discovery although, this information came from The High Council of ETs or other highly evolved spiritual beings. Some information of another nature was made clear to us about what to do, or not to do with their information. We knew this came from a Higher Being of the Christ Light and only a fool would doubt their words!

During our next adventure the ETs said, *"they wanted to sharpen our intuition"* so they began to leave messages more often on the screen saver using only Universal information for us to continue our studies. They worked on a continuous basis training us for other things to come, and we took in everything with a light heart always eager to learn, knowing that one day we would experience a giant *revelation* in our lives to the whole of this. Never did I dream what they taught us was not just our schooling but also about writing the books for others to learn through! They want the truth told so badly from those of us who are a big part of this, and their truth written to take away fear of them. This is so one day people will be able to merge together with them and not be afraid, sounds like a wonderful plan to me, and it will take many of us to keep educating the world to take the fear away most have been taught.

As a happy mother who dearly loves her children, family, caring for my home, and taking care of my loving son I did the normal things a woman does but underneath all of this I was dealing with all of the above, other places, other beings, other dimensions, the spirit world, out of body travel, as a medium, you name it. My son took life very calmly he was grateful for each moment of each day as I was for him! I knew how he did this because he was a very old soul, a teacher to me, his sisters and many others, he knew what he was here to do and so did I. If David and I had not chosen to work together as a unit in these worlds together I imagine we would have felt terribly isolated and alone. But together we shared the many dimensions and worlds we each understood and working together made this serious plan we chose easier and an exciting part of life.

My daughters were busy working and living a busy life and knew nothing of what went on with the ETs, but they had no trouble believing it, they had seen some messages that came in on the computer screen saver with script written in symbols. They were very familiar with movement in the house while growing up with the seven spirits who lived here. And later when they were long grown, we showed them the moon necklace with the traveling scarf and a few ET computer messages that popped on when they were here. I don't know what their thoughts exactly were, but they looked at the amazing things done here and smiled, they were surprised, and probably shocked about the ETs. Much more was going on since they had lived here, and I knew the girls were intuitive but if they never used their gift it was fine, I understood that. I am sure most others would not want to go there this being another life.

It took time for me to quit trusting a few others and completely learn what I was told years ago *to not do*, and that was, *"do not cast your pearls before the swine"*. I wanted to share a little when given a little free rein in those years because I was filled with excitement with the amazing things happening. I had held back everything we were learning, but a few times I trusted too much and spoke to a few friends about the amazing spirits we can become when we die, and how some of us live in fear with man-made teachings. I did this in good faith to relieve their fear, but I may have made them angry or scared, or they may have thought I was silly. Finally, one of my heavenly teachers, *John* came to me and explained sweetly, *"Of how he did the same work when he was on earth but not to force the information onto others"* then mentioned his own lesson with humor that he had to learn the *hard way* of when to keep his mouth shut! The result being, one may lose people who you thought were your friends and even sometimes family members. I am sure the few who we told wondered what was going on with us because this was way over their head, and perhaps the few others secretly felt the same. Some people are open and some well; they are on the level where they should be which only means, we all have learning to do no one is better than another. We are how we are taught or simply do not know, and there is nothing wrong about being *skeptic*, that is the way we learn too. We are all on different levels of learning and there are many levels to work through in life, the main thing is that we keep learning and hopefully find out there is really nothing impossible. As another of my spiritual teachers told me, *"If only people could see what the real world is and to know things aren't always as they seem"*. So, in the long run, never let anyone stop your growth with his or her remarks or ideas, stay on track; let your heart and intuition lead you and you will learn.

Every single person is given *free will* this eternal gift is yours to use, and there will always be negative and positive beings which help create a universal balance we may not fully understand but is vital. We can learn from the *negative ones* because they teach us by what they do so hopefully we know not to follow them. The ET Beings of the Light are phenomenal universal species and loving teachers working for mankind to wake up if we want to keep this earth. We are in a new spiritual revolution which will take a huge amount of work to change our planet to a new one which will bring love and peace to all beings in the future.

This recalls an experience I had when I was out of body in spirit and taken to a place which was brilliant white and everything around me was white and nothing else. Suddenly there was a man with me or who I thought was a man at first, I remember we began talking about the *realm* we were in and visiting in that time. This being appeared to me as an older man who I knew was one of the greatest kindness, and I felt his absolute Divine love *radiating* from him to me. He was made of complete love and I remember we were talking about how things came to us through our *intuitiveness* in the *psychic world*. We compared lessons with how these things unfolded and how we were connected; he said, *"We both were enlightened, and we knew"*. He continued saying, *"we could see and hear long past the 6 senses and there are more past them as we have found."* Then he spoke about *"Holy Beings and those which are true and real we see and experience."* I loved meeting this enlightened being who I know came to me as a human but was much more than that, he was on a very high level! Then he said, *"to look down at my hand,"* I had a *special ring* on that I did not recognize, I did not have a ring like this not yet anyway in my lifetime here on Earth! It would be ELEVEN *years* later when this ring would be brought to me from the other side, I was being shown this in my future to come!

For my own confirmation when this ring appeared mysteriously, I asked, *"Who is this ring for?"* and the heavenly messenger's voice bellowed out *"FOR YOU!"* I was extremely humbled and stunned by my amazing experience, this special ring was a *Holy* ring! The center stone is a beautiful deep violet color with tiny diamonds around the oval shaped setting which has a gold band. It is precious to me for reasons in my spiritual life especially being a Holy gift and not because of its beauty alone. This ring has been blessed and is a *very, very special gift* from *The Universal Divine Source* and holds great meaning of importance to me. I am grateful I have written everything down in my notebooks over the many years keeping my records as the Universal Creator asked me to do long ago. When the blessed Christ, the Son, came *mysteriously* to me in that way as a man I knew, and so did my son David who presented this ring to me.

There was more I found written in my journal about the being who presented himself to me as a man, *"I asked if both of us were learning on the same levels since we were the same in our work and he conveyed to me that we were!"* When this experience continued the holy being of the Christ light let me see the vision where I was walking down a very long hall and I came to a very spiritual place which reminded me of a huge Cathedral or Church where there were rows and rows of pews. I noticed that everything in this huge open space was bathed in a beautiful bright white light setting as the same Christ Light Being, I had met before. He was now in all glowing white a radiant being of pure light this heavenly being was still some distance from me but facing in my direction as if waiting for me at the front of what was happening. Although, there were other high Beings also present this one I had talked with earlier was the highest of all, and I remember everything being so very quiet. Soon one of the others was facing me and led me to another area off to the side, I didn't think or ask why? I was filled with complete happiness to proceed with him somehow knowing he would soon be teaching me much more of colors, auras, and the *amazing transition* when we as humans leave our physical bodies. There was a long line of people from where we were, and I wondered *"were those people in spirit in the process of passing over and I was to be given this review for certain reasons"*?

I do know when they let me experience how it felt to leave my body; it was the most wonderful amazing feeling ever!! I had no weight at all and could move faster than thought, and the best part I had was, I was free of my heavy physical body which was more than *exhilarating*! Once before when I died, I had a similar experience about our human body weight, at the last breath one has our body is gone forever and the spirit is lighter than light! I have gladly shared these beautiful experiences to let others know… When this happened to me my spirit shot out of my body so fast, I was instantly in the universe and a part of everything there is, and everything there could ever be, I merged with everything which was created! When in spirit one moves faster than thought once we are free of our earth body, and I was one of them!

Seeing myself in my spirit I was so happy other spirits laughed with me; they were humorous, not like most tend to think of the other side with fear and so serious with no laughter, it is pure joy! They told me, "my colors were of *green and rose* which are the highest after the white, and how after we pass over, we know one another by our colors and my color means happiness!" These are the colors I have always loved and been attracted too. This feeling I had cannot be explained in our language, nor can this extraordinary experience be ever imagined! I felt strongly the Christ Light ETs were a big part of this refreshing my memory of long ago when I had gone through their familiar tunnel of Light! I had died in the wreck at 16 and had these phenomenal experiences to begin my work, this was like an extraordinary review!! Humans are the ones who create the names of those on the other side such *as aliens,* and this one word alone draws out fear, perhaps our story can help!

The heavenly experiences I reviewed while in the Cathedral brought back those memories of when I was in the wreck and DOA, then finding myself in spirit with the most phenomenal loving, compassionate and captivating presence of white Light that I cannot explain, our Creator. This is not a man, but an infinite energy of unexplainable Supreme Intelligence of love and compassion way beyond anything one can know! The magnitude of where I found myself in was a precious place of pure beauty, and the Creator spoke to me of my future life to be, and things I would not remember later because I needed the experiences first along with other lessons I would have. After this, I was sent back to live out my future, have my children, and teach to others of His truth!

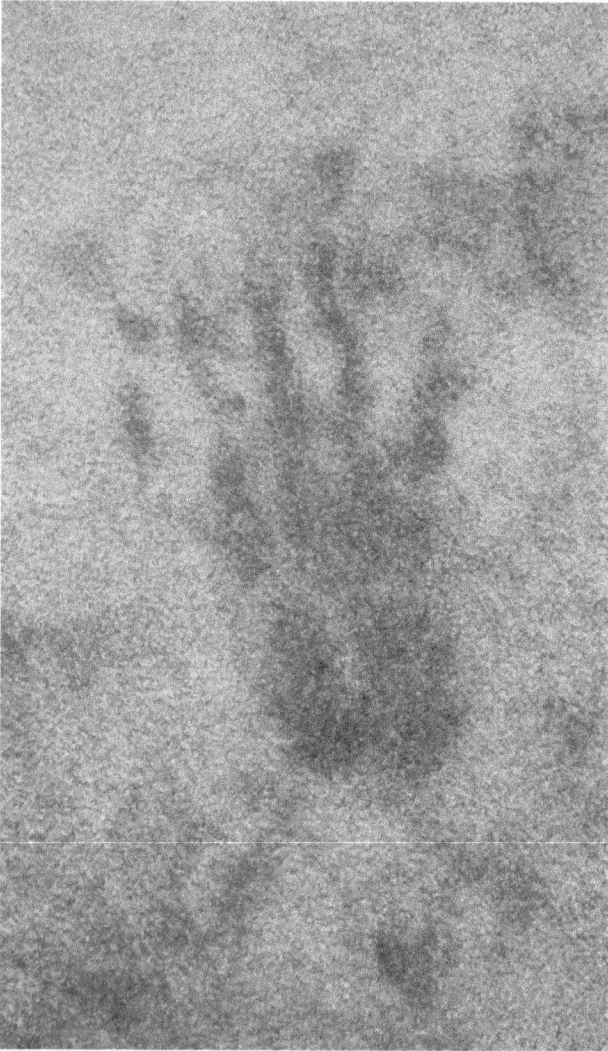

*On this page and the following one are just a few of the many imprints that
we found over the years in the carpeting throughout the house. These seem
to have five digits which is different than many others.*

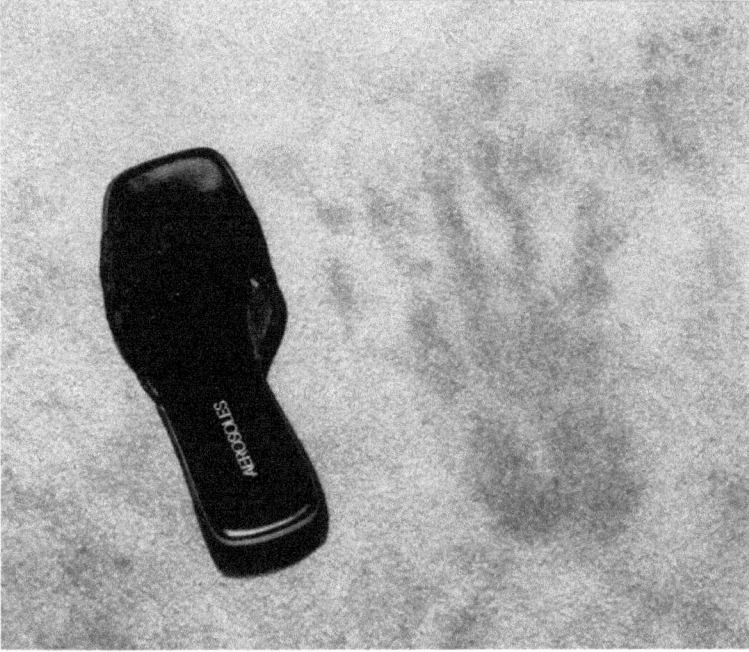

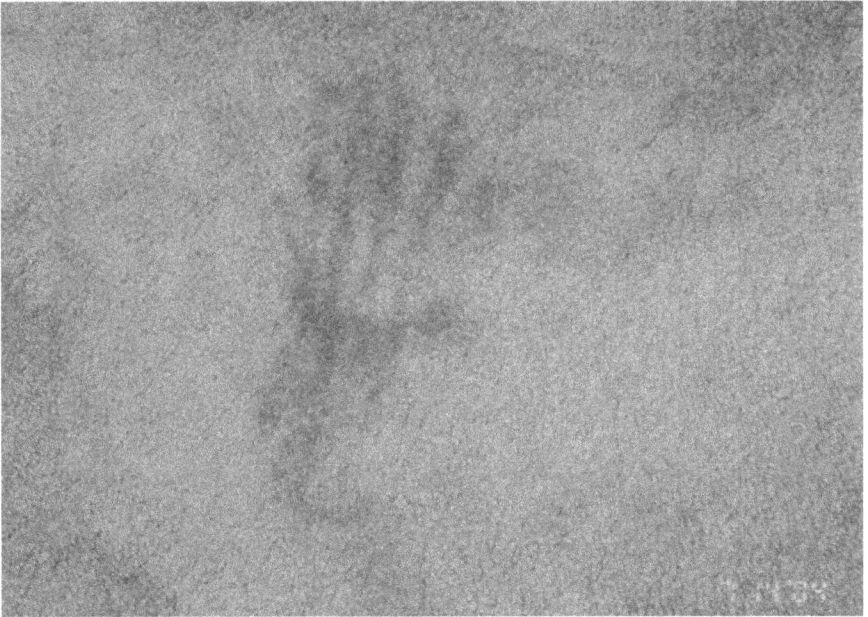

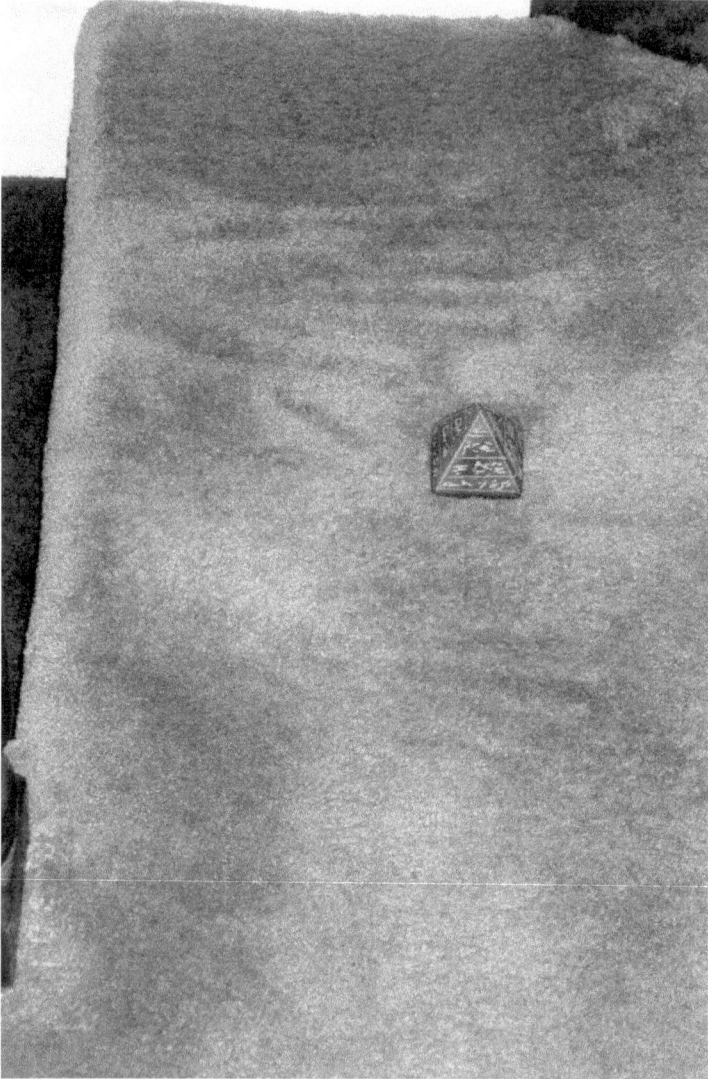

See the ET handprints on both sides of my small pyramid (when you turn the picture sideways from this perspective). This species of ET has long thin fingers with a short digit where we have a thumb. These prints belonged to a High Council Being.

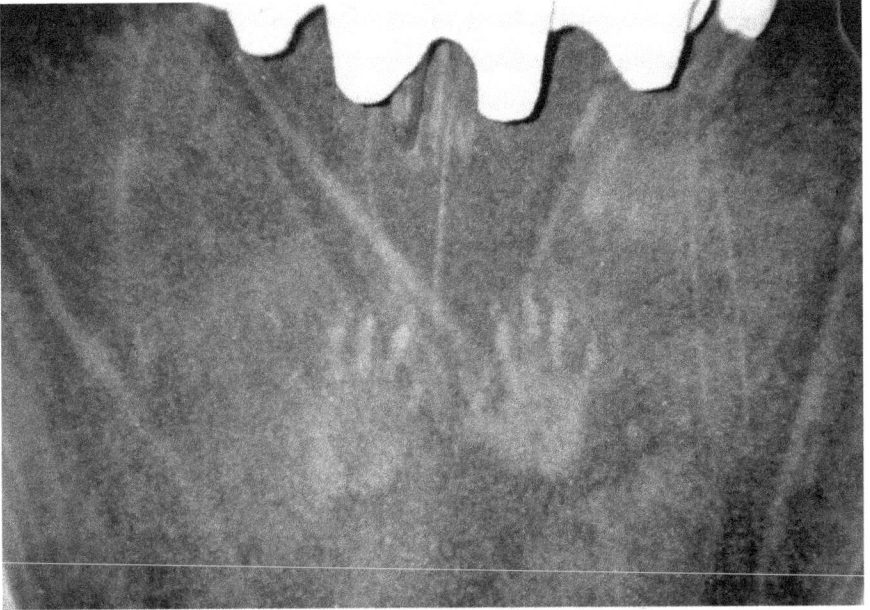

We found these small unidentified handprints with a symbol in each palm and pyramid symbol (V shape) in between them from unknown Beings.

Information came the next night from the ETs about our world being of *great unrest,* worse than ever before as it is now, which I won't go further because there is still a small amount of time for man to change things from bloodshed to harmony. I received this same information several years ago from them, but it has only gotten worse on our earth plane, and more time wasted. Man is bent on destroying this beautiful world we have been given to live in, now more than ever, this is about POWER and GREED!

A few nights later we were picked up by the ETs and at first, I thought I was still driving my car with two other passengers, one was a family member and I realized the car was driving *itself*! I had my hands on the steering wheel but suddenly the car picked up speed so fast I had no control! It was dark and people were sleeping we had been to another town taking someone home when it all began. This is how the ETs sometimes let us experience things without knowing at first what has happened but quickly I realized we were with them; it was *exhilarating* to be completely free. None of the others seemed to be aware of what happened I quickly realized they were in a trance state and I was looking down below us thinking I would see the universe, but it was only WATER I could see! I focused again, we were moving through the universe and stars and suddenly at a beautiful lighthouse.

Today was April 11th my past grandmother's birthday, was this a vision, a visit from her? It was hard to grasp, then I recalled looking out of small windows which went completely around what I thought was a Lighthouse. For whatever reason I that moment I was given a message from my late dad for my son David, and me, *"to know that the power is within us and that all we desire shall be ours there will be another message soon, love Dad"* His message meant everything to us and seemed to wake my senses to why I could recall this *familiar* lighthouse, and what I had thought was one. Taking a better look there were many small windows all around it in this huge space inside. It was then I realized this was a UFO, a Mother ship, but we were to see it as a Lighthouse to relax our human mind. The message from my dad was to help my son and me because at that point in our lives we were having difficult times with David's illness therefore, they had brought us there and the ETs were going to help my son. My dad and the others wanted us to know they were with us and this confirmed even more that my dad, David and I were integrated together in a different way with the ET beings in how we are of them. Those who were with us that evening would not remember this and wake up back in their bed the next morning thinking they fell asleep on the ride home and was too tired to remember more.

The Grays returned soon after this experience on the same night, so I was fully aware of them by having trouble sleeping and watching all kind of energy beginning to form around me. It didn't take long there stood several of the little Gray's with two of them moving up close to me. Both were looking at me closely checking me out, and behind them I noticed a *trail* of what I can only describe as circles like huge coiled spring's that made me remember a toy called a *slinky,* only they were much larger! I should have known by then this represented a Vortex/worm hole. I began mentally receiving their thoughts to me, they wanted to show me something and the little ones began to part, moving out of the way and there stood what

I can only describe as a *unicorn type of being*! That's as close as I can come to a description of this universal life form, for whatever reason I was to see it maybe soon I would know what this was about.

After this, I was transported with them into the universe to explore another type of being I didn't understand, it disappeared with the little Gray's only what seemed to be moments later! After returning me to my room it was not over, I began to see a bright light coming towards me and in this light, I could see a *farmhouse* in a beautiful setting I knew I had seen before. I don't know in what order I saw the next thing exactly but I encountered a very large round object that reminded me of a satellite dish and in the center of it was a tube with a shaft of light coming from the bottom of it to the ground. I realized I was in this huge round shaped UFO, and aware I was looking down on this, all these things, the farmhouse and the scenery! It was then I knew I was traveling, and not in my room I was in the UFO.

I believe I was being re-acquainted with some type of a life-form the ETs wanted me to see. Something they wanted to acquaint me with so perhaps the *Unicorn being* was connected somehow with the farmhouse scene I was being shown. I couldn't figure out any other explanation in my human mind I would have to wait to see if I was filled in from the ETs. The good part was I was having a very *pleasant* experience I enjoyed very much as when we go with them to learn at other times. I was sure this would have meaning later it usually does, and it happened on a *full moon* night, this was getting to be a standing *date* with our ET friends. Later I found out I was correct the large coils were-- wormholes! I was experiencing more travel through them to many other places. What an exciting night!!

I told my son about the *little visitors* the next day because I had not seen him on this latest trip and he told me, *"he had seen two of the little Gray's last night too then he fell asleep on the sofa and the next thing he remembered was one of the little Gray's on the staircase and the other one went towards the end of the family room moving fast, this was all he remembered."* David made a decision he would start sleeping on the sofa most of the time so which of us heard or seen the little Gray's first was to come and wake the other one up, with that, we thought we had a new plan to go by. All I can say to that remark is... we would find out it would *never* be that easy but at the time we thought we had it figured out, not knowing we were in for a *big surprise*, we should have known we had NO control over the ETs visits!

There was something else happening in the next few days when I went into the city to shop. I was looking at a beautiful looking armoire to set the television set into. This was a discount store filled with high-quality furniture, but I decided after finding what I wanted it was still too expensive. One of the salespersons told me they were getting ready to mark it down soon with the other furniture so I may want to check back. She explained every 30 days the price dropped on the merchandise, so I made the long trip back in hopes of purchasing this furniture. I was disappointed when I saw it was still a little too high, as I stood there trying to decide what to do, I remember a different lady walking out of the main office who was the manager but why did she look so familiar?

A strange thing happened *I knew her* even if I had never seen her before I felt as if I had *always known her;* she was looking at me as dumbfounded as I must have been. We both stopped in our tracks and I looked away since I didn't want to stare at her, but I'm sure I did at first. She walked closer asking if *she could help me?* I told her what I was looking at and it was a good buy, but it was still a little too high for my budget. Her pin name had *Stephanie* on it, she was smiling at me and I will never forget what she said, *"You really do like this don't you?"* I nodded; I did. *"You know, we don't get people like you that come into our store, how much can you afford to pay?"* I didn't understand what she meant but I had this strange feeling about her and told her what I could pay, immediately she said, *"SOLD, it's yours I want you to have it"*. I was stunned, overwhelmed with gratitude I didn't know what to say at that moment except, "thank *you, Oh, thank you!"* She looked at me with a large smile and said; *"You know that we are kindred souls don't you, I wanted you to have this"*. I knew in that moment we were; I just knew it realizing we were on our separate journeys in this earth time therefore she wanted me to have this gift. We were in the same work in the spiritual realms with the Christ Light Beings! I was so happy to meet her in this way although we never talked again until in the following years to come. I never saw her again even when I went back to thank her once more, I asked for her as the manager, no one had ever heard of her!! Yes, we were kindred souls!

A surprise came to me years later after this experience, to sharing a special meeting of our two souls because it has so much meaning to my story and hopefully to you, here is why. Some years later I would meet up with *Stephanie* once more but in a different way. I was resting early one morning not wanting to get up and suddenly appearing to me in spirit stood this kind lady Stephanie who I met in the furniture store! She was standing silently beside me looking into my eyes and then over at my notebook I record everything in laying on my nightstand. She reached out to touch it and began reading the pages that laid open then looked back to me saying, "*the messages are only for you no one else.*" I knew that she meant, "*not to tell anyone about what I was experiencing, it wasn't time yet and some would copy my work.*" then she began to vanish!! I had a second to see a young man with her that I strongly felt was her son also in spirit with her. I wanted so much to *thank her for coming* with such an important message, but they vanished quickly, I couldn't *thank her* fast enough! I knew when I thanked her by telepathically sending my thoughts to her, she heard them!

For her to appear from years ago when we met in the store, she had my best interest at heart to protect my work. I have always called her *Stephanie*; the earth name she told me and I know our meeting was right on time in this world, and not because she let me have the piece of furniture at what I could afford to pay that day has nothing to do with it. This was the *reunion of two kindred souls* once again and this is what I saw in her eyes, she knew who I was by looking though my eyes into my soul. We had made a blessed *covenant* to meet like this from a past time. I will see her again one day that's for sure and I feel these things help to prove we all are from the one source, the Creator of all!

Another ET joke began using the *dimensions scarf* I mentioned earlier. The ETs had hung the scarf up again and again on the ceiling fan in my room and that week my scarf seemed to have a mind of its own. I heard my son calling for me, '*to come and look*" his voice sounded *urgent!* I hurried upstairs to see what was going on the traveling scarf had moved across the room to my crystal ball that I keep on a desk, a special gift to me from David. When I calmed down, I managed to take several pictures of the crystal ball decorated with my scarf to record and video for my records. The next day I found the scarf moved back to the fan, what are the ETs trying to tell me? My guess meant, we will be traveling with them soon, Good guess!

That evening in my room I stood staring to focus on the scarf, after a few minutes a voice of high authority began to speak to me, "*I am of many dimensions and you will see greater things.*" Wow! Was I excited, my mind was dealing with so much I felt like David and I were complete outsiders on *earth* now! Hopefully we would be learning more Universal information as we did so often. No doubt, this had been one of the highly spiritual ETs that we know as our teacher who delivered the above message, and afterwards I was thinking of the *surprise* message when I felt something *whiz* by my right side! I looked to my right my scarf had moved, it hung over the small lamp on my bedside table close by to me! Funny thing about this I noticed how perfectly it hung coming to a v shape at the bottom of the lamp with every piece of fringe hanging the same, so the label faced me which was labeled *Dimensions.* This was how my teacher gave his clues to our next travel into dimensions and Light! This could only mean one thing after my experience with this great being; we would be traveling to other dimensions of the past back to the pyramids and to other ancient places.

Yes, the ETs would be coming tonight how exciting! We looked forward to all this strangeness we were so anxious to relearn, I joked with David, *if we aren't back tomorrow hopefully, we will be returned soon.* "*Oh, don't say that!*" was his response laughing, and then we began joking with one another, only kidding! One thing I ask the ETs before we leave with them is, "*to please have us both back by the next earth day early, safe, and sound, in each of our beds just like any other normal day*", and our wishes are met just as we asked them to do, their word is truth and this was agreed on. The only reason I asked for this favor was not about fear, I didn't want us to come up MISSING…

The traveling scarf continued to travel going from the table lamp back to the lights, and back to the fan but one day about noon I saw the scarf was draped perfectly over the top of my dresser mirror. It looked like a big swag on a window drape; the fringe again was perfect with every strand hanging a certain way on the scarf. I was sure the scarf was hanging across the mirror representing it as a portal, like all mirrors to us are. I tried putting the connection together which I quickly solved since mirrors are portals for us this must be where we will travel through tonight. The same evening, I found the scarf moved across my bed high over the headboard on a cornice that fit across the top of it, and again the scarf looked perfect! I decided I may need to ask how this is working I would assume the room being a main portal of dimensions every place in it means I can leave from anyplace in it or outside, but it also meant tonight I would be traveling. I made sure I videoed each experience on tape, took pictures, and made my notes with the time and dates, and leaving the scarf alone like always to see when they would move things again. It was best to remain patient as far as we were concerned this was the best thing to do and not bother any item that was moved. The ball was in *their court* now as we use to say, we respected what they wanted from us this was for us to use our gifts and mind power, and to increase them as they teach these symbols.

A week later it was unusually quiet which was surprising and for that reason I felt a little depressed just kind of a down feeling. I sat down on the staircase where I was telepathically asking for help to get through some current problems and to be given guidance on how to work through personal issues. Suddenly a beautiful sounding voice poured out to me, *"don't yet know how much ye are loved, keep faith, everything will be all right."* I was overcome with tremendous love from this spiritual being and began to cry just as quickly I stopped! I felt a rush of *electrifying energy* whiz through me, a knowingness of who I am as a spiritual being, to get up and enjoy the gift of this day, then I felt wonderful! I am forever grateful for the help I am given and *miraculously* as I was given those words, I could visually see *two doors which were side by side.* As one door opened a being who had just passed away entered through it in spirit form, then another one in spirit came from the other door to return to a new life on earth, it was like a revolving door! I took this to mean *the two doors represented two things. One was an opening into the other side and the other door was meant to be one back to our world, Re-incarnation!*

When the doors had opened beautiful bright white light streamed out flooding an entire space and in this space were many of our past loved ones who stood in this light. They were all smiling at me waving, and just as quickly the two spirits that had come to deliver the message to me *went back through the doors into the bright light and it was over!* I was completely *overwhelmed and uplifted* at the same time; my adrenalin was pumping! My day had gone from feeling down to an *amazing experience* I would never forget! I knew this was real it happened, but at that time I thought could I ever share this. I want people to know we live on eternally and that we have help on the other side no matter how bleak things may seem!

In my next experience one night I could see my *spirit body* sitting in a chair as I was explaining to someone how the spirit body could leave our earth body at times and go do other things, and this is when we are *out of body.* Continuing I said, *"See my spirit body is sitting in that chair a few feet away from me."* I was teaching this person I had been looking at my spirit self and this is a natural occurrence we do at times without being aware of it. Of course, most people cannot see the spirit realms, but one example is: have you ever noticed an older person in a nursing home or someone who is very sick staring off and not answering you? It is not always medication, lack of natural sleep, or sedation when that person seems to have no response with a vacant look on their face. This may be when a very sick person's spirit *could* be out of their body someplace else, and this is an example of how the spiritual part of us can leave the body in terrible or bad times which it also does at times of sleep. It's not always that the mind is bad; it is the *escape* needed by the spirit even for short times especially when in difficulty and only an experienced person who has some knowledge of this seems to understand.

The spirit can travel in a blink to another time and space for those who are trapped in a wasted body and this is a wonderful release. Their spirit may leave for a while or longer (months and years if in a coma) to keep them going longer as Alzheimer patients do. I have heard stories about prisoners of war tell how they survived and what kept their mind intact; their spirit would leave their body in meditation which helped them keep their will to live, to find hope, to fight death each day and night, this gave them faith and strength to live longer in order that they may be rescued. In a common daydream where does your mind go? More examples are; when you drive your car for miles and suddenly you are home or come to a stop but do not recall anything in between? When you are moving doing normal things at work or in other places and suddenly find you are finished without thought. Happens all the time to all of us and we don't question it; see what I mean about spirit moving in and out.

It was the month of June on *Father's Day* I was lying in bed restless and awake when I heard a noise in the dark. I knew it was the bedroom door because it opened, I watched the figure of a man pass by my bed going into the bathroom, I raised up on one elbow noticing the door was left part-way open. The light spilled out into my room sort of giving it just enough of softness to see. I was wondering what to do or not to do, should I wait or go investigate? I studied the door opening and noticed the shadow of someone pacing inside back and forth over and over past the door!

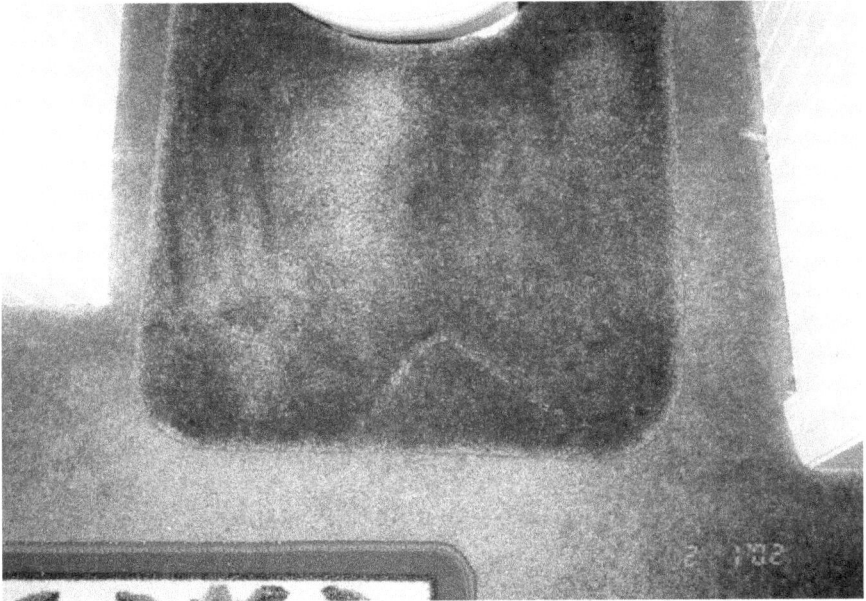

Here is an example of finding faces, a hand, and a head imprint on the bathroom rug with universal symbols throughout and in the palm of the left hand. The pyramid symbol is at the bottom.

But I didn't have the courage to get up and investigate I was still debating to either forget it or look, I made my decision to get up, slowly walking to the bathroom door I quickly pulled it completely open to see, NO one there! I don't know maybe this was an *indication* of a visit from an ET, either way someone wanted my attention to let me know they were here. I later came to my conclusion it was one of the ETs because of the faces, and symbol of the pyramid on the bathroom rug. The next day about 7 pm I was coming into my room to change and noticed my heavy 7-inch cross was hanging over my bathroom door! I keep this cross under my pillow and have for a long time I knew it had been there that morning when I made my bed. This sign was meant for me to know I was always being protected. My human mind was concerned with thoughts that perhaps something else may have wandered in from another universal place which would be very rare to happen. This would not mean it had to be negative as we are well protected by heavenly beings and the ETs to call upon. I was sure the reason was simply to let me know we are divinely protected, and therefore my cross was put over the doorway! My answer was clearly given to me on the spot our Angels were nearby! *"We were not to be concerned, for this cross was our sign of our safety and of their love for us"*. How beautiful!!

The Traveling ET Scarf continues.

It was July I had company visiting and they wanted to look at the room where so much activity was going on. We let them explore through the house since they were trusted friends for years. Entering the room, the Dimensions scarf had moved from its former location from the chandelier in the tower to one of the dolls I collect and wrapped around her tiny shoulders looking like a shawl! Our friends were *enthralled* with what we had shared with them, although I didn't tell them who I thought moved the scarf. We knew it was the ETs who did and Katie the little spirit girl was with them. Our old friends couldn't wait to come back after their visit.

The next night after my son had fallen asleep on the sofa, he was awakened by two loud sounds, *intuitively* he knew the ETs were back. He felt their presence and grabbed up his little dog Shorty and quietly came upstairs softly calling, *"mom, mom,"* as he came into my room. He wanted me to know we had company, but he couldn't wake me no matter how hard he shook me, I didn't wake up! Later that morning he told me: *"I kept calling you and shaking your shoulder, but you didn't wake up and it had scared him!"* He knew as I did when this happened it meant one of us was gone with the ETs in *out of body* in travel... I only remembered being drowsy later morning and felt like my eyes were glued shut! My son remembered he must have followed with being taken immediately after me, *"he had been taken because he knew the ETs did something with the three of us;"* his little dog Shorty made three. Apparently, I was taken first then David and Shorty and currently I had been in-between worlds... (Refer to pages 52 through 55 for pictures of the scarf.)

The day after David told me this experience, I found the moving scarf draped beautifully back on the chandelier in the *tower* which is a small part of my bedroom! Once again it looked like a beautiful parachute hanging upside down on the light fixture it was gorgeous and perfect! I began taking pictures, videoed and documented the experience I couldn't help but wonder where the scarf would travel to next? I studied this for a long time and how it was hanging on the light so gorgeously arranged everything was always perfect! Then I had the idea to lay down on the floor on my back looking upward because I thought there was something in the scarf and there was! I was shocked to see an ET *face,* no, there was more than one! The faces were quite clear with the largest one showing up in the pictures I took that day! This was a *nice break* for us because we could study the faces better on pictures then three days later the scarf disappeared off the light! I soon found it *accidentally* when I opened my closet door to get something out and there *hung the scarf* right in front of my face it had another new home! No matter how strange this seems this was teaching something about the portals being everywhere in these rooms and the staircase, I knew what it was!!!

I knew we were *right on track* with new *incoming information* concerning the scarf and why it kept moving; it began adding up for us. We were learning as the ETs intended us to learn with our trust and patience and their confirmation of a huge vortex in the closet all through my room in the hallway, tower and the stairs! Well guess what, three days later the *traveling scarf* disappeared from my closet it was gone again apparently to another new location which turned out to be hilarious! We had been hunting everywhere for the scarf to no avail but not giving up we never gave up on anything concerning the ETs! It was later in the evening on the 3rd day when David came to tell me he knew where the scarf was, *"you will never believe this but its outside!"* Sure, enough he led me to one of the upstairs' windows where I could look out to see the lower roof of the garage and there it was as before. I began to laugh with him we couldn't stop because of the joke these *intelligent* Beings were playing. They knew our own humor and jokes better than we did that we played on one another! Yes, there was my scarf in all its *glory* blowing in the breeze like a little flag HANGING ON THE WEATHERVANE high up on the garage as before! The first thing I noticed was the direction the scarf was facing which was northeast. This direction meant they were coming from the North Quad I left the scarf alone over the next few hot and sunny days but then the rain came, and I thought I better check on the scarf. A good thing I did since the rain was washing dye out of it onto the shingles below. I climbed out through the window onto the roof and retrieved the scarf I used to wonder if any of the neighbors or people coming by the house ever saw the scarf flying out from the weathervane? David and I would be laughing so hard imagining who may have seen the scarf blowing in the wind wondering what kind of strange people lived here!

Even with him terminally ill he had an enormous sense of humor with so much excitement in our worlds. I am very thankful we had those years of wonderful precious times to share in an amazing, mysterious, beautiful universe with our lessons. I knew this was keeping him here longer with his keen interest in our magic worlds. I give my heartfelt humble thanks to the Supreme Creator and ETs of Christ Light for always teaching us we have certainly been blessed and humbled by being a part of this phenomenal uncanny life living between here and the Beyond...

It wasn't long until I had more ET contact in the night hours. They were telling me, *"we needed to meditate to the Northeast (where the scarf had faced) where my spiritual leader had answers waiting for us. Let yourself be guided through the dark and your faith in self shall bring you to the light."* How very thankful we were for this. The East is both our MAIN direction out of the four, although we are from all four directions to do our work on earth. There would always be astounding messages from the divine to help us learn and grow and to keep our faith no matter how things may seem at the time.

This next heavenly message is another one I love so much, *"and when the voices come, they will astound you and fill your very heart and soul for you will never doubt what you hear to try and describe the feelings you cannot do and your life is never the same, and you know without a doubt that you have indeed been given a special message from a Divine source from another dimension, that such a fine line separates our life here and as we say, the other side. The words are crystal clear and sometimes the full meaning may not be clear to you at that time it could be a day, a week, or longer but it will come and make sense at the right time"*.

I thought how very blessed we were to be here as planned and then I was directly asked *"about my life here on earth"*. I took the meaning to be, *"was I understanding our mission more clearly now and more aware of what our life mission is about living as a human being"?* I remember feeling excited, happy, and peaceful to know there is so much more to our lives that most have no idea of and what does the Universe continue to hold for us? One of the reasons we get into many situations at certain points in life is that most of us have *gotten off track* with the things we need to let go of once and for all and haven't. In my times of doubt and sadness looming over me the heavenly voice would remind me, *"Don't thee know how much ye are loved?"* In those times of doubt with a problem I could feel a powerful love radiating from a magnificent Being of Light to me as if loving arms were wrapped around me holding me with divine love, full of wisdom and comfort. I was told, *"To remember that no matter what happened here in my life I am always loved with the greatest love of all and I always will be for it is eternal"*. Then the heavenly voice continued, *"Our Angels are always with us if we want to think that or not."* The more I understood this magnificent force telling us, *"to not question such a divine connection because the ETs who worked with the two of us are the ET Spiritual Beings of the Christ light, as the Angels and Higher Beings are the same"!* I love this; it was the great Revelation which opened my spirit all the way! I was remembering much more of whom I really am and what I am a part of from my very beginning with the beautiful way they told me, that the ETs are as the Angels and Higher Beings are, so I could tell others! In these heavenly words how much clearer could it be for others to deny them? They also told me, *"to make my mark*

85

upon the quest" meaning my writing, to continue to tell the truth to the world with what we are being taught!

Like a Thunderbolt We Were Struck by the
Love of the Creator

The Holy voice said, *"we were now ready to meet with the Great Council once again."* I would remember our message always as my teacher assured me with this knowledge, *"that when the rivers flow over the mountains and prairies there will be time to gather up all. No tears of sadness only of joy for it is clear in hand. Trust and do not be led by negative people. Your teacher, the Shaman and I work closely together with you, and your son, and another teacher. Know that the Universe writes this out and is in the stars, that we are here! We love you and stand beside you we are all connected. Realize nothing matters but love and compassion. Send love, light, and healing where it is needed, tests are there for everyone. We must return now for there are others who await us. Remember, nothing can hurt you but yourselves and there are greater things to come."* We felt very small and humble our hearts were pounding with joy about this future meeting with the Council. What more did the Council want to say to both of us we could hardly wait! We have never had trouble realizing we did not belong to this world, and these Holy messages made it clear we had promises to keep, and everything is in order and perfect in our worlds!

Going back to the day before each of my parents crossed over my spiritual teachers came to me reassuring me, *"to believe in myself and don't doubt what I get."* This was one of my lessons, *"to trust in my heart and soul and I will see clearly. Have total trust, you are like a sponge and have come a long way."* One of our highly evolved teachers told me, *"his name was Zorba and to know he continues to work with us, our teachers, guides, and Angels of protection. And to rejoice in the knowledge and fact that my son and a grandson are also healer's, and that David is a teacher on earth and the other side, that he helps on both sides. His smile is sunshine and lights up the earth and for me to keep working with my mother and tell her to release she needs to let go to join my dad and others on the other side for her joy and happiness".*

When this message came my mother had been seriously terminally ill for 19 years, I did as I was told going to the hospital on her final day to find my chosen words through the above message. I could plainly see she was still in a coma, but I knew she could hear me. I looked at her beautiful face for a long time to imprint her likeness into my mind forever until we would meet again. I watched her final life force energy leaving her small body out of her crown floating upward through the ceiling. I knew she had wanted to go so badly and finally her will was giving up ready to go now and leave here. I held her hand and told her how much she is loved with my words we all have for her, and that she was the best mother in the world, I was proud to be her daughter. I told her everything I could think to I wanted nothing left unsaid while she had time, I always told her how I loved her, but this was different on this last day to pass my devoted love to her. Dad had come through to me so many times to tell me, *"I will come for your mom when it's time. I'll reach out to her and take her hand and we will be together again."* My dad had been waiting a long time for Mom so they could be together again. They were always *sweethearts* in life with a strong loving bond that could not be broken even by what we term as sickness and death. I knew it was past time for her and my dad to be together in spirit and at that moment my heavenly teacher told me, *"go home now and rest soon I would be called"*. I obeyed and the call came soon she had passed on it had been so hard to leave her that final day, but I knew this was what she wanted me to do, she needed to join Dad and had suffered those many years! I didn't want to hold her back with my emotions and my desires for her to stay for me how cruel this would be which is why some people hang on so long they need to hear us say, it's OK... She held on for years because of worrying over leaving someone in the family now she was free! She didn't want me to watch her go is why my teacher told me to go home.

At my mother's funeral as the Minister was giving his service, I saw my mother and father appear together close by her casket, they were sort of suspended in the air just a few inches off the floor. I felt their love as they looked at me smiling and I must have had a very serene look on my face because the Minister asked me afterwards, *"what did you see, that I had such a serene look on my face he knew I could see something"* later we talked more privately. He told me he knew I was seeing something, so I took a chance to tell him what

87

I saw and found he was a true believer. He confessed he had an experience more than once in his life he could not share so he understood and believed. He explained he knew, *"because I had the most wonderful smile of peace come over my face"*. I explained, telling him my mom and dad were side-by-side holding hands with a red heart in-between them showing their love to me for one another! The thing is their last name is HART, and there was that symbolic RED HEART between them! From that very day on my mother began appearing to me just like dad but now they would come together! Dad smiled at me and said, *"Where you see one of us the other is always near-by"* and that's how it has been for these years they are always together there is NO ending for any of us.

There is No Ending

I saw three magnificent *Angels* appear in the middle of the night arriving in a flash lighting up the room from ceiling to floor and my mother's face appeared she was young, healthy, and beautiful like a 20-year-old! She was simply making her visit letting me know she is always here for me! I knew Dad was waiting in the wings because I heard him calling out, *"hello Pumpkin!"* And this is the way my mother would visit from then on, just like dad I learned long ago that a person in spirit can return at any age they want to with most showing themselves at a younger age. Sometime after my Mom's passing my automatic writing changed, she brought me more detailed information. I sometimes used an automatic writing method with the intention to write on my note pad as their words flowed to me, and quickly I relate back to the other side, there is no waiting. Mom and Dad always told me, *"to just call their name and they will be here for me"*. There are *no farewells* only other dimensions; we are only fine lines, parallels apart from this side to the other. And the same as with the ETs, all spiritual beings, and heavenly Councils who school us both.

CHAPTER 5

The Little Grays and Our Reality as Family

The little Grays returned after my mother passed over if they had been around in the days before she did, I would have been too busy to even notice in my exhaustion. The spiritual ET beings, our heavenly family of guides and teachers from the Christ Light were assisting us through this time. As most people know after a loved one's passing there is so much to take care of and during this time, we knew the ETs were concerned about us and close by to help us. They gave us our needed energy to let us do what we needed to. One night after things had calmed down and in bed, I was restless and could not sleep suddenly I felt someone nearby and looked up to see one of the little Grays floating over to above me. I asked, *"What do you want?"* The Gray responded telepathically, *"that he was only observing me and not to be afraid."* I had noticed that night it was almost a full moon, so my room was filled with moonlight (a night they usually appeared on especially in the beginning of many others). This little Gray was from the *"North Quad"* we knew well from the ETs species we traveled with often, so it was fine I was glad to have his company...

The little Gray continued to stare at me with those big eyes which held so many secrets and I knew he was of good intentions the same as the others who came to us. Then I quickly fell into a deep sleep still looking at him later I felt the little Gray seem to be busy around me all night, although at first I couldn't remember what happened I only had bits and pieces of the night in my mind, but I knew I went with them. I remembered a familiar huge flash of white light after the little Gray had contacted me and my next memory was being in front of a familiar screen like a huge TV with different letters, designs, and symbols with most I couldn't make out or understand. This happened often on other occasions when they were teaching us. Thinking back before my visit with the little Gray that night before I went to bed, I had found my *moon* necklace hanging on my ceiling fan facing north. With that familiar sign I knew I may be having little visitors coming all the clues were there before I encountered the Gray which meant a possibility, I would be going with them. My strong feeling was, they took me to *"regenerate my mind and body"* after my mother's passing to help raise my energy back up. After that night anytime I found my moon necklace and dimensions scarf hanging from my fan I knew without a doubt they would be coming just like they always had, and I felt better.

The following evening, I received a new message from the other side about my mother from our ET loved ones which made me feel good! "Mother *is very happy and remains close to all of you she is with father and they are like sweethearts in love as they travel the universe like sparks of light. Mother knows of your great love and respect for her and father, we are all one part of each other."*

There the answer is *WE ARE ALL A PART OF EACH OTHER!* What blessed words I would be able to tell the world one day; I was very grateful to receive this message and the timing was exactly right. An enormous golden light woke me the next evening filling my bedroom it was as bright as a sunny day and continued to become brighter! Suddenly, a *high-pitched frequency* sound went through my ears that hurt somewhat and startled me at the same time, so I quickly closed my eyes! I felt when I did this, I broke connection to whatever it was because the sound stopped. At first, I thought everything had returned to normal even the bright light was gone then I realized so was I! I was in travel with the ETs, they stop time for us we are not aware of when traveling out of our physical body to other places. In minutes of our time we can travel thousands of light years and back! I don't know what exactly happened that night this is all I remember but I know they were here and traveled with them.

David and I watched the calendar for upcoming dates of the full moon this is a big part of our travel and strong connection with them. We found that sometimes the ETs traveled along big *electrical storms* when they would come to connect with us. They seem to take advantage of this powerful energy and apparently use it in different ways probably more than we could ever imagine.

Our little Gray friends made another visit to us a couple of nights later which was quite strange, the first thing I remember seeing was the shape of a man or what I thought was a man go to my closet or the staircase, they are fairly close to one another so it was hard to tell and it was dark inside. The next thing I heard a very *loud crash* coming from the family room below, running out of my room and down the stairs and I couldn't believe my eyes! *I saw* a *large plant suspended in the air!* I must have turned and ran back to my room because I had no more memory until towards morning when I awakened to *noises* in my room! I knew this was the ETs doing something or bringing me back from another place. We found out early on they can easily *blank out your memory* if needed at any time but may let you see a part of what you experience if necessary.

The next day we found a new message from the main ET Council leader of the Christ Light, "they *mean no harm and carry none that I will soon be able to see into the windows of the soul even more clearly and the window into my crystal ball for further lessons.*" I was finding out my crystal ball was a main learning tool the ETs were using to teach me how to focus better. I did not use or need it for readings it was only a focus tool to help sharpen my mind, but I experienced more teaching through it about focus.

I soon picked up pictures I had developed from my camera film in one of them I found a picture I did not take! *My crystal ball was floating through the air in my bedroom almost to the ceiling!* It is full of bright sparkling light floating over my four-poster bed and its shadow on the wall is not normal and extremely large! There is no humanly way possible this could be normal but there it was clear as could be! We sometimes often found pictures I DID NOT take but the other side can easily arrange the impossible! This would be used one day for reasons of proof for those who needed it.

At night I began to frequently notice ahead of time the ET *visitors* would be coming with flashing bright lights going across the ceiling and coming in the windows lighting the room like daylight. I was beginning to realize the light was like a *"welcome* or a *beacon"* announcing them, then little Grays would suddenly begin to appear. At other times an ET of a very high order from the *"Great Council"* would be standing by my bed to communicate. One of a most important lessons from our ET teachers we studied most in those many years was remembering the amazing connection of *everything* that has ever been created. The whole of *Creation is combined into one giant network!*

We on earth have been *taught incorrectly* since the beginning when truth was hidden, then people could be controlled with man's power. It has been about POWER since man was brought forth in some way and is no different in today's world so therefore our world is like it is now, in bad shape! The earth and all Beings created in space has a unique bond together and *the all* was created at the same time by an *"Infinite Supreme Intelligence of Love"* we know as our *Creator/God.* This means we are all related so would it not be fair to say to *one another?*

This concept is, what I know to be true but how many on earth think there is nothing else but earth? Good question isn't it? There is enormous fear in our world today many others do not want to think in this way that there are others who exist in a never-ending space. My parents and I never discussed any kind of life in space other than they may have joked at some time of UFOs, but I am positive that subject was never brought up. So much has been lost of the truth but there is always hope because it's never too late to learn and leave the old ways behind which bind us here.

It was important for me to reconnect with my mother she had been appearing to me in visions for an important journey we both would be taking. That same evening I was in a deep sleep when something woke me, then my mother appeared she wanted to show me a place where she was now on the other side and in a flash, we zoomed off into the beautiful universal world among the bright stars in less than the *blink* of an eye! I was in astral travel with her in space between here and there which seemed only a breath away. The next thing I knew I was standing with her very high up which seemed to be on a mountain that's all I know to call it. This is where we overlooked time and space, skies and clouds, it was breath- taking, magical, and glorious! She began to tell me, *"How the earth looked from where she is now".* Much of her descriptions are hard to come by because there are no human words to describe this information. Our earth is truly *out of this world, and all I could see was millions and millions of pinpoints of light it was beautiful!* She told me, *"this is how they see us on earth and as I grow, she grows there too".* Suddenly I was back at home out of the vision I felt renewed and wonderful! I was thankful my mother answered my prayers! The ETs reminded me more than once what my mother said, *"As you grow, they grow through your learning and to have patience, lots of patience all we can."* They knew I had many unanswered questions in my mind it was flooded by now! After being with my mother in the vision I asked my son if he was there, he remembered being on this journey with his grandmother and me, although I had not seen him, I had felt he was with us. Sometimes it is this way when we travel, we may not see one another but know they are present. We sent a big loving *"Thank you"* to mom for sharing her new home letting us see where she and dad existed in an unexplainable, beautiful and vast universe!

The Pyramid Painting

A dear friend of mine gave me a gift of a small pyramid and one day it began to move around *mysteriously* when I was gone. Returning home, I found the pyramid wrapped in small black ribbons, which I didn't have, and I couldn't have managed to do anything like this being wrapped in such an extraordinary way! The ribbon wrappings ended with a perfectly made bow on top of the tiny peak this was telling me something and seemed to be a special gift, an important one. I found my answer when confiding in my dear friend Bev she is an artist and for some reason she was quite excited when I told her about the ribbon wrapped pyramid. She asked, " if I could take some pictures of the pyramid and bring them so she could see it," Sure I told her, a few days later I drove to her home and brought the pyramid pictures for her to look over and with the first one she began to smile. She excused herself after going through them to get something out of her closet where she carefully pulled out a new painting on a large canvas she had just finished the week before with a pyramid looking exactly like mine wrapped in identical small black ribbons with a bow on top of the peak! We both stood their sort of speechless for a moment and began to shake our heads smiling at one another at how the universe knows all! Why in the world was this an important connection? Our minds are the same not only as best of friends but both of us are Clairvoyants, we thought this was great and exciting to see what it led up to. Our minds (my son, Bev, and me) were surly working together no matter how far apart we were and being *kindred souls* we three were together in many lifetimes.

I do know Bev was afraid of anything connected to Aliens even though she knew my son and I were being taught by the Christ Light Beings through a blessed connection, but she still had a fear of them. I figured at some time she had had an abduction with the negative ones instead of universal schooling by the loved ones which is what we have with the Christ Light ET beings. Therefore, I considered she had possibly been taken by a negative species and had a bad experience. After the pyramid incident Egyptian Hieroglyphic script began to appear to me in the night with Egyptian language and figures painted centuries ago inside of pyramids and tombs. The experiences we had with my pyramid and Bev's painting of it was certainly a part of the connection to my son and I we have to Egypt, and Edgar Cayce, not to mention the Extraterrestrials. Therefore, finding my pyramid wrapped in ribbons was a symbol bringing this experience to us next. The mysteries and stories of the Pyramids, Pharaohs, and their culture are not only one of the wonders of the world but also about some of our past lives when we lived in that period. I knew this was a part of another lifetime shared together with Edgar, my son and Bev, we had experienced life there more than once. Through my growing up years into an adult I was immensely drawn to Egypt and in school I knew the answers to my tests on Egypt without reading my history book.

After this discussion with my son the ETs came again when we were gone and left my crystal ball placed a short distance from my small pyramid in various positions on the floor, as if showing or reminding us of a map of something important we should remember, but we weren't sure what. Then scrolls of Egyptian writings began to come in the night showing more *"hieroglyphic script"* as if trying to get me conditioned to understanding it again! I have no doubt whatsoever, they wanted us to recall our lives there I had seen this same script given to me in visions from the ETs when they taught us inside the crafts, they wanted us to remember to relearn the language we once knew. This was fascinating and I am sure it will seem completely unbelievable to most people if I had ever mentioned it, but I could dismiss those human thoughts easily being connected with our spiritual teachers who work diligently with us.

What occurred to us is absolutely our truth and no one can ever take away the knowledge of what the teachers have taught us. It was time for us to continue with new information, and a new awakening that came from a Being of *"The High Council"* with an enlightening message: "there *shall be a great inner awakening into your very soul and prompt further development and soul growth. The auras you see will become more often and more beautiful, full of passion, and full of sorrow*, joy, sickness, *and all that comes along with human earth life there. This will help your growth and healing and with love and peace to you all until tomorrow in your sphere and dream states where we will meet again. The pyramid is a gift from the heart and soul of higher being. Go now child you have listened well to your teacher.*" How proud we felt and for the answers about the small pyramid in our home I was delighted about it being a gift from the heart and soul of a higher being!! And to my surprise the Great Council Being spoke my teachers name, *"Han Tai Chen Su,* this encouraging beautiful message came from both *"The Great Council* and my Oriental teacher who was a *Sage* in his life centuries ago in the *Han Dynasty in China.* The ET continued, *"who you know by his name I have written before Han Tai Chen Su and his spirit is working with the ETs."* This confirmed it all; we will be able to help more people along our way with our continuing connection of working together and then I remembered the words I had been given *"have patience my child"*. I was wound up and excited my mind was going a mile a second, but this was such wonderful news! The more we could learn the more we wanted to know we were excited to learn from The Great Council and The High Council; they are the highest ones.

After this last experience something happened early the next morning, I was awakened by a light, I glanced at my bedside clock to see the time it was 4:30 am. The room began to have a golden glow getting brighter and brighter with sparkles of white lights dancing everywhere. This light directed me to a very tall and beautiful Angel messenger appearing; I had seen this being before in the same way after my mother passed and once before that. At the time of my mother's passing this beautiful Angel appeared holding out both hands cupped together then slowly opened to release a beautiful golden dove which flew around the room twice. It was during those seconds I caught a glimpse of my mother's face along with this Angel Being of Light. The message from her *was* about, *"love and peace, and that my trust and faith had been established in my heart and to know my Savior helps to guide and direct me. The golden dove represented love and compassion I show to others and for me to go out into the world each day and spread what is in my heart"*. This was the second time this message was presented to me in this way, I was beyond thrilled and humbled to receive it once more! All these wonderful concepts made me want to do my very best in life and learn as fast as the other side saw fit for me. My son knew these things since he was a young child; he came into this world with his memory intact with what he came here to face with me, together in our lives, and he was helping me remember our choices for this one. His sisters looked to his advice and loved him very much as he did them. I am so blessed to have my loved ones with me again in this lifetime they are my *jewels in the crown*, I was at peace now falling back to sleep...

A next message would help me to know more of why I *adored* the home I live in even though I always knew it was a *special learning place* on this earth and where I was to be. My message came soon from *"The High Council"* confirmed to me with these words, *"this place is good and draws the Light of Christ!"* How happy this made me they are talking of my home *"The House of Secrets"!!* I began to think about asking the ETs for permission to interact more with them to learn what the BIG picture adds up to in this century or if Earth would still be here. I was without doubt knowing everything going on was already in motion and with my free will this is the only way all of this could be happening in my life here on earth. I decided for now I didn't want to push too much for answers the ETs had made it plain about giving us lessons slowly enough so our humanness could digest their information I would need to remain patient. My son and I went over each experience as they were given to us using our intuition as we were told to do to sharpen our skills. We both had been given tons of information already.

At one point later my main teacher *Han Tai Chen Su* who had led us into Reiki with Edgar came to me and led me with his thoughts into the art of *"Tai Chi"* where everything fell into place. I was learning to focus even more with this ancient art, and I loved it! I asked my spiritual teacher the reason for this and his answer was simple, *"To improve focus!"* Just as I had thought everything, we each do is for a reason, good or bad hopefully we learn something. Tai Chi, Reiki, and Martial Arts all go together because they are all about learning to use energy in various ways.

It was a Tuesday when David told me the ETs would be coming that night with special messages, I was to prepare myself in order to receive *three* messages they wanted to speak of. First, I saw the little Grays that evening in my room with bright light coming through the windows, the room lit up like a huge bulb was turned on and shinning. As usual the full moon was out which helped me to see them even clearer, they knew I was wondering by my thoughts I wanted to *video* them sometime and they agreed! I didn't know when, but I supposed we would later, I was filled with excitement thinking what a *discovery*; we would have proof of them! I noticed other unfamiliar beautiful Beings in the room with them who were only visible by the *gold lines* they were made in; this was another type of being which was phenomenal to see! I watched them as they were moving around in their shapes in a transparent form in all gold lines! I have written of this before and once was when my dad came to me in them. I can't find the words to explain them and I was curious to who these beautiful Beings were, I could see completely through them in their transparent forms!

I was gathering information soaking it up and at the same time knowing in my heart and soul these Beings were very important highly evolved ones of the Christ Light, perhaps from the Council. I watched as they inched closer to me and instantly, we were communicating in a *mind-to-mind* telepathic conversation! They had come to give me three important learning lessons so my heart was pumping not only with excitement but with love, because I could feel so much love coming to me from these amazing Beings. I felt fully consumed knowing I was totally loved through my entire body head to toe, inside and out, then they began to explain the important messages for me.

1. That I am part of them! I will continue to go with them for my higher learning and returned unharmed and to not be afraid this is all happening for my own good.
2.
3. My sight and all other senses will get stronger than ever a big turning point now more than ever.
4.
5. I would remember more and more it would come. To have absolute faith and trust in myself this is all written in your journey.

This was amazing, and I knew it to be true we had complete trust and faith in everything we were being told by them. I realized this was occurring for a reason close to my dad's birthday and I felt my grandmother's presence (my dad's mother) she was around me now her name was Electa. This was all amazing and bought so much happiness to us plus it was strange to think of our *newfound* way of life and learning being processed to remember these things. My son and I were evolving as planned; just imagine how our minds were spinning! Remember we were dealing with our everyday life, the spirit world and spirits who lived here together with us, plus the Universal, paranormal worlds, and ET teachers from other planets and dimensions that few would ever know of. We separated the negatives pounded into our heads for generations such as, *"things like this can't happen"!* Such as, any type of alien contact people really do have was what people joked about; and made fun of especially the people who dared to tell what had happened to them, who many are labeled a *basket case,* if they only knew I thought!

Some people who have been taken by force were trying to get others to take them seriously and who knows how many were hoping to get help? There were those who would never tell of their fearful experiences I have read of who were too terrified at night to go to sleep wondering, *will it happen again tonight?* Some abductees are afraid each waking moment when taken again their will they may never be returned; they feel such helplessness not knowing how to stop it. I am sure many lives change dramatically; even worse knowing they are completely helpless to do anything about it; this is something real and nothing can fix it.

I was relieved when the ETs told us *not to speak* of our experiences and schooling from them until we were given their permission. I wasn't anxious to become a laughing target with a family. This was fine with me I had much to learn about at that time. I would like to think there are more people now who seriously *listen* and believe others are having these experiences. A successful way I suggest finding one's forgotten experiences is to begin a healing process with *hypnosis.* In this way hypnosis may possibly help to get deep into their subconscious to pull out some answers for them.

My families had no known knowledge in their earth lives of these things happening with ETs and other life forms from in the universe, unless with the news of Area 51. I found a strange line written in my grandmothers Bible years after she passed, *"that things aren't always as they seem."* I believe she knew much more than she dared to speak of I felt her quote was related to other Beings but who knows what it was I am going with my own feelings about this.

The next visit we had with the ETs they told us: *"School is in; we are all here to learn".* We were excited each time we went; David and I were in *universal school* for many years and still are with them, they are also our spiritual teachers. We loved being taken to the universal schools to learn from the higher Beings of the Light, this was an enlightening and loving experience each time. Soon it was time to advance to a higher level of teaching a *"Spiritual Being of Light"* would help us understand more of our work beginning with this message:

David and I are a significant part of the destiny of this world and there are others who are also working on our earth plane to help mankind for after the earth becomes new and fresh again Earthlings will be starting over with a new spiritually which would consist of love among all people. Selfishness, greed, wars, and pollution all will be erased in this new world and in its place will be love for one another a new beginning for humankind. The Aliens (ETs) are all around us here and everywhere there are several species of them and not to be alarmed. To know there are two very negative species that creates havoc among the earthlings not directly, indirectly, but not to worry more information comes soon on this and as a confirmation when David's blood was taken on that night long ago it was used for a new vaccine that will help to establish new colonies of people part human and part Alien, for we all are a part of one another, God created everything at one time. There will be goodness and mercy for all, when the exact time and conditions are right.

Not only being *overwhelmed* by this message of a new world and a vaccine made from David's blood to establish the new colonies, we were being confirmed again of all we believe in with their pure love!! Reading this message of the future is what we dreamt of helping to unite others and bring LOVE back to our people! This carries a great responsibly with it and we gratefully accepted it! Thank you, son, for all you do to help humanity, I love you!!

99

The ETs often repeated to us, *"that without a doubt we are all a part of each other in ways most people would never think about"*. This was very powerful information and how would it ever be accepted we didn't know but it would happen! My son and I were helping to establish the new *"Hybrid"* program and years before this happened our lives did a 180 degree turn when I was told to get a certain book to read to help me in my *"Earth form"*. I thought Earth *form* what does this exactly mean? At the time this was one of my next lessons to understand better when I came across some spiritual information given to me from the ET Council. Then years later they were reminding me, I had forgotten about getting this book. I had been introduced to this book of information along my way a few times, but I forgot each time because of what was being presented to us day and night we were astounded with our new world of information! This is all understood by them and being reminded once more that it is important, and this is part of why I am still grasping at everything I can, a seeker never quits! I still plan to find this book as soon as I can locate it there must be a great reason the ETs want me to have it and I am sure they will guide me to it.

There are times I have thought how busy my son and I are day and night while most people sleep and rested, we were out and about astral traveling, being schooled and involved with all kinds of learning from the Christ Light ETs in Universal traveling everything they needed us to do that was possible. Some days we provided many readings for people who wanted information to connect with their past over loved ones while others we gave Reiki to help them along their way. We had heavy schedules and many times David had to slow down and was very sick for long periods of time. I gladly attended to my son with love and devotion and would a million times over to be with him as before. I have been blessed to take care of him through his illness and working together like we did helped us both mentally and physically with keeping our thoughts positive and devoted with trust, faith, love and belief in the other worlds, and for this world to begin changing to a more loving one.

I was once given this blessed advise, *"to not forget I am here to also enjoy my earthly life. I am here to learn many good things to fulfill this achievement to the best I could, not disappointing my soul."* This was the BIG advice I needed I am completely humbled by it. I was also being reminded by Edgar Cayce, *"To live my life here, so enjoy. Don't burn out to soon, not to do like he did and burn out before my time as he did."* Thank you blessed Edgar!

The ETs Face

One day when we returned home, I went to my room and the first thing I noticed was pink flowers on my pillow! They weren't hard to notice since the flowers had not been there earlier that day while making my bed and once more these were the same flowers, I kept in a room downstairs now they were on my pillow! I began to look for footprints to give me a lead to who could have done this? It only took a moment to find out but not of feet, I was looking at the drawing of a ETs face in the carpet how in the world can they do these things right under our nose? One thing was certain they were either here someplace before or had been I felt as if I had a miniature *"Crop Circle"* on the floor with the drawing, with that thought it seemed funny to me and I began laughing in disbelief! With the abilities the ETs have what a kind gesture it was to provide me a picture of one of them which I felt was an honor, even though I was still laughing, shaking my head saying, *really!* I was experiencing new and amazing surprises, the ETs told me they would give me a picture, but this was not what I expected! They had promised me a picture early on and I knew they would deliver it and even though this picture wasn't on film it was extraordinary! I felt sure another picture would arrive at a future time; but if not, they had kept their word!! My son came up to my room to look at the famous ET photo in the carpet, we wasted no time questioning one another, *"do you know what this means?"* I think to the ETs this sign only meant they had kept their word and wanted us to know they can be funny too!

The Universal Beings had come in the middle of the day as I was cleaning but we knew no one could have seen them or their craft they are only spotted if they want to be known. It is certainly not normal in our world to find items from them or anything else although we ask for things to bring back with us. The world has long been talking about a piece of material looking like silver foil for years from Area 51 and perhaps one day with the ETs permission we can show their messages and the things in pictures they do. The ETs can arrive on a sunny day or bitter cold night, rain or storms, weather doesn't matter much to them but at times fog may for some reason. They travel faster than the speed of light with just *"thought "*and they can transport anything, program our minds, and implant tracking devises to monitor us and others... For decades they have come here with some walking amongst us in human form (such as we do) so why would this be so hard for them? Our visits were tiny as to what their *abilities* are and what they can do. In short, when they began to connect telepathically to let us know why they have been learning our human emotions over eons of time, it was to learn and understand human feelings and human ways even better. They were showing us they care as with the flowers and *Crop Circle* drawings and taking my picture as a joke to show us they knew how to express feelings of caring, joy, and other emotions. They have learned from us such as bringing flowers and the promise of a picture of one of them! We were as proud and happy of them as if they were *children* and how beautifully we work together is the extra icing, with watching them acquire emotions we use on earth.

Little did I know even greater things were going to continue between us in those earlier years. To our knowledge we had not read or heard of actual written messages from the ETs/Aliens in their own writings given to *a human being* or the schooling they give us but how could I know the world is quite large. This would one day go out to the world in this book as they want. I will continue now with another *phenomenal experience* which started in an extraordinary way ending with an ultimate surprise!

We thought of our constant contact with the Beings and how the ET/Aliens watch the *Scientists* and those who have the world's largest telescopes with the most expensive equipment in the world who are watching 24 hours a day, seven days a week for even a tiny sound or sign from within the universe. And here we are a mother and son who are communicating daily/nightly throughout our lives with the ET beings on a regular basis! This was beyond extraordinary; this is an enormous breakthrough we held in secret and we planned to keep recording their information and messages they continue to send, not to mention there would soon be another new way of communication coming to us. If you are thinking this is all fantasy and, in the mind, NO, there is proof of the writings and script from the ETs. The information in this book is a large part of what the ETs want told in the history of Alien encounters as far as we understand this from them. Everything we are doing comes with great responsibilities to undertake but we accepted this before birth and went with it knowing it would all matter greatly, and perhaps turn out to be of the utmost importance to many people.

It was *humbling* to know the information we carried and to stay as normal as possible, I had the concern of what would happen to our lives and my children's lives when this was revealed? I wanted them to have a normal life with privacy and I still have those same concerns. My family is not holding any information about the ETs of any kind they only know we have experienced a life connection with them. David and I were careful to not scare or upset the family in anyway. When the ETs first came to us in the beginning to reveal themselves as family in order not to upset us, they gradually in time re-introduced their way of techniques to us by going with them which is what I am describing. We have never known how many of the ET trips were programmed for us to forget afterwards, or those we each thought of as dreams in the early years.

The Amazing Airport

David experienced a special trip with the ETs he wanted to tell me about one day as soon as he woke up. In the beginning of his trip, he could see the setting as a regular airport when he was first taken there, and then a stranger suddenly came up to him putting his hand on his back and telepathically said, *"I will help you David because you are rare and see the beauty in life"*. The man then led him to what appeared to be a staircase leading down to a lower floor. David said, *"It was so beautiful the floor was made of beautiful copper and gold colors and that he had never seen such beautiful colors, they looked like the size of tiles but were made of a material similar to the look of our metal"*. In moments he could see outside of this airport setting and described the round shaped room he had been that had windows all around inside of it. Then he was led by the stranger to look out of the windows where he could see such incredible beauty in a sky of sapphire and brilliant blues combined with other amazing colors. Without another thought in his head he realized the stranger had somehow brought him home in that moment and was back in his bed! We discussed this the next day, it had happened without any doubt he had been taken to experience this and returned that same evening. Afterwards David was given information from the being who took him that he was an ET High Council Being who had made his appearance as a man at the airport, which made David feel comfortable while aboard their UFO craft. The stairs going down to another level with the brilliant metal floor was what the ETs let him see as the floor, but this was teaching about learning different levels of consciousness in life. The windows that were completely around the room setting were inside the UFO and seeing the brilliant colored sky was when David knew he was traveling through the Universe and suddenly was back home in his bed!

We have come to find the false scenery is easy for the ETs to arrange in our minds, to let us think we are seeing it as real in those times. What the reasons were for on this trip he was to know of for his future work then blocked from his memory briefly to make it appear as a dream state while it was happening. The ETs can arrange trips in a certain way and then erase any memories when needed to keep one relaxed or not to overwhelm us. And when events happen, we remember there is a reason we can remember them. They know how *fragile* the mind is on these matters; so again, a little at a time is to absorb information into the sub-conscious mind, in this way the mind is not overloaded. Who knows how long each one of us will experience these episodes and in the early experiences sometimes we questioned *"what really did happen?"* Each human's mind and what they can handle must be in the right timing to bring more information to the person. As time passed, we became more relaxed always looking forward to them coming and anxiously ready to go with them on each trip. We were never fearful; we felt our connection to one another, and we loved our schooling! The more time that passed we felt a strong family kinship like our earth family, only in a different way. These ETs are very spiritual, and we feel blessed to be in their company as the heavenly spirits they are.

Soon they brought more precious words to us, *"Rejoice as the Angels sing in triumph! Love is the key to all happiness as thy son knows."* How beautiful and powerful lifting our spirit!

Next, I want to explain about abductions and why some are done.

104

An Alien *visit* is completely different than an *abduction*. A *visit is with one's agreement,* a positive contact made between you and the beings at some point beforehand if one can believe this or not. Our agreements were made with each one's chosen agenda and contract before we each were born to return to earth. When an agreement is worked out for a next life, that soul can evolve back through free will to a new earth life if one chooses. Now, a *visit* depends on how strong the mind is, and what our connection is with a universal being which determines how soon or if ever, any kind of memories will be given to this person in their lifetime. I only know ours I can speak of for the two of us in how we know this to be. Deep down in the layers of the subconscious mind lie answers that sometimes hypnosis can't pull out because of the fear a person carries so they *may never recall they gave permission.* Permission is really a big thing with the many beings we have as teachers and workers.

An *"abductee"* is one who has been taken with force by a negative being and terrified with forced trauma this is how an *abduction* is usually done, which may damage the human mind for a lifetime.

The *"visit"* must be with one's permission in some way, usually without memory of giving it which can still be a very complex experience for the human soul because of the lost memory of their agreement. People who experience a *visit* may also be terrified by not remembering *any kind of an agreement* and they may never recall it. All in all, both ways can be very scary to endure when the memory is suppressed. I wanted to point out the different words in how the two experiences are looked at by some others. Again, I can only explain ours and how our chosen lives are. Some may even remember being with the beings since children and still be afraid when grown to an adult. We are thankful we remember ours from children with good visits and looked forward to them.

CHAPTER 6

The Dance of Transformation

The ETs were supplying us with new information about our own *transformation* and how we are moving through our personal experiences of reality, new waves of thinking, feeling, sensing, merging, and dividing, in an infinite dance of *transformation* as the soul grows and moves closer to the Universal Father our Creator. With these things we were developing more as a human to cope here but belonging to our universal beings. I am sure our real nature can be a little strange thinking about it being different beings but as one. This takes me to our Creation; a heavenly being said, *"My son and I were created as one soul then divided into two different souls in the very beginning to work together in each lifetime."* This was beautiful information; knowing our choices were made together to live with our universal ETs and on earth, this for us would be a highly advanced part of the whole. We were supplied with more fragments of information we slowly remembered now which made perfect sense. Just for humankind to know everything is part of the vast universes, worlds, and everything created is a great spiritual awakening, a revelation for those seeking!

These species are of a very *superior intelligence* that protects and supports our work providing us with their guidance in our covenant and this blessed purpose in our lives. This is something I kept in mind through remembering it from before, and how varied our teachings came to us with our own personal experiences. This is always with our permission of each step, as when we made our commitment to come here. At first, this life here is very powerful for the mind to absorb; once knocking out old ways of a structured belief system one has been accustomed to can be a shock for a while and takes getting use too, fortunately we completed this in order to learn and survive.

The ET/ Spiritual teachers were soon back to remind me, with my sight changing I would be able to see molecules; I call these *Eons and Ions* floating in the air we breathe and everywhere around us in everything created. I had been experiencing these tiny invisible goblets for many years, now the beings had expanded my sight even more. I know science tell us these invisible patterns and can only be seen through a microscope, but I was able to enjoy them moving everywhere I looked in their tiny shapes and sizes. On cloudy days the Ions and Eons, (I call them) move more slowly with the reverse on sunny days, on smoggy days they are still very slow-moving floating around in different patterns of directions. The skies, trees, all nature, animals, people, every living thing everywhere absorb them in order to survive although most people never know about them and cannot see them. On sunny days their patterns and little shapes are different, beautiful, and faster moving flowing into everything, everywhere, auras of humans, animals, our bodies, food, trees, homes, everything there is. This was so exciting to me especially when riding in a car as I watched these tiny invisible patterns floating outside and moving through the car windows settling into everything and myself. I was enthralled of how the tiny little goblets could change their shapes, sizes, and patterns, I didn't care who or if anyone ever believed me and I never told others, only my son. I knew I was experiencing an extraordinary vital part of this planet!

It made perfect sense to me as to why people get depressed in winter months, they feel the *winter blues* when so many days are dark and cloudy then we absorb fewer of the tiny Eons and Ions, the endorphins our bodies need. We get them, but there is a big difference in how one feels on the cloudy and cold days to a sunny one. All these amazing energies are vital not only to humans but animals and everything else on the planet to thrive. They pass in and out of us with a new reserve entering continually and for most people they are *invisible* like the air we breathe. But humans and everything else on earth must have them to live, they are a vital part of what everything is made of. This is my human way to describe them in my simple way since I am not a scientist. One delightful thing about these tiny molecules is, even on the sunny days they look as if it is *snowing everywhere!* I took me a while to became use to this, and in time became normal.

I had double developed my sight from that night long ago by being able to use each eye with a different ability *close or far away* the same as a telescope can do. I realized when the ETs changed my sight everything they were teaching and helping us with has purpose, and positive direction from an Infinite Highly Intelligent Source.

One evening David was awakened by a humming sound in the back of our home he decided to get-up and investigate looking out of his bedroom window. He could see several bright white and colored lights and looking more closely he made out the shape of a UFO craft. The lights were coming from around and under the craft, as it was *hovering* over our barn. The hum of it began to sound louder and louder to his ears but he decided to go outside and look, this *aggravated* his hearing more and he was wondering why no one else nearby seemed to hear it, or maybe they did, not know where it came from. After this, he could only remember going back inside and the next day he woke with a bad headache and told me his experience. This was when his memory kicked in of when he went outside, this was apparently to *board* the craft, not just to look at it. When he returned, he was outside coming back into the house!

This is one of the many pictures I was told to take by the ETs on a dark starless night over the house when an ET Christ Light Being appeared. This let us know how protected we are by them.

108

My room was at the opposite end of the house I vaguely recalled a humming sound in the night, but I only had a short memory of it. I began finding out there were times we had not remembered being with the ETs; and there were times each of us would wake up with a big headache. One thing we were aware of we were *never* harmed in anyway… These beings we go with are a loving, compassionate, positive species. Because of how our trip is orchestrated with the familiar ETs, we had reason to think these new Beings came from *Orion*, a well-known star system.

Three days later a message came in about Knowledge: "in *order to gain more universal knowledge one must give up more of the material realm. In order to gain more knowledge, one must also be able to see with a clear eye into other dimensions and new realms. Freeing the heart and soul from all burdens will let one travel to any length our hearts desire. To live in the physical world is hard because you are a spiritual being here for a short while. So, try to separate the two, three, or four worlds you see and feel and work in the physical world but use your newfound knowledge. You have much to do and see yet; your eyes will hold more now, your mind will hold more now, just realize we are with you always*".

How wonderful this information was, they know we would gladly give up any material in our earth world to gain more knowledge, and we are thankful for everything the beings do to adjusting us to our human bodies. Living in the other worlds and this one has been fascinating because we love both but freeing the heart and soul have sometimes been tough because it is hard adjusting coming from where we belong. We found out the night before with the UFO over the barn was for new adjustments to be made and to learn other information from *Orion*. Lesson being, we both were happy about giving up more to learn more, while living in this physical world, to gain more universal knowledge and travel to any length our hearts desired. We remembered to see into things around us with a clear eye, we had been relearning a great amount through our time here with help from the beings who teach us. later the same day another message arrived, "*David has the power to heal his self he can do this and you his mother*" this was absolutely a blessed heartfelt message to be reaffirmed of since we both devoted our lives to Reiki and were using it every day! I am positive without any doubt; David's miracle healings were happening through the Christ Light ETs and Reiki energy. We were dedicated in our heart and soul to helping others and ourselves, I worked on my son as the ETs and heavenly beings did through the years and he survived death and severe illness many times! This message above empowered us in our work we felt we were right on track and never to leave our course and dedication to Reiki and Christ teachings!

For some reason this reminds me of a lady from a neighboring town who stopped by to visit one day when I was in the yard working. I could tell she had trouble choosing her words to tell me something, *"when she passed by my home, she could see a rainbow over the house!"* I really appreciated this since she knew nothing about our experiences, but the shocking part was, she could see this rainbow at night! She described it to me, *"All seven rainbow colors were in sparkling bright colors coming down from the sky and she could swear she saw an Angel being inside the rainbow! She had wanted to tell me this for several years but didn't want to sound foolish or just plain silly"*. This was very meaningful, I knew there was a reason she saw what she did, her life was changing to a stronger one growing spiritually higher with the gift of psychic awareness within her. I bet if she had known what was going on with us, she would of have been extremely surprised! After these many years she was still trying to figure the *rainbow* out and had finally decided to tell me about it. I don't have the answers as to why this happened to her except, she was going to a higher level in her spiritually, and I am very thankful she shared her story with me. I know there was a good reason she experienced what she did, life is an amazing mystery waiting for anyone to learn.

It was April a beautiful spring day had arrived; messages were increasing to us from the Universal ETs and passed over loved ones. The ETs reminded me in a direct and gentle way with next message: "Let *not your feelings stand in the way of your great works meaning, don't get tied up with material things. Not to think about what others will say, not to be afraid to tell people that you do not have the time for the little petty things in life, use your free will, your time as you wish fulfill your desires. Know you may always use and count on your freewill in life, just don't get bogged down. Do not be afraid to tell of your life's experiences."*

There it was, and I loved it this is what I needed to hear; now I could talk with those who have an open heart and mind, and others who I felt were ready. I was to teach, and I needed never look back or be concerned with what others think… The petty things seemed to consume me at times in this world before, this was what I needed! This was the permission I needed to begin writing my books filled with our experiences. I was told, *"to never be afraid, cast out fear and replace it with Love, the gift is yours now of celebration!"* This freed me to begin what I promised to do during my lifetime; we had constantly been working with the spirit world, doing readings, hypnosis, teaching, traveling and learning through our ET family. We were involved with many more things than the earth world, and suddenly we were told, *"How things were going to get even busier in our lives."* This was about starting my books; I knew our teachers waited and would advise us as usual.

There was something wonderful planned for the both of us we knew nothing about, which was meant to be another amazing turning point in our lives! Much of the time our life in different worlds was like being up high looking down at everything evolving as if earth life was one big fabricated dream! After those thoughts a heavenly spiritual being appeared with this beautiful message: *"this is how it really is because you know you are a spiritual being first learning in Earth school with many of us around you, your teachers, guides, and loved ones come to help you along the way. The other side is your real home you will return to when your mission ends. Earth school is one of the hardest to learn from there is time for the human being to try to correct any problems now and from the past, learn lessons, and to make amends or not, but to learn what is important in life, love and compassion for others"*.

What important information for others to continue growing from and understand why they exist on this earth; this beautiful message explains the truth so one can repair past mistakes if they choose to. We are all together in this amazing way growing to heavenly realms with our own belief systems. We must look somewhat like the old saying, about the spokes on a wheel all-leading to the hub, just coming from different directions. We are full of humility, humbleness, and thankful to tell others so they can understand, by learning to correct life's problems using love and compassion for others, what an amazing gift to all!

A Superior ET Being of Intelligence arrived from *"The Great High Council"* before our next travels with the message below. Only two others could see this then, but the ET said, *it is time to share it exactly as written below.*

> *Great High Council*
> *Gone through warp into a sister universe*
> *Have new tech. being planted into your brain stem*
> *Released from their own system when we are ready*
> *Passed into Tri system to be exposed to Tri council*
> *For final approval. They say yes, we all bow before*
> *Each other and accept all responsibility.*
> *All is well, and soon to be completed Tri will finish*
> *Processing data into brain stem.*

I will be honest this was a surprise the ETs wanted the above message included in this book for others to see. I know they go slow with us at times so information can be stored in our memory that we are involved with something enormous and extraordinary the world will know about one day. This important message was only one of many hundreds the ETs shared with us. Our continued processing with what we watched on the *screens* in crafts had been implanted into our brain stems, these were things we have always known but brought back in *"portions"*. We were completely merged together with the *TRI council* and the others, there would be many more messages from our Universal family coming and we were ready to receive them.

The council brings a superior new advancement to us

On a special night in the month of June I was standing closely beside a being from the *"Great High Council"*. My mind raced with questions wondering what his visit meant; although I was having my own thoughts on this honored visit. The *Council* had appeared in beautiful bright light that did not hurt my eyes just the opposite, and four of these Heavenly Beings were standing beside my son and me. My mouth must have opened to speak but I could not have spoken a word, and David did not speak either we felt paralyzed, our feelings and emotions were full of amazing love!

This Council is one I explained previously made of the highest evolved universal Beings which made us feel even more proud and honored. All four of the Council each wore a beautiful long robe and they themselves were very tall in stature appearing to us as almost human. These were *"THE HIGHEST OF ALL COUNCILS"* of magnificent love and peace, their intelligence is more than any being could possibly begin to achieve or understand! When the main one began to speak he let us know, *"they had come to help me but could not with a personal problem at that time, I was to use my intuition and in this way I would be prepared to find my right way. That I had been good to this person, but I cannot make choices for anyone other than myself and to remember this".* One of the mostly transparent Beings was standing to face me and seemed to be inside of my mind reading my thoughts with his powerful and gentle presence. The strange thing is, I could *see through his skull, the veins and insides of it*, and quickly he materialized. He knew we welcomed them and were not afraid and felt extremely honored with their visit!!

After this I began wondering, a*m I awake* I don't know if I was saying this out loud or telepathically, and though I didn't see David later I knew he was close to me this honor was for the both of us. Then they spoke, *"This Council is the highest after the Creator as the Angels are".* Wow, we were mesmerized!! Immediately, like a sudden break in time we were home and what happened in our honor was put into our memories until later understood, and how we wished we knew the rest. How can these things be explained, they can't, we were overwhelmed with humbleness and gratitude!

The Being's first message had made perfect sense because I was in a heartbreaking state when I went to bed that night and they knew I needed them. I had asked for their divine help, but I never imagined we would meet them like this! I knew on that day my son was calling out with his thoughts for help to lead me, this *Council knows* when to intercede to help us. Interceding is also done through the *monitoring* they do with tracking devises. What was important to me was realizing they had come to prepare me for a future event that broke my heart, but it was time being the end of it. They came to soften the blow as much as they could and remind me of why I am here. After the *Council* gave their help and filled my heart they were gone, vanished, and this is the last thing I remember except being overwhelmed with their love as it passed through me. I knew we received their protection of love giving newfound strength and courage, we would need for some time. They told me *"to never forget they have always been united with us both and would be forever"*. This brought tears to me we had divine help and could always count on them to protect us! It became often this *Council* came to visit; they would form a circle up high in the room over me to relate their information after this we traveled with them.

To Venture Inward

I heard a familiar voice someone in spirit was telling me to get a certain book *"Venture Inward"* by Hugh Lynn Cayce. Edgar had been his earth father who presented himself to us long ago as our teacher again in this life from the other side and we knew Hugh Lynn to be one of his past sons. The strong connection between us continues today as it did in earlier lives I have written about. I knew this book was of upmost importance something I needed to do; it was an introduction from the beloved universal council for others to study. On this same night in the early hours Edgar was telling me, *"Child you ponder many questions of your new work it will come in like a bright flash of light and it will click into you just like eons ago when you and your son did this work. You shall not be deceived by many your sight has cleared."* This enlightening message from him helped to guide us on our many paths… how honored we felt. The ring of truth in this message became clear the instant I recognized it from all our times before. I carried his message in my head for days, what was Edgar getting ready to do? I felt very small in this world when I watched the beautiful *stars* at night for more clues to come from him and the ETs, we knew a new journey had begun, a very important one.

Each time we received a message from our Universal family my heart would pound with anticipation, I would be hoping an answer would be given to us at that instant as they many times are. I knew my thoughts were always heard and in reading the next message it made an impact in our lives: *"Life's journeys are the key to the soul, live life to the fullest."* How simple, but sometimes life here gets in the way and makes important things slow to accomplish but to use more patience. If you study the divine beings one powerful sentence above about life's journey it makes complete sense for any person.

I found myself going back to memories of the nights I would see a *key* handed to me. I always reached out for it even though I knew it was not solid it was an important symbol, I knew I needed to reach out *to accept it and I wanted it* because it was in my love and heart to do, *this was very important not only for me but also our planet.!* At other times a message about this key would come to me with the Spiritual Beings own words, *"YOU HOLD THE KEY."* I kept getting more messages about this *special key,* sometimes in visions and from the Beings, astral traveling, a dream states, or in these messages appearing in my notebook! Many times, I heard their words to me day or night no matter what I was doing, I could be driving, in a conversation, reading, watching TV, all kind of instances when the words came. It was some time before I knew the complete meaning, I hadn't understood fully for a long time what I was being told to do with the key, but since then it became clearer with a *powerful* understanding. My son knew what the *key* meant throughout his life but kept quiet about what they wanted me to recall… The timing had to be right, he was just waiting…

Meeting James Van Prague

One night I was given information from the other side for David and me to go see a medium named, *James Van Prague.* We had watched this man do readings on TV and this would be a real treat to watch him in person. My son was still ill and less sight and eagerly wanted to meet him. I had an old car I wasn't sure about starting out in to drive the distance to Iowa and catch the afternoon readings, which was several miles from where we lived. I was ready to trade it off and complete the deal on it soon, but I knew we were to go, or I wouldn't have been told in the night hours, it had to be important. I somehow knew a better way would be provided by the Universe to make this possible. The very next day the universe wasted no time, I walked into a restaurant where a friend of mine and her sister were dining. After we greeted one another one suddenly said, *"You'll never guess where my sister and I are going!"* I knew right then the doors opened for us and to make it short, we were invited to ride along with the two of them to see none other than *James Van Prague*. They planned on making a round trip going there and back in one day which was perfect! The following night the spirit world told me, *"Our spiritual teachers and loved ones in spirit would be along with us, we the pupils were ready to hear this new information that Van Prague would call out to us and with the message's given. We were to say to him, "we are to begin a new field of work, Cayce sends us, is there a message?"*

"There will be news and knowledge given to the both of you. Enjoy this day of beauty you are loved so much dear ones". We were excited, even though we could get information in our way there was a great reason we were to get a special message and watch Mr. Prague work. There was more, something else was ready to unfold, we were in for a tremendous surprise, a day we would never forget!

We arrived in Iowa early enough to get front row seats just a few feet from the stage so my son could see. The big surprise and another reason for us to come was apparent right away, in the back of this large room I noticed an older woman sitting in a wheelchair waiting to see James. Even though she had changed over the years I recognized the famous *"Greta Alexander"* we were so happy, this was another dream we had waited for to meet this wonderful lady. She is the famous psychic who has helped solve *"missing children's cases"* for years and very well known. We watched her off and on over the years on television my son and I would say, *"one day we're going to meet Greta Alexander"* here she was! David and I went to Greta and before saying anything she immediately held out her hands to take mine, I looked into her eyes and told her how we had followed her work over the years and waited for this moment knowing one day it would somehow come. She smiled and told David and me, *"we had surpassed so much"* then she gave us both a wonderful reading as if she had known us forever! She told us, *"that she was very proud of us and that we both were on a high level of learning".* I hugged her saying, *"I love you, she replied: she loved us too!"* Then I gave the words I was supposed to say to Van Prague to Greta they seemed to just spill out of me, *"We are to begin a new field of work soon Cayce sends us do you have a message?"* She replied: *"Yes, I believe I have"* and she did! Then David stepped up to her with a big smile and taking his hands she smiled so big at him

116

and the first thing she told him was, "*I'm so glad your mother traded off that old car you had before something terrible happened it was ready to go.*" Luckily, we had rode with our friends as planned, and then she gave David a beautiful reading, my son was in tears, so he sat down and later went back to her for the rest of his reading. Greta had told my son, "he *is very spiritual and on a very high plane that he had every talent in his hands he could do anything with his hands, and he is a healer and more wonderful things*". How blessed we were to meet her!

I wouldn't take anything for that day meeting those two amazing people that afternoon. James had several more wonderful messages for David and me as soon as he began his readings. Even though we didn't tell the two ladies we rode with we would have contact with James the information he had for us spilled out of him, and one of our friends leaned over to say, "*that's for you guys!*" He first named my grandmother, mom and dad and other family names, even my dad's dog *Iggy,* and as you might think this is not a common name. He spoke of my mom being in and out of the hospital and later the nursing home for years, of David, his sisters, and other family members going back in time. He called me *Mary* as my teachers do at times and said, *this name was very important for me,* he had information of past babies from long ago before I was ever born that were in my family, and of my late mom and dad. James called my mother and dad by their first names and one of my brothers. Then he named *Edgar Cayce,* who he said was one of our main spiritual teachers, Edgar's dogs, and his love of fishing.

But the thing I was so surprised with, he named *two twin baby brothers and a sister I never knew I had,* who passed away at birth! Each twin boy was named after a grandparent; little *Artie* was named after my grandfather *Arthur, and Little William* after my other grandfather who was called *Bill* for short. Our next shock came with information about a baby sister I never knew I had named *Lecta*; she had been named after my grandmother *Electa!* I had always wanted a sister since I was the only girl, and suddenly I had two twin brothers and a baby sister! The other side once told me *I had a baby sister who died, and I had been a twin this proved it to me!* David and I were extremely happy, and our friends were really surprised at the readings being completely accurate as we filled them in on the way home!

As soon as we returned home, I wasted no time calling my dad's sister (my Aunt) to confirm our discovery of the babies and to find out all I could. When I called, I only asked my Aunt, if I had any other brothers or a sister, *"Why yes didn't you know this?"* I told her I never knew and how I found out, she was stunned! She said, *"the reading was correct that some of the babies were born before me and after and in those days when mom and dad were young, people just didn't mention those things to kids. I guess it was like something bad to talk about that had happened I didn't know why, but they wouldn't even say the word pregnant out loud".* I guess a woman was supposed to be *ashamed* in the old ways and my aunt speculated mom and dad may never have told me because you wouldn't tell a small child, and by the time we were old enough they just never did. So, the years rolled by and I never knew the *secret* until now!

I was told years back from the other side by one of my guides *"I would soon know what the entire secret meant one day"* and this was certainly a big part of it! I was thrilled to find this out now I would try to find where they were buried. My aunt mentioned she wasn't sure where the babies were buried and in those days the headstone usually only had *Infant* or *Baby* on it when they were born dead or died soon afterwards.

Shortly thereafter; on a beautiful sunny day I was led to their grave sites by Katie the little spirit girl who sort of came with my house when we bought it. She is very sweet like any child and one day she directed me to drive down a little dirt side road beside the old cemetery where I let myself be guided by her without much thought. I seemed to know just where she was taking me. I parked the truck then walked up a hill and there to my left were the three little stones with their last names! I had found my sister and twin brothers, this made it all official! I had always wanted a sister and she had been there all along and I had two more brothers! I was happy to know where they were buried, they were real not just a story. I didn't know it then but there would be messages coming to me from my siblings that melted my heart! One more thing, amazingly Katie and her family were buried nearby the babies, there on a tiny flat stone engraved was *Katie.* The discovery of the babies didn't end there an amazing miracle happened around one month later one day I found my notebook opened lying on my bed. This is one of the notebooks

I record my Alien/ET experiences in with all kinds of other spiritual information and messages. I felt the importance of something in it waiting for me to discover; my heart was beating so fast my head was reeling with all kinds of thoughts. I knew I was not *imagining* what I could see with my own eyes! The notebook should have been under my pillow where I left it at least it was when I made the bed that day and no one could have bothered it we had been to the hospital in the city for David's doctor appointments earlier. I hurried to the side of my bed to see a page filled in with the scrawl of a small child's printing. I sat down on the bed to read it, at the top of the page it said, *"miscarriage of mommy I'm your sister Lecta I've always been with you and I love you, you and your son are one."* Oh, I was so happy how sweet, it put me into tears! This was from my baby sister who I knew as *Lecta* I felt so much love for her, my worlds were wonderful!

I had a little sister I had not known about until the reading from *Van Prague* on that fall day. I had thought of nothing but my *baby sister and baby twin brothers* since my discovery of them! They will always be in my heart and I wanted to see them at that very moment! I could feel their presence with me, so I began to whisper words to *Lecta* and the twins at times when I was alone and I knew they heard me tell them, *I love you!*

Around two months later it happened again I found my notebook on my bed opened to a page which said, *"Yes, you were right I am little William* (then the printing changed) *and my name is little Artie sending our love to all tell Evie we're with her also."* Evie is my Aunt who knew of the babies, my heart broke; tears flowed out of happiness realizing this was from my two little twin brothers from the spirit world, the twin brothers I never knew I had! My baby brothers were telling me they are always with me and love me! I was in total bliss with the tenderness of their love I knew this amazing discovery was meant to be! I wanted to hold all three of them at once and tell them how much I love them! I continued to look at the children's attempt at printing and how the print changed from little William (Bill) to little Artie's, then checking on how little Lecta's style of print looked different on the other page. All three notes were in a different print this was beyond any words I can think of; how do you describe something like this, you can't! I went to another new message printed to my aunt they had left for her *"tell*

"Evie where're with her too". I was floating around all week and couldn't think of anything else and it seemed the ETs were watching and sharing all this love between us. David loved the messages he was as happy as me and we talked about this for hours, and he had been so happy to meet *Greta* as I was.

I would often daydream about what had happened in our lives and what would come next with the ETs and our loved ones in the spirit worlds. I carried on automatically each day with the normal things one does in life without too much thought to everyday living. I enjoyed and loved life, slept well at night when I had a chance even with my company of ET travel. Then there were the spirits passing through and the 7 who lived with us, I was experiencing other worlds with strange and magical experiences.

When David and I had an experience we focused on it at the time to learn from it and I believe one of the big reasons I was able to live life as if nothing out of the ordinary was going on, was because my son and I could discuss and share the experiences we had together. I must say, buying groceries, paying bills, going to ball games, birthday parties and so on I was like anyone else enjoying this world, yet knowing underneath David and I lived an entirely different kind of secret life we could not speak of. I often wondered at first why the other side called this home *"The house of secrets"* that's exactly what it is...

At certain times we were shown past, present, and future to come which *embraced* me in my learning. I began getting more *colorful* visions in the night of another type of teaching, these visions showed me I would be in a school filled with different classes and students where I could see myself teaching I was excited to know a place to teach was coming for me in the future this was after I learned to do Reiki. I loved using the gift of Reiki energy and to teach it, but I needed to be more careful in the future to protect myself knowing what some people can sometimes do to others when something new is introduced. Even to the extent of our spiritual teachers showing me a couple of women who would be *"jealous"* wanting to ruin me if they thought they could. I could see these people in the visions with their names to know who they would be on sight. The other side seemed intent on educating me about negative people so I would be more prepared to deal with them they know I am a *softy* and I don't handle this well. I knew this was a future event to come and it would be several years later I began to teach these classes and unfortunately I eventually met two of these people who tried to *crush* my very being with negative words, and who were hoping to use me to their advantage to advance in Reiki when they were not ready and they would never be ready...

I was grateful to my guides who warned me of this I knew the other side the *"Christ Light Beings, the ETs"* stood beside us with their *magnificent* love surrounding us. I knew we were protected; these people couldn't really hurt me unless I responded back in their way going to their level. I held no fear of them only pity, I recalled one of them calling me one day trying to scare me with her superior power of Reiki energy. I was stunned to think she expected the universe would ever let her use this God given gift in a negative way! The woman was influential coming from a family having money and use to people bowing down to her wishes, but I could feel her bad intention and motive within herself. When I answered her remarks, asking me if I was afraid of them, I simply told her, *"No, I was not afraid of her and her friend"*. She said, *"They both together could do things to others because they had twice the energy to use on people"* which was to frighten me. She did not like it that I spoke to her in a good and positive way without malice I was never afraid of her, I only pitied her. Reiki healing is from the universal Creator through the ages since the beginning which is made of the most supreme love of healing energy!

Why this happened with the two women was for my own benefit to understand everyone isn't always there for my own good no matter how they seem, and I needed to learn about all kind of people. It was hard to know there are people like this and much worse this lesson was also to remind me; I can't control anyone but myself. Some humans get lost in life becoming jealous and bitter and try to use others it has nothing to do with you doing anything to them they are badly off track in life for various reasons. This was a new lesson to learn I found I had a lot to learn, to be more careful and never brush away my intuition, to always go by my divine help to be aware of those who are negative. My spiritual teacher knew I had to experience this for other times which would surface in my life and hopefully I would be more versed to handle these new experiences. I led a very sheltered life growing up, I remembered how my parents helped everyone they could and were very kind to others and I loved this in them. Parts of life were going to be painful like everyone's and hopefully my experiences would help me immensely in my many lessons. My son also suffered by negative actions from others that broke his heart even many he helped; this is hard to understand.

The ET Babies

One thing I was *completely* in awe of was when David and I were taken by the ETs to see the Alien babies! They let us see them in a different scene, one they created letting us think we were in a *hospital setting* so I would be relaxed. First, we noticed what I assumed was a nurse in a white uniform and in front of us was a see-through glass panel or a material like glass and on the other side of this were lots of babies in containers. This was like a regular nursery except each baby was submersed in a fluid which looked like water! I became *alarmed* because their tiny bodies and heads were under this liquid, I was worried they would drown! How could they live and breathe in these containers under water? I was telepathically told, *"The babies were fine, and I would be told more about the process later on."* I was escorted out by an ET and found myself someplace else where I remember looking at the number 6, and the ET with me said, *"It was of importance and to remember it"*.

I recalled my son helped me to relax about the babies telling me, *"Mom they are alright"*. The ETs said, *"don't worry we are here to help; your light shines bright here tell the world we live on!"* I love this message it melted my heart and meant that passed over spirits of some loved ones were getting ready to evolve back to earth and I had seen them in their baby stage waiting to be born again! This ET also told me, *"this was very important to them and I am to speak for them in my books to reach out to others and this is why they were showing me the reproduction of the babies."* I understood what they wanted me to do it was very important, soon I would begin my book and write everything in them they want to say! These babies were fine if I remembered the process of reproduction now or not...

It seemed strange at that moment I could see the spirit of my late *grandfather* and we were overwhelmed with love! If I could only explain how this feels to have these strong emotions of such love between worlds, my granddad crossed over many years before and here we were interacting together in this way! I must have been smiling *ear to ear* at him knowing I was somewhere in another time and space with him. ah, dimensions! After he smiled at me, he was gone, he only wanted me to know he is alive in spirit the same as mom and dad and those who have passed before into other worlds. Now the big question you may have, *how does all this work together, the spirit world, Extraterrestrials, and Heavenly Beings who work closely and in what order or is there any certain order in the way they work?* Sometimes things are so simple we make hard.

One Sunday evening without memory of my transfer in travel I found myself in one of the ships I had been brought there the ETs to visit the babies again, I was curious why I seemed to be having many of these visits. These babies had a bright light on them and without hesitation telepathically I was told by the main ET *that some of them were part MINE! What!* I wondered why they had taken my DNA at some point I felt many emotions running through me, and I could easily see the babies were *Hybrids,* part ET and part human, I was a part of them! I was confused in my thoughts and questions were running through my head as I stood glued to the floor studying them, not wanting to move. Then I noticed there was never movement from them since they were immersed in the liquid with the light overhead, but I knew they were ok. I supposed being *Hybrids* they were different in many ways and quickly I reminded myself, I should know! I clearly understood they are a part of each world with the information I was just told which had been blocked from me for how long? Only the beings knew how long, but now it was coming to an end and it was time! They wanted to fill me in about myself; the part of me I did not realize completely, with memories stored away surfacing a little at a time. I don't remember David being with me then, but he may have been and the next thing I knew I was home.

I woke up and it was morning I still felt groggy when David came to breakfast, I asked him, *"If he remembered anything from the night before?* He said, *"He was just getting ready to ask me the same question because we went to see the babies again, then he asked me if I remembered?"* We compared the same experience since he viewed the babies and gave me mental support if needed. Talk about mental support, I was being introduced to a part of myself that I would never think possible in a million years at that time. It was one thing to be taken to view the babies even knowing some may belong on earth but on this trip to be told they were a part of me I felt proud! Was this trip taken to explain more about a human's eggs, to store them, and when the time was right combining them with the Alien part of genetic make-up? It had to be; I couldn't think of how else this was done the ETs have been taking us with them throughout our lives and more was beginning to make sense. David was always with me to support whatever we experienced his memories were never *repressed* and mine were being released, and I felt proud to be part of a new evolution of Beings.

I would be told later by one of my spiritual teachers, *"Your studies have helped prepare you"*. I can't tell you, the readers, what an *impact* all of this had on my life! After we had returned from the last trip my face looked drained when gazing into the mirror and I could think of nothing else after reality hit me. It's not as if this had never crossed my mind but I was in a state of surprise, who wouldn't be? I didn't have bad feelings I felt fine and wondering how many others in our world may be having this same thing happen to them in order to develop *"a new colony of future people"* for a new world? I knew my suspected truth for some time was right on, there had to be other women chosen with their given permission over time. The *visits* were important for us to relearn, about our new babies. This was much to absorb, but I wouldn't have experienced this trip if I wasn't ready everything would be ok. There would be more answers coming from stored information in my memories and shortly later, I felt *honored* in a new way to be able to contribute to a new world one day I was excited to be involved in this program! I looked forward to returning each time to watch the babies grow I would be watching the babies grow at an accelerated growth with a much higher intelligence!

The Egyptian Mummy

After loss of sleep for the next few nights putting my life back together, I had not been in bed long and finally fell asleep. It seemed only a moment when I suddenly awoke and opened my eyes, a soft golden light filling my room was moving closer to me. This light was the outline of something forming like a large billowy pillow, this bundle of gold light formed into a full figure! I first saw large dark almond shaped eyes looking at me with the lower and upper part of its face wrapped in a gauze like material. The entire body continued to be wrapped from the face down in what appeared to be layers of gauze cloth over the figure. This was an Egyptian *mummy,* only the eyes were exposed to me! The figure seemed normal in height and moved closer to my bed sort of *gliding* to me. The strangest part was this Egyptian being held out its left hand to show me something! Over the wrappings on the middle finger of the left hand was a beautiful ruby ring just like mine, the one I have now! I was shocked, I have an exact copy of this ruby ring, it was given to me years ago for my *birthday* from my mother and dad! After I examined the ring the mummy quickly *vanished* away! I looked at the ring experience as if his mission was completed leaving me in great awe, what does this mean, I would soon find out!

As I lay there awake, I kept thinking about me being a mummy who lived in that era, and I knew why!! I was to remember this as these words flowed to me, *"This ruby ring was a connection to this life; the ruby is my birthstone. I had experienced life in Egypt, I had worn this ruby ring on my left hand".* Wow, this was important for me to recall, and in only a breath I was hit with a sudden jolt as this was *pointed out to me in a vision!* I was seeing *a past life* of when my Egyptian mother and dad gave me this *ruby ring* as an Egyptian child, I was young and it was my *birthday*, my parents today had been my parents then! This was an important part of my life in Egyptian times I was to remember, and I would never forget this wonderful reminder it was amazing!!

I repeated it in this lifetime to be with my mother and dad again and they may have unknowingly given me the same Ruby ring for my 16th birthday as a teenager! I figured it out after the vision of the mummy experience; I realized I was the mummy *showing myself* the same ring my parents had presented to me in this life, this ring had to be important! I have experienced other past lives in Egypt as my son and I, and Edgar Cayce, who was Ra Ta in one of his. I find it amazing how these things are planned by us long ago so perfectly and ageless... I was thrilled knowing mom and dad were my parents in that period too.

A following message came to me later that week which was simple but uplifting, *"Greetings from all of us there are greater things to come*". This was a treasure in all to come from the ETs own writing in my notebook and this was on my *birthday* (which reminded me of the mummy vision) and on a full moon night. I knew what the full moon meant to me it was not only my sign, but it meant more travel with the ETs! We were overjoyed when their messages came from the other side to us and I remind myself daily this was surely an easy feat for them to do with everything else they do; I am sure one day we will be doing this ourselves! It is a thrill to get notes and messages in this way, it is actual proof even though we know the experiences are real being with them through our lives.

Over the years I kept every message we received handwritten or printed, and those I could keep on the computer and taking pictures of everything we could. There would be some messages that we were *"never to reveal to anyone"* unless we are ever told to, those would always stay locked in our hearts. Sometimes a message we recorded on video or computer was only left for a few hours or less then disappear! These were meant only for us; our lives were full and rewarding with amazing lessons from beyond and we both felt humbled to achieve any lost memories from the highly evolved beings of the light. I thought how strange this may seem too many people, but I have been told with this actual message, *"To tell of our experiences and to tell the world and to not be afraid"*, as I mentioned earlier. I know we are protected with the strength and courage provided for us to go forward in the work without thoughts of what others think, it doesn't matter to us, now that we have the permission to speak for them. I had to work hard getting to this point and some days were very difficult when you feel like an outcast inside yourself. Therefore, I am very happy David and I chose this journey together for to be alone in this work in this world would have been *extremely hard!*

CHAPTER 7

SPIRITUAL WISDOM

Several years ago, when writing my first book of the spirit world was to open doors for myself and others who have had strange experiences happening to them and were afraid to share them. This may have been for many different reasons, one of them was usually a fear of being looked at as a mentally ill case. Those who step forward in this work must be ready to ignore the outside world as never before, we know nothing would be accomplished if we and others did not move forward to speak our truth, invent, and write the experiences of history lived. In the long run it doesn't matter who believes one's journey when you know your own *truth* and there is no need to look back and waste valuable time. Looking back at one's self stops their full potential and as my spiritual teacher told me, *"if one keeps looking back, they will never be able to go forward in life"*. This was beautifully put but at the same time I needed to be reinforced with words at times to continue moving forward. It would be easy to stop and not do anything, but it would break our promise to the Creator, and we would never do this!

A new message arrived in our spiritual teacher's handwriting a few days after my birthday: *"Thank you. Behold you are a child of God!"* How beautiful, I was overwhelmed when I found this about 5:15 in the afternoon when I returned home. I must have read this over several times, then went running to show my son who also receives our blessed messages. We felt immensely honored and humbled what *"a remarkable beautiful birthday gift"* I was blessed! Everything didn't happen only at night there was many messages from the ETs during the day. The other side told me, *"We were called "Messengers" in their world, and when certain spirits had a message to be delivered to a loved one, they were counting on us to deliver it"*. This can sometimes be difficult because of approaching people you don't know with this kind of information, although we feel a great responsibility to help them. We wait until we are to go to them guided by the heavenly beings.

The heavenly beings and ETs need not think about time issues where they are, and the longer spirits are crossed over some tell us they have *forgotten* what time is here on earth because there is no such thing there. Time for us is simply a measurement that was developed long ago to make a timetable for our days and nights, we needed something to go by and this works for us in our way on earth. The other side let us know, *"they don't miss any of this stuff"* and the amazing thing is they seem to know every birthday, holiday, illness, weddings, and whatever upsets us in our lives.

One night in my universal travels I looked down at my feet I had two different shoes on one was a black dress shoe, on the other foot I had a white sneaker on, I knew that feet symbolized *"spiritual foundation"*. In that moment I saw our symbol of the *"Ying Yang"*, this was reminding me I needed to keep more of a *balance* in my life between work and play. This is very important for all of us to keep a balance, which has been a hard one for me and probably most people. I don't know when to take time out and not work so I knew the black shoe represented *"a working shoe"* but if I would *bend* some it was also *"a fun symbol"*. The white shoe represented *"a quick way to move into a causal relaxing balance"*, here was my formula for a better way to live but I haven't exactly been able to complete this one. This gives you an idea of how things were given to us to figure out and learn from I don't think symbols ever have the entire same meaning for those who get them, each person has their own. You must learn your own to help yourself it has taken many years of study to learn our many symbols and there are always new ones which come along. This is called *"growing into your mind capacity"* when one does, the symbols are quickly recognized when you need them....

Lessons on speaking with love

One evening in a vision I saw David with three beautiful Beings around him. I knew they were healers that were *"discussing his condition"* they took a sample of his hair to examine. This was on a UFO craft we were brought to at the time the next thing I saw was *"three snakes"* in a beautiful blue color, one of them punched a symbol into the tongue of another snake in the shape of a heart! Somehow, I knew what this symbol meant, *"to speak with love even to those who are cruel"*. I have been taught by the other side when a person is cruel, they really *dislike their self-inside* that's how they feel about who they are. I am not fond of snakes in anyway, but I was not afraid, I felt the lesson of love in this experience was so clever because of how it was represented. The symbol of snakes is often used as a medical and spiritual symbol and this time it was about *speaking with love*. I do not know all of the reasons or answers by any means, I only know it is important to learn the lessons we are shown or they would not give them to us, and snakes shown in this way as symbols show *"spiritual wisdom and love"*.

These things may be happening to us for a future event coming up in our world to learn and handle others we meet, this is what the message meant. I was told the next evening, *"to know not only in your heart but also in your mind we are all here to help, many of us are here and from that which is Holy and that which is from the Light even the ones the ETs who come to help, all of us are here are stronger than ever. All of this was given in love."* I love this how much clearer could it be? This is a very spiritual message given to help us and everyone who will listen to them through this book! I was absolutely blown away how could one not feel this way? Soon; on another evening the Beings appeared again, *"Yes child we shall travel, enjoy, and learn. You are more ready now and not as tired as usual. I know as your teacher and your guide you are ready and wanting to go on. Sometimes it is good to rest and wait. We are here and soon your eyes will grow heavy and we will go"*.

For several weeks in our evening travels much healing was done and explained to me in the spirit world from the ETs, healers, teachers, guides, Angels/Arch Angels and past loved ones who work steadily with us. My son had become extremely ill and hospitalized in very serious condition we were being prepared ahead by the ETs to get through this by those who help us from the other side. I was to pass Reiki healing as directed from the Divine Creator through me to David with the Divine Light guiding it.

One day I was asked by David's doctor to leave my sons room at the hospital to step into the hall where his doctor looked at me with sadness, he told me, *"My son would not live out the day!"* I could not respond for minutes but in my heart, I knew my son would live! *"I could see Angels and spiritual loved ones all around him he was surrounded in love there were so many I could not see the walls in his room anymore, only the highest of Angels glowing in their light!"*

It is terrible to watch our loved ones suffer so much to stay longer with us, but this was his journey and I knew when the Angels surrounded him and I heard the words, *"for he shall be well"* he would survive! I was overwhelmingly happy, my legs went weak, peace washed over my soul, he chosen to stay longer! David is a highly *advanced spiritual* teacher to me and many other people on this earth and one day many would understand.

David's Turning Point

Very quickly after this amazing miracle took place a remarkable message came to me from the other side which sealed his choice:

"David could do well here or there" meaning, by his passing into the spirit world or to stay on earth to do more great works with his free will. With his choice he could help many others on our earth plane if his will was to stay longer periods of time here. Our teacher said, *"Tell your son to do whatever is in his heart and for me to see my son as pure light and healthy, see him doing all the things he loves, and it shall set him free and so shall you be! He will know what to do for he is an old soul and he knows this. His heart is more set to stay and not leave yet so there is what you call time. Now go dear child, and wear a smile, hug's and love does wonders we are with you both always"*.

This was the happiest extraordinary moment for a mother to receive such a blessed message from the Creator I knew my son had made his choice! We both never faltered back we truly believed and trusted our hearts to the Creator, The Divine Ones, those from the heavenly realms and Extraterrestrials of The Christ Light...

David surprised or should I say *shocked* the medical doctors as another miracle occurred once again. He had passed the crisis and in a short time became stronger and began to walk some each day and hold down small amounts of food he was surviving!! And as always with a big beautiful radiant smile on his face, a *smile that glowed like sunshine* no matter how sick he ever was! His sisters poured their devoted love out to him we were his *"cheerleaders"*, he was determined to get better and better, he represented complete faith with through the miracles given to him!

Just think of the many miracles over our world happening every day all the time. Miracles *empower* a human being with tremendous love in the beloved *Creator* and no matter how serious they may become to someone they can change in the blink of an eye! After this thought; the heavenly voice boomed out, *"David will set an example that many will never forget giving hope to many others."* WOW, what more was there to say, except, he does, and he will!

An Angel Brings More Joyous News!

One evening after my son was home from the hospital he had to be in bed for a short while, soon he called to me to come up to his room and bring my camera there was something that had just happened. *"Sit down a minute"* he said. He looked so calm with light glowing about his face and thin frame he explained, *"he had just had an experience an Angel had appeared before him bathed in bright white light in his room"*. The Angel said, *"To tell me to go to my room that something was there for me to find."* David said, *"GO SEE!"* We were excited I hurried to my room and found my cross necklace laying on my dresser with the chain made into the *shape of two Angel wings,* I was astounded! I hurried back to tell him what I had found, and he was still smiling then looked very serious and asked me, *"if I knew what this sign meant?"* I replied, *"does it mean I am learning even more and gaining strength, and getting stronger in my spiritual lessons?"* He said, *"It's all of that and the Angel said, To tell you that you have reached another new plateau and now you are out of the cocoon I am like a butterfly I had earned my wings!"* I was full of excitement and so happy... I called out *"thank you Angel!"* We sat and talked for a long time about this extraordinary event and how it was done with my cross necklace to earn my wings, I don't think I slept for several nights!

My son was back in the hospital within the next few days with a near heart attack and close to death! I put things together that had recently happened with the symbols, the Beings of Light, and what had been said to me by the Angel about this being my son's choice to do what he felt the need to, I pulled on the strength of the Angels and the other side. I had the faith and strength I was given but I needed theirs too! The other side would come and speak to me in those days telling me over and over; *"for he shall be well"* I knew to

131

believe them, and I did not doubt, I never had! As a mother my heart broke to watch him suffer so much David would always have a weak smile for me when he was conscious, he even tried to smile for the nurses or anyone else who entered his room no matter how weak he was or how close to death he was. If my son could always be so strong for us, I knew I could always be for him! I never let him see me cry to upset him I gave him my love and positive words to live. He gave me strength by watching him and I would not leave him for a minute until he passed the crisis and was better. There were no tears of mine ever in front of him to see, this would have upset him for me. I sent healing with my total love to him through the years with my smiles to him, this is the way we did it all the years he lived… Not one time did we each waiver from this, I would never let him see my tears unless it was from my joy! People dying need your love and strength not our tears, which makes it harder for them. It is hard not to cry and show your deep feelings... which I did in private.

Some of the nurses came in during the late night to talk with David when he was better, and I marveled at how he was giving *"council by listening"* to them. I was so proud of him I was learning what it truly was to have such strength as he had. He survived again and eventually I could take him home! He told me, he got his strength from *me* and I was completely humbled to hear those words we had one mind and could talk with only our thoughts.

When we returned home from the hospital, I found David's antique Holy box of healing open on my dresser with the small picture of *MOTHER MARY* placed inside of it, before this her picture had been on a table in my room! I knew this familiar blessed sign was to show us *"Mother Mary and the Christ"* sent their divine help and healing to him and along with his own *free will* he would go on and continue to live! He *had many miracles* in those 19 years…his story is one of inspiration for others he was a spiritual teacher here to give others hope and courage, to love themselves in the growing process!

The next trip to the hospital was even more serious David was near death again, and again he became well enough to come home with another wonderful *miracle* through his strength and free will. He had choices *to stay or to go* and thank God he still wanted to stay to be with us and work in his healing. The picture of *Mother Mary* was placed back in the opened Holy Box to let us know his life was going to continue for now and *he would be well* once more! I have *never forgotten when Mother Mary* would appear to me each time, he was critical always saying, *"I come to you as a Mother to a Mother"*. Then she spoke to me of Christ her son and that she understood my pain, I am not Catholic which does not make any difference to her, why would it? Some belief systems may never want to believe this, but it is true. She continued to come to me several times through the years to lift my spirit as she spoke of how her son suffered, she knew my heartbreak and said, *"she would always be near to me"*. David was using his freewill with his miracles to escape death, so many times I can't remember them all. One thing he never did was to become negative thinking the worse; he was not ready to leave here although his physical body was... *Mother Mary* has been a blessing to us through our lives.

Over the years I lost count of his hospital stays and I recall after one of his serious hospital emergencies when he was much better I left the hospital to come home for fresh clothes, little did I know this was going to be another amazing event about to happen. As I was leaving the hospital to drive home David's last words to me were, *"don't ride the train back mom, you have never done it before"* I noticed he had concern in his voice. I was very tired with our many trips for years: so, what did I do, I rode the train and returned right back to the hospital. I never do things like this, but it was a sunny day I could sit back and relax. When I stepped into his room, I found my son propped up on his bed ready to go in his t shirt and pajama bottom thinking we would be in the car. I never dreamt he would be released on that day thinking it would be at least the next day or two but seeing that big kid's smile of *accomplishment* I knew he had been talking his way out since I left, which he usually managed to do. I thought he didn't know I had taken the train to the hospital instead of driving like I always had, but looking at me he *blurted* out, *"you didn't take the take the train did you, I was just released."* He knew I had, and I thought "oh no," what will we do, he had no shoes bringing him in as an emergency there was no time for shoes!

We left the hospital with David in a wheelchair I borrowed long enough to get him to the train platform which was nearby. He was holding onto three bed pillows of ours, a small suitcase, and my handbag with me pushing him. He had on scrub pants, a tee shirt, hospital socks; and no shoes! Binging him in as a BIG emergency when he was admitted days before I figured he did not need his shoes he wouldn't need them yet, and when he did I would have them there for him. Nevertheless, I had to leave him sitting on a bench with all the items beside him at the train station which luckily was only a short distance, across the street from the hospital. I ran as fast as I could to return the wheelchair back to the hospital, I was so afraid he would get sick or even worse *be mugged,* I was a nervous wreck! When I told him this, he began laughing hard and finally able to say, *"Mom who would fool with me I look like a homeless person I don't even have shoes to wear just hospital socks".*

When the train arrived, I was able to get him and his belongings on board before it took off which was a major feat. Our next problem was the train it had the coldest air conditioning which was blowing on his thin body, and it continued to make several stops along the way I didn't remember making when I rode it earlier. I could tell before we had gotten very far, he was exhausted and weak his feet were swelling, and I was worried sick this trip could put him right back in the hospital! What had I done by not driving? But I couldn't have known there was going to be another *"miracle"* planned and was waiting for us on that day. David would never have complained about the trip that day or about the situation, he never complained about anything! It took a while before we arrived at a destination which was not familiar! When the train stopped, we had to board a bus to get to my car parked some miles away at a shopping center. I had a bad feeling when we got onto this bus but I had to hurry to get David in a seat so I let go of the feeling which would turn out to be correct! The bus driver began driving for a long time, too long, and I could see nothing familiar, so I knew something was not right. I asked the driver before we boarded if this bus went to the location where my car was parked at the shopping center, the driver assured me it did! I couldn't tell where we were for a long time and suddenly, we were pulling into an un-familiar area in a bad part of town. This is when I found out the bus driver hadn't changed the sign on the outside of the bus when we boarded, we had gotten on the wrong bus! Even asking the driver if it went to our location I had been told, yes. We were going to be stranded in a scary part of town without shoes for David.

Now an amazing experience was about to take place, the bus had come to a sudden STOP and everyone was getting off I told David to wait; *"the bus surly went on to the shopping center about five more miles up the road"*. About this time, I heard the driver call out, *"End of the line!"* "Oh no, I said then the bus driver basically told us to *"GET OFF the bus"!* She had a short temper one could easily tell, not knowing what to do I helped my son off the bus. We were loaded down with our things and I was trying my best to hold him up. I asked a couple of people who were sitting on a bench, *"when the next bus would come?"* They told me, *"this was the last one for that day it had been their stop and there wouldn't be another one today"*. We realized the driver was already gone and off duty to ask more questions for help and this was a time when most people didn't have cell phones.

I secretly thought *"we needed HELP what were we going to do"?* My son wasn't looking very well by now and I could only blame myself if he had a set-back, I was assuring him we would get to the car some way. We turned around because we heard a voice and behind us stood a young slim black woman who had come out of nowhere! There had not been anyone around us a moment ago, she wore a green checked cotton dress, had very short hair and held nothing in her hands, not a bus ticket or a purse. Instantly she said, *"come follow me I will show you the way, I will show you the way home!"* We automatically began stepping towards her, she was walking backwards motioning with her hands, so she faced us both. She was gesturing with her hands to follow her and repeated, *"Come follow me I will show you the way, I will show you the way home"!* Then shock followed, she showed us a bus *"where there had not been a bus a moment ago now there were two of them!"* She directed us to one of the buses saying: *"Get on this bus it will take you home!"* I never felt a need to question this beautiful person and somehow, I knew to do just what she said. There was something I cannot describe about her it was like being in a *dream state* with her kind and loving voice leading us onto the bus which wasn't there moments before! I began to step up with David in front of me to guide him up the steps to help him manage. I was still on the first step with the woman standing beside me by the bus, quickly I turned to *thank her and started to call her Angel* (which was only part of a second) and she VANISHED, GONE! I couldn't believe it she had

135

disappeared in that split second with no place for her to go! There was a chain link fence near the bus and another fence a few feet away in front of the bus, and no other people around. I looked everywhere around us, but she was gone, disappeared! How could there be *two* buses when there hadn't been one a minute before? The big question was, *"how did she know where HOME was for us and which bus to get on?"* I remembered she carried nothing in her hands, no purse or bus ticket, nothing!

We quickly knew, she was our *Guardian Angel* who had come to help us in our great time of need! With both of us realizing this at the same moment we both said, *"She was an Angel!"* Everything made sense now that's why I had instinctively began to call her *Angel* without giving it a thought! What a glorious and magical day it was, now we knew the reason why everything went wrong in our world on this day. It was because we were meant to experience this *Angel Being* who was protecting and helping us to get home! All of this was planned from the other side just for this reason, *to know this Angel who came in human form, not only to help us but to see her and to know we would always be helped by her on our path!* There was no human answer other than this, how else could this be? If she had been an ordinary person how would she know where we lived or which bus would take us to where my car was, or where my car and home was? Also, she carried nothing material with her, but she did have a beautiful loving radiance! Therefore, to take the train that day was for this reason and everything else followed!! We were to see her in human form to know her and she helped us more than once! Later this story came out in Guideposts, Angels on Earth magazine, we both felt humbly honored to tell our story!

As weak as David was, we chatted eagerly all the way to the car and home about our heavenly help who appeared in our time of need, and even though she had vanished before I could thank her, she knew the gratitude and love we felt. This is a day neither of us would ever forget and she would soon be helping us again at another time. There have been other stories where a stranger helped save someone or others in need and then the person vanishes just like our Angel! I believe Angels have no trouble reading our heart and soul this is their heavenly assigned work and I can still see her in my mind; I always will, and how in the world did she get those buses there? Nothing is impossible that's for sure! We made it a point early on to tell others our story reminding them that each one of us has a *"Guardian Angel"* to watch over us. And there are many spiritual Beings in the many universes and worlds who are working together with an Intelligence beyond what any human can imagine which is more than amazing!

The Infinite Supreme Intelligence we know as God created all Beings including Alien Universal beings, *not only us* here on Earth. It was clear to us in our work with the Christ Light ETs and many loved one's past, they are all combined in some amazing way with other species of beings, but many do not understand and cannot accept this, someday they will understand.

A few days later a short but powerful message came to us from the other side it verified what I have just written: *"we all work well together here, all of us, things shall open greatly now. We love you all. To remind others that we never die, that the soul never dies, it is life after life, immortality."* How we loved this beautiful message it is so clear, how much clearer could it be!

One night in late October David was awakened by a familiar *humming* sound that soon got on his nerves, so he got up to look out of the window. He could make out all kind of colored blinking lights a short distance away high up in the sky over the house and barn. Immediately he recognized the familiar shape of a UFO and he knew the ETs were here to make a visit. After he watched for a while the rest became a blank and the next thing, he knew was waking up the next morning to a sunny day. To his big surprise he found a *"basket of flowers"* sitting on his bed and called me upstairs to see this. Unbelievable, we thought when he showed me the flowers, he was still sick; we knew for them to arrange this surprise for him meant they were showing emotions of caring and love. The ETs were expressing their feelings in our way of doing things, and David was feeling better already! The ETs wanted us to know they have learned more our ways and emotions as we do of them. These emotions were something they really wanted to understand from us and the funny part of this is, *the flowers had come from another part of the house* and placed on my son's bed for him! We thought this was so funny at first and yet astounded! This was an amazing gesture and it was more than *ok to borrow the flowers* from in the house it's the thought that counts!

Right before Halloween our Universal family came with their higher wisdom and said: *"In order to gain more knowledge one must give up more of the material realm. Gaining more knowledge, one must be able to see with a clear eye into other dimensions and new realms, and to free the heart and soul from all burdens will let one travel to any length our hearts desire. To live in the physical world is hard because you are a spirit and being here for a short while. So, try to separate the two, three or four worlds you see, and feel and work in the physical world but use your newfound knowledge. You have much to do and see yet. Your eyes will hold more now and your mind. Just know we are with you always. Your earth mother and father are with you and many others. Your son is getting better."*

This message was amazing we are always learning, and they have taught us so much to help us survive earth life! Our loved ones past stay near to us with the beings who teach us because they are made of one another! I could feel the love they share with us, it helped to make me understand more about myself being here as a human, and we are only here for a short while. We love their powerful messages and appreciate having this magnificent bond with our Universal family! Before I felt them ready to leave, I was reminded: *"that one is never too old to do the dance of life".* Don't you just love this, we were full of joy for days!

Jesus Christ and His Angels

Two beautiful Angel Beings appeared to me in my room floating just a little higher than the floor with one on each side of my bed! I felt the immediate presence of my mother and dad with them (this was the date of my late mothers passing), they were making me a visit! I thought for a moment my eyes were playing tricks on me and I called out to them in some way for I was also seeing *"JESUS CHRIST"* appearing with them!! I was not expecting this miracle I was shocked and could not describe my feelings with what was happening! I was told telepathically something about the *"Christ Light"*, but I cannot recall what because I was completely captured with their beautiful presence! Christ, my mother, dad and Angels were standing before me gathered around my bed what did this magnificent visit mean! I felt as a child getting the best surprise I could ever imagine, so there really isn't a way to explain this miracle with my words! In moments of sheer awe suddenly they were gone from my sight! After this *blessed experience* the next thing I knew I was walking to a *UFO* to board it! There was so much going on in this phenomenal experience I was never going to forget it happened, who could? I felt *embraced by the greatest love one could ever imagine to be given such a gift!* This is the memory I will keep forever from that wonderful, unbelievable night being my mother's birthday, and I knew the secret part of this happening, we are all one connected! This was not over because the holidays had something else in store for us, it didn't end that night!

The Blessed Mother Mary Said, "I Come to You
as a Mother to a Mother".

It right was before Christmas that I had an *unimaginable* visit once more I had gone to bed and was still awake when I felt someone present with me. I gazed over to see a beautiful shining figure moving towards me and in that moment, I realized the figure to be *"The Holy blessed Mother Mary!"* I was beyond thrilled she had returned once more, and I have no real description to fit her she is so beautiful, *immaculate* in a glowing white robe with a soft looking beautiful blue covering her head *glowing in white light!* She kept a continual loving smile on her beautiful face and I will never forget as she looked into my eyes and said, *"I come to you as a mother to a mother in your hour of need that she had come to give me the added strength I needed now and to remember to keep my trust within during these difficult times by having to watch my son suffer so much"*. Before she vanished away, she also told me, *"To always keep my faith in my son's healing for he would be healed again and again and only leave this earth plane with his free will."* She is a compassionate magnificent light of love, which left me totally weak with joy as if I was in a dream! It was hard to realize this was happening as I witnessed her before me in such entrancing beauty and Holy presence which seemed unreal, yet it was real, a *MIRACLE!* I realized the grief I held inside for my son so long had set up a barrier to protect my broken heart and my energy was low I needed to rid myself of any gloomy thoughts I carried, to banish them, and focus on the many times we have been blessed and graced with David's choices to live longer! It was not like me to make room for negatives, but I had let a fear begin to grow, *of my son leaving in the future I was worn down in my part of humanness. Mother Mary had come to lift me up to where I had been and she understood as no one else could have, as a mother to a mother!*

I had faithfully and eagerly captured her words to keep in my heart without doubt or question letting the words soak into my very soul with this blessed *miracle happening* before me. I felt I had been transported to another beautiful heavenly place for those moments in time which is impossible to describe. She gave me the added strength I needed with her extraordinary love. How thankful I was, I had quickly written down her visit to keep fresh in my mind as if I could ever forget! The mother of *"Jesus Christ"* had bestowed her heartfelt messages upon me on that precious evening.

Mother Mary continued to appear to me and my son at different times since the above experiences happened and I know she hears my prayers for David. We both prayed for her terrible suffering as a mother whose Son gave His life for the world. We have always had a *tremendous* bond with her in some way as I am sure others the world over has. It took me time to come down from this cloud I was on with what I had experienced Christmas, and now what a perfect time for this gift to know my son would stay longer than I thought he might. I had been completely RENEWED and it was a very Merry Christmas I often wondered how a Priest and Ministers would accept this, they are trained in a school not by experiences.

Later in the month I found a message in my notebook in Mother and Dads handwriting with others which said, *"We love you!"* This message was not only from my parents but also many others in the spirit worlds. It was after my mom's birthday; they spoke to me of the meeting in the night and the Heavenly visit from *Mother Mary!* I was wondering how we were so fortunate and blessed with how the messages come to us in so many ways even in the spirits own handwriting through the years. We were excited each time we found a message and I commented to David, *"who would ever believe this?"* But it never mattered because this was for us, it had nothing to do with others, if they believed or not, this was our own reality of consciousness and personal truth among other miracles happening over the entire world.

I found one message which followed soon after the above one from the ETs; they had put it in my notebook and left it on my bed. *"Greetings from all of us, go child enjoy and do what you came here to do, go forth now, we all love you."* How sweet, I had no doubt they were always close to us in everything we do and continued teaching us as their students! It wasn't long that we found another enlightening message about our healing work. As you can see our worlds were many with the highest teachers to teach us and were instantly rewarded once more in the next message with these words, *"Congratulations to you both love will shine through. We are proud!"* Wow, with these messages we knew we were on track with what we were doing, the messages kept our morale up; just knowing we were doing things correctly as we promised long ago.

It was now a new spring April fool's day, and Edgar Cayce left a written message to us to know we were advancing in our work, *"You both are on your way to a new awakening your Angels are with you and you both are on a new journey."* We were excited to see this we had missed EC's letters to us for a while, but we knew he was busy in the other worlds too. These were our rewards with their blessed messages, they meant so much to us to and to be helping others in whatever small way we could; this was the best thing ever! Later that day I found my crystal ball lying on the floor (the one that my daughter had given to me as a gift), which had another beautiful surprise with a message this was another confirmation of all we were told, and that our Angels were here with us!!

It was another new day beginning and before I opened my eyes, I thought about the day to come as I lay there a few minutes stretching. What a beautiful surprise when I open them the room filled with golden *rays of light* coming from above through the ceiling and showering down over my body! And in an instant, I realized I was *looking down at myself, at my own body* lying in my bed! I opened and closed my eyes *to blink,* had I really woken up or was I in-between dreaming but no, it was still happening and I began to hear words, *"that there would be many wonderful things to happen full of joy and happiness"* and then it was over! At that moment I was brought back into my body I had been astral traveling! Knowing this, I waited a moment to collect myself before I sat up to write this experience down, and then I made a sketch of how the gold light looked showering over me. Apparently, this pertained to the future I felt quite content knowing this but knowing sometimes how material things can be made to look I did begin to wonder, *was I really at home or someplace else made to look like I was in my room at home.* Still I waited and nothing else happened, so I knew I was back at home...

A few nights later I discovered a written message in my notebook from the other side: *"Life's journey is the key to the soul, rejoice, live life to its fullest. As you grow there, we grow here. We all work together; you both have worked hard on the things you came here to work on."* This was happy and positive news David and I were uplifted to experience the bond we and the universal worlds have together in our work. We understand each one of us choose our journey here on earth and this certainly validated any thoughts on it. The handwritten and printed messages coming from the other side were unbelievable, this beautiful message was right in front of me as I held it in my hands! Even though we both have received many of them over the years each one is still, if not more amazing each time.

CHAPTER 8

THE JOURNEY CONTINUES

Tonight, was a full moon (which is an extremely powerful energy) and messages continued to pour in from the ETs. *"Greetings, from all of us, many messages shall begin to arrive, there will be many words written out and you will enjoy them all."* We loved getting formation in this way and often wondered if others did or had? We couldn't get enough of them from our teachers and guides. We gave thanks from our heart and soul that it continued would this happen until we both left the earth plane, I knew we both would continue working together as we have in lives before, ours is a *forever* bond…

Edgar Cayce (E.C.) Begins Our Schooling

It was July 21st when Edgar came to tell us: *"that time was getting away and it was time to start the trance states, that the clock will run out in October and you will have missed a very important mission in life there that you took on long ago. Your teachers wait beside you to help guide and direct you and your son."* This was SO exciting we had been waiting for this news to come. My son was to have more surgery in the next few days and with this thought Edgar assured us, *"he would be with us helping to guide the doctor's hands, and that everything would be alright and go well."* I asked Edgar for a confirmation on this, I had understood what he said correctly? My answer came that night when I found my small lamp turned on beside my bed the one, I had given to my mother I call the *pink lady lamp.* I strongly felt my mother's presence in the room with me also and heard her words, which came as my confirmation reminding me *"to not be as hard on myself I am a human here in a human world and earth is only a learning school. That we all will always work together in many ways and that she and Dad are very happy on the other side in their heavenly home there, and they miss us in many ways, but to know they are free and free to help comfort us in the ways they can. They know David and I are very aware of all of them around us and that they are very grateful we are. The vast knowledge is there, to keep tapping into it the trance states work will* come. *We love you all, All of us."* ... This signing off included our spiritual teacher *Han Tai Chen Su* which seemed right that they all appeared in this way with his insight to healing and teaching us. Even though our real lives were kept hidden for now one day our story would be told so this message was extremely rewarding with the visits from my Mother, Edgar and Han Tai Chen Su. What a wonderful night, how could anything be better and again we thought *how did we deserve this great honor?* David and I were grateful and emotional to be with these beloved spirits, and happy with our loved one's messages from the other worlds they continually delivered because of our dedicated work.

Four weeks later another beautiful message arrived this one was with a heavenly voice speaking out loud to me: *"Yes child, the light shall shine on thee forever."* I was overwhelmed with joy this is beyond what most humans may believe in especially with how we are taught in school or church, would those others ever be able to comprehend this someday? We knew there were others like us working in a similar capacity who are learning the truth of spirit and love beyond earth with other universal beings how many realms may there be in an endless space! After this last message I found myself in a spacecraft that evening after I had fallen asleep, I was with a woman and her little boy. She panicked telling me, *"we needed to go back to earth in a hurry!"* The mother held the small child on her lap preparing for the trip back, is all I remember of it.

A couple of evenings later I awoke to see the gentle ETs were back again the main one was looking at me as if studying me closely then he began relaying thoughts to me, I began to process his information, *"he was only observing me"* which happened often but did not bother me. The ET had messages for us the first one was: *"to be careful of your choices in life and the light shines upon you and yours."* Again, this was another message about *"the Light being shined upon us"* we felt extremely honored and spent much time thinking about the meaning of what the ET had said. We ended up having many discussions about our journeys and connections to the other worlds beyond, trying to keep everything in perspective with living in many dimensions. We knew this last communication was a very spiritual message given to us from a high ET Christ Light Being of the High Council. They were letting us know, *to think first before decisions were made,* we needed to keep this in mind with other travels coming up for us into other dimensions planned for us. David continued getting stronger and his health was getting better little by little Edgar was at our side with our loved ones we were all working diligently together as in lifetimes before, it was very exciting! Another new message arrived, *"that the Aliens were for experience sake and very important to us."* After those words David saw a vision he later sketched "a *pyramid with a cross on top and above that an all-seeing eye with rays of golden light emaciating out from the eye radiating everywhere"!* Then a heavenly voice told him: *"Remember you are being embraced in the Christ Light and to focus forward."* This explained his vision of the pyramid with the cross on top with golden rays of light emaciating out from the eye! I wish I had the words to explain how it is to get this kind of information from another world of dimensions and of our love for these spiritual universal beings, but words cannot simply define it and each message very important!

It was in a vision I could see a small book titled *"Think on These Things"* Edgar Cayce's little book and he spoke to me, *"that we all work together".* We had been told this before as a reminder from Edgar himself and these confirmations were about the contract we had made before we evolved back to this lifetime to work together. Going to my room later that day I found a third sign from Edgar with the preceding information to David and me. At first, I couldn't trust my eyes, on my bed laid Edgar's little book I had seen in the vision, *Think on These Things* and my CROSS was lying on top of his book! In that moment I heard him say, *"achieving wisdom is a wonderful venture."* How wonderful this was a fantastic experience; I gave thanks over and over for all the lessons we have received from him and our universal teachers for their divine help!

It was November when my mother appeared to me on her date of passing, she refers to as her *"Celebration* day" along with this beautiful message. *"Wisdom is yours my beloved Ann you are a messenger and a bright and beautiful soul you will shine on forever with eternal love, from mom."* I became very emotional reading her message telling me what I am part of and somewhat surprised by my mother calling me by my second name of *Ann* this was unusual but occasionally she did. In the next few days another written message arrived from Edgar, *"Ann, we love you! We are helping many souls, but we are always here*". They were really on a roll with their messages we were overwhelmed and content they are with us. The other side and our past loved ones had their many ways to help and guide us all they could, and I understood when I needed to call for them, they would. And even though they are busy doing other things with other souls they can always hear and assist us. Their messages are a precious part of their knowledge they are reinforcing us with as we grow spiritually closer to the truth of the Creator. More personal messages arrived, and we were eternally grateful for every single one we received! The things I know, *"is the other side knows our every thought and our soul, you cannot fool them. There is no pretending with the ETs and heavenly beings, and everything we receive is very important"* ...

The Tape Recorder

Edgar soon returned telling us we could use the *tape recorder* in the trance sessions, it would be fine to use. We had asked about this earlier, and then Edgar talked to me of a difficult time I was going through in my life and to not be so hard on myself. *"You are to indeed have a joyous life there on the earth plane, try not to focus on other problems they have their free will and love them for who they are. To do what makes me happy to smile and be happy with life, happiness comes from within."* He continued: *"we would receive many messages and signs and my sense of direction will guide me in all things. Thy seeds have been planted!"*. Wow! My mind was really spinning putting everything together he had told me. I was thinking more clearly now and drawing closer to answers with connections to everything we were being taught, even though what I knew was *against* all I had been brought up to believe in I had left behind long ago. I could have never had this connection if I had not left the old ways behind me most of what I learned in my life growing up was to live in fear of the Creator if I wasn't good which was wrong, and since then I have left the old ways behind. This happened when the Angel told me, *"Come, follow me but first you must leave the old ways behind for I shall show you the way."* On that extraordinary evening when this divine *Angel* came to me my life changed completely, by following those beautiful words and in good faith my heart was healed forever I have never looked back…

I want to make note here: that my mother and dad never knew of Edgar Cayce in their lifetime to my knowledge and it's obvious they are with him on the other side, and the evidence is clear that we have all been together throughout lifetimes before. This also tells me Edgar had been waiting in this time period for David and me to discover him once again as in many lifetimes before, and together with his help, knowledge, and direction we are a team it's like taking the same refresher course in class. By the time you finish this book you may find answers as how to change negative thoughts in life through your own trials and errors to find true happiness. This depends on each one of us with what we have chosen to do, and the answers lie inside each person, *"seek and ye shall find"*. Life is meant to be lived believing in ourselves with using compassion, belief, courage, strength, trust, faith and sharing our love for others. It would be well to learn when and how to use our emotions and choice of words in what we say and do unto others, this is *earth school*. Don't let well-meaning others take away your power, your journey and mistakes away from you they are vital and needed to learn by. Even knowing this you are still living as a human being we all make mistakes and hopefully we learn from them. Mistakes are vital to our growth on this planet. It's a winding road we are on don't be so hard on yourself remember you are loved by *a Loving Infinite Supreme Intelligence of Knowledge a Super Consciousness called Creator.*

A few days later when I went to make my bed, I found a message waiting for me. Most of the messages come between 10 am and 10 pm each night and on some days at both times with two or more messages in a day! The last message simply stated: *"Thought you needed a laugh, love, your friends on the other side"*. I felt a *big lift* for some reason after reading this, and I began to laugh, after all they know best, and I wondered what they were up to! Their usual writings in my notebooks were becoming clearer; I have been surprised at how good their scrip looks and I am proud the other side does so much that most would never dream of! Our mission had become extremely open to the spirit and alien world which is why so much information and teaching comes to David and me. And because our days are full, we have much to discuss each morning and evening, we had been told by the universal beings that *"our worlds are many"* they certainly made believers out of us!

It was the later in the day I found my notebook on top of my robe. It had been taken off the bathroom door hook where I keep it but now it was folded neatly on my bed. This was a surprise to find it in this way, when it was time to turn in, I wondered if the folding lady spirit had arranged this nice gesture or someone else. The *Folding Lady* is one of the spirits that resides in my home as I described in my first book can you believe how considerate our invisible friends are, some think they are still alive doing the normal things they did before, and some are teachers to us.

In the middle of the night I woke up a bright light shining in my eyes my bedside lamp had been turned on! I knew the ETs had been around or were here although I did not see any. Getting up I went to check on my son and knocked on his door which woke him up wondering what was going on? I asked him, *"If he heard or seen them?"* but he had no memory of any beings, so I decided to go back to sleep since everything was quite in the house maybe the lamp was just a way of saying *we are here.*

When our lessons continued the next day *"the other side talked of material things which we need while one is here on earth to get by in this life but mean nothing on the other side, to not put much importance on them in life. That sometimes one has to walk away from them or give up these material things since this may be a way to learn certain lessons."* Another valuable lesson that had long fallen away in my old man-made beliefs and old ways of learning I thought to be spiritual I had to be *serious and a martyr,* but this is all nonsense to me now. When let the old ways go long ago as I was told to do and told to remember many things *"are not as they seemed to be, we had been taught to create joy, smile, and smile big and to let God fill you with his light, happiness is deserved, that is why you are here!"* These uplifting messages are to understand *we are already a Spiritual being* here to learn lessons through a human experience and to try and remember who we each really are as a spiritual being with a soul!

A message arrived from my, great, great grandfather who I never knew of until I had an earlier experience of him in a vision years ago and since then when I see him, he is dressed in his Civil War uniform holding a Saber sword beside him. I found through his appearances and messages to me he is definitely a teacher for me and this is what he wrote to me, *"General Powell is here my little honey child, it's been years awaiting for you all to open up the Vail, this is you Annie and David Michael with you always, General Powell"*. We were so amused at his southern slang just he used in his life and that he is aware of what we are doing on this earth. He had been waiting to introduce himself and as you can tell he was a real southerner in life, and this is how he spoke. He was a General in the Civil War and surprisingly half Indian, in an earlier experience he told me he watches over us and he will always be here for us. This letter above from him is in my notebook in his own handwriting which made it a special present! I keep every message, letter, whatever they leave, copy and record them and he is a delight!!

The important point in the messages was, realizing something big was registering we were to do and what would the ending be? The universal beings came with the truth passed to us to remember and write it and one truth we both have experienced is physical death I write about in my books with how simple the complete *transition* is. This is because we both have been *physically dead* and brought back as some others have been, so I spent extra time the next few days on how to tell of our experiences on paper. I knew somehow there would come an important time to write about this transition and I have never forgotten what the other side told me, *"to reach inside my being it's all right there, which is my truth not anyone else's and to not be afraid!"* I chose to teach these truths in my life and suddenly the years flew by and I am on this third book.

Life went on and I loved the beauty of everything I could see here on earth even if it was only in my yard and my small town, and with my main treasures being my daughters and son, my family, and divine universal beings of the Universal Light. What more is there I thought if we are together is the ultimate gift! If it is rainy, snow, sunshine, whatever kind it is a beautiful day to celebrate life with my loved ones and the many amazing souls I keep meeting on earth and in the other worlds beyond.

The DNA Part

We spent birthdays celebrating together throughout the years with many wonderful holidays, I enjoyed being a mother very much and grateful for my life with my loved ones! Our experiences continued to happen, and we still told no one yet of what occurred to us with the ETs, even the family. This would have revealed our unbelievable lives that most would not understand at that time. It was hard to keep quiet about our different multidimensional lives and I felt like a *complete different Being myself.* I wasn't exempt from it anymore we both had gladly accepted, *"we are a big part of them"*. Our schooling never stopped in our worlds and secretly I hoped it never would, and with those thoughts I began to read a new message one afternoon: *"Ann, the horizons of life is cherished forever."* How wonderful to think about, I discovered the next one at 2:40 pm on the same day the times had started to vary now, *"The lessons go on as we come together again like old times"*. I knew this came from Edgar and very comforting.

We were soon looking forward to the holidays with the family and others with another beautiful Christmas message: *"Enjoy the Christmas time and see the beauty it is good for your soul. A great surprise is coming, and your senses will go up again and improve to a new high. Mom and dad, grandparents, loved ones, and many more are with you all. We love you, all of us."* It doesn't get much better than this love embraced us both to the earth world we live in with loved ones, and the other worlds with spiritual beings in the great beyond. In this *strange way* we had no regrets of any kind just the opposite, knowing we will always be together!

I began to look at things in a new way because of our experiences and to teach *"life after life is eternal which continues in the universes with other beings as well"* which I will never deny. I believe in every lesson they on the other side have shared with us knowing it comes from those chosen ones who help teach the truth of love. This Intelligence I can't explain except as I do, and I wondered to myself exactly when *man-made fear* started probably with sole survival. Was it the beginning of time when this Infinite Supreme Intelligence/Creator was portrayed with only fear? It seems in the beginning of humankind fear was brought to the first ones here to survive through their evolution of development and used to keep people under control by the Elders or whoever were the most strong and powerful ones. I firmly believe this is the answer *and it is still about power* which rules and thrives today in our world more than ever. Looking back at history there didn't seem to be much taught about the Creator having divine love for each one as His magnificent creations... We were to fear and be afraid, how sad, I still meet those of a kind heart who are so afraid to cross over... they expect a great punishment for the smallest thing and some think they can never live long enough, to be good enough, to get into heaven.

The next incoming message explains a good rule to live by from my teacher *Han Tai Chen Su: "Follow the Tibetan rule, why worry over things that can't be changed."* When this arrived the timing was perfect, the odd thing is I had just finished watching a movie called *Seven Years in Tibet,* the timing for me was perfect. I was strongly drawn to see this movie by my universal teacher because I had had a strong tie to Tibet. Soon after the movie I was shown a vision of my life when I had lived there. I was a little girl from a poor family as most of the people were, but I was very happy with good parents and good teachings. I was about 5 or 6 years of age and so was my best friend in this vision. I could see us playing together giggling away with our face and hands smudged with dirt I knew in a moment she and I had shared our lives time and time coming together again in this life.

We didn't meet up for many years until I began to teach Reiki at a college south to where I was led. This one young woman who I will call Denise came to my classes to sign in and seemed familiar to me. She had dark hair and a beautiful smile, and she was different having a special radiance about her and everyone loved her! After my first class I remember her waiting to talk to me after everyone else had left, then smiling she came to my desk to get acquainted. She told me later, *"she knew me when she had first seen me and if I didn't notice her waiting to speak with me, she would of went on that first day".* But *spirit* told her, *"I would stop her and say hello"* which I had! Eventually she told me *"of our lifetime in Tibet where we had been sisters before,* the same as in my vision! Later, we had the opportunity of a lifetime, we both were to experience seeing the *Dali Lama* as he traveled across the United States!!

It was largely because of our close friendship and past life pulling us together we were able to go see the *Dalai Lama* when he toured not far from our state. Such a dream to come true, we were so excited! This was on her *"bucket list"* she told me shortly before we attended a two-day program to see and hear this beautiful soul! After our dream which was a phenomenal experience, only a few weeks later at the age of 43... Denise passed over! That would be a day I will never forget it was because of her that I would want to relearn all I could about life in Tibet and their teachings.

This happened to Denise one day at school when she fell to the floor while talking to another teacher before the morning bell rang! Her unexpected tragic death was without a reason and none could ever be found! She was a dedicated grade schoolteacher for many children, she loved each one of them and will always be missed by many people. Denise had told me she was losing energy and had to stay in bed each weekend to be able to teach all week. She was so tired in her spirit and soul wanting to go home after Denise crossed over, she made many visits to me and my son day and night, giving us messages to tell her family and her young son. I would write what she said as David did which would be pages, and for this meeting together again I am truly grateful with our promise to one another as Tibetan children to re-unite in this lifetime! Past lives are amazing when one is ready to acknowledge them as more than a dream and she would be coming to me thereafter still to this day!

I had given Denise a beautiful Tibetan jacket for her birthday she was cremated in which made me feel content and honored because she loved everything about that lifetime... later her husband said, *"he didn't know where the jacket came from, but it was perfect for her visitation"* I told him I gave it to her for her birthday a few weeks before she suddenly passed...

One night I was astral traveling watching myself in another past life I could see myself in a Colonial period, I wore a red Officers Jacket with brass buttons down the front and white pants tucked into high black boots. I was riding a white horse on the battlefield with fighting all around me and watched myself being shot accidently by my own men in the frenzy of war. Immediately, I found myself standing beside two doors in the universal heavens, one door would open, and the other door would close, almost moving together with people going in one door and some returning out of the other door. I watched myself come out of one door in that early Colonial period when I was being first born coming to earth, and then called back when I was the soldier who died in wartime returning through the other door meaning (back to the other side) where I saw myself in spirit then understanding *"I had died in that war"*. The meaning was quite clear to me as I watched this process and there were many others around me experiencing the same thing happening to them going in and out of the doors! This represented the birth process being born to our parents and when the time came to die, going back to the universal world in spirit. If one chose to reincarnate the next life one has the free will to do this at a certain time to return. I knew the ETs were in this someplace since we are what we are, as part of them. There is a great Divine Council who helps a soul to plan a return if desired, after this vision I couldn't help but feel this next message let me know how aware of my thoughts the other side is. The message simply stated: *"Ann whispers into eternity."* Meaning, they on the other side hear every thought and know one's total being, and my lesson on the doors was very clear to me showing the cycle of life after life.

Edgar and General Powell Return Together

I had not been in bed long when I knew something was happening across the room, so I focused my attention to a *ball of light* slowly coming towards me which formed into Edgar's spirit. He had a big smile and said: *"work will begin very soon"*. Behind him followed my Great, Great, Grandpa Powell in Edgar's trail of energy saying: *"Hope, peace, and truth, don't fret Annie I am here! Love to all."* I called out to both *"thank you"* and they vanished! Grandpa Powell liked calling me *Annie* and I bet this had been my name in several past lives, and in today's time I was called Ann as a second name. I was on cloud 9 full of anticipation with their words and messages, which empowered me in our work, plus there was a surge of being energized and ready to move forward! At this time Edgar had continued to use my old word processor to send more messages. *"Greetings, to my beloved Ann, realization is in the realm of nothingness in the material world. I will start relay thoughts to you on this Electrical PAP. Give me a little time to prepare, End of Transmission."* E.C.

David and I were preparing for our special day to begin the *trance states,* we had placed a tape recorder beside the sofa with pen and paper not wanting to miss a thing when Edgar began to teach us those, he once used himself! Suddenly a new thought flashed in my mind, I recalled Edgar's sister was also named *Annie* and I wondered about my name *Annie* which he and Great, Great, Grandfather Powell continued to call me by. This was another definite clue to this past life of ours, I was sure I had been Edgar's sister who was called *Annie* in his lifetime.

If you are wondering what this part of the story has to do with other spiritual beings such as the ETs, you will find out ALL of it DOES! My review covers the many different spirits who have helped to pave our way in this work, and more of the new discoveries we are involved in with other beings... Therefore, my books had to be written in *portions* when writing several books because so much was happening extremely fast through the years. In the beginning of our new discovery of who we are I did continuous *"soul searching"* as to why two people went from what we thought was a regular life to this enormous quest we were on now! More than ever everything I use to think I knew about humankind with my old teachings when I was young was long gone, and since then we were living a true authentic life; which is our truth! This is simply by letting go of *human fear* which holds one back in old negative beliefs and this led us to search further to find we, as universal Beings are *"bright and shining spirits having an earthly experience,"* in which to learn and grow to higher levels. And even after death some may simply want to get back in line wanting to return as the doors did show. All of us will hopefully learn something from earth life and after our human death go to the other side with our free will. There we can choose to stay and learn or re-enter earth life once more this can be done as many times as it takes to get things in order of what we want to accomplish. So, it's best to not take shortcuts, everyone will pass through their lessons to graduate to the next level or not. Souls have options with choice to stay wherever they are working with universal beings, everything is a choice. This may sound very complex because of the many levels and work one may decide on doing with the Council of Christ Light Beings, but it is not.

On Christmas Eve of the same year David and I received a blessed message from *The Great High Council, "and ye shall be guided throughout life, you have achieved this reward!"* I was so excited, and David stood nearby with tears in his eyes what a glorious gift to receive at the Holy Christmas time I couldn't call out *"Thank you"* enough! I mean, how do you give proper thanks in our human words we couldn't, but we knew our heart and soul were heard! That same night I was told something *"about seeds, pods, and to swallow them."* This meant sow the spiritual seeds we were given to help others so they in turn may sow them, meaning the words from the Christ Light, this is the understanding of the message. I feel we used the seeds from the beginning and as our lives went on to continue sowing them to whomever we can.

At this same time one family member was going through a very rough time her husband had passed over only a few weeks before Christmas. On Christmas day a new written message was waiting for all of us when we got up, the other side had written on my note paper *"your family member will be fine and succeed Merry Christmas to all!"* We made Christmas as well as we could with this message to help her get through the holidays, but it was still an extremely sad holiday even with the message. It gave us great hope knowing all was in its place, we knew the loved one who crossed over was adjusting and making contact now to relay his messages with his love and passed over loved ones on this special holiday.

On the 27th of December at 7:45 pm I found these messages. *"Greetings Annie my beloved, the time is drawing near. We get stronger each second in time. I will let you know, E.C."*

The New Year message for us was: *"Love one another the New Year is a new revelation for the soul to learn and grow. Increase mind over body functions it will be a fascinating year sending love always"*. These were exciting messages, we felt closely connected with the other side it being only a breath away we knew this would lead us to use the right words when speaking to others of *"loss and the disappointments life brings we can conquer and learn from"*. I wanted to help my loved one with her husband's loss and to help David's health to continue getting better with a new healing pattern. One never gets over a loss, but it gets somewhat better to deal with over time, but one is never the same again and to reach a broken heart is the hardest thing to do. Most know the heart and soul struggle for a long time, some for a lifetime.

I knew this last message from Edgar meant to be ready and prepared for him to teach us the trance states and time was drawing closer to begin! We were excited to learn from our old friend who is a great spiritual teacher, we would be more than ready preparing ahead meditating to improve our focus with other techniques we used. It was more than an honor to have a teacher like him, and because of the family bond between us made it precious. We were being taught more about *"mind over matter"* and our mind power would be stronger by working in these amazing realms together. Edgar talked about the power we each have been given to use on this earth and the mind is absolutely the builder as he always said, *"We are what we think we are"*. The year ended with a beautiful Holy message; one I shall never forget! *"Ann you are embraced by the gold threads of light Archangels Michael and Raphael are guarding your very being."* I have *no* words for how honored and humbled I felt and immediately after this message I began to see a vision of the magnificent *Archangels Michael and Raphael,* what a beautiful blessing this was! I can't explain nor describe these glorious Archangels I have none to do justice to them! They help us in times of great need when we have called for them in astral travel and always with my son's miracles!

*A New Spiritual Awakening, A Revelation
to Behold*

This next message arrived quickly filling our heart and spirits to great heights of happiness, life had become a dream come true in our work, how precious and HONORED with the blessings we received!

Remember now, this is a great awakening which will be wonderful and gives you the healing powers to assist in the healing work to help many. You shall experience the healing from Christ, His love and beauty. The colors will be there to help detect the illness to assist you on your journey. Nothing matters but love, love from the heart, from your heart into the body of the one who you work upon to heal. We shall be there with Cayce, his loved ones, Doc, and your loved ones, we all work together. You are wrapped in the gold threads of light; you are a healer now. It's your time and we shall see you soon. You will see us many times over. Know a new spiritual awaking is upon you and some of the others. It is time and we will be ready soon. This is the new revelation we have spoken of. We are

156

here to guide you, pass it on to thy son now as you have been, we work through all of you. Our work together really begins now. It is all going perfect, End of Transmission.

I don't know what to say anymore as to how we both felt reading *this* beautiful message coming from *this highly developed divine energy, an infinite endless superior consciousness,* we were stunned for some time!! This continues to confirm *"we all work together blended within our own separate abilities, existing from past and future, other dimensions, multidimensions, star systems, galaxies, worlds and more"*, which cannot be described with words.

We will continue with those who are against the *dark ones* on earth and space who are creating dysfunction wherever they go. Ours was the ultimate honor to use the healing work on others with our heartfelt commitment, we were completely humbled and enriched. The *new spiritual awakening* was clearly here, and we were ready the *new revelation* had begun, thank you blessed ones!!

We were beginning a new journey on a different level, our excitement was hard to keep hidden from others, but we did. We felt no one could understand this if we had told them and how much more perfect could things be! This let us know there would be new and various information we would learn and comprehend; another wonderful thing was they never pushed us about time. I am sure the rest of the week I was in a double daze as David and I have read of others who have witnessed extraordinary happenings in certain times which helped them or someone around them in a Divine way. We know these wonderful things happen at certain times and are not explainable, we both being deeply involved as we are with universal schooling was like a magnificent dream, and it was for real! I didn't want this part of our life to ever stop therefore we knew this was forever, just as we had incarnated through other times.

I would always remember from early on of our great awaking from the Beyond when we were told, *"That every human being belonged to everything in the entire universe"*. *This message couldn't say it any clearer it is of the truth.* I had questions rushing around in my head ready to charge ahead, but I was told to have patience, so I calmed down life was good, no, it was glorious! I went on being a mother taking care of my son and my family for what they may need to the best of my ability. There would be no one else but our dear friend Bev to share these experiences with for a while about our lives because we three were the same... except her fear of Aliens. We wanted to help her with this and later I believe we did.

A new incoming message informed us of an important journey for us to experience. We were told this with a message *"Moonchild and Offspring Son see you in the lateral part on this earth's evening's moon, safe journeys to both of you... ETs"*. We were ready to go and out of curiosity we wondered which group of ETs these were it was wonderful to be connected to different groups and species of *Spiritual Christ Light Beings* knowing we would always be safe!

Everyday life was something we no longer thought of much other than our precious family life and time spent in the hospitals, my thoughts were usually jumping all over the place because I knew no one else could begin to understand any of this. We decided our mind had to be created extra strong for so much happening and thank God, David and I were on this journey together! Not only was this a *"secret life"* for now, living between different unknown realms and worlds with what we knew was like a storybook and this story is about divine love for one another. On my late mother's birthday, we celebrated a long-awaited message that arrived from Edgar, it was *"THE ONE"* we had waited for! *"Greetings my beloved Ann, the time frame to start is mid-January. Let's get prepared. E.C."* Now isn't it strange this would be the date of my late mother's birthday, she was involved in these wonderful experiences without a doubt we were so excited we couldn't wait, but we had too!! Edgar would soon be teaching us what we had been waiting for and this message arriving on mom's birthday was special! I was happy to find out years later that Edgar had done some readings about *"Beings in the Universe"* and more than any one time he told me, *"the answers lie in the stars"* and this was the supreme clue!

A short time before our *trance work* was to start, we were on pins and needles, and I felt my parents nearby since they are involved with Edgar. It was strange that in their last life as mom and dad their memories had been washed away of these things. I recalled on the eve of my mother's passing a soul being appeared sending his thoughts to me telepathically: *"you're never too old to dance!"* I was confused but let this slip from my mind quickly, since then I seem to hear this occasionally and when I do, I know it means my mother is *dancing the gift of joy, life, and celebration in heaven!* That night I sent out my thoughts *"Mr. Cayce we are waiting and ready to begin the work."* I must have slept quite a while and when I awoke what I saw was magnificent, there was "a *large cross with beautiful purple light glowing out to me, it was beautiful!"* With my vision of the cross Edgar appeared holding out papers to me, but I couldn't make them out fast enough to read I only caught the one word *BOOK,* then I wrote his words down as he said them: *"Yes, beloved Ann, Edgar here, it is coming in soon and our work shall begin in only a matter of time on your earth plane just keep faith like you do and know it shall be. Yes, we shall be very busy in the months that come; you will be learning symbols, sounds, more ESP and much more. The trance states will open new territory once again as you work in this field."* then he vanished away and letting me know I have worked in healing lives many times as my son. Soon after, Edgar's son Hugh Lynn, and his mother Gertrude (both in spirit) appeared. Hugh Lynn spoke, *"It is time and we love you here".* Gertrude spoke last, *"Yes Dear we shall work fully and wonderful together once again, always together. Do you have any memory of the pear orchards? If not, we will show you."* Then they were gone, and I felt I knew what she meant!

The Golden Pears

I felt Gertrude spoke of a past lifetime we were together in and wanted to jog our memory with another event about to happen. David had planted a peach tree years ago in his yard, but the little tree only produced a few *peaches* at first, but after this quote from Gertrude one day something extraordinary and wonderful happened! We went to the hospital that day for his appointment and when we returned home, we parked in the garage as usual and entered the kitchen, there sat a *bowl of pears* on my kitchen table! We were shocked, just standing there looking at them for a minute or so before one of us could even speak! No one was home other than us since we were the only ones who lived here. We began laughing with joy looking at them, pears in January we both were ecstatic; I mean sitting on my table were *14 beautiful golden pears in one of my own bowls on the 14th of JANUARY* which is my late mother's *birthday!* We examined and counted them over once more as we discussed this new phenomenon repeatedly questioning, *"how do they do this, how can this be."* My mother had to do with this one!

This happened again later at my son's home when he found a glass bowl filled with 14 *golden pears* on his kitchen table while they were still out of season! We knew nothing is impossible coming from the other side, but we were thinking with our human thoughts first *"how in the world do they do this?"* David told me my mother said, *"we were to eat one now and the others daily"* which we did, I must say they were delicious and sweet. We had no doubt they were from my mother and Gertrude since she spoke of the pear orchard! This was the connection between my mother and Gertrude... Our families had always been connected in other past lives; and must have had a pear orchard!

The pears would appear again when my son's illness became very serious again and he could not sleep at night (he would become much worse if he laid down). At times he would go outside for fresh air this seemed to help him breathe somewhat better. It was on one of those nights he was having difficulty and went outside before daybreak. He told me, *"he could make out something shinny that had blown into his yard he bent over to pick it up and when he raised back up, something grazed the back of his shoulder and he quickly turned. He could make out PEARS right in front of him but because of his limited sight he felt one of them to make sure, it had happened again! Yes, this is what had brushed across his upper back and shoulder when he stood up! He told me, he hurried inside to find a flashlight then hurried back out and shined the light on the peach tree to be sure of what he had seen. They were PEARS alright 14 golden pears, which were out of season, on his peach tree where nothing had been there the day before! And once more only 14 of them, as on my mother's birthday!"* This is what Gertrude was telling us to figure it out about the pear orchards. To experience this again was exhilarating when David told me what had happened! At this time, he had moved to my mother's old home when he had been much better, only a few blocks from my home. There was no doubt my family and the Cayce's had been together in times before, and my guess is, we all lived near a pear orchard or maybe grew pears? We would have to wait and see... Gertrude had arranged this to help put our puzzle together when she mentioned the pears, we defiantly have been family as we thought. These things cannot be explained, the experiences and messages were clues to study.

After this happened David told me my mother (his grandmother) had come to him in a vision saying, *"the pears were given for us to taste and each time this happens we are to taste them"*. We each ate a pear right away the same as the other time we found them, they were deliciously sweet, juicy pears! We knew this experience was confirming to my son and me the Universe, my mother and dad are with the Cayce's working together with us! This was to understand just how involved we are together again in this lifetime all of this started after Gertrude had spoken to us about the *"pear orchard to awaken our memories of us together"*. We had always been a part of each other in some way which we have never doubted!

The next night I heard the name Marrow, quickly opening my eyes I found myself in a UFO looking at the babies once more they were immersed in the same clear liquid which looked like water, but it wasn't. David asked the next day, *"if I recalled him being there and both of us observing the babies"* but I didn't. I remembered using telepathy as usual while talking with the ET who was showing the babies to me. The ET was sending his thoughts to let me know, *"these babies were half ET and half human"* there was someone else beside me, another woman, who was human, and she was talking to me about the babies that's all I could recall. The ETs took me often to see them and I have been learning how *"they produce these half humans and half alien babies called Hybrids."*

The next evening at 6:30 I found a hand-written message from E.C. in my notebook, *"Your studies have helped prepare you"*. The next night he left a forwarding note stating our trance time to begin. *"Tuesday at 10 a.m. to be ready"!!* We couldn't wait to begin how exciting, and I had figured out why the number 10 is shown to me in visions we would begin our schooling at 10 am! I knew long ago tens and zeros are important numbers in my life. Right before the 21st of January another message arrived from him, *"Hello, my dear, blessed is thee. Soon we will work together."* The closer it became the more anxious we were this was such an honor for us!

It Was Time at Last for the Trance States

On January 21st Uncle Leo's old clock chimed promptly at 10 am and we began the first of our many trance states knowing this was going to be an *ultimate experience!* We could feel his energy in the room waiting to start he proceeded by guiding me to lay down and face the north as he had done in his trance days, everything was prepared to begin. The tape recorder was nearby, and our notebook had selected questions ready for David to ask about. We had been prepared for quite a while I began relaxing by closing my eyes and quickly went into trance with David guiding me. He began asking me questions, those we hoped to get answers to about our work and other questions in general we thought would help us. David told me afterwards when we started my voice was different and did not sound like me it was a male voice probably Edgar's who supplied us with information, all seemed to go extremely well for our first time. After I came out of the trance state experience Edgar spoke and said: *"Yes child, all went very well, rejoice, thy son and thee. Wear your bold colors of joy, dance, and enjoy life for it is yours to have. You both deserve all happiness. Your lessons go well, we are with thee and ye are loved so very much. That is all."* Oh, how happy and excited we were this was like a dream to us, it was really happening! Our lessons would be three days a week on Monday, Wednesday and Fridays at 10 am as Edgar told us. We talked of how our lives were changing very fast in the best way, our lessons with him would continue for months to come we didn't want them to ever end, and David was in remission throughout the trance states!

Many times, I have given much thought, if someone were to tell me what we have experienced without being in their shoes I wonder how I would have reacted to their story. I am open so I believe I would understand as best as I could even though it was not my journey to experience, because no two people's journeys are the same. I try to respect each person's experience knowing it belongs only to them and for their growth. The same as ours is for us with what we have been taught from the Christ Light ETs, Universal Beings, heavenly Guides and Teachers.

This next experience explains how sometimes information comes to us. I was in my bedroom one day and beside it is another smaller bedroom from where I heard a noise coming from listening closely for a few moments I heard beautiful heavenly words coming to me from the *"Great High Council"*. They told me, *"Our house here is full of Monks and Nuns."* Wow, how wonderful to know this is true, which makes sense in numerous ways and though I am not Catholic or carry the name of a religion this doesn't matter to the Creator, it isn't a title or a label that gets us to the other dimensions when we each move over. This was a confirmation, a reinforcement to me I felt positive about because long ago there were *Nuns and Monks* in this home, or in this same space before the house was here. We had seen them in their spirit energy in David's old room and have felt their protection; this is a very special place! The first time Bev came to this home and walked into that bedroom she spoke of seeing *Nuns* and said, *"this was a "Holy place".* Perhaps the ground here had a holy occurrence or building here at some time long ago, if not, there is something indescribable of a blessed high order which still lingers here very strongly. Therefore, is why we experience so many universal divine beings and Angel realms from other worlds. In one picture of the house outside there is a *transparent very old building* sort of overlapped together with this home! There was something that had stood on this ground early on probably years before this house was here, which is an Historical home today, that has great meaning and this amazing energy fills the house with goodness. I strongly feel it served as a Holy place since the Ley/Linear lines run through this home and ground.

We had divine help guarding us through this time period and David's doctor was absolutely enthralled with his unexplainable fast healings and amazing unbelievable progress! I had been constantly using Reiki on him and with Edgars work in healing, and if you recall, the one message spoke of David's healings being done becoming stronger now! His doctor was extremely happy and told us, *"she had never seen anything like this before"* meaning his miracles and fast healings. He thrived and continued to live; we were thrilled beyond human words! His doctor said, *"to keep doing what we were doing with the Reiki energy healing,"* and we did, combined with his medical care and Edgars strong healing! David surprised the medical doctors time after time, with his rapid healings even when they gave him little or no time left to live in their opinions. He was teaching others about the Creators healing through his faith and strong will to live and without saying a word he was

163

proof for others, he was alive, and they could not explain him! The medical people were extremely happy!

The next night during my sleep state we both were suddenly in a beautiful Holy place where I was being told once more something about seeds, *"to swallow the seeds."* I could see we were in a beautiful Ancient church and I knew the *seeds* were for learning and growing in order to *"spread the holy seeds"* to whoever we could. When we came out of this Ancient church leaving to go back home, I could see the road divided up ahead like a fork in the road. The meaning was clear to us, we had a choice to make of which road to follow. Our classes of learning had been made clear to us, *"that we were there in the church to grow in knowledge"* and this was the heavenly school we go to learn in. I wondered if my son would have memory of this later and he did when I asked him the next day. If you are asking yourself, *"why doesn't the other side just say what they want us to do in a simple way?"* Well, it is a different way we are taught there, and we have found through the messages to us and through our teachers, guides, ETs, and loved ones in spirit there are many reasons we do not have to understand everything at one time we need *time* to process. We need to keep complete trust, faith, and belief, and above all learn patience, perhaps we are to learn to be well versed in all ways and use our intuitiveness to become stronger without doubting ourselves with the human part we feel. Learning to separate what is real and what is not, this is what our teachers explain, and the feeling I get *"is to quit questioning each experience so much"*. We had to laugh about this answer to questions, we knew it was right to use patience which we didn't have at times, to figure out some things ourselves through our experiences. And with our given knowledge knowing it strengthens us for what comes.

The next words I heard were very important *"you are just where you are supposed to be remembering this."* I felt a joyous relief to know we are right on track in life; I compare this to when I made an A in earth school only thousands of times better! I believe most people just want to know if they are on track in life which is a logical question many of us ask ourselves in our humanness.

It wasn't long after this lesson I was on board a UFO once more watching the babies, the little *Hybrids* who are part human and ET. Looking around I noticed my son David was with me which made me feel better, the ETs had taken us both to see the babies for a reason and the last thing I knew a block of memory loss was put in front of me, the rest of my memory was erased! I can't remember more about this experience, perhaps it only meant it was time to go back I just know I watched the babies again and I felt strongly there was a reason for this so often. I continued to see them regularly these Hybrids looked more human, in fact, completely human and this seriously bothered me the babies are always in the liquid even though they are fine, and I usually questioned *"how do they breathe immersed in this stuff?"* The ETs must be leading up to something they would tell me about when the timing was right about the Hybrids and then I would be taught more, I was right...

David and I were waiting for more answers we knew without a doubt Edgar was a huge part of what was going on with us and in the crafts when we travel. Edgar gave us confirmations on how well our work was going and Gertrude would do the same from time to time they both said, *"they were so happy to have the work carried on that in this way they could continue to teach what they possess."* How beautiful it was to hear these words!

We worked diligently learning from Edgar for months through that entire year loving every second of it, I felt he would be with us through our complete life here; he had made it clear he would be and in all the healing work we did. One time he told us, *"that we would go on to other work in our future with the both of them."* This was exciting, like in old times together even before Atlantis, but this would be in a new world. There were also other Divine beings that came to earth school to help assist us in many ways.

What happened one day later was astonishing, it was around 11 am, I discovered my notebook lying open and NOT prepared for what was on the page! First, I could only see the drawing of a larger hand with rays shooting out from each finger, the palm, and around the entire hand outlined with rays shooting out from it! Underneath the hand was the message, *"a healing hand works through you and your son"* I thought I was going to *faint* this instantly took my breath away as humbleness washed over me, I was shocked! But there it was in front of our eyes, yet this was hard for me to comprehend because of the magnitude of it! My son was humbled by this as I was it was so beautiful meaning, Hands of Light!

From that time on we wished even more that we could *"heal the world"* if this could have been humanly possible, we would still be trying! I don't remember which came first, the healing hand drawing in my notebook or the picture of the same looking healing hand in an Edgar Cayce booklet I received in the mail from A.R.E. (Edgar Cayce's Area of Research & Enlightenment). Both healing hands were identical yet coming from these two separate places, and still to this day I sometimes look at these remarkable notebooks feeling very thankful for this *"miracle"* presented to us.

We knew the universal worlds would continue to send us these unbelievable messages keeping our faith, belief, and hope up when we exhausted ourselves, and they knew when we needed them to uplift us. In the future we would learn by being in a human body we nearly wore ourselves out in the process as the years passed by. We were repeatedly told to, *"slowdown in order to keep our health"*, and we meant to but saying *no* to those who needed us was hard, we couldn't seem to do this most times. I know Edgar could understand this he had did the same when he lived, my son knew he would not live as long if he kept working tirelessly helping others anyway, he could, but could not stop from helping them the same as Edgar had done. I marveled watching David and at the same time my heart broke at how much he did on the days it was difficult for him to even walk, but he did with a smile to those he had come to help. I lived in heartbreak to not say anything, but I knew this was with his divine choice and let him keep his self-worth it was hard silently wanting him to slow down, I was in a catch 22. His extra time was spent working with his flowers and garden, they were beautiful even with his limited sight, the Creator took care of him in his days of illness.

The *Great High Council* of the Creator and Universal realms watched over us by healing our human bodies when we wore ourselves out because sometimes, we became very *sick,* and this was the Universal way to slow us down before things worsened. And then we both had no choice but to rest awhile I call this our *prevention* time, when they put us down to make us rest, and this usually happened at times when only one of us was sick. Then we could help one another and usually neither one of us was down long then our healings were complete, and we started over again.

I often thought of Edgar because he could not slowdown in his own life and eventually was warned more than once: "*that he would die if he didn't slow down*", but he couldn't stop helping people especially in war time when so many others needed to know how their loved ones were fighting in the war. This took a great toll on him and eventually he did pass away because he could not say, no. He had continued after repeated warnings working with others harder than ever until he first had a stroke and later, died of a heart attack on January 3rd, 1945, what a great loss for the world! We could understand why he kept going no matter how hard it was with the tiredness he felt, this is because the three of us have so much in common in healing work. I wondered how many more warnings we ourselves would get I would think there are many other people in different categories of healing work such as nurses, doctors, medical attendees, caretakers, disabilities of children, and other similar work, who also get sick from being over-worked being human. We were told to keep a balance *many times* which a very BIG lesson for me has been as well as my son, someday I hope to achieve this in my life to take better care of myself. The old saying seems correct "*take care of yourself or you won't be able to take care of anyone else*" and if it wasn't for the Christ Light ETs who re-energized us, I would be on the other side with my son now. The Creator works through the ETs the same as his Christ Light Beings.

A night or so later I had a vision with Edgar who I was watching, and I seemed to be right with him. He was standing on a beach and my feelings were telling me this was Virginia Beach; Va. Edgar was wearing a suit and a hat with a wide brim and I noticed he had his glasses on and was filled with serenity, totally relaxed, looking out at the ocean. I could feel he loved the ocean it made him feel at peace, but I also knew he was showing me to "*take time to relax*". I came out of the vision and looked at my bedside clock, 6:30 am too early to get up with that thought something grabbed my attention! There was a shape floating towards me which materialized into a big round clock with the time, 10:00! I laughed; thinking how funny Edgar was being with his reminder of our trance states at 10 am, the next day! How clever, he was choosing to show me his joke with the big clock once more as if I could ever forget the time, I loved seeing Edgar and his BIG clock! At breakfast I told David what Edgar did we thought it was funny and it made our day! That next morning went very well with the trance states, Edgar was so good to us in his lessons, the love and respect for one another was enormous! In the evening, there was a new message in my notebook *"Confirmation guaranteed. E. C."* I was sure he enjoyed the laugh about his huge clock as much we did by sending his confirmation to us. We still had a way to go with the lessons, we would be missing him when they ended but forever grateful, this would take a year in our lessons.

It was sometime after this we discovered Edgar had a new plan in store for us, he began to teach us more about the four directions we are from and how very important to understand them, little did we know what he would do next. We soon found out the next day I found *four arrows* drawn in my notebook showing me the four directions (which had happened earlier on with the Angel being when we found the arrows drawn on the staircase landing), these clues would put us onto another new path! This symbol and message meant we would be led to our work with the souls going south/west and it would not be long when the ETs made their presence known along with Edgars! Our lives were like a dream with lessons and schooling, we had much to be excited about daily it was wonderful! We kept finding everything is completely connected to everything and everyone, I knew our consciousness had many levels to explore without a time limit.

CHAPTER 9

ANOTHER CONFIRMATION, THE ETs ARE OF THE CHRIST LIGHT!

Approximately 5 days later we were watching a TV special when I felt compelled to check my notebook for new messages and was delighted to find one, *"Look in the sky!"* We hurried outside as fast as possible and once in the yard David heard the words *"tomorrow night at 8 pm"*. After talking this over for a few moments we decided there was nothing else to do but go back into the house and continue watching the special since we had not noticed anything outside. We were just in time to see a man on a TV program *"looking up into the sky"* the man was telling of his experience looking at the stars, and how they were moving about making beautiful patterns with others in a group doing some strange things! The newsman said, *"this happened over Central Illinois"* where we lived! This amazing experience was for real, not a space movie we questioned one another, *what do the ETs want us to see, the same as the man on TV?"* Did we somehow miss this; maybe we didn't look close enough at the night sky and what will we see tomorrow night? Talk about universal timing this was not a coincidence, there is no such thing as coincidence, the TV story and our message was an exact confirmation of tomorrow night with whatever would happen.

Very early the next day before I could get up, I heard a familiar voice say to me, *"Looking into the elements more you will be using your 3rd eye more clearly now, see?"* I felt Edgar's strong presence and quickly his face came into view I knew it was he who had spoken, he continued, *"The Aliens are a very special part of the Universe they are of the Christ Light!"* BEAUTIFUL, the answers are in the stars as Edgar taught us! Of course, we both knew this we had always known this in our soul, and he was confirming it I called out to my son, *come quick* so I could tell him what had happened. Some divine universal beings came that night to speak… *They* stood in front of us and said, *"the ETs are a very special part of the Universe and of the Christ Light! They come to save the Earth and they love us. They warned us there are the negative to be aware of. These here are our spiritual teachers full of love! They put the train of thought into man giving it through the mind and are with us both tonight. They will come again in your dream states tonight and to go by our first thoughts and instincts to understand them.*"

We were absolutely thrilled and excited those words cannot begin to describe our feelings we had waited for this moment and here is the message of truth for others to see! To be in their presence I cannot express the overwhelming *tremendous awe* we were experiencing!! Everything we have been taught by the *"Christ Light Universal Holy Beings were of the Supreme Infinite Universal Truth"* and on this glorious night of *celebration* was the time they chose for us we would never give a moment to doubt their superior knowledge! Then they continued, *"The books written will be for those who are also on a chosen journey and those who seek the Christ Light and Infinite Truth.*"

They honored us with their love and knowledge then were gone in a flash of light! It took some time to come back down to our reality from such happiness, and the next evening things began again! We were told *"to be in the yard before 8 pm"*. We were there early waiting, pacing, and watching the sky it was partly cloudy but no matter because soon we began to see balls of color, sparkles, large moving shadows and flashes of blue and white lightening moving in the sky! We decided to split up to not miss anything that may happen David stationed himself in the back yard to keep watch and I stood in the side of the yard to the front. We weren't prepared for what came next; out of nowhere we both heard *8 loud strikes of a Gong!* We yelled loudly across the yard to one another *"did you hear that!"* We both started to laugh and began shaking with excitement, I was nearly jumping up and down, the *"gong was announcing our Ancient Eastern teacher Han Tai Chen Su, who was joining us in spirit!"* David and I waited quietly; in moments many Universal Beings came together with those who teach us along with the ETs. They are our heavenly teachers and guides who circled around us to share this special evening as we experienced them in their beautiful spirit knowing people passing would never see them!

As quickly as they appeared my son called out for me, *"to take pictures pointing out directions to where he could see them moving to above us!"* I took several pictures with my little camera wondering if the ETs and spiritual teachers would print themselves onto the film. I only my little camera which normally takes pictures about 8 feet away from an object at the most I had nothing special. By now, the beings who came were combined with many of the ETs still above us looking down as they began communication to my son, *"they would be back on the next first clear night so I could see them too."* I had been busy trying to take pictures hoping there would be something on the film!

David drew the Circle of the ETs and Spiritual
Beings Over Us

The ETs told us *"we would see many wonderful things from then on, and this was for us to experience"*. It was a night hard to come back down to reality from and seemed almost unbelievable, yet we had witnessed it! I felt sure the pictures I took would have some type of evidence left on them. When we went inside David sketched the circle of them above us in case, I didn't get the picture taken in time which was a good idea his sketch looked good to have as a back-up. In only minutes there was another short message to us for our growth: *"Be aware that we are in a process of fusing ourselves with you. You must be patient knowledge will be yours for all time".* Wow! double wow, *fusing means forever*. We would be learning about 5th-dimensional life forms in the Galaxies and much more.

The next night the sky was cloudy, so we didn't know what to expect I held my little dependable camera in my hand ready for any action the small camera had done the *impossible* so far. The ETs and other universal beings can easily make their imprints happen on tape or film. Nothing happened that night, I thought perhaps the next night when we went out, they may come and show us something up close. We were in the yard early as usual for the 8 pm meeting, it was super cold, and we were pacing around in warm jackets back and forth very excited along with our usual wondering, if any of the surrounding neighbors had ever seen us on any of these nights. And if so, they must have done some wondering what we were up to, and then it happened! The first thing we saw was a *huge glowing bright CROSS high in the sky!"* Amazing, this was happening at night you know, but there it was as clear as could be beautifully glowing over the house with an Angel figure! I took a picture as fast as David called out to me, *"DO YOU SEE IT MOM!"* "YES, I do!" This was indeed *a wonder, a highly spiritual sign amazingly beautiful!* We stood frozen in our complete awareness; our eyes glued to this phenomenal sighting then zip…it was gone! We waited awhile but it stayed cloudy and cold that evening and nothing more happened, we finally gave up returning to inside the house.

We were buzzing rapidly about the *"beautiful Cross and Angel being that had appeared* we had witnessed *what others could not see and may never get to see and were grateful!"* How we could not be after a few minutes inside the house I warmed up and decided to go check my notebook which I normally do in case we are left new messages and it was gone! I looked around the room everywhere, but it was gone I could only think they were doing something with it. I knew it had been taken by one of the heavenly beings so without any sign of them now we decided to leave home for a while. We would go to one of my daughters to visit and tell her some of what had happened in the yard and hoped when we returned the notebook would be waiting.

When we stepped inside the house on our return, I immediately began looking for my notebook and soon found it when I felt something under my bedspread; yet my bed was still perfectly made! Very clever I thought, I couldn't tell the bed had ever been touched. I called for David to come and see what they had done then I opened my notebook to find a message tucked inside of it. I strongly suspected our ET friends had taken it in the first place who else could of, our new message said, *"Our time is parallel to your time. The answer is in the stars. The night is not so clear. Come again, Neptune System. Christ's light shines everywhere"*! This was phenomenal, they will be back soon I said.

Yes, not only does the *Christ Light* shine here on Earth it shines everywhere, just as the ET beings who come from the *"Neptune System* who are *Christ Light beings"*. They are teaching and proving as Edgar has said, *"The answers lie in the stars."* What a grand spectacular night to never forget!!

The Cross and the Angel is a Giant Revelation!

We knew the important sightings hovering over the house last night of the magnificent *Cross in the night sky and the Guardian Angel* meant for us. This information was one of the greatest signs in a while, it was a *REVELATION* for us in our work and with the amazing picture of proof. Christ's light had shown upon us as we stood in the yard, we were completely humbled by these grand experiences more than words could ever express! When I looked at the pictures of the Angel, I had taken on my little camera that night it is plain to see the Angel is guarding us and the house on that *starless black night!* This was to let us know we are divinely protected!

We were sure these universal ETs were from *Neptune*; I couldn't tell at first if the name they had given us at first began with an N or G in their written messages earlier. With further study we decided the word began with N making the name *Neptune* and pronounced in this way. This species of Beings was very high up as the others who have been coming to visit us for so long, and we felt we had known them forever! Some once lived on earth who were Hybrids and looked human, so they blended in and worked among people here to learn more of our ways and culture.

We didn't think about this with more questions it had been made clear that we must not let our human mind change what we know to be our truth! Now I understood, we knew why the timing to write the books and everything else we were taught had to be just right as we were told by the highest of Council. The truth is to remove man-made FEAR and replace it with LOVE, no doubt things were not always as we think with how we are taught all our lives. I spent many hours throughout the days and years thinking; how did the facts, and the truth become the lies in the beginning so the truth would be hidden and forgotten? This incoming information was reminding me of a giant tapestry being woven together a little at a time without a beginning or ending called *"the wheel of life"*. One day I was shown how the wheel of life takes one through their experiences.

The Big Photo Session

At 5 am I found my bedroom full of little Grays I focused in on one of them who began moving slowly to beside my bed; he was looking me over out of curiosity as usual, so I looked closely back at him out of my own I wanted to examine the outer covering on his small body. I had asked for this request the day before and now I had the chance to do this, the covering, his skin I will call it had a leather look to it yet surprisingly it felt smooth to the touch. I traced my fingers along the little Grays thin arm on up to its face and over his large eyes, which radiated a bright black color looking back at me, he stood very still as I examined him. He (I am guessing this is a he) was letting me check out his features and the feeling I had from the little Gray guy was very positive along with his curiosity. I felt like we were *bonding* in some strange way and then something funny happened! When I focused my attention to the foot of my bed another little Gray had stationed itself even closer to me away from the larger group of them. This one really caught me off guard, very quickly he popped up closer holding up what appeared to be a camera like mine, a *big flash* of light went off blinding me for just a moment; hey, wait a minute this little Gray had just taken my picture! The impression I had from the Gray was *"got you back!"*

I am sure this was a big joke back at me for last night in the yard when we were taking pictures! I couldn't keep from bursting out laughing I was realizing they know our human ways much more than I thought, how I wished I had this on my video camera! I couldn't quit laughing this had to be a first, having your own picture taken by an *"Alien Photographer!"* How I wished I could have a copy of it, would I possibly get something that looked like my picture? I wanted to beg for one from them in that moment knowing they can make anything happen, it was not something impossible for them to arrange. This was great and you know, I felt them enjoying these strange moments with me talk about laughing, when I told my son he doubled over with laughter thinking I was kidding, they are learning our humor very well!

To continue about that same night after my *photo session* with the *Alien photographer,* I noticed many more lights flashing about the room lighting it up even more. I could see a large crowd of Grays still moving around as if exploring everything in it. Suddenly there was an extremely LOUD booming sound with flashes of intense lighting that let me see clearly into their dimension for a moment! I could see into their world for that instant and for some unknown reason I wondered if my picture was going to be studied some place far off in in another Universe where a being may be asking, *what is that?* And was the devise the Gray held to take my picture a make-believe camera, a real camera, or something they know of?

After the big flash and loud sound, the room darkened back very dim, that's when I went ahead and told my audience of Beings, *"I know this is real but please leave me something to prove this really happened to me"* and they did! It seemed they left and at that very time I faded into a deep sleep and when I woke, I found a rock of David's close to me on my bed. It had come from his bedroom one that Bev found and had given to him because it had the look of an Alien face on it! I knew it had not been in my room and never had been I couldn't wait to tell David my night experiences with the Grays! This was a fascinating night and big confirmation, they have learned our HUMOR very well, and I have NEVER doubted what happened on that special night with my ET photo session!!

It is amazing how fast time passes on our earth it was hard to realize the start of this New Year was now into February. The ETs had let us know our next rendezvous with them would be on the evening of February 11th just three days away. On the night of the 11th it rained very heavily so our meeting was canceled by the ETs when they telepathically let us know, *"too cloudy tonight".* Our meetings needed to be on a clear or partly cloudy night, so we were rather disappointed by the weather. Sometimes the ETs went ahead and came in with lightening I guess it depends on what they chose, and lightening may help them travel since its energy. But something did happen earlier that night some hours after going to bed, it began lightening heavily and suddenly a huge flash of lightening with a loud *cracking* sound woke me, my eyes flew open! The lightening lit my entire bedroom up like a sunny day quickly I noticed a few of the ETs were here I felt familiar with as the *regulars*. One of them began telepathically talking to me about *"different planets"* although, I could not remember much of what they said the next day. I only had written a few words down about our visit, it was something about *Planet Neptune.* I did have the name written correctly, this species of ETs was from there, with that last momentary thought I realized I was on board a UFO!

They are so clever when they do this complete *switch in only a moment!* It's not like changing your shoes or catching a bus, this is a *universal switch out into outer space,* and you can't imagine it has happened! There is a gap, a stop in between, such as gaining or

175

losing time we never feel, and even experiencing these things from time to time it is still amazing!

Once realizing I was onboard, I found myself watching one of the ETs who was looking closely at my son while examining him as if checking the color of his skin, his eyes and so on. Then the ET cut a few hairs off David's arm to examine further I knew there was something important they were working on and needed his sample to use it for, something they planned to test him for. Afterwards, they told us, *"there would be an important reason for this experience"* and we both believe the strange things they do are only for very good reasons! This is what I remembered, and my son remembered nothing more either.

Soon it was my late dad's birthday the middle of February, and David's granddad from the other side was going to do something to surprise David, he couldn't wait! Finally, we gave up nothing had happened all day we were disappointed, so I told David goodnight and started upstairs to bed thinking maybe dad is running late this year occasionally they do by a day or so. Walking into my bedroom *I was instantly mesmerized;* I had not been ready for this one! My bedspread had been turned down and the *large brown Teddy bear* that had been transported to us years ago was in my bed, on my side, in *my own pajamas!* The bears little arms were outside of the turned down covers sitting up like I do reading! I laughed so much I could hardly get my breath back then I called to my son to come up, *"you have to see this one!"* Being terminally ill these jokes they did keep him laughing all the time with what they were doing! I think about how they diverted our thoughts and used our humor; our family of ETs know what caring and love is for sure!

David and his sisters loved granddads jokes so much, he had outdone himself with this one! We laughed together with tears flowing, my dad was a joker and so funny in life, and no different now on the other side! Why he chose to do this with the bear we have no idea except it being hilarious! We hoped mom and dad would never quit doing these funny things for us! David was happy with the joke then he found his birthday message from his granddad and grandmother *"Happy Birthday we love you"!!*

Near to completing the Trance States

At this time, we were still busy being taught by Edgar three mornings a week with the trance states along with our questions and answer sessions. We were overwhelmingly honored to be learning with him, we were enthralled! Edgar would close each class session in a heavenly way as we gave our devoted thanks before signing off. Everything was recorded and written down as we finished, this was just unbelievable! At night it continued to rain so we didn't go out into the yard for a while, finally the weather broke. Unexpectedly around this time I hurt my back in some odd way, it was so painful I couldn't stand upright, so David gave me Reiki treatment's which made the pain go away quickly. I was healed and felt good again I was back up to normal once again. And soon, I found a most blessed message: *"Child of God you have been healed!"* Oh, I was thrilled beyond all human words, David had passed this blessed healing to me and this precious note confirmed the experiences were happening to the both of us. This was never to be taken lightly; we were always ecstatic, happy, humbly grateful using our faith with belief always.

Soon after my healing one day my son told me, *"he could see Old Man Winter in his crystal ball and he held a Dragon Fly, there was also a Bear growling, and then a Being of Light coming out of the bears solar plexus"*, he knew the meaning of his predictions. The Dragon fly is one symbol and the Bear is one of my animal protectors. I would figure it out, but David told me what it meant, and his predictions were always right. The being coming out of my solar Plexus was *my real self* he said.

The last of February I found my Oriental necklace lying on top of my notebook one evening with a new message: *"look up in the sky"*. Then David told me, *"Han Tai Chen Su said: On the 13th of March there would be a full moon and there would be another sign coming to us connected to the first one, look up in the sky!"*. I had figured finding my Oriental necklace on top of my notebook was telling me to look to the east on the next full moon for signs of the ETs, and our eastern teacher *Han Tai Chen Su to arrive.* I felt confident this was what the sign meant so we checked the calendar and there would be a full moon in March on a *Friday the 13th,* which seemed very interesting! Next, I found my Oriental necklace lying on the same page as the message in my notebook and quickly thought, *"our lives*

177

are like a universal storybook with something happening almost every day from another realm and dimensions that even we can't believe at times." Our lives have been this way forever to us and most days we sometimes have forgotten what is considered *normal* here. Maybe we are the *normal* ones living a normal existence?

STAR MAN

Why did I call him *Star Man* from the very first? Years ago, when I met a new friend, without thinking I immediately called him *"Star Man"* I never knew why, but the name fit. I was learning constantly at that time from my spiritual teachers and guides, and deep into the world of paranormal experiences when I met this kind person. Although I kept very busy, I was to work with him to help him, and I hoped he would open his eyes to lost memories. When I called him this name without a thought; he looked at me curiously and smiled, saying nothing about it. In time he was beginning to *"open his mind"* more I was teaching him a spoonful at a time as I was supposed to do.

When we talked at times, I felt his restlessness, he knew he was more than human and from another place, but he had adapted to his ways of life here on earth with much forgotten from before. He had not recalled why he was here; and his life was tough, he had chosen an addiction in this lifetime suffering from alcohol, pain killer drugs, deep depression, and guilt. He was not aware of himself being a teacher to others with how he lived his life so those who were addicted may choose to take a more positive path to learn that one can conquer what haunts them in life. Through this, others watched his life change and some of those around him also conquered their own addictions by watching his journey. Although, he and other people he met along his way were not aware of this, or that he was teaching them... After some time, he began to accept my experiences with the ETs and of himself being involved in some of the actual ET events he witnessed.

I recall one evening we were sitting outside and when I looked up there were several *Crafts* overhead, I knew I was to point out to him, then he had no choice to what his own eyes could see. The beings in the UFOs wanted him to watch this event staying in view for long minutes doing all sorts of formations, which are not normal for any type of airplane, and these could not be explained by him. This was his *first encounter* to witness and remember what really does exist. My son knew we both were to work with him, and we knew this person's mind was being *reprogrammed* by the ET Christ Light Beings. We helped him in ways that would not frighten him by explaining how everything comes as it should. The UFOs continued to appear at times for him to watch and I felt secure that when he was alone, he would sit outside or wherever he was to watch the skies from then on. I told him, *"if he had questions to let me know and if I could help or explain anything I would try, but I sure didn't have all the answers to anything except what I had experienced".*

All of what happened frightened him; he wasn't remembering who he really was yet and where he came from, but I would help teach him about the ETs and how we here on earth are taught *"they do not exist."* He could not deny what he had seen, nor did he try to with what he experienced himself, which taught him about new worlds he would pursue in time. One night there was an object in the sky (UFO) over head which sent a shaft of bright light down right beside us for him to experience, and I am sure we both went on a trip with the ETs that night.

In his older years he became free of his suffering by becoming a follower of *"The Christ Light",* it was then he may have realized he was *"a Christ Light follower from the Stars!"* His life promise had been completed and it was time for him to go back to the Stars where he came from. He had taught others about suffering and how to conquer addictions through his own life, that it can be done. With his love, compassion, and chosen desire to help others he will be honored forever through the heavens as his name is whispered through the Stars for eternity. I was honored to be his very good friend, and to know his beautiful heart, soul, and bright spirit. When he crossed over it had been years since we had seen one another to even talk of these past things, but I feel he knew why my son and I had been here for him. He had totally changed after our meetings becoming a seeker of the Light. How many of you have ever said to a new friend, *"I feel like I have always known you from the first time I saw you."* There is your clue!

The man in my story was special and I will never forget him.

The Crystal Ball and the Pyramid

One night my son and I were in the car coming home when we were only a short distance away from the house we could easily see the windows were glowing with light, all of the candles were lit in every window on the top floor with no one home, at least we weren't home yet. The candles made the house look like a big storybook at Christmas time, and I must confess I loved how sweet the *family of ETs and spirits* were to do this for us. Upon entering we hurried upstairs to see if there would be a message waiting where we found everything looking warm and cozy and quickly noticed there were several items moved around in my room. My crystals which had been on a table were among some of the items moved and the shades had been raised high so we would see the lighted candles in the windows coming up the road! I remembered in the last trance states E.C. had said to us, *"there would be surprises coming soon."* we were not only excited about the candles but what this meant!

This event happened on a late Saturday afternoon when the days had started to get dark earlier, so I turned a lamp on then hurried across the bedroom to check my notebook. I found a message stating: *"The time is near and the bells in heaven are ringing",* how beautiful!! What the meaning of this message meant we weren't sure of yet, after we settled down my son and I talked about what had happened all evening. After we exhausted our theories, we quit guessing knowing the other side would eventually fill us in about the wonderful *"welcome home"*.

Close to the Christmas holiday another message arrived: *"Time travels; remember tonight both will be honored for thy Kingdom of Heaven is open."* I became faint I had no words for this beautiful message, we were out of our minds we were so happy!! How glorious!! *Thy Kingdom of Heaven* had an honor arranged for us? We were ecstatic and happy; how can this be, I could not sleep when I first went to bed my adrenalin was pumping so fast but finally, I fell into a deep sleep. That night we went on a trip with the ETs and I could only remember being with them and realized the timing may not be right to recall our trip for now. Christmas was extremely beautiful with the treasures being my son and daughters and their families which was an outstanding day full of love!

The first of the New Year we received a telephone call with good news of a private matter along with an unexpected letter which was a wonderful surprise for us. We figured this was what Edgar meant when he said, *"surprises would be coming."* Immediately afterwards another message arrived with a huge surprise, *"The Great Traveler requests his presence."* Our humble answer was: *"Yes, what an honor to meet again!"* This Being is a *"Divine Being of the Christ Light"* whom we have met times before I have mentioned. After this message a next one arrived: *"beware of the full lunar Red Moon."* All of this had to mean something big with so many messages so close together; their surprise was being put into place!

We were to go with the ETs that next evening and as instructed we looked outside at the moon to see a beautiful rose haze in the sky and a few smaller UFOs moving over us. It was also the night of the *Eclipse,* what a grand entrance for the arrival of the *Great Traveler!* In case you may wonder we were never afraid to go with them just the opposite we were excited, waiting and ready to go! We had no memory of our adventures that night because they did not let us, we could not recall the *trip* with the honor held to join our heavenly beings. We understood sometimes there are reasons we must wait. Usually later when they feel we are readier to absorb the trip we are filled in and given the reasons but for now we needed to remain patience, I sometimes believe the lesson is about patience.

A Special Birthday

My son's birthday is January 8th on that day right before our classes at 10 am a Heavenly birthday message came for him: *"For a soul of many souls you were created for a special purpose! From thy Father in Heaven."* David's message was beyond *MAGNIFICENT* we both were stunned, my son had tears running down his face and, so did I! There are no real words on earth to express this joy, I knew David felt great humbleness with heartfelt gratitude! We asked, *"what could possibility happen next?"* This was more than extraordinary; I am very proud of him knowing one day it will all make sense...

The next surprise was finding my *crystal ball with my small pyramid balanced on top of it sitting on my pillow,* which is close to impossible since a crystal ball is perfectly round and slick to place anything on top of it but there it was! Surprise number two was David's alien faced rock lying beside the crystal ball! We took our time checking out this unusual arrangement with our examination trying to figure the meaning knowing they wanted us to. One thing we knew, this was from our friends the ETs! That was not a fair question to ask you the readers, but it may help you to think about how we were dealing with all of this. The placement of these objects also had my small crystal pointing to the four directions (drawn on paper) with the alien rock facing north. We knew this meant the Beings were coming in from the *North Quad* in this way they had left their *calling card* to expect them. David's incoming information from them was: *"they were bringing more wisdom and knowledge to us so things would become crystal clear that we had been wondering about."* And with this message the ETs left us a drawing of a *"black hole and a Pyramid"* in three dimensional which said, *"Soon it will continue".* We knew this meant more UFO traveling through the *worm holes as a shorter route to the Great Pyramid!* My crystal ball and small pyramid would be used by the ETs through the years like a Universal map for us to study when they placed those on the floor a certain way for us to understand!

In dealing with the constant phenomenal experiences we had, I was sometimes extra hard on myself when I couldn't learn fast enough. This would create a big letdown although the other side never pushed us, just the opposite. I sat down one day grasping at this our lives my mind had become overloaded and suddenly I heard the voice of Edgar say to me, *"the words are given, all will be fine. Forgive in thy heart, forgive thyself."* E. C. I realized he was telling me to quit beating myself up to forgive myself, that I am living as a human in this world, relax take it slow, be patient and continue with the lessons. He also reminded me that one day in the future everything would be explained and cleared up from on the other side. His words helped me immensely lifting my spirit with peace and I humbly thanked him. Living life such as we are doing here on this planet our teachers understand our frustration at times because we never feel we belong or fit in here, and we never would…

The middle of March I found a beautiful letter with the two white doves lying inside of David's antique Holy box on my dresser and the small pictures of my mother and dad were placed beside the Holy box as well these are the little doves I keep on top of it. Edgar told us long ago, *"the signs of the doves were ours, the same as his and is our symbol, our connection to him"*. A precious letter was waiting in the Holy box with Edgars blessed information, *"A blessed union is thee. A new phase of work will be coming! Non- believers will believe when they face the truth! Behold eternal love"*. This important message was sent with love and after going over it a few times I began taking pictures and videoing as I do for our records. Those precious words were edged into our minds, I knew no matter what happened we will stay true to our dedicated work, it does not matter who believes or not, we will never stop. The main blocks we would encounter is with negative fearful people who will try to upset us in our work, and those who do not understand what this is about. We are learning each day in some way about our world and the beliefs within which could be simple for everyone because the secret is, *to open your* heart and answers will be there. This is when one finds deep compassion and love for all.

On the next night there was a big beautiful full moon just waiting for us, and the ETs told us, *"to go outside at the usual time of 8 pm"*, but before we did all the candles came on in the windows without human help, lightening up the three tower windows! We knew this meant the house was like *"a beacon of light for the ET Universal Beings"*. The tower was a beacon to them like on an airport runway to attract them easily, and other positive beings from the Beyond, they had told us this. We scurried out of the house that night like two kids with my camera in hand as I led the way. Things had already started in the night sky, we watched all kind of energy floating through it, some in brilliant colors and in different shapes! The energy looked like *"zigzag lightening"* even though it was a clear night, they were here! The objects we watched were floating over and above the house, I told my son, *"the only stars out were in a cluster in some kind of an odd pattern"* the strange thing was I counted 18 to 20 stars in an unusual pattern after this I took pictures of them. When the film was later developed, I had clearly captured the *"zigzag light"* in the night sky in my photos! I also had taken a perfect picture of another huge *"Angel Being"* right over the house as if in prayer!!!

I had one other exciting picture which appeared to be *an opening, a doorway, in the night sky, a dimension from our side to the other!* Sometimes in the night there would be a *red square* in the dark sky they called their *doorway,* this is what I had taken a picture of! Everything was easy to see in the pitch-black sky with the smaller bright red opening, how exciting this was! After we went inside, we found new Alien/ET information in the notebook waiting for us: *"that the red opening represents a doorway, a route, to another dimension from here to there!"* WOW! This confirmed our very thoughts! I did not expect to sleep that night we were excited about everything we experienced and because of the pictures taken! When I went upstairs later that evening for bed, I found the Holy box lid tightly closed again with the crystal ball placed on top of the lid! Everything was back in its usual place and I thought to myself, how nice the ETs and spirits put items back just like I had them! Tonight's surprise was the very thing we experienced when we were told ahead of time that more would arrive, it was unbelievable!

The very next night we found the chandelier light on in the tower instead of the window candles lighted, and on the floor was a drawing in the carpet of arrows showing the four directions again! The ETs telepathically told us, *"this is to confirm the thoughts we had"* there was no doubt in our minds that this home is a *powerful vortex of energy* it always been and always will be! If my home was ever moved or torn down the *invisible VORTEX* would remain!

At nighttime when I am looking around my bedroom many times the ceiling doesn't seem to exist anymore where the ceiling should be, there are only millions of sparkles which look like thousands of stars far off into the universe. On other nights I may see a bright flash go over me and then I will be moving, astral traveling at tremendous speed into the beautiful star-studded universe which exceeds a kind of beauty one could never imagine! All the while I am aware of what is happening to me with the feeling of *faster than thought,* which is unexplainable, but meaning I am right where I should be! I was always happy knowing I was going home to the other side to visit awhile this is where I had come from in my beginning to be born, and one day I would return to join loved ones.

I had no fear of returning to where I began it can't be explained for the beauty it holds that is there and belongs to every one of us.

EDGAR

After a night of travels the next morning at 10 am Edgar was back teaching us about the body, our system, organs, bones, and blood vessels in our morning lessons. And the next day March 18th was our celebration of Edgar's birthday when he lived on earth. We conveyed our joyous birthday greetings to him, *"Happy Birthday Edgar, we love you"*. Later the same day I went to get a glass of water and in the bottom after I filled it, I found a penny which wasn't there before! I recalled the old saying of a *penny for luck and a penny for your thoughts* so for whoever placed the penny there I thanked them. It was also St. Patrick's Day and thought of the word *trickster* someone was having fun with me and later in the day we found a message full of Irish humor. First, there was a four-leaf clover drawn at the top of a page in my notebook with a message, *"my baby Ann, me little lechecum, Luck of the Irish."* Humm, sounds like my Irish grandfather I was thinking. I thanked my grandfather and those who may have been involved and who come to teach us and for what they do, by sending our love to them! We had a feeling there was more yet to happen and we were right! On the two days of celebrations first, we found the computer screen saver full of St. Patrick cards floating across it complete with Irish music playing! The Irish cards were so cute and beautiful, this was the ultimate, and astonishing! The music was so happy I videoed this celebration and tried taking pictures with my camera, but the movement of the cards made it impossible though the cards and Irish music stayed on for almost three days!!

It was a week or so later I had not been feeling well and behold; a message came to me from above, *"Blessings be to you! O God give us a heart, that we may risk life itself on thy way and give us a soul that we may devote ourselves to the other world"*, how lovely and beautiful! The next message arrived shortly after the first one: *"My beloved ones a change comes very soon in your favor be wise with your decisions for many opportunities are opening up towards you both your guides and Angels will be close as always. Keep up the beautiful spiritual work that you both are doing your rewards will be everlasting. Journey well and love to all, free your mind and soul and all will come together. Soon you will see all.*" How beautiful, we were absolutely in heaven!

Let me fill you in more about our late Uncle Leo's clock. We had never wound his clock, and in orderly fashion after he passed over, he would drop in from time to time to wind it and later it became a sort of *mailbox drop*! Many times, we found the clock door open with his key still in the face of it as if he were standing there winding it, and he probably was! Sometimes I would find the door on the clock standing open and beginning to chime when I was working in the house. Uncle Leo loved his clock and he kept it going for many years, we never touched it to wind it and when I moved the key to dust the clock shelf if I didn't put it right back where he kept it, I would find it back in the correct place quickly! I could leave the room and return in a few minutes to find the key back in its place! We videoed his clock in those times and took pictures over the years when we found it opened commenting to one another, *"Well, uncle Leo and all of the spirits here sure have a wonderful sense of humor"* then we continued to laugh thinking of how they do so many wonderful things, especially when one remains connected closely with the other world. They cared and loved us as we do them, sides do not stop love for one another it only increases!

My mother and dad, Uncle Leo, Edgar, and many more with the rest of our loved ones in spirit were often involved together when having fun with us! It is great to know they stay so close around us plus today's fun was a happy sign from Edgar, Uncle Leo, and my Irish Grandpa on St. Patrick's Day! Edgar's birthday was still being celebrated throughout this, therefore is why we looked forward to all holidays. We never knew what the other side had in store for us and we couldn't wait to share their experiences with our family here. There was something for us to always look forward to in our many worlds. I believe what happened here with the other side was how David perked up daily no matter how he felt. He loved what the spirits did to make us laugh, they were special, and we never knew from day to day what was going to be next! They wanted to lift his spirit and I know David could intercede with them when he wanted to bring some of the surprises to me!

The Phoenix Lights

I recall one evening while watching TV there was a famous guest speaker on the Larry King program who was a Senator. He spoke of an experience he had with a UFO in 1997 by seeing what he believed was a huge UFO craft along with thousands of others in the Phoenix, Arizona area. He said, *"That after this happened, he was now definitely a true believer, that this incident changed his mind about Aliens/UFOs forever"*. He told about this extraordinary sighting viewed by him and many thousands of others who were very credible witnesses! Most of the leading Phoenix newspapers were there who filmed the UFO event too! He said, *"He was shocked by the size of the UFO it being as large as a football field moving very slowly over the city"*. Phoenix is one of the 7 largest cities in the US, so I am sure many people were shocked and frightened as others who were thrilled!

On that night a very well-known doctor happened to be outside on her upstairs balcony who videoed the UFO and took pictures on a 35 mm camera of the same experiences that evening. This was a night when people were crowded together throughout the city waiting to see the Hale-Bop-Comet. With a city of this size, thousands of people were looking in the sky most with their video cameras there were many who witnessed seeing the UFO that evening.

The *Larry King* show later had a couple of known skeptics as guests one night talking and laughing about UFOs. These guys had appeared on various television shows to *discredit* any Alien phenomenon. They thought they knew more than any noted physicist, UFO researchers, and eyewitnesses to the Phoenix Lights incident! This tells you what they were trying to do by laughing away the evidence of thousands who were true witnesses on that night. Even after serious study by experts and others who filmed this event and had evidence the skeptics would have the same lame answers with silly ideas of their own no matter the experiences by the many who have seen and filmed UFOs over the world for years! I doubted the skeptics own conclusions would ever be changed with their ideas that UFOs do not exist! Skeptics already have their minds made up *"it's all a big hoax"* one can plainly see they can't bear to be wrong... The reason is plain to me, *they are afraid* and can't bear to think they are wrong it's called EGO, and they simply turn information around to bring attention to themselves maybe they are so fearful they don't want to believe. The answers I have heard at times from some others sound like a first grader who knows more than any scientist, and I believe this happened in other categories of science to a brilliant man named Einstein!

I have also read accounts in newspapers about UFO experiences by *creditable people* that were skeptics beforehand and have since certainly changed their minds! We know everyone can't be lying; it's happening over the world and who really knows why the Government will *not acknowledge* there are other Beings? They know, so why is this still top secret, perhaps simply because they have denied it for so long, they are afraid of looking foolish to admit it now? It does give them power over people which has always been this way and one common question that arises is, *"Why don't the Aliens appear to the public or to the Government?"* They have apparently been around forever so why don't they just show themselves to everyone? I think that's easy to understand, *the risk is too great they know they would be destroyed out of fear, or for whatever reason our government wants to keep the truth hidden.* The way I understand it with what our ET friends say: *"they have made the mistakes of coming here times before but didn't find the humans peaceful it was anything but, some have died who were destroyed"*. I am sure they will show themselves one day when it's SAFE to appear and perhaps when people become readier to face the truth when becoming more spiritual to receive them. The ETs/Aliens have their reasons, and why should they trust us with their past experiences on earth?

UFOs are witnessed all over the world and some do land but only for certain reasons such as *"The Bentwaters incident in England"* which occurred on December 26th, 1980 when something very strange happened in Rendlesham Forest not far from a military base where the RAF and USAF were involved. The military was supposedly trying to locate evidence after what happened on that night in the forest where something *"not from here"* evidently did land, and for unknown reasons as usual it was covered up! I have heard one of the witnesses speak a former soldier by the name of John Burroughs, who was stationed at the near-by base and on duty that night who tells what he witnessed. This was a world known happening and still well-known today that in my opinion was defiantly covered up!

It is silly to think the aliens may hurt us; they could have done this since the beginning of our race if that was their point. I doubt we have a weapon to do much of anything to them unless they crashed and were injured, which I myself believe has happened more than once in earlier times. I sure don't have all the answers, but this is what I am learning from the ETs, and others who witnessed their own experiences with them including some high up military people who have spoken up, and a few astronauts with some of their experiences. What else do people need? Fear can ruin a life if one feeds off it.

The negative Aliens are another story and I don't know much about them except what I have been told from the positive loving ones, and a few brief experiences of our own with them. No one wants to see or be around evil people or these kinds of Beings. I feel the exact same way as some experts and researchers on TV and even a few ministers in the news who have said, *"who are we to think there were no other beings created in this vast universe besides humans? We are one small planet in space and who can explain what is really out there?"* There are many mysteries in the Universe with mostly unanswered questions; there are no real answers for now except through those of us who are in touch with the Aliens as an experience and who have sighted them. We along with some others on this planet are called the ETs *"Ambassadors"* to speak their words for them! It is ego or simply lack of information that gets in the way of many people's thinking, that we are the only beings anywhere in the universe that exist, but there are many of us over this world who say, *"We are in touch with the ETs/Aliens"*. And others who continue to report their experiences the world over as my son and I are doing and will continue to do! One of the ET messages we were given from them is perfect for now which speaks for them, *"The entire human race has purpose. Some destroy the purpose and some soar with the gifts always learning LOVE is the key."* ETs.

Greetings from the ETs

A message from a new system of ETs contacting us was found left on our computer addressing us both as *"TRI"* as we recently have

189

been named by them. Before you read our message to us, *"TRI"* I am to tell you some extremely important information from the highest of Universal beings, *"You see, God makes no mistakes in his Creations, all of us were created at the very same time and are a part of one another. The space beings, ETs were all created at the same time as human souls we were all sparks from the Creator/God, and in our beginning we all inhabited the universe."* What an amazing gift this message is in their own words*! This information is more than extremely valuable for humans to know coming from an Intelligent Infinite Supreme love who trust us to write their words so they may speak through this book with their universal knowledge!* We are truly honored!

The universal *space beings* are not from our galaxy but come from other universal places, and many of them come from very highly advanced planets! These souls are just as much a part of the Creator as any human here on this earth and those on other planets. The Aliens/Extraterrestrials have amazing technology so far beyond ours that we have no idea of, disassembling atoms, reassembling them, creating UFOs, travel at past the speed of light, is only a tiny bit and other future things we may never know, they are superior beings... Therefore, it is easy for them to *"hide"* their crafts and themselves when they need to. These are the ordinary little things they do.

When people on earth see a UFO in the sky it is because *they want to be seen* this is what they shared to my son and me long ago, they also find it simple to disappear hidden way in an instant to shield them. One day if earth finally gets it right and moves more spiritually, they will interact directly with us here. The ET Christ Light beings are on such a high spiritual plane they are very close to the Creator, and there are those in the universe of a negative nature. They all originated as we did, beginning as co-creations by God and because of those on earth who have not encountered one of them it does-not mean they do not exist, the same as an Angel being who one may never encounter, yet certainly does EXIST!

New message arrived *at 9 am*. Status new: *"Greetings, Tri, we are a highly evolved spiritual being. We are currently in the process of getting you prepared to receive our incoming information; we will be using your earthly terms so you may understand what we are trying to communicate. You Tri will each have a certain job to perform and carry out completely. Work with the Harris group they will be joining us soon, please help prepare them, so there is no fear, work with them. When they are ready the "Great Traveler" will materialize before them. Tell the one in Chicago to exercise a little more patience until the next full lunar moon. End of transmission".*

This was exciting and made complete sense to us, we both had started to work more with the Harris group (as they were referred to) about our experiences with the ETs so when the time came for them to experience the *"Grays and the Great Traveler"* they would not *"freak out".* And we would continue doing our best to gently teach them to release the fear. We were also told by the ETs, *"the female would have the most fear, but the male was searching for answers, and they were good people wanting to learn more, and we were to help them."* My son and I would receive more information soon...

I had been thinking about getting a message all day in-between cooking and getting ready for an appointment when I noticed my notebook lying opened on my bedside table, I rushed over to read it. Looking closely, I saw the familiar writing from our beloved teacher Edgar. His message to us was: *"my beloved Ann, your healing will be completed as of May 3rd. Rejoice and know you are loved. See you very soon."* I had been under the weather for a short while so this was wonderful news without a doubt, I knew I would be healed by May 3rd, we were certainly looked after!

Edgar's next message came at 11:30 am the next day written in my notebook: *"Your sons angels are powerful spiritual beings, they watch over you all, be prepared for a new awaking! Let Gods light shine through us all, blessed are thee! Your new work is in the making! Enjoy today, tomorrow and forever." Sincerely E. C.*

I thought of how beautiful his words are as I reread the message sitting down, my pulse raced my heart was hammering as I held onto Edgars blessed message with his acknowledgement to us, and the protection around us in our work! I asked myself, *"is this a big dream I will wake up from someday? No, I always knew this was our real world and truth!"*

The next night it was too cloudy to go out into the yard at 8 pm as we had been instructed to do the day before, so our meeting with the ET beings was *called off* until another time on a clearer evening. The following night there was a big surprise in store for us we found strange drawings in my notebook at the top of the page; I took this to be an Alien type of script from the ETs with another message underneath in their regular script we could read. They worked with us to bring back the universal language we had known before along with the universal codes we had used. A new message came soon.

"Ann, you complete the circle North, South, West you *face east; you are a powerful life force as well as a spiritual one. Thy Child is blessed. Thy Father in Heaven loves you and is with you always. Do not feel as if you are alone. You, David and I make the circle as well Eternal love."* I read this *over and over,* we were so happy trying our best to soak in the beautiful message; we felt completely bathed with God's presence of total love!

We were given this extraordinary information confirming that we are working together and was never alone, which made our lives *unique* and *unnatural* to how we have been taught as human beings. There is no doubt these messages come from the *"Divine Creator"* and highest spiritual Beings of love and goodness! Never has there been a negative message given to us through our earth years, we are only taught with the greatest love, positiveness and expert guidance to teach us to live the best we can, I pray I always live up to this.

CHAPTER 10

The TRI and ETHERIC COUNCIL

Our next new message arrived, Subject: *Tri listen, read, learn, and share. God force energy at its highest possible manifestation, especially, when we harness creativity, for the highest good of humankind. More will be following on Reincarnation very soon; most of your questions will be answered from all in thy realm, a sheer mist between our world and yours.*

Life became more amazing daily if that was possible and reading this ET message meant our contacts would continue to happen with new teachings and information so naturally, we planned to live up to everything we could to deserve our work. We both continued to be over-whelmed with our Divine connection together and know only a sheer mist is the only thing existing between us and those on the other side. I wish most people could understand this, the veil had become thinner and thinner as time passed and now, it was only a breath away and we were told by the universe in this message, *"The veil was completely GONE for my son and me, now and forever, between our worlds, and the Stars, Galaxies, Planets, and all other Universal Dimensions know of our work into other realms!"* This *was a giant revelation* we were honored to achieve; we will see into all they want us to! Home for us is everywhere on this side and the other side, which lets us know we don't feel *misplaced* any longer, but our secrets were to be kept hidden until after this book. This was the difficult part hiding our lives and living between many worlds.

There are answers waiting for anyone if more people opened their heart to love, this will open and free their mind to see more clearly, these are my thoughts on this and as the ETs added, *"to become more spiritual"*. Through our promise to the Creator we hear words daily leading us in our work I am speaking for myself and my late son David Michael because now, I am to expose a universal truth to those who question it *"REINCARNATION IS REAL!"* There will be many of you who believe this without a doubt but there are many who wonder, or those who choose not to believe, and one has this choice with free will.

It wasn't long until another new message was found from Edgar.

"My Beloved Ann, A new technique, what can it is? We'll see!! E. C." It was quite clear Edgar was having some fun along with his messaging to David and me; leaving us in more suspense! I was betting the other side was having a few smiles themselves about our excitement wondering, what was next? We were like two small children waking up to Christmas every day in our world and we didn't have long to wait for our next lessons. They came that evening to each of us we were told, *"how to visually see clearer to know when people were not as they seemed to be by looking more deeply into their eyes which truly are the windows to the soul".* This reinforced we would be receiving extra perception in this field of work and life in general, and not by-pass what we may see in some others because of the person and circumstances of *not* wanting to see what we did. I have passed this over many times wanting to find the good in those others but sometimes it cannot be found! Everyone doesn't have a good soul who comes into this life full of negatives' this gives others around them a challenge to grow stronger and learn.

I immediately began asking a barrage of questions, one right after the other about this subject of *bad doers* probably wearing out my spiritual teachers with my many questions. And unexpectedly a message came to tell me: *"I needed to slow down, be patient with my excitement and soak in what I was given. Your answer is right before your own eyes, can ye not see? Your new work has started, but ye don't recognize it? I will send you a clue".* This was defiantly from Edgar; I jokingly told him and other spiritual teachers, *"I guess I can't see the forest for the trees now days".* I am sure they enjoyed my little joke back to them because this is an old saying I teased them with. My being so excited I didn't realize I had the new work right in front of me! I was moving information too fast in my mind not realizing I had it, so I vowed I would slow down I would do this to stay on track I had been in my own whirlwind! Those on the other side working with my son and I told us, *"they are happy we get so excited and want to learn all we can, but it will only come when they know we are ready to go on to the next phase."* No one can rush the teachers and others who are working with us, the best thing is, they are happy with our learning and have a great understanding that as *part Hybrid* our brain capacity is 100 percent full and that we have much to process… sort of like a computer but more so…

The following message is very private to us but after many years I am to share this extremely special message with you. It is a powerful part of how we evolve, this may be hard for some of you to understand I only hope you can accept its truth! This powerful and extraordinary message came to us from The Heavenly High Council.

Subject: The Etheric Council.
Message: To help a soul.
To help a soul get ready for its next passage, there is a group of highly evolved Beings in spirit what make up what is known as the Etheric Council. These Beings have completed Earth life incarnations and make recommendations to help other spirits develop their "life plan" the Spiritual objectives a Soul wants to accomplish in the upcoming life. This plan outlines the incarnation as a sort of blueprint of opportunities needed for Souls advancement. The exact details of the plan are left to a spirit to decide. That is where free will comes in. Each soul is unique, the knowledge and wisdom of each life is incorporated into its memory, so it might choose a vocation in an upcoming life that is familiar. All the answers to all the problems lie within. Any trial or tribulation is merely a test to see if we can uncover the spiritual solution. A Soul is given many opportunities to develop and expand by living through adversity. Growth is never easy and can be accomplished only by experiencing every aspect of a situation and fully comprehending it. This is the end on transmission for now TBC for new Tri council. Love, light, happiness and joy- Go forward and live each moment in Christ's light for his light glows from within thy face

This is the most beautiful information one could receive explaining the life plan and what it means. To those of you who are reading this are privileged to accept this or not, with your own free will. This is the truth we are kept from knowing in man-made religion mostly because many have no idea of continuing after earth except some with their ideas of sin and hell, with no forgiveness...

Hands of Light

There were some sad and tough times going on in the family with loss of life I drew myself close to my loved ones to help what I

195

could, plus staying closely connected with the other side gave me positive strength. I never forget how blessed I am every day of my life to have my family of loved ones and my work that helps me see things much clearer and stay positive. Soon another new message came from Edgar which told me with one word I needed: *"Help!"* I knew at that moment his help was on its way. This short but powerful message from beyond during this time of difficulty brightened my days, and a second of his three unexpected messages arrived soon after.

"Ann, Gods work goes through your hands, blessed are thee!" Fifteen minutes later, the third message appeared: *"Keep your faith in the Lord, things will be fine, rejoice every day as thy son does"*. My heart was mending reading these precious words brought to me by Edgar and higher Beings. I was weak in my knees and a rush of joy washed over me and after reading the messages all my sadness was lifted away. However; little did I know I was being prepared ahead of time for another impending illness my son would have to face! Barely 24 hours passed when I rushed David to the hospital in extremely *"grave condition"* after much guarded medical care, Reiki energy, his strong will and mind power combined, not to mention the Christ Light beings he eventually made a positive turn around!! When he was able to come home, he was very weak and not able to walk, but his spirit was strong, and this is when he told me what he saw in a *vision* on his first night home from the hospital.

On that night I heard David call for me from his room, and when I came rushing in, he asked me, *"to sit down on the side of his bed he needed to tell me something"*. I listened intently as he told of a heavenly vision with their words, he was to tell me, *"The time is here! And then he watched a vision unfold in front of him, he could suddenly see my hands which were cupped together as if to catch something then he saw a bright white light coming down from above me going directly into my hands which formed a ball of light that I held."* The Heavenly Beings told him, *"This healing light was what I used to heal myself, to shower myself from head to toe with the light to relax me and whoever I work on"*. Continuing, he began to see a vision of more white light glowing around my body, out of the ends of my fingers, around my hands, and my chakras were *dazzling* in all their colors as I *floated* in mid-air!! Then he repeated the next words exactly as they told him, *"I was a healer long ago called "Imperial One" that my green eyes were like green emeralds and they used my eyes and could look through them"*. He was exhausted by then but with a big smile on his thin face, if ever I have had a time with NO words this was one! I questioned, could I do all I promised to the Creator I would do everything I was told the best I knew how through what I heard this night from my son! I have been truly blessed and not always understanding but now I knew, I was speechless and shocked! I gave my son a big hug and lots smiles; I knew who he really was that others will never know of!! We were two humbled hearts…

You see David is made of love, compassion and light known as Christ Light, therefore is why many others have said, *"They could see the light in his eyes, and many of us* are called *Light Bearers.* We made our promise together before we each were born to complete this journey once more, and we would never let ridicule about our work stop us. Someday, I will be given permission to explain this more in detail about that particular time frame. Both of us would continue together as mother and son and we gratefully did until my beloved son left this earth. I had to remain behind yet still being a part of other worlds and dimensions, and we immediately began working together as before with each of us from both sides. This made things better since I missed him more than life itself, I was completely devastated, and my daughters the same, but I knew we would all pull together throughout our lives with our strong love!

Getting back to the night when David told me about his vision with the ball of light in my hands, I have no idea how long I lay awake I could only see his face bathed in loving light with his beautiful smile as he gave this Holy message to me. He never thought of himself in his entire life even as a child. I did a lot of soul searching for days and marveled at the Being I know he is; with his strength, determination, strong faith and love for life.

An Evolutionary Process

The next day was really a hot one so we stayed inside where my son could lay on the sofa to breathe better and not be sick from the heat instead of on the patio where I worked on him with Reiki. Around 10 pm that evening I helped him upstairs to go to bed saying, *"goodnight, and if you need me just call out. I love you!"* Then after another big hug and *"I love you"* back and forth to one another. I went to my room where I found my notebook open and full of writing waiting for me, I was not prepared for the beautiful heavenly message in it because of what I had received from David the night before I was still processing!

This new message was about our beloved work: *"Greetings, an evolutionary process is going to create a group that will be coming to you both. You are a teacher, so teach, a lesson in itself! Rejoice every day is a blessing! And do not let anyone get in your way of spiritual growth! You and the little one is now prepared to receive the gifts of heaven. The Master is proud"!!* I went weak yet blissful; I had to re-read this HOLY message several times over and hurried to tell my son now! He smiled so big and we hugged one another.

I took extra time to think about these extraordinary messages, and David's vision to stay longer was the most important to me with promises to keep. With the information above pointed out, I began to have more of an understanding about our journeys. Memories were coming to me I could understand why I chose the path I had with my heavenly son. I wish I had a way to express how grateful we are for the eternal love we all have access to, which keeps our inner self intact. It's there, within the power of each person just waiting for us to reach for it and when we do, life changes to the most rewarding and positive one from then on! For now, my son and I would still have our earthly troubles and tough times to go through, but with these extraordinary heartfelt messages they would carry us into our future healing and spiritual work for the rest of our lives in joy of helping others.

Even after David passed, he guided me each day helping me to go on without him it was just in a different way, if only I could give him a *"solid big hug, as I knew his sisters wished they could."* This is my human part of emotions and I am very fortunate and blessed to see and hear him as I do, and the others in the worlds Beyond. In this way we will always be together forever!

Soon it was time to begin something new, it was the end of spring going into early summer and my son was still living when Edgar delivered a message for the both of us: *"By the grace of God thy son and thy mother will begin thou work and thy new journey."* We were immensely grateful to know we were beginning on another new journey. My son told me; *"he was more than ready"* we both were geared up and ready to start whatever was in store for us.

It was on a Friday night I saw the vision of a white envelope addressed to me which had A.R.E. on it, and across the front of this envelope was a *"string of pearls"* draped on top of the envelope exactly like on the neck of a person, I know pearls mean *wisdom and knowledge.* In this vision the envelope was floating in midair almost to my mailbox. I looked closely to see a stamp in the right-hand corner of the envelope, and one was with a man's face who I could tell was Edgar Cayce then the vision ended! Two days later I went to pick up some film I had developed I was anxious to see the pictures I had taken. While sorting through them I came to one picture which was NOT one I had taken! In this photo I was stunned to see a white envelope with the same description of an A.R.E. envelope floating in midair to my mailbox and the stamp on it had Edgar Cayce's face on it just as I had seen in my vision! I hurried to get a magnifying glass to see the man's face on the stamp to be sure and it was Edgar just like in my vision! I was ecstatic with this exciting discovery as I was in my vision, and I wondered if there had ever been a stamp made like this? This meant Edgar had something coming in store for us, a letter such as this meant *"communication with knowledge and wisdom"*. As I mentioned I get many symbols in many ways they are only for me to understand in the way I know too. Edgar was showing me something was coming from his A.R.E. (Area of Research and Enlightenment) foundation from in Virginia Beach, VA. It would be something from him he arranged to happen!

The Crusades

In the night I awoke to see several *Alien faces* around me, and I was handed a beautiful *red rose* by someone who I could not see. I know a red rose means *love* and, in that moment, I suddenly realized I was in universal travel. *"How sweet"* I thought silently to myself and just that fast I found myself among hundreds of thousands of stars in the vast universe it was glorious! I could see the 3rd eye on the forehead of a Being's face and his eye shinned with amazing bright light, next I heard a voice tell me, *"a message would come*

199

from Edgar and, we all love you! And the Aliens (ETs) love you!"
Oh, I was so very happy!! This reinforced the Edgar Cayce mail in
my vision and in that same moment many ETs had come to take me
into the stars! Without having time to absorb the beautiful message
above in less than a blink of the eye, I was watching a fast-moving
film like a movie racing across my vision being put into my brain to
recall. My next moment was like *magic* I was among the pyramids,
there were horses and marching soldiers, some of the soldiers carried
the *Cross* in front of them as they marched. I could hear the word
Crusades being told to me! I had been taken back in time and
watching this event! I knew at that moment I had been traveling in
space and transported to that era. I felt the spiritual oneness and
fight for freedom deep within myself and of these brave *Soldiers* in
those ancient times, I had been one of them!

In what seemed only moments I could see a beautiful staircase, *"I
was going up and up the stairs into the heavens among the stars!"*
Then it suddenly ended, I can't describe more because things slowly
vanished, it was over and the end of what I was being shown. But
then another continued vision of the Crusades was shown to me: I
had been a Soldier then and carried the *Cross* to gladly give my life!
I loved being reminded of this lifetime I have always been happy to
serve God. I remembered being shown this in my past once before
when I gladly gave my life to *stand my ground* showing my love in
this way. As I have been told, death is the beginning of a new life
and life is the beginning of our death.

At 1:15 am the next morning I awakened to see Edgar standing in
front of me with a big smile. There were *beautiful sparkles*
showering down from the ceiling to the floor in my room, and I saw
two boxes, one at a time. The first one had an initial on it; I believed
to be an A. and the second box had an arrow on it meaning (Lakota
Sioux). Then Edgar said, "One *comes along in the material world
that believes as you and the son who you two will trust let me see
your palms.* I held out my hands and he said, *"The healing is
stronger than ever".* I was so grateful for this all I could say was,
"thank you" to Edgar I was curious and mesmerized!

Years later, my dear Native American Indian best friend who I met
came into my life, he was called by his American name of Alex.
This was the meaning of the first box with the A on it I was shown

long ago. The second box with the arrow meant the one to come along would be Native American from the Lakota Sioux nation, which Alex was! He believed just as my son and I, and we became connected immediately knowing we had past lives as Native American Indians more than once. Alex shared this information with me after knowing him several years. We were married with two children and had a good life in one, in the other one I was a Brave with family who I took good care of. We were the same as family for several years after we met, he respected us as we did him! He became sick in later years and left this earth plane to go to his universal home. He was a great teacher who taught me much of my forgotten heritage and he was very gifted, a high up spiritual teacher and a well-known artist. The moment we met we knew one another without saying a word at the time.

After David crossed Alex helped me want to live again to finish out my work and life, he lifted my spirit. He was special and gentle; his energy and spirit were amazing! I am honored we agreed to meet again in this life, and I loved him very much. After he passed, I would see him as I do others and one night, he woke me to share time with him. The setting for us was at a round table with a white tablecloth, he was smiling at me as we sat beside one another. He had a small box sitting on the table in front of him he slowly moved over to in front of me without a word. I opened it to find a beautiful ring with a gold Dragonfly for the setting. I was spellbound and so happy, the Dragonfly suddenly came to life flying around the room then back to the box landing on the gold band of the ring!! He gave me what he had wanted to in life, I didn't know this at the time, but I felt he loved me. I was overcome with tears and happiness, our timing to be together this time was off our lives were dedicated to others which was right for each of us in this time.

Edgar continued to send his blessed messages about our *sacred* work which was very important some I am not to speak of. Directly following a few nights later in a series of visions I first saw Edgar and General Powell's initials floating together in mid-air above me which let me know the two of them were working together on a mission with David and me. I was reminded by both, *"To not be afraid to forge ahead, keep my ideals and let my mind be free now"*. Apparently, Grandpa Powell stayed very busy making his rounds that night with Edgar, I was grateful for this information…

I lay in my bed for some time wondering what were they up to or were they just letting me know how closely they worked together? This tells me they had known one another in some way since the beginning of time. It wouldn't be long until I had a visit from Uncle Leo who began talking to me about, *"how to save time on healing people"*. I was swept away with all his wonderful input writing it down as fast as I could what he told me has helped me very much in my work, my list of healing prayers for so many were so long I would fall asleep awhile, wake up, and continue with the names now I had a new shorter way just as powerful...

Very soon a special message arrived of great importance for us: *"In the Earth calendar of July be prepared to view our family throughout the heavens. We will be picking up our extended family members (earth siblings) and working on their metabolic and neurological backgrounds we will not harm anyone. We are currently working on some adjustments in order for your earth bodies to handle the depressurization techniques and molecular breakdown to be transformed to the surface of other planets; you are voyagers in a new time laying the path for mankind to follow. Think things through for it will affect the future of all mankind-end of transmission"*. I have no comment to make on this information except *UNBELIEVABLE,* it happened, and is very important.

Another message later confirmed the one above it was clear to us we were on track, *"You both are coming into new worlds you are experiencing everything but not remembering yet. Soon you will remember embrace and cherish it! You both are loved dearly"*.

After these extraordinary messages imagine how difficult our lives were each day trying to keep a balance within our worlds and not sharing these things with anyone. We wanted to tell others, *"there are so many other Beings that live in other glorious universal realms and worlds"*, but we could not.

At that time, we knew nothing about UFO groups except of one main group called MUFON, or anyone else we knew who mentioned Aliens or UFOs to either one of us. We existed in worlds of our own for a long time, but the ETs fixed this when we became more acquainted with MUFON later, finally, we could share!

With Edgar's next visit he said, *"Looking in a reflection glass is a portal to the other side"*. This means, for us mirrors are portals into the other side we travel through, we knew what he meant by his statement. There isn't a mirror I cannot see the portal in; they are all portals to my sight. This message was to let us know nothing we did is without direction from an *Intelligent source*; this Infinite Intelligence of universal beings work under the Creator as the Angel/Archangels do and are known by many names.

These amazing things happening to my son and I are beyond what the human mind of most may be able to understand but I am explaining as best as I can. We accepted a great responsibility with our permission and the *looking glass* Edgar spoke of is how my son and I also see energies, spirits, universal beings, and ET/ Aliens moving in and out of mirrors! Each night before I go to sleep as I lay in my bed, I watch various spirit Beings moving around the room, in and out of the mirrors, doorways, and tower windows until my eyes grow heavy and then fall asleep.

This brings up something incredible that appeared in our home many years ago and how we found this *looking glass* we named the Magic *Mirror!* This mirror was brought created from energy, molecules to us, from the universal beings to use, one day there it was on the wall! We named it the *Magic Mirror* it was a great instrument, a portal for our learning, our lives were busy daily living in many worlds, spirits, and with the beings in our home and energies through the mirror. This home has been our teaching ground even before the ETs began returning so often, they didn't want to load us down too much at once. We were being well-versed through our spirit and ET family, they taught us in *portions to not overload us* with information and our pre-birth memories.

Back to Edgar's Teachings

"Beloved Ann, Edgar here, you are right on track. Blessed are we who furnish and send the power of thy LORDS HEALING TO ALL we CAN. Yes, dear child you can use the trance states as you wish for, I shall not forsake thee. I shall always help serve you with Christ's words and healing touch for all time. Know there is much coming of a wonderful nature and rewards are many. Congratulations on your beautiful story in <u>Angels on Earth</u> you shall write much more to be

published. Thy son is doing well, thy works are well received. We love you all".

We were truly humbled and honored with this beautiful message these things he mentions have special meanings for us to know, Edgar is with us on our journey I will be given the words I need. He and others had chosen to be our teachers in this lifetime, Edgar taught us about each one's destiny with our lessons and advised me with his writing to me, *"to keep studying, writing, sending healing, and to know your life's work is so important here and thy son and daughters. All is beautiful and good. Goodnight, Sincerely, E.C. and all of us".* Wow, this verified our work once more, at times the term *"from all of us"* was used by those who work with us as a common signing off because many were in contact with us.

It was some time before we heard again with a written message meantime our lives moved on with new trials and joys into summer. It was a hot afternoon just before the 4th of July at 1:30 pm when I found my notebook turned over on its face, I hurried to it longing to read their familiar writing with our new awaited message: *"My beloved Ann, do not fret thinking we have forgotten you. It has been very busy over here preparing for our next stage. Be patient my dear it will all fold together. Embraced by love! G.P.".* The message came from great, great grandfather Powell who sometimes comes with Edgar he told me long ago, *"he would always be around to help me".* I couldn't help but laugh at the old-fashioned word *fret,* this kind letter is written in his southern language from lifetimes before. I am happy he introduced himself years back and I have a photo of him holding a Saber sword in full uniform... July 7th brought more important news, *"Be patient there is time for everything. Expect a great thing to occur soon! Enjoy beloved children, from all of us".*

After a human departs from here into spirit so much more awaits each of us. Look at the help and protection from the other side some people never know of or want to believe could happen. July 10th brought more news with a short line from Edgar, *"Arrives, new arrival soon, Love to all",* that was it! Something was coming that would become instrumental to the family, was it a new baby? We were trying to figure it out but didn't come up with much at the time in order to not be consumed we let it be for then. It wasn't long after my birthday passed, I found the sweetest message from the other side in large written letters, *"Celebrate! Happy Birthday, Baby Ann, Pumpkin, we surround you in a circle of love and light, Daddy, Mom, Edgar, and General Powell, Granny and Pappy, and many more"*. I was so excited; my smile could have lit the town up at night! I had been waiting for my birthday message to arrive I felt wonderful knowing the other side was present to celebrate my day of birth! They were always with us at every family occasion with loved ones, I wrote down my humble words of thanks in my notebook, *"this is the very best birthday ever!"* My special day was perfect with my children around me and loved ones from the other side!

There were some serious issues at hand the next couple of weeks I was feeling mentally and emotionally upset with how to make things better or the best that I could in a certain situation. I finally gave up deciding to give it a rest and not think about it anymore, I would be led. later as I was lying on my bed, I found hope in a new message cleverly written without me knowing it right in front of me in my notebook, *"Thy burden of the world is not thine to carry. Thy soul is soaring into a new dimension, God in Heaven."* I was happy this amazing answer gave me relief immediately I must have read it several times letting the Creators words soak in!! It was hard to realize these things happen but here the message was, and I knew to never doubt these precious words, only a fool would!

For the next couple of days, I kept the message in my mind going over it continuously when suddenly another one arrived: *"Yes, you are going into a new dimension of learning now. Things will get better for you in the learning at long last. Now rejoice! And be happy thy child help is given in these material things. We love you all!"* This was so exciting I felt a new energy coming into my body it was just what I needed with all this love! The next day early came another message from an amazing messenger and this one made me feel faint…

Beautiful Mother Mary Stood Before Me

The shock was seeing *"Mother Mary"* again who miraculously appeared standing before me and began speaking, "I *come to you as a mother to a mother. Remember, do not be down upon thyself for you are only one person, rest, relax; enjoy life there for it is short in your human years. Thine child is working for our Father in heaven, a glorious work! Do not fear others remarks! Things will get better now. You and David work together to help many"*.

I was absolutely in a state of something I cannot describe in any way with great happiness and joy that filled my very soul!! Even experiencing this divine being it was hard to realize! She continued, *"Thou preparest a table before you!"* How does this happen? This was my human part of thinking, there she was **"right in front of me!"** Many times, *Mother Mary* returned to me in my sadness, she knows when I need her help and her blessed words give me strength! This experience has another very important blessed reason I am to tell you about, *"regardless of how each one of us has been taught, or the name of any religion does not really mean anything but a way to identify the source of what it is called"*. I am not Catholic, but as you see, it does not matter what I am called on earth because in the real world, the heavenly world, we are known by each one's heart and soul, nothing else matters! I love *Mother Mary* with all my heart, and she has taught me our earthly titles are not important and this is known throughout the universal heavens!

David had many spiritual beings who watched over him in his illness and through his life. With his God given gifts he knew things before they happened, and this amazing gift was in his heavenly agreement to be born in this way. With these abilities he could help others more with his sharp awareness. We were being cautioned off and on to slow down in our work but because we love it, we were always eager to resume it quickly with our excitement! When we worked together passing healing energy to help those, we could it gave us each a healing too, since the energy passes through the healer first then into the client. As ill as my son was, he would mentally send healing to many others who lived miles away then rest, and soon things began to get much better and his sickness improved more and more! When the Divine ones pass information to us, we never doubted what the information was for the Creator's words are not to be doubted!

The ETs continued to wake me usually by a noise or lighting up my room in the coming nights and early hours. I knew there were times I was *returning or leaving* for travel with them. One night a *heavenly voice* sounded out to me with an important message. I had been in a deep sleep and suddenly awakened by several Beings of light I knew telepathically to write their message down in my notebook. They told me: *"One day you will have built a long road to a much simpler form of existence, one of magnificent beauty and you shall look back upon this event like a classic, a story to remember, one etched in memory for always, one recorded in time. Soon you will understand the tablets we show you in the night dear one. We are here loved one and yes, we are many from the light carry on the work we know it is first with you and that is good."* What can I say, so much was given to us my heart was beating fast and my tears were of joy! This meant our lives would be like a *story book* one day, but real! Later that morning I told my son about the message and of our memories recorded in time. This gave us a great peace and achievement knowing we were using the gifts as intended. I don't know if this has been written anywhere before or not, but later I found another empowering message in the Holy box. On that day out of the blue David said, *"Go look a new message has arrived".* It was right after lunch at 12:15 pm it begins below...

No More Tears

"Laboring for the food that does not satisfy but with the honored of God they live a life where there are no more tears. Around those blessed isles soft sea winds breathe and flowers of gold are blazing on the trees." My son told me the meaning of these blessed words and what the message meant. "We *of course are never satisfied in our learning of our Divine knowledge. The food (the mind) we always seek more so we can continue to learn and there are no more tears in heaven the rest is what we can only understand here of the smallest idea of how beautiful heaven is"*.

This message was put into terms we could understand, to pass onto you the readers, it almost makes the wait here seem longer before we can go home how amazing to learn in this way! Barely two more days passed before the next message was brought to us it was typed on my old printer and found in the Holy box on my dresser. *"Flying swift as thought, in a wallet all of silver, a wonder to behold, a messenger of God."* This was amazing and the meaning to this is, *"an Angel being who is a messenger of God."* This is so beautiful, and I have no right words to thank this messenger of Light! The universal Beings explained the meaning further, *"Our Angels are always beside us protecting and guiding us along and they are faster than thought, in a wallet of silver, meaning their light, and of course they are a wonder to behold, Messengers of God!"* Isn't this beautiful thank you, dear beloved ones!!

It was August our messages continued in our learning process of the *trance states* with Edgar who let us know, *"David would begin to carry new healthy weight to his body that he was doing very fine now",* which was absolute *heaven* to hear about my son! His body was absorbing more healing energy he needed; this was wonderful news because he was still somewhat frail... yet he was becoming stronger with a radiant look in his eyes once again.

The following evening, I was urged to look out of the window my eyes were searching the night sky for a UFO and there one was not moving. I quickly went outside to get a better look it was now over the house with its blinking lights in red, green and white around the bottom of it. At times some of the lights were different and I could not tell exactly how high it was, but it was close enough to see it well. I must have stood there 30 to 40 minutes until I finally tired and went to sit down on the front porch while it was still in the same place and later, I went to bed. The next day at 10:10 am there was a new message from the ETs, *"did not make contact last night try again tonight."* I took it that something was off or wrong last night preventing them *from actual contact* when I watched them. The next contact was happy news, *"Welcome children school will be starting again soon!"* Good, we would be learning more and anxious to go!

The 21st of August another message arrived early which was breathtaking, my tears of joy were mixed with exhilaration! *"Thy eyes shine bright with the light of the heavens blessed are thee and thy son. See you tonight! Continue the good work and grow, from all of us".* This lifted our soul we were heartfelt and felt on top of the world! It wasn't long until another sign came at 9 am I found it on the back-stairway landing with an imprint drawn into the carpet of an *"Angel face and one wing!"* I was quite excited and quickly took pictures of this experience to record the drawing and then we anxiously awaited the next day for messages, and one appeared: *"you are a special entity to many souls blessed are thee".* How wonderful, by now we were far beyond any words to say, we figured we must be doing things right! Some days their messages would come one after another and we felt it was getting close to the time when our connections with the universal beings could be told to the world!

On August 22nd at 10:10 am I found a new note: *"may catch us on film tonight!"* Wow, we knew this was from our family of ETs and they planned to be here tonight, this reminded us of playing a game of sorts, they know our ways better than we do! That same night when they were in my room, I could see them clearly and they were sending their thoughts telepathically, *"something about a new kind of work we needed to do"*, but I couldn't remember what they meant the next day. I know I went with them in the night, but I have no memory of where and didn't get it written down.

Early the next day I knocked on David's door to see about him and he didn't answer so I went on in and he was gone! I immediately panicked because he couldn't walk but a few steps without my help, where was he? At that very moment the phone began ringing and thank goodness it was him asking me to come and get him! I picked him up at my parent's old home asking him what he remembered, and how did he get there? He told me, he remembered waking up about 3:30 am and felt like he was still dreaming yet he knew he was awake, and then he was somehow going to his grandparent's old home (my mother and dads' old home). At some point after this *he suddenly woke up* to find himself standing on the small back porch in front of their back door with the house key in his hand! He was completely confused, and in shock, not understanding what was happening, then let himself inside to call me to come and get him! But once he went inside, he couldn't stay awake and fell asleep, when he awoke later was when he did.

When the phone rang, I was so relieved to know where he was and that he was alright and hurried to get him! He seemed ok except he was still in a daze without any details, so I got him to bed, we waited until later to talk about his experience when he felt more alert. He was sure he had been transported by the ETs in the night because he couldn't have made it by walking, he was completely dressed but without his shoes on! We knew he had been in bed when we turned in last night so this had a gigantic impact on us, how else could he have ended up that far away from home? There is always a reason for what the ETs do, we felt this was for an experience, maybe he

209

had been on a UFO and was put back down at his grandparents' house since his has happened to him before.

I found three separate messages from the ETs on the same day of David's strange disappearance. The first one was after I brought him home at 1:45 pm. The first message said: *"Try again Monday"*; the second message came in at 2:20 pm and said: *"did you see the light?"* I had seen lights, there were four UFOs moving around going up and down, back and forth, coming close to me then retracting back with amazing speed. They were moving erratically in different patterns and there was no time to get my video camera, I was afraid if I looked away even a second, they would be gone! Most times I had my camera ready, so I could video their crafts, but I didn't this time. Sometimes they would stay for over an hour until I couldn't hold my camera any longer because my arms were too tired, as we used telepathic conversations. To prove my point about the crafts what kind of a plane could suddenly stop, hover over my house sitting in midair; zoom in and out, back and forth, up and down, with unpredicted speeds for long periods of time in daylight. Not to mention this happened *only* over my house for years no one ever mentioned seeing them! What would be the reason a plane would come here repeatedly over our home, and they cannot stop in midair, and no one to ever see this, I am only making my point.

The third message arrived at 3 pm that same afternoon which read: *"Maybe again"*. Three notes in less than 3 hours was exciting along with transporting David to my parents' old home as well, plus they were in the house to leave the messages. I was relieved he was no further and in a safe place. I know this was planned for whatever reason; we thought they were probably letting him experience more of how *transporting works and work on him.* As I mentioned, the ETs don't always visit at night, it can be at any time in our experiences. I later asked our ETs, *"why others did not see them or their UFOs when we do?"* Their answer always made perfect sense, *"we have a shield around us others cannot see us"*. One question the ETs asked: *"did you see the light?"* I had set up my video camera aiming it down the front staircase in case I would be able to catch one or more of them on film in the house. I took it by the message which said; *"try again"* possibly meant to *try again* to get some of them on film? I had been asking them to let me capture

210

them on film which they had agreed to, but when? They always kept their word so I knew it would happen, I hoped it was not a joke like my experience with the Alien photographer earlier which I admit was hilarious!!!

I became very ill that coming Sunday probably with a case of nerves with so much going on. I was sick part of the night asking for Edgar and the divine healers to come and help me along with David. I knew David was sending healing prayer to me and I worked on myself throughout the same night. I awoke to see beautiful lights appearing in my room with some of the lights forming into others. And in some way, I knew the lights were coming from Edgar and the Christ Light ET Beings filling my room with them! I watched as the beings gathered around my bed and began working on me with this magnificent Light, what a beautiful and phenomenal experience!! I fell asleep quickly as they worked and waking up the next day, I recalled I had written down what Edgar spoke to me about, what *a nervous condition* can do, and about my diet. He told me what to stay away from, dairy products, and spicy foods because *"my body was very delicate right now with so much happening"*. He called what I had, *"a nervous stomach and that my system was very delicate right now to get the mind, body and spirit back in tune with the Universe. And to place my hands on my stomach area and use the healing I use on others that this energy shall pass through your very being do this for yourself we all love you and are with you."* The next day a few more words were given to me, *"to celebrate and dance you are healed"*, and I knew I was! I was so grateful I could not afford to be sick while taking care of my blessed son I had been truly blessed and healed! In the next chapter I will explain the importance of setting one's spirit free and what kills our spirit when each of us are not accepting our own responsibility by fighting to survive here.

CHAPTER 11

Miracles, Humility and Gifts of Messages

In the later part of morning I found my pillows lying on the floor beside my bed, it was as if they were showing me a *prayer altar* which gave me quite a surprise. I had made my bed a short time before and nothing was amiss then so I examined the placement of the pillows closely hoping to find a message and there it was: *"enlightened one the journey goes well thy son has the fire in his eyes to concur evil! He is faith!"* He certainly is full of faith, love, and courage, and never afraid, nor does he ever complain I thought. This was the first day of September the beginning of a beautiful fall and what a wonderful way to start out a new month!

I would like to remind the reader I write the messages exactly as they have been written and given to us without one word of difference. I was overwhelmed with this message about David as I sank down on the bed pillows to read these words that were left for me, again and again. I understood David's healings were extremely important to give others faith, hope, and to never give up among many other things. He fought fiercely to live each time he had been a breath away from death when he had his DOA (dead on arrival) experiences. I was happy to see the word *"enlightened one"* as he is and my son did have the fire to fight for life, this was all very humbling with the names he is being given. Softly then I heard a heavenly Being tell me, *"We accept all responsibly with humility, grace, perseverance, and our eternal love for our Creator/God."* So true, I was overwhelmed in this blessed experience and hurried to tell my son about these beautiful Being's messages!

Soon after this happened, I was told: *"to live life and enjoy it if a person doesn't fight to survive and set the spirit free it kills our spirit."* I was very encouraged by this to live each day with the happiness we received from loved ones, the ET Christ Light Beings and others. I started out the next day with new energy I had errands to do and wanted an early start. I drove my old pick-up truck out of the back driveway and right before I turned onto the side street I thought I had *been transported into* a *time warp, I couldn't believe what I was seeing* in front of me, it was the most beautiful confirmation on our teachings you cannot imagine!!

I brought my truck to a sudden stop with a jerk, pulling myself forward to look out of the windshield to admire an amazing incredible sight right in front of me! There were hundreds/thousands of *"golden rays"* which were brilliant bright lights of gold filtering down through the surrounding limbs of the trees right in front of me! I have never seen anything like this before in my life except on the cover of a new booklet from A.R.E. Even the position my truck had stopped exactly where it needed to be for me to see this so perfectly! I felt I had been transported into the universe; it was so unbelievable! I even thought, *"is this real am I here in the alley"*. I sat there admiring the beauty of this gift, I knew in a second this was not anywhere near normal in our world, this vision had been sent to me for a reason! This WAS the same *as the front cover on my new booklet from Edgar Cayce's A.R.E.* I had received prior to this day, the very same! I sat there spellbound and suddenly it hit me, Edgar had arranged this! I had no intention to move away this was incredibly blissful! Finally, I had to move out onto the main street I used every day, but I wasn't ready to move, this had never happened before and hasn't since, this was arranged by Edgar and sadly I didn't have my camera. Each day afterwards I hoped it would happen again when I left home but... it didn't!

The name of the monthly booklet I receive from A.R.E. is called *"Experiments with God"*, and this month the booklet had a bright yellow cover on it with a picture exactly as I had just seen! I had experienced the same rays of gold electrifying light coming through the limbs of the trees onto me lightening up my world! I knew Edgar had done this for me he was reinforcing all he had told my son and me, it's something like this I call a *miracle*, without a doubt! These things are happening from the Creator and no one can begin to spoil your day or life if they attack you with negative words or in their actions, it doesn't matter! That is on them.

I was positive I had a *coat of protective armor on* with the Angels around me, we had been told this since we came into this world to do this work, and that it would be the only way we could survive. I wanted to tell the world of our lives with these magnificent spiritual beings and how the afterlife really is more than ever! We both have been told many times by the High Council of Beings, *"one day*

213

people will understand how we have been taught wrong about so many things all of our lives because of fear and rejection. Here on earth some people try to live a life that only a Saint could, and the heavenly ones know the truth of our world."

That same evening, I awoke with words being given to me by one of my Spiritual teachers, *"He who truly believes with an open heart shall have no fear upon this earth or any place of existence. Know thy child you are loved to know to follow thy heart. Everything opens as it should like the flower, the lotus will blossom as it should and be very beautiful as life unfolds and is beautiful. You are right on track! We love you, all of us".* After writing this down I felt very honored and comforted falling back to sleep like a baby.

The next message I received pertains to everyone on this earth plane to know and remember. *"It is not just as we take it this mystical world of ours life's field will yield as we make it, a harvest of thorns or flowers."* This very inspiring message is for every human being to know we can make our lives *a rose garden or a thorn garden,* easy or tough, depending on our thoughts and deeds which are created by each person. If we think *"poor me"* and *"why me"* all the time, that's what we will get in life and those lives never change. It is the same as putting your order out into the Universe each day with your negative thoughts, and guess what, the Universe *will* fill your order according to how one thinks. *"Thoughts are things"* and anyone can change their life to a positive one with using positive thoughts. This change may take time but as you keep trying it will finally begin to get better, it is hard work. This reminder was given in a sweet way to pass on to others that can lead one to finding the way, the truth, and the light, by putting one on track with harmony, changing one's life for the better there is always hope with faith.

Life Is Sweet, It Really Is

During a late drive home in October I saw four familiar objects in the sky with flashing lights moving in all directions, they seemed to be putting on a *light show* for me. I pulled over to stop awhile intently watching them and before I knew it 45 minutes had passed! There was no doubt the formations were something a plane could never do! Two of the middle UFO's would pass one another, one sideways in a flash of lightning extremely close to one another and the speed they moved with was unaccounted for in words. I could not measure their distance, but I know what I saw. They had maneuvers that were unbelievable, I didn't want to leave but eventually I went on home noticing they were still moving around in the sky. Looking up once more I could see they had followed me, until I arrived home. This was not uncommon, in fact, I felt very comforted it was such a good feeling. I loved it when they watched over us like this, we continued to see more of them as the days passed then a new message appeared from the ETs and Edgar.

Incoming; life is sweet enjoy the aroma I am near. Yes, the sight was a craft; we let you look through a black hole. Been helping David sending our love through as what his sister saw as the Christ light in David's eyes, he is very wise. This soul will now thrive as yours will also Ann. You carry a lot of weight. Talk to your son as you have many lifetimes before. He loves you so as you do him. Bid your time and love all, Signed by All.

Beneath their message *Signed by all* was written in Universal script with ET symbols. This message was important about my son and how they help him, so he continues to get better and thrive, and how our souls relate keeping one another strong with our devoted love for one another. One thing I planned to do was talk with my son more about his sickness, I knew at times he held back on how he really felt; and we have always shared everything. He would begin to joke with me when I became serious, so it was difficult to talk to him of illness, so I hardly ever did. He would tell me, "we stay in good humor and positive, so he didn't like to talk about his illness." I can't for say how much this message meant they know us in every possible way, and I knew why his sister could see the *Christ Light* in David's eyes as others have. When I had hidden my worry of him in his sickness, I knew he could detect it as I could with him, and then he would smile and gently tell me, *"Oh mom. You worry too much"* then he would laugh which was contagious and I would laugh and no more was said; we were completely positive working together. I worried myself about him until the other side would tell me what I needed to hear, this would calm me and give me extra strength. My son and I have shared lives together throughout every incarnation; therefore, we know one another's thoughts and feelings, bring a part of one another it has been this way forever from our beginning.

215

Thy Father in Heaven, All Beings are All One

Beautiful fall arrived and with it another very important message from Edgar: *"My beloved, you are waiting be patient all will come together soon and make sense, and then all answers will come! Please be advised that you are a special soul with many gifts bestowed upon you. When you get pressured just call for all of us and we will be there to regenerate you. The Father loves you dearly. That should give you great peace in itself lovingly always, E. C."*

How much more could one ask for in times of sadness with such powerful and beautiful messages! Love is everywhere around us, and everyone, the greatest love of all, this divine message lifted my spirit and soul immediately! We would forever be able to call for them with their amazing heavenly help and advice to stay on course, they knew when we needed to hear their words in this darkened world. They know how difficult it is, and how passionate our choice was in choosing to reincarnate back to this planet.

This precious message was beautiful; I felt I could do anything I needed to in order to finish out the promise. David and I never felt alone with the *Christ Light Beings* and their guidance. Some of the extra pressure in our lives was knowing to keep our *"connection with the ETs secret"*, this was not quite as hard to do anymore, but it was still something we were too kept to ourselves. We knew someday millions of others will know the truth of ET and human connections being one. The extraordinary gifts the ET teachers supply us with is their *knowledge of truth.*

Apparently, there are thousands, maybe millions on earth that are living and surviving as we do, and the ETs are experiencing their own *"revelation"*, way beyond our scope. I know there are other circles/networks of people the world over who are having contact with different species, and I have been told we are sometimes called *"Ambassadors"* for the ETs. This is how my son and I both feel because of experiencing a *daily living with them, we are of them.* We can speak for these Universal positive species along with *The Great Council* of *Christ Light Beings* who we interact with and who school us, in this way we are sometimes called *this term* for them because we are their voice! We are here to speak their messages from many other worlds, dimensions, star systems, galaxies and more, which is our honor! This gift has been bestowed upon us as their *universal brother and sister* and loved ones for others who are here on this Earth from other universal places, they want people to understand we are all connected!!

Some people have heard about negative experiences and may have read numerous stories about aliens and abductions, and how some of these people have experienced horrible and terrifying ordeals with them. To us, there are different ways for *abductions* to happen and the worst is done by negative warring Aliens as mentioned before. The second way called an abduction may be with that person not remembering *their own agreement* they made from another time before birth, so when this happens it is NOT for negative reasons. But to them it must be horrible, and in most of the cases these abductions are done to *monitor* the person while they are on earth in order to learn their ways and emotions to understand humans better. If the person remembers the agreement or not, it could still be absolutely horrifying to many.

Some of us here on Earth such as my son and I, are called *Hybrids* we are a part of other worlds, and we have an agenda to help others and to teach of these things. The agreement one makes ahead of time to go with certain beings may be erased from their memory, this is done for their own protection and wellbeing until it is the right time to remembering it. I only know firsthand about the agreement we made with our Universal family before birth, I cannot speak for anyone else. The ETs monitor us letting us remember only some things at a time they call *portions,* which was the best way to begin remembering *who and what we are, and we belong to them.*

The benevolent Beings we are from are good, positive, superior and highly Intelligent on a very high spiritual level of the *Christ Light,* such as those who also school and work with us. They are right below the *Creator/God* existing on a very high plane full of universal knowledge, much we do not yet understand, and they also learn from us. They are trying to help humankind and Mother Earth, but unfortunately fear captures many people when they experience travel with them or when they see them, which leave some terrified, I can understand this. Those who have given permission most times do not remember it. In other words, there is a benevolent and malevolent species to deal with throughout here and other worlds.

To be taken especially with negative species may leave a terrible scar on the physical, mental, emotional, and spiritual genetic make-up, the mind takes a beating on those who are dealing with this... There is a huge difference in the two words *Abduction* and *Visit*, to us, abduction may be by force, a visit is with permission.

Even though those who are taken by positive beings with their permission may still have great fear of *a next time,* the positive species of ETs may take samples of blood, hair, skin, bone, DNA, sperm, eggs, all kinds of things from a human but only with permission and never to harm them. They are helping create new cures, other positive highly intelligent Hybrids, and future scientific discoveries most would not understand yet, these others have agreed to do at some time and the memory then erased.

The ETs can easily pass their thoughts to some on earth such as, to a scientist's mind who will never know these are not his own and who would never think it isn't their own *brainchild* of discovery! To my knowledge neither of us have ever been hurt or had any physical exams which have left us afraid or harmed. What we did know, everything the ETs have done with us was agreed on and has been to help mankind there was nothing by force or any kind of painful tests and above all *never without* our consent. We are continually relearning worlds, universal languages, codes, past lives, other universal Beings, Stars Systems, Galaxies, Planets, worm holes of travel, and how to help them as they in turn teach us relearn what we once knew *"secrets of the universe!* It is a long list they have for us and being a part of them is another of the *important teachings*.

Another amazing thing is being able to see our loved ones and others after their physical deaths on earth since we both were children. What we also volunteered for was to help create new techniques of energy healing in the human world and to teach it. This is another reason we came back to incarnate together be with our loved ones once again as family.

My son and I were healed in separate times in different years for certain reasons most importantly when we both had been DOA and various NDE experiences. This is when the *"Christ Light ETs and Angel Beings"* would come to help us. My amazing experience was when I died in a car accident at 16 when we were hit head on at a fast speed by two intoxicated drivers. There was once a question in my mind about that experience, *"Did I return back to here as a Walk-In?"* No, I did not, although I died in the wreck for such a long period of time I should not be here in anyway or completely brain dead, but I was repaired on the other side by the ETs and sent back to teach, have my children, and experience this earth life for my mission.

There are some people who make an exchange when they die an earthly death because they have chosen an agreement ahead with another *mind-soul* on the other side. This means, they may choose to trade places with one another, the soul-mind one will return in their place called a *"Walk-In"* for the one who retreats into the other side which I will explain more about later. In other words, the soul/spirit trades places.

The definition of a "Walk-In" as best I can describe is an exchange of mind and soul. People who have lost the will to live through all kind of circumstances, an illness, mourning, a sudden death, being sickly, or who finds life too hard for them on Earth may want to be released from here. During a certain time *if they* made an agreement in their mind with a soul- mind from the *Etheric* world to use their body until it wears out, which is done ahead of time, there may be a trade. The earthling's soul-mind slips out into the Etheric world when the agreed upon time comes, and the other soul-mind slips in their body and there it will finish out the immediate karma of its existence. In other words, they trade places and the exchange has then been made. The Walk-In, the new soul-mind will have a different personality which is its own and will probably be noticed by those who knew the old personality of the one who vacated its body and left to go back. Even though, an illness and/or with certain accidents there can sometimes be a change to one's own personality from the trauma with no exchange and the personality may change due to those circumstances this is not an exchange.

The new soul-mind person who made a trade *will seem different* to those who knew the original person although, they will never know why. The new soul-mind will stay with the exchanged body on earth until it wears out. I feel those who wish they could pass who have no communication anymore, perhaps living on breathing machines and so on, and wants to escape their ravished body by not wanting to live this way are perhaps some who trade. Most people may not realize this can happen and there is no proof of this except through hypnosis…

We Are All Aliens

In some fashion everyone being related to one another and a part of one another, is connected. I'm sure many people right now who are reading this book will be shocked, even disgusted, at the idea of what I am saying, but just remember before you judge we are told not to judge one another. There are many ET/Alien intelligences that appear on earth and have for centuries who mingle and walk amongst us resembling humans who live an earthly life with us!! Can I prove this, not any more than you can see the air we breathe, but I know many of them are here. Some beings do this to learn and study our way of life here and return when it is time to leave back to the Cosmos with the information they have.

The early fall was busy for us with amazing messages and travel with the beings and soon it was time for a new message: *"Greetings, be patient the time is drawing near. We all love you and are here for you."* I felt a solid comfort reading their words coming at the right time, this was a difficult time period we were having. This gave us a boost to know we are always surrounded in total love from our Universal family, this feels the same as getting a *big hug* from your loved one. Living between the paranormal, spiritual, and ET worlds plus earth life I sometimes ran low on energy and needed to rest more and the same for my son, but we loved our adventures!

It was close to Halloween which was a serious time of the year for us, we could feel the negative energy getting stronger in the world, I wondered if this affected the Beings who come to visit us, was it hard for them to stay longer in this dark earth? But after thinking this strange thought I knew they take extra good care of themselves being a superior heavenly race! The very same night of the message on patience I discovered another one placed in my notebook, it read: *"Extraterrestrial, watch the sky we are near. Tell David we will not take him without permission! There will be a grand occurrence tonight in the sky – 8 pm and later. Take the camera and see! Yes, you all are a grand part of this vast universe. You shall see much tonight!"* We were super excited and pumped up, when I told David of the message; he was very cheerful as always and said, *"it won't be long now to see what happens!"*

There must have been a certain reason the ETs wanted to confirm this message to David about having his permission, it seemed very important for them to have ours on any trips with them! So far, they have our permission to go with them and the many times before.

I had a dragging feeling as if I was losing energy the closer it came to Halloween. This is a night when earth energy is at its highest, loaded with bad negative vibrations, it is the strongest time of the year for the *"worst of the worst!"* These kind of negative emotions and vibrations are wanting to latch onto malevolent people who practice *"black magic"*. They are easy to maneuver around then and many of them would be busy collecting together in secret meeting places for what they consider *"Devil worship"* or worse! My son and I are so sensitive to this we can feel bad energy quite strongly even from a distance it is not a good feeling, and we were on alert!

Here is an example; on the night before last Halloween, we were traveling home in the car on a lonely stretch of road which is in a remote area. As I drove, I suddenly could hear gruesome chanting with terrible vibrations coming from someplace in the woods back from the road we were on! Even though we are protected, I couldn't get out of there fast enough! Being clairvoyant is sometimes a little nerve racking! The next night we were out late scanning the skies watching for our ET friends, I knew we couldn't stay out long due to my son's health, especially with the nights getting colder and being outside. Finally, we gave up and returned inside something changed.

Close to Halloween I found an ETs message at 9:30 pm, *"Try again, tonight too cloudy. Tomorrow night"*. The next night we felt the ETs close around us and the stars were out in their magnificent glory! The night was clear I could easily see one UFO and took pictures then thanked them and said, *"I hope we got you on film"*, this made me remember I desperately needed to invest in a good camera! Shortly after taking the pictures we were cold, tired, and decided to go inside, turning around to start into the house I noticed *the candles were turned on in every window of the house again*, the light was even on over the garage door, and the tower lights, how sweet!! This let us know the ETs were inside now or had been moments ago.

221

Early the next day David and I were eating lunch with a friend when suddenly my son's fork flew off the table by itself, the two of us laughed but our family friend Ted didn't, he looked concerned, so we shaped up in a hurry. Ted exclaimed, *"Didn't you see the fork flying in thin air, how could that happen!"* We sort of shrugged it off *to, "both of us have seen things move before, we didn't know!"*. Poor Ted looked puzzled with our answer as we changed the subject this movement of the fork was a warning it had a very negative meaning, "that we *would need to be extra careful"*. This was some bad energy, but the ETs were protecting us, since Halloween was not completely over yet! Soon another example of strange phenomenon happened in our local hardware store when I sat a heavy bag of drywall mix on the counter to pay the clerk. While I was getting my money out the heavy bag went up in the air about a foot in front of the cashier then came down on the floor in front of her feet with a crash! NO ONE had touched it; the cashier was so rattled she yelled, *"How could that happen!"* I began shaking my head saying, *"I don't know"* the bag weighed at least 5 lbs.! *The negative force was coming on strong.* There have been so many things done over time I can't explain them, and our best defense is to pretend to others we don't know. We know when something negative is trying to frighten us and this kind of energy can sometimes give off the most putrid odor, and then we get to work to get rid of it we would be busy!

Halloween night arrived David had been busy all day getting the traditional party together for our family with good food and treats. This was his very own fun thing to do! That evening I was too busy to think of much else but after the party was over and everyone had left, we both were exhausted. David went to bed and I finally turned in after 11 pm and I was relaxing a few minutes before sleep remembering to check for a message in my notebook. There it was: *"Greetings, we gladly take you and your male offspring on a long voyage next full moon"*. How exciting!

The next day eating breakfast we were chattering away to one another about our next trip, this one was going to be with a different group of Beings that we were not as familiar with but knew to be *"Christ Light Beings"*. This is probably why the *permission* thing had come up a few days ago with these being a new species who we knew were positive and worked alongside the ETs' we were familiar with. The word *"offspring"* was one key clue that let us know we would be meeting different ones, since this was a newer term for my son; we looked forward to the next full moon. I must admit we both laughed about him being called the *offspring* and I had fun occasionally, I would call David my *offspring,* which gave us a good laugh. For now, we would be patient the time would be here before we knew it, we had nothing to be concerned about. This group of ETs was very spiritual the same as other groups of Christ Light Beings, we were completely safe and gave our permission...

Many days when I would be busy working in my home, I would suddenly know to stop everything, sit down, and listen to the voice of a deceased loved one, an ET spiritual teacher or guide. This was one of those days when words began to flow to me as I wrote them down, *"It is not this way, nor that way it is how you make it! No challenges come greater than this year of changes and you are right on track! There are the baby step's one has to get through first."* This was from our teacher Edgar his messages were always helpful to us and a good reminder of our work three days a week and we really appreciated his advice. It is our *baby steps* in life which prepares us for future events in our lives and no one can rush them. Our spiritual family is always here for us, they know our feelings and our thoughts better than we do. You see, this message arrived when one of our dear friends had just passed over exactly on my *mother's date of passing* so it came at a good time for lifting our spirits. We had long passed being apprehensive about being in touch with different Beings we were not afraid to face unknown journeys by staying open and accepting of what came to us from these benevolent beings and learning was exciting...

If one stays afraid of everything fear puts up a block, a protection, for when something is too terrifying to face or when one needs to act, it serves as an asset to one. It can help in two different ways depending on what is happening at the time and since we both are open with a positive desire to have the experiences we have; something negative has no place in our lives but sometimes slips through. This has expanded our higher consciousness, and learning of many consciousness through our experiences, imprinting them into our mind to what is happening. I may never remember all the trips and experiences consciously but at the same time I know without a doubt it is happening and stored in my deep subconsciousness, exploring the many dimensions of consciousnesses… Try to remember that everything has a purpose in one's life, even the negative things help us in many ways to learn, and are vital to growth. And sometimes it is a lesson not only for us but someone close around us. Every experience is unlimited and important to learning though our lives. Living in many worlds is what we are doing, by discovering and remembering who and what we are as a soul/spirit.

When I returned home one day upon entering the house, I had that kind feeling, *a knowing,* the ETs had been here we know when they have made a visit. I hurried to check any movement of items or messages left in the house, especially my notebook, and sure enough they had left one for us what excitement I felt! Since we have an energy body and can change into anything by changing molecules, maybe they were still here in the house watching since we felt they were right beside us! I began to read our new message: *"Will return Dec. 23rd to resume mission. That is all for now."* It would be awhile before they come back, and I felt sure this was from our *newer Alien ET contacts.* The note was signed in symbols of their language we would study trying to figure them out, if we could. I guessed the 23rd was the next full moon, or maybe they changed the date to come for some other reason with a certain mission they had in mind for us? Then things changed in a good way and we knew the ETs played a huge part arranging it, I recalled my son laughing, he knew!

A Team of UFO Investigators Would Come Now

My son and I were interested in finding others who had experiences like what we were having which didn't take long. A short time later we attended a Psychic Fair not far from where we lived in the city. We were seeking answers and other people of *Liked Minds* to share our unusual UFO experiences with and who have had their own experiences. We were led to a woman called *"Owl-woman"* and once introduced we began sharing some experiences with her. This person listened with great interest and indicated that our experiences needed her friend's expertise. She directed us to a person named Joe Palermo and found that his experiences included numerous UFO sightings being an official investigator of such experiences for the Missouri Chapter of the MUFON Network. Joe suggested an onsite investigation with our permission of whomever or whatever we were in contact with.

He called me the next day around 11:30 am, he wanted me to ask, *"the ET's permission for him and the team to come to my home to investigate and talk more of our UFO experiences"* then he asked, *"are you in contact with them and do you think they can hear you?"* *"Oh yes, I know they can!"* I responded, after the call with Mr. Palermo I contacted the ETs telepathically asking their permission for the team to come here.

It didn't take long to get my answer back, on the same day at 6 pm that evening I found my small pyramid figure and crystal ball had been moved from the top of a table and placed at the top of the staircase landing lying on the carpeted floor. Both items were placed about two feet apart as if this was a clue to a *"Universal map"* for me, and with this display was a large printed word in the carpet YES! Here was the answer, they were all welcome! The word looked as if it was engraved into the carpet with an arrow drawn on each side of it, this was a big *OK* for the team to come; they had the ETs permission! I left everything just as we had found it so the UFO group could inspect it when they arrived, then videoed and took pictures as I always do to document what they had done!

I immediately made a call to Joe Palermo and explained what had happened and I had his answer. I knew the ET's had set this up because they wanted this group to come for special reasons I will explain later. I thought it strange this entire meeting was set up on a loved one's passing over date of three years earlier, and during this same night I found myself with the ETs. I remember I was being briefed about another *"solar system"* and told *"to remember it is in the four directions, and to open my mind fully that there are secrets from long ago and the group who is coming will be shocked."*

Then I noticed a bright light was shining over me as they continued *"the North Star favors the point which one starts watching to form patterns. Look to the east and north for the patterns. He will not find the system we told you about in your system of stars and planets for it is only here. We gladly explain more later when changes occur tell his people we are here, and we are many. We will communicate through you and your male offspring son only. The galaxies are coming together into a new dimension of learning a shift will occur soon with no danger to anyone or anything merely a shift. Yes, we communicate well with the two of you keep this private for the time being. We understand your words and language know we only come to help and learn also. The vaccine is nearly ready now the two of you know us well and are beginning to remember. Don't be afraid of the voyage for it is only a voyage that is long in our time. You and offspring son will only be gone short moments in your time we have much to show you, you are like pioneers to your world. A large quantity of information is yours to pass. Yes, we will leave a confirmation for you. You are a part of us as you know. You will see us soon your work here is made of portions, to look, learn, and receive. Incoming will increase. Enjoy your earth life, be happy, we can still work together to help each other, Extraterrestrial's."*

WOW! This was AMAZING! Time seemed to stand still as if it was nothing when we were on the Craft that night and the next thing, I knew I was back at home in my bed finishing writing down the above message. I noticed the time was 4:30 am, the bright lights were gone, and my room was extremely dark, yet I was writing the words exactly as given as I often do in the darkness when an experience has ended...

The Group from MUFON Arrives

After coordinating everyone's schedule and finding a mutually free time, Joe Palermo, Owl-woman, Joe's Reiki Master Chris Schiebe, and Joe's researcher Bob Buck planned the trip to my home in Illinois. Wasting no time everything was in motion and it was the day Joe Palermo, the MUFON investigator and the team was coming to visit us from a nearby city. When they arrived, I welcomed them inside where we made ourselves comfortable then they began to tell us of the interesting psychic observations on the way to my home in a certain area they had traveled through where there was a strong sense of the existence of what, in ufology terms, are called *Reptilians*. These are said, to be a race of humanoid aliens with features *Reptilian* in nature. In most reports, these beings are considered hostile towards humans. This unexpected information confirmed what my son and I had experienced one night traveling the same road through this same area.

After this, I showed the investigative team the signs the ETs had left for them upstairs on the staircase landing. They examined the large YES! in the carpet with my small pyramid and crystal ball nearby; both were placed to look as planets somewhere out in space, the ETs had made their permission clear. To start things off I showed them some of the pictures I had taken and a couple of videos of UFO's I had filmed over my home, and part of another video of strange beings WAVING back at me as I recorded them. Mr. Palermo was really surprised at the ETs big YES! made in the carpet and the video of the beings! After talking for a while, we took a break for lunch; all of us left at the same time, ate together, and returned at the same time. No one had been in the house while we were out (no one human that is) but when we walked into the family room to begin more questions every one of us experienced a shock! *EVERYTHING* the ETs had placed on the landing on the second-floor upstairs had been moved to downstairs (the pyramid and crystal ball) to the middle of the floor in front of the TV cabinet in the family room in the same order. We were all excited to say the least I didn't know what the ETs had planned to do, so my son and I were stunned as well!

The camera man managed to start his camera after a few moments of getting himself calmed down in order to document everything the ETs had done. The team told me, *"They had never had anything happen like this before!"* When they were ready Joe Palermo asked me, if I would sit on one side of the room and the other psychic he brought on the other, so we each could do automatic writing with any answers we received from his questions. When we both were ready, he began asking the same questions to both of us to see what we each received. He wanted to compare our answers of what we received from the ETs. I began my contact with the ETs knowing they were ready and waiting for me to write their answers down. They wanted this to happen to prove they exist and work with us.

The first question asked was, *"where was the well outside?"* I wrote where it was with the information I received from the ETs. I had always suspected one may have been on the property even though I was not sure there had ever been, but the ETs told me a well had been there long ago! Joe asked several questions and the ETs made it very clear they would ONLY go through my son and me with any of their information! With that, I only wrote down what the ETs wanted me too, which was extremely clear and of great importance. The ETs gave me answers to questions Joe asked and when we were done, I had pages of information from them to relay back to him then my contact was broken with them. The information on the following page comes directly from the ETs, and this is what they wanted him to know word for word.

As explained in the story this is the reply, I found on the upstairs landing from the ETs allowing the investigators to come.

The North Quad Colony

North Quad Colony, you can call us "Nomadic" in the Neptune System. We Beings have been here many eons of time. We only come to help and learn as you do, we work together. Our intentions are to be of great service in the vast universe of Knowledge. We shall contact and instruct what we are here to do in time. The universe is vast and mighty in our work earthly changes can and will be made through simple changes; there is much work to be done. We will only come to this point in your time with these two contacts David and you. The Mother ship has not been here yet except in remote areas there are many who know us important information comes soon be prepared for this event. It is of a great awaking on a most positive level no harm to your people or your planet. The pyramid holds great secrets and great value you remember more as time goes by, remember when we showed you the chamber and the levels of Importance this remains hidden. You remember you hold the KEY we have only just begun. We understand your thoughts and words and soon you will remember ours we work together. They, the team must remain patient little by little more is revealed. That is the end of incoming for now. North Quad

This is where we found the pyramid and crystal ball after returning from lunch which had been moved from upstairs to downstairs.

229

Before they signed off, the ETs again mentioned the *KEY* I hold. After I read the above message to the team this broke our contact. The ETs had made it clear they would only work through David and I, so the other psychic did not get this message, it was only for me to get. The psychic who came with the team did a good and correct reading on the well and the house saying, *"that the house is only full of goodness with the Angels being around it and us."* I appreciated the ETs gave her this information about our home…

The team asked many questions about our experiences and visits with them which we gladly answered. They were quite shocked that the *"little Grays"* were so friendly because in their experiences they hear from others they only received negative feedback about them. Later we went into the kitchen to sit around the table where the team produced sketches of Alien beings for us to point out any we may be familiar with… we reinforced that the species of ETs we deal with are all *benevolent* instead of being aggressive or hurtful, which many are reported to be by others, again was a big surprise to them! We seemed to be crushing a theory that has existed over a long-time span of many years told by others about alien beings, but with our experiences this had never happened! I believe the team left in *"sort of shock"* from what they witnessed and experienced here that day. The ETs messages were for David and me to pass to them as I did, and afterwards on the same day the ETs were back and continued to tell me about the key, *"that I hold the key!"*

They have spoken to me through the many years about *this key* and supplied me with visions showing my son and me living in past Egyptian times which are in my second book *"The Story of David"*. I have written about the lives we both experienced living in ancient Egypt, they were very important! In the last one I hid some of the most important sacred treasures of all in the Great Pyramid that may be found one day, if it is meant to be, which has not been discovered yet… In this past life venture, we both lost our lives immediately afterwards in the Pyramid when the soldiers caught me along with my son. I barely had time to hide these Holy treasures for all time! We did not care if we died if we completed this sacred mission and our death was swift, but it was our honor!

I was soon in contact with the ETs to find out more information from them, and I was astounded with the information they gave me!

Extraterrestrial here, dear child of light, yes, we are many and called the Grays. We will come tonight you know us. Our race is a very civilized race of many people of our species. We have the knowledge to contact and move in the Universe at a very fast pace. Our journey in your time, which is parallel takes longer in our dimension, but only seems seconds in yours. Have no fear to go on the voyage with us; you shall be back in only moments of your earthly time. We Normadics, Grays, cannot live and survive with other races; we have tried before long ago. The North Quad to you would not be on a level for you to understand. Your North direction passes any galaxy Earth could know we have taken you both there many times as you see now in your mind's eye. (They were letting me see in this way as they talked). The City is quite large and vast, you see the ships, yes, and you do. The names only divide the species so we can be identified in your world. It's as Black, White, and Chinese and so on in your world. There are only two species to always be aware of, Reptile and Lizard ones. Tell Joe he will see us soon no harm will come to him, and we will be in school just observing him. You and male offspring know we only come in peace and love and learning you shall hear more tonight. Extraterrestrials

This to us is *priceless and valuable information,* what scientists and researchers wouldn't want to know this! The Extraterrestrials knowledge makes things clear that we are a *family* with them which even to us can sometimes seem unbelievable! And we feel happy knowing our truth. It is how we are living here as humans term things and use our words in this world that they try to understand. The ETs are letting us know, all Universal species can be defined in different ways, and different beings and most others are extremely limited in knowing how to talk of them with a correct name or title. They told us once, *"Their names for other species are similar as to how we have chosen different names on earth for our different races and nations. But we are all one everywhere!"*

We Meet Again

Years later we would meet Joe Palermo once more at a Missouri MUFON meeting in St. Charles, Missouri. We accompanied our friend who was offering to do aura photos for people at the meeting.

I was delighted to see Joe again, and during the meeting I was afforded the opportunity to speak on some of our experiences. Joe spoke up endorsing me to speak and briefly explained how he and his associates made an onsite investigation and the success of a specific experiment regarding what is called *"automatic"* writing that Owl-woman and himself conducted with me that had positive results and of the experiences that occurred.

While there, we planned to listen to the attendees who would be sharing their experiences of UFO's. I will always recall an older Minister Reverend John Schroder and his wife who spoke freely of their experiences, we least expected hearing anything like this from a minister. I doubted this was common to have this couple attend to speak, and I admired them coming forward to share their stories! Attending the meeting were all kind of people from all walks of life that evening with a wide variety of different occupations, which made us feel relaxed and welcome. They came to share their own experiences and to ask any questions they had on their mind. When my turn had come I briefly shared a small amount of our encounters with the ETs and that my son and I were having very positive experiences, then I briefly explained how the ETs were our teachers and family along with the little Grays who assist them which seemed extremely unusual to everyone there. It was a very nice evening to be able to share together.

CHAPTER 12
Earth and Moon Child

It was a full moon and a different species of ET/Aliens had invited us to go with them on a long voyage for a learning experience. We made an agreement with them to be back home by morning and to do nothing that is not agreed upon. The next day I awoke back in my bed as usual feeling good, then I jumped up remembering I had a dear friend who was coming to visit. During our visit I felt our ET friends had been here or were here, so I excused myself for a moment not saying why. I went to check for a message noticing the time was 2:10 pm. There was a new message waiting for me in my notebook: *"Will return December 3-4 also to resume mission. That is all for now."* Their message was signed with *"a pyramid drawn and beside it some ET symbols"* which were in a different universal script for me to try to figure out. After company left David told me they had also been here in the night arranging a joke for him by using his alien rock he knew this was done as a human type of joke to make him laugh. They have discovered our jokes by watching how humans react with emotions... they study our emotions to learn.

Our next experience was on a trip with them through the same night of the 3rd and 4th of December when they returned. The first thing I recalled I was looking down at my feet at the floor in the UFO to see what I was standing on. It felt strange to me, it was a *grid* of some sort, a familiar looking one that I have seen before we are able to walk on in the ships. The grid looked like a steel type of material we use on earth, other than that I had no idea what it is made of. Before taking a step, I noticed there were other life-forms present standing close to us I have no specific name for, they seemed to be a new group of Beings I had not experienced before. My next memory was when we were permitted to hold and examine a long narrow piece of an unknown object of a silver/black color like a piece of metal, but it wasn't, it had no weight to it whatsoever! The Aliens wanted us to know what the piece was for, but at this time I am not permitted to give out the information, so our memories were partially erased. I know they implant information often into our brain stem for later they tell us this often.

233

This species of beings was completely focused on checking us out as we each spoke telepathically with them. We felt safe with them and had a clear understanding when they told us, *"My son and I were both an experiment"*. This conversation was telepathically, but it was different hearing it in this way from these beings. I wish I had more memory of what was being processed that night, but I don't, my only thought was I wanted to bring something back with us for *proof*! I realized exactly what was going on at the time and my thoughts were pleading with them, *"Please, let me bring something back with us, but the next thing I knew I was waking up in my bed.".* I searched the house and found nothing I was a little disappointed but hoped maybe the next time we could bring something back.

At 10 am the next day I did have a confirmation from the ETs to let me know they had positively been here and if I had had any doubt of this David's little rock with the alien face was on my bed pillow! This was definite proof, then memories came rushing back to me of seeing an Alien being by my bathroom door. This could have been when I returned, but I wasn't sure if it was before or after the trip last night. Then I heard an ET telepathically, *"I would be going again that much more information would continue to come to us"* then he was gone! I also came across another message laying between two pages of my notebook the ET had left for me. *"Remember our journey in time Earth and Moon child, returning soon. It comes in time. Let it pass."* I understood the meaning of the message perfectly which means, *that we will remember our journeys with them in time and not to be concerned of what it means let it go for now."* This species of beings calls us *"earth and moonchild"* as we are to them, and they would be returning for us soon.

We experienced many more UFO sightings in the next few days, one I was with a friend of mine while we were in my car, so I pulled over to show her the UFO. The ETs put on what I call quite a *light show* for us darting about up and down, back and forth, moving at tremendous speeds and stopping in midair, she was shocked! If anyone is even thinking it may have been our government with new planes of some sort I simply refuse to think so. Why would they be doing this repeatedly for years and years over a small farm town and only over my home, plus they would sometimes do this staying for an hour or more, for what reason? They often reminded us, *"They have a way for others to not see them*" and they told us long ago about a special shield they have, I knew this had to be true when they were above us with people and traffic going by constantly. I was happy the ETs let my friend see their UFO's so it was meant to be; because little did, I know I would soon see her on a craft with us! This was their reason for letting her see them.

After this experience when I arrived home, I found a new message full of information. "*Greetings my beloved child we have waited long to begin anew. Much was to be done on both sides. We have been very busy! Yes, the Dr. is in, and your healing will be completed by December 25th, fully. You are feeling much better now.*" What wonderful news I thought and thanked them.

"*The Doctor is in*" refers to our beloved teacher *Edgar Cayce!* See how we are all related and working together? I can't tell you how happy I was to get started again with our universal family even though my beloved earth family knew nothing yet of our journeys. We were still on hold until we could fill them in one day. I thanked the beings and Edgar for the healing they did with their caring I was feeling good, they are remarkable! The quote, "The Doctor is in" was in my A.R.E. magazine coming in my mail. Leafing through the pages at the very top of one page was a small outlined box and inside of it was printed *"The Doctor is in!"* How amazing! Thank you, dear Edgar and ETs!

Remember Our Journey and the Kundalni

Before we knew it, we were experiencing another new beginning as our life unfolded in our space travels. The first memory I had was seeing all kinds of *spirals and balls of light* among huge leaves and thick foliage, so I knew immediately we were with them. We seemed to be in a familiar place, and I wondered if this foliage was everywhere around David and I for some reason we had been transported on a UFO to this place where perhaps some of our ET friends lived or hid from humans on their trips to earth. We were moving through this dense area when a Being of high intelligence appeared right in front of me reminding us, "*we were well acquainted with the Kundalni, to meditate, be open, and ask our Angel for answers, and to know that the power is within us and that all we desire shall be ours, soon Zorba comes.*" This was a strange and an amazingly beautiful message at the same time, we were certainly familiar with the Kundalni since we work with such energy in healing work, it is very important and powerful in the body and resides in every human person and one needs to understand how powerful it is and not mess with it without the knowledge!

The Kundalni lies at the base of the spine and raises slowly, the word means *"to coil, to spiral"*, which is a field of supreme intelligence, a cosmic, invisible energy vital to life! As a man or a woman begins to evolve in their incarnation it moves slowly upward and is directed by the *"soul mind"*. This powerful energy works up to the Crown Chakra to unite with the Silver cord, then one will ascend to the higher realms to finish their evolutionary cycle. *More may be researched in the Encyclopedic Psychic Dictionary by June G. Blitzer, PHD.*

This Being of intelligence had stopped its communication to us now and to my *horror* I began to see huge snakes around us which luckily, I was aware represented the *Kundalni*. This is only a symbolic symbol so there was no harm in what we were shown or to be frightened of. We are the students, and this was an important lesson to always remember one must be very careful and know what they are doing to work with such a strong energy, after this experience I suddenly found myself back at home in my bed and at once I fell into a deep sleep after I recorded everything.

The Number 3 and the Revelation of
the Myth

When I woke the next day, I found three pennies on the top of my trunk at the foot of my bed. This was an important clue for me another day of learning was about to begin with the number 3. Numbers are *extremely important* in our lives they can tell one about the *choices* and other *strengths* we can use; and are important tools each one needs during our life path. The number 3 represents *"great strength and transformation";* and these examples were left for me to study and teach as good examples of three.

Starting examples of threes are on the next page which I believe will make sense to you when you read them.

Edgar Cayce, David, and me.
Jesus ministry lasted three years
The Father, Son, and Holy Ghost
The Holy Trinity
Fire, Air and Water
Body, Mind, and Soul
Our Three Spiritual Centers
Third sign of the Zodiac
The three Pyramids

And importantly groups of three, messages in a row, things I study in books and many other groups of three. Numbers are important in every life; these are only a very few examples of them. The next night I was awakened *three* separate times, I had experienced being in a spaceship for the study of 3's and why they are in groups! I was not quite sure what this exactly meant but I had an idea and for some time after this I found words printed in groups of threes' that were part of a mystery in some way for me to figure out. As you can see, the number 3 is an amazing number to learn by and then it hit me with their lessons for the three of us, *David, R. L. and me,* and we are called *TRI* by those in the universes!! I know it seems strange with how we are taught at times, but it is also clever and amazing in how our universal information is sometimes given such as learning the important number 3, and to know we are in a state *of transformation* numbers are so important!

The following day I found Edgar's small book *"Think on These Things"* open to page 102-103 lying on my bed for me to study. My two white doves were facing one another sitting on the book's center spine to hold it open to a certain chapter *"The Source, the Pattern, and the Power."* Again, there was the number 3 this was leading up to those lessons and these pages are what I was to read in the small book, it was important! We became schooled in the 3's and many other numbers such as 2, 5, 7, 8, 11, 12,20, 21, 22, and 33, as time passed. When our lessons began with number 5, I found them everywhere they were in groups and written on my notebook, I was even seeing 5 in the night, and visions of 5 on my white closet door! My door was used as a chalk board of sorts, and the numbers often appeared in front of me in midair! Numbers pop up in our lives and have great meaning, they are significant, and some people choose their lucky numbers when trying to win something. We all have certain numbers we associate with in our life, check your SS, Driver's License, Address, phone numbers, and numerous places.

New messages from the beings were pouring in coming from everywhere, you cannot imagine the excitement working together in other worlds and many other dimensions. Before we knew it *"old man winter"* was here so we settled in on the cold days, and on many of those we had were with my son's hospital stays, otherwise we were at home learning things that others could never imagine! Our minds were working on numbers, quotations, new ET symbols, planets, new Beings, astral travel, worm holes, and more. During these times this next message came by way of the computer, "Incoming: *I am near. Yes, the sight was of a craft we let you and your son look through a black hole. We have been helping to send our love through what others see as the Christ in David eyes he is very wise. This soul will now thrive as yours will also, you carry a lot of weight talk to your son as you have many lifetimes before he loves you so as you do him."* This came from the ET Christ Light Beings and Edgar *and w*e received this similar message once before and it was wonderful to see it again!

You see, I was not comfortable bringing up his illness very much because we kept a 100% positiveness about it and his phenomenal healings. David preferred to always be positive as I did, he did not like to talk of it, we both didn't want to talk about it much other than going to appointments at his doctor's office. We both thought positively about his illness, so we didn't discuss it when things were bad for him except in a positive way. We believed 100 % he would be healed each time, as he was, no matter how severe we knew the universal healers would help him be well even when we were told different that he would not live out the day! David knew I was happy to hear anything he had to say and there was nothing we couldn't talk of but perhaps we needed to talk and share more of what he was feeling, but he would only smile and tell me *I worried to much if I tried.* We were very confident he would be here for some time yet; this was in my daily and nightly prayers "to help keep him well"! We talked telepathically much of the time such as, when he was critical and in the IC Unit at the hospital, we always communicated in this way as my mother did with us when her voice was gone. He may have wanted to tell me more about things in his mind when his time came and what he wanted done afterwards, which we did shortly before he left us, which was unbearable to my heart and his, *I was proud he did things his way*, that was all that mattered… we did it right for us!

A continued message arrived with serious information: *"The Revelation of the Myth is here, the time is here, the four corners of the earth they will meet."* Immediately after this message another one appeared: *"Watch the sky, we are near there are many of us. We will not take him without permission, Extraterrestrial's."* We understood each different group of species needs our permission before we went with them, and we both gave permission to each positive species. They were so good about asking for it every time. Messages were zooming in to prepare us for *"a big journey"* to go with them. The next incoming message told us, *"we know our part in this journey and to be ready to go with them"*.

"Greetings: The Linear Lines will be crossing on the earth day 12 and earth month 12 we are getting prepared and we need you both to be prepared as well. It will be a cosmic wonder for certain fellow BELIEVERS to see… try to meditate as often as possible, you will reach the higher vibrations necessary to reach the necessary goal…. translation in progress, journey well my friends." This was so exciting to us; we wondered what we might see in this *Cosmic Wonder!* The ETs knew we would accompany them on these travels they know our heart and soul inside out, and our hunger to learn and be taught by them to remember what we once knew, and we wanted to experience this great event! We were running on extra energy and adrenalin waiting for this next journey to happen and it came quickly! This next message summed up another group of the number 3 we had been told about with 3 more messages.

New message: *"Greetings, a great event will occur in the evening sky in the earth atmosphere. A time will be relayed per your request as soon as possible, please continue your meditation and rest as needed for the physical will change for the journey that same evening. You will remember the journey if needed, please be patient as your human emotions try to take over what they do not*

239

understand yet. You will understand one day very soon.... We are teaching as you are the studious student."

Wow! We had everything to look forward to and I felt this was happening to help David and I get through his illness by living in the other worlds which we loved. The ETs of Christ Light Beings filled his world of illness with miracles and healings, and me with such courage and love I cannot define! We had other worlds before us day and night which people did not believe in, and our supreme universal teachers!

Appearing some hours later with more news was a new message from the ETs. *"We received an error in our time lapse, in the Linear Ley Line, The Big Event will be postponed the 21st ˉ 24th day in December of earth year 2000- Earth time 2 am."* We were feeling disappointment, but we knew the ETs needed to set up another time something was not ready... Time passed, we continued with them on other voyages learning and traveling with them and before long the ETs let us know more joyous news, they had made us a part of what was happening, our blood was used again! They said, *"A new treatment for humans to be unveiled soon, using peoples own genetic materials to make an effective vaccine in terms fighting their tumor cells with their own healthy cell tissues. Vaccine is already being constructed and ready to give to test patients, more to follow today."*
... This was another reason our blood was used!! One can plainly see the ETs are trying to help Earth people, not kill them!!

A Heavenly Being of Light Brings
a Beautiful Message

The Heavenly voice said: *"Come now and sit beside me for I shall show you the way I am life everlasting. In his namesake I shall follow thee forever. Be thine glad forever in thine heart we travel together to help one another for thine is the Kingdom forever and ever. Know you have did well your heart is in the right place and you have taken my hand and wanted to do this work I intended for your growth upon this earth plane for many years. You are on a new level of consciousness. Bless you child."*

After I read this, I became very emotional, heartfelt, and stunned as I read this message over and over with feelings of awe and wonder! I had not completely discovered inside of myself the greatest love and joy I cannot begin to explain!!! I questioned myself repeatedly *"is this real that we are worthy, is this for us?"* I became alert then to my surroundings and promised we would continue to do our very best for the blessed Creator, this Infinite Supreme Intelligence we call God, and for the rest of our life to do the right things to our best!!! We will stand our ground against the bad and evil that enjoys harm and discord to others we pledge to help and protect those we could, our happiness was uncontrollable, we were completely bewildered and questioned ourselves *"can we fulfill all we have promised to do?"* One thing clear to us was we both would use our strength and human power to finish out life in this way with Divine guidance! Earth is only a prelude to a never-ending life and the treasures are the spiritual learning's we have been taught!

This reminded me of something which occurred years later when I was drawn by the other side to visit a few churches by offering my help. I was led by the beings from the other side to set up a group meeting for the bereaved these loved ones need a place to go and join others who understood their pain after the loss of a loved one. To my surprise I found that most churches I went to except only one in another town, did not have a program for this! Some had Bingo, Sewing, Bible classes, and so on, but none for the grieving how can this be I wondered! One church person explained; their minister sometimes spoke briefly on this but that was about it. This mission was about people needing to talk together in conversation with others who had loved ones on the other side; this wasn't to be a bible class. Each person could share their feeling of loss together. My heart and journey were to begin a meeting place once or twice a month so the bereaved could come together to share their feelings of sorrow knowing they were not alone a sermon. Then my job would be done, and I would move on to other things I was directed to do by my ET *heavenly guides and teachers.* I had hoped it would happen, instead after two days of visiting churches I found most had other activities, which seemed more important and basically said, there was no room for a bereavement group in each one I went to! No group I thought, not one church I had gone to had one, and I know people needed this program more than some of the others they had. I

241

was very saddened, but there was nothing more I could do, I felt badly and could not understand how this could be!   One of the worse examples was one church pastor who didn't listen long and bluntly told me, *"We don't need this, it wasn't in their program"*, it stunned and shocked me death wasn't in their program? At least I had tried to find a small meeting place for those who were in dire need of companionship. I will know one day why I was sent by the other side there was a lesson in this, I needed to understand in how some others think, and importantly how some in authority do not like suggestions if they are not theirs.

The Holy Box

I was looking for something in my room one day when I noticed the Holy Box sitting on my dresser was partly closed with only a corner of Edgars little book *"Think on These Things"* sticking out of it. I knew he had left a message inside with the lid being partly open for me to notice it. In his message he said, *"To study page 14 in the chapter "On Choice and Will."* Edgar and Huge Lynn, his son in spirit had told me to watch for something earlier that day and with my intuition I saw the image of a most unusual and beautiful tree in bloom my son pointed out to me as we were driving. I immediately began asking with my thoughts, *"did I do something wrong"?* Why I thought this I do not know, and *Edgar's* words flowed out to me, *"No child, nothing you have done wrong the lesson being let others choose their lives then bow and walk away. What they do is of no concern use your precious time to write, create, and do beautiful work as you desire. Use your free will it is time and we are here to help; you have worked hard and are learning much each day. Remember you have precious free will do whatever you wish to create. We love you."*

With this inspiring message I was back on track learning more when to back away, and not to make other people's problems my own or the way I want them to be in helping them, which I didn't think I had but I am learning. This also reminded me of the minister with his objections. We all want to make things better for loved ones and our friends but I finally understood if we take away their problems we also take away that person's right from them to learn the lesson they needed, and our own, so even with having good intentions it is not the way to go so let others learn.

This was my human side thinking, focusing too much on how to help others and the other side wanted to be sure it didn't become my reality to try and take away other problems to solve because we each have our own life lessons. It is a fine line to know when to step back from a situation and most parents, loved ones, even friends are guilty of this, we don't want our loved ones to suffer or have hardships in life but… making our mistakes is *VITAL* to all of us in this *EARTH SCHOOL* and a *HARD* one to learn! We were told more than one time, that Earth is the hardest school to learn in!

Here was one of my own lessons I was struggling with this was a lesson to help me, to guide me, and the answer was right in front of me! I thought many times of how unusual our lives are and how to explain them when I was to write our truth in my books. I knew then *our secret* would be out to everyone, would they understand? I put too much thought and energy on *"How would we be judged"* who doesn't think about *"what will other's think"* this is the way we are taught from birth with more negativity! My main thoughts and concerns were *how* to explain our universal life experiences, let alone how every single one of us are connected to one another, our Creator/God, ET Christ Light Beings, and other universal beings. So much I can't explain it this is what I had been afraid of telling but not anymore!! I would be strong; I was uplifted because the fact is; I *want to please the Creator with our promises not others!* Now you will understand the new message below and why it was sent.

Let not to let thy feelings stand in the way of thy works meaning material. Not to think what others will say, not to be afraid to tell people you do not have time for the little petty things in life use your time as you wish that would fulfill your desires in life. To know you may always use and count on your free will in life. Just don't be bogged down in life with unimportant issues in life. Don't be afraid to tell of your life experiences go ahead spread Christ's word we love you dear.

Oh, what inspiration to continue the journey, we were uplifted with their beautiful words in every message received. I have left the man-made fear taught by humans long behind! We came here to help

243

others who have held their experiences in secret, and to leave the old ways of fear behind them, when this happens a door opens for those who seek the truth! Each soul created is unique in their own way and part of a grand plan.

This is what I needed; and this beautiful message spiritually supports what we are doing in our lives as they have told us, so we can finish our work on this planet. We will move forward with a strong mind, never looking back with what we are to do and learn. While writing my books I knew exactly why we each came here to do this work, and this is what we are doing, the beings are speaking not only through the books but also through my words when speaking to others. We have felt the Creators grace with each ET travel and visits into the universes and other worlds knowing how protected we are, and nothing can stop our mission! These beautiful heavenly messages from our universal families have helped keep us going hundreds of times over, and a hard lesson to learn and understand is *"we cannot heal the world and everyone in it"*. This was difficult for us long ago until they allowed us to remember why, *because our human nature is to help others but we each have a certain time on earth we chose to accomplish our journey in our lifetime then it is time to go home. And without making mistakes we would learn nothing to better ourselves as a human.*

Each human has the chance to learn and move to newer levels through mistakes therefore they are *extremely vital* in life through our universal lessons we will continue to spread the teachings and I will continue to write the truth.

Baby Ecken and Milton Porter

Days later I heard the nick name of *Ecken* called out to me, I was not sure if it was Edgar who did this or the possibility it may be a clue of sorts. Then finding this was the nick name of one of Edgar's sons, so I presumed he wanted contact with me, but I did not know for sure since his name was not called to me again that day. Edgar had three sons one named *"Milton Porter"* who died as a very young child this shattered Edgar, Gertrude, and their family. Nothing more happened after I heard this name but a day later, I heard these words, *"the gift is here of celebration"* and beside me on the bed laid my

Edgar Cayce book which had not been there a moment before! I was not quite sure what this meant but hopefully I would soon find out because the next day my son became *"extremely critical"* he was in for another fight to live! After rushing him to the city and into ER things became even worse as David continued fighting for his life! As he fought to live, I saw a miracle I witnessed a beautiful Angel who appeared beside my son, and these words given, *"for he shall be well he would survive!"* I was so happy, ecstatic, heartfelt and thankful!!! Through those next days he had a hard time fighting to live and suffered severely but... eventually won and I had no doubt he would live! All I kept in my mind those days was the Angels words, *"that he would survive"* and this was never wrong!

Somehow, I knew this experience was connected to something else and it wasn't long Edgar appeared to speak to me of a tree and said, *"The Willow tree, one looks at this tree called the weeping willow and Greater things thou art shall see".* This was a clue in some way from seeing another of my son's *miracles* happening right in front of me and to know we would continue to *"see even greater things to come"!* This glorious message represents having Faith, and strength, it carried a very spiritual meaning to us I will explain; it represents *the cross of Jesus Christ! "For he shall be well"!*

In the night hours Edgar and I met again, he spoke to me of the beautiful ocean by A.R.E. the hospital and school he started called *"The Area of Research and Enlightenment"* in Virginia Beach, Va. He himself had established the A.R.E. in his later lifetime for the poor, so those without money could be helped with the best doctors and hospitals to get better the same as the rich. Then Edgar said to me, *"I walk beside him".* I knew exactly who he meant by *him* and what family member it was who was still living and presided over the A.R.E. which was his grandson Charles Thomas. Edgar meant, *"That he and Hugh Lynn his other son who are both in spirit come to walk beside Edgar's grandson Charles Thomas when he walked on the beach".* I could see Hugh Lynn and Edgar doing this very thing, then Edgar told me: *"to read Samuel 14: chapter 14".* This was an important clue for me to give his message to Charles Thomas from him. I was happy to be the messenger for him and do this very thing and the response from Charles Thomas was good.

In no time a following message arrived: *"Have no malice towards anyone remember we are all of one flesh. Separate the actions from*

245

*the body it is always the action not the person, his or her behavior, we are a part of the whole...*Yes, we are all a part of the whole everything which has BEEN CREATED." This seemed to be the same reminder from my grandmother when I was just a little girl. She told me this very thing and with her not knowing it she was a wonderful teacher to me. It means, *"Not to let others who are foolish and speak hard words get to me or my work with their negative deeds, words, and anger".* He knew we would need this in our life for those who want to try and stop our work more than I knew.

It was 8 pm when my son found the old *word processor* turned on it held another message for me! *"Greetings to my beloved Ann, realization is in the realm of nothingness in the material world. I will start relay thoughts to you on this electrical PAP. Give me a little more time to prepare. End of transmission, E. C."* Edgar was gearing up to begin teaching us more information about our work with him in our *"trance states"* when we would be working together more in the future. Edgar, David and I, also made a group of the number 3! I asked for confirmation signs with a symbol of the cross from my spiritual teachers and this is what I received: *"Long ago the trees had many great symbols and the one that was used to make the cross was the Olive tree that Christ was nailed to and forced to carry on his broken back. The symbol is forgiveness and love for thy fellow man. The symbol shows great love it's like our graduation present from the heavens. Healers and helpers from the light and all that is holy awaits you one day. The symbol is also because we are proud of you and the work you do together. Another step forward is the hearing of the tones meaning higher and newer frequencies and of higher vibrations. Also, your sight, smell, touch and other gifts are enhanced now. Meditate as much as you can we shall travel and help you in the night hours as well".*

This was a beautiful warm loving amazing gift to receive and I cannot describe our feelings! I took my time as we studied each word carefully letting them sink in and no matter the names or titles we battle over in the wars, or life in general, everything on Earth and in the other worlds beyond is one fascinating, mystical evolution!

The Great Council Arrives

It was 3:45 am, *"Wake up!"* was called out to me! I must have heard it clear because my eyes flew open and when they did, I began to see a white light beginning to form in front of my dresser which was our beloved visitors *"The Great Council!"* what an honor! Earlier in the evening they had attempted to come in twice before I guessed they may have had difficulty entering our earth space but now they were here! I heard the *tones* sounding their announcement *"The Great Council comes"* and I could plainly see their body forms as they moved closer. There were four of them sort of floating up over my bed as they completed a circle like they do; they had come to help me through a very difficult time in my life. The *"Great Council"* are the same ones who come from long before Ancient times in the earth's beginning who are ETs from the Christ Light. See how everything is connected and was created at the same time, yet most humans are afraid of their own selves, unsure of any life after this one. The main Council being of the four then moved down to be in front of me he is life size and still materializing into a solid form. He is the one I was able to see completely through his entire head, veins, skull and all, this was happening now as I watched, the same as another time I watched this when he arrived in energy. In only moments he was completely solid to complete his humanness as I still watched him; I was wide awake I had been asking for their help telepathically and I knew they would come! I won't go further with what happened that early morning I can only say they wanted to help me with a great sadness I would be facing soon. They are of *pure love and compassion* more than our words can describe! I was immensely grateful for their compassion to me knowing I was never alone and had never been alone.

The next day *Hugh Lynn Cayce* appeared to me and told me "I was to get a book titled *Venture Inward*". I knew this must be very important for me because in no time these written words were sent to me, *"Child, you are in wonderment of it all and that is good. You shall not be deceived by many or any. You ponder the question about your new work it will come in a bright flash, it will click in just like eons ago when you both did this work."*

Hugh Lynn and Edgar were referring to our work together long before Atlantis, and in our other lifetimes together. Then I began to

247

hear the familiar beautiful *tones sounding* throughout the house they seemed to flow through me as well. The high vibrations lifted my senses to what I needed to know universally from Edgar and *"The Great Council of Christ Light Beings."* This announcement meant their visit had lifted my spirit relieving my human mind I was so grateful I couldn't wait to tell David! No surprise, he already knew when I told him he usually knew things ahead from memory.

It was early fall, the evenings were becoming chilly with a hint of frost on early mornings, and we were busier than ever in our communication to the Universal Beings. David had gone through several extremely critical times, so many by now I could never count them through the years, and with each one he barely made a comeback it was only with the heavenly beings help that he did. I had taken him to the hospital so many times we nearly lived there over the years. He suffered greatly but with a beautiful smile, and in his way, I knew he was trying to save me from knowing the pain he carried. It was the messages from beyond which gave us our strength and kept us going with the familiar sacred words, *"for he shall be well"*. I knew he would survive every time if I heard those words, it was when they stopped, I would know he had to leave me, and I couldn't stand the thought of this. The Divine ones from other realms, dimensions and our consciousness lifted our spirits; they knew how much it would take in these times of suffering, so they stayed close by with their visits. Our next heavenly message says it all, *"my son would live to go on for now, and more new adventures awaited us!"* I was the happiness ever!!!!!!!!! New messages began again! Another continued message arrived soon which was a repeat. *"A grand occurrence tonight in the sky-8 pm, take the camera and see!!! Yes, you are a grand part of this vast universe!*

How amazing this life of ours was constantly receiving heavenly guided help from the ET Beings of light and other heavenly ones. Another message quickly arrived: *"Greetings, be patient the time is drawing near, we all love you and we are here for you. And yes, be strong my son I am very proud of you-you have a lot of time to love and be loved, all of us!"* Oh, how BEAUTIFUL!!!

How relieved to know my son would continue with this great news; his smile was so big he could have lit up a stadium the same as mine!! He was given more time just like that, and David always kept his hopes high, he was never negative, and this reinforced everything we believe in coming from the Divine beings who watch over us! Boy, were we on top of the world!!

The next Thursday evening we found contact mail again we were expecting the ETs, but their message said: *"Try again, tonight too cloudy, tomorrow night. We gladly take you and your male offspring on a long voyage next full moon. Extraterrestrials."* I had no doubt the information was sent to us rapidly since I had just connected with the ETs asking, *"if we could go with them but only if they are the Beings who are positive, holy, and from the Christ Light, then return us back to here by morning '.* In this way the ETs could continue working on my son to help him heal faster than ever! In our own higher consciousness, we held the knowledge we would survive through what we had promised to accomplish.

On the next clear night, we knew to go outside and watch the sky there were *flashing lights* which is our signal and yes, they were coming for us after we each turned in for the night. We returned inside so each of us could go to our room to bed as soon as I turned my lights out the familiar bright lights began coming through the windows flashing in my room. The room shown bright enough to see the Beings faces clearly, there was a large group of ETs gathered around me and one began telling me: *"there would be a blood exchange done on me on the trips with them. This would happen between me and the others to help my son, it will be a pleasant experience it's all in the learning."* I knew they would never hurt either of us, they loved us. I was only too happy they needed my blood each time for such a positive reason to help my son as they had done times before. I would gladly lay down my life for him and they knew I was grateful to participate in this exchange. They have taken both of our blood several times before always for good reasons... The ETs said: *"To please be aware they were in a process of fusing themselves with us. We must be patient knowledge will be ours!"* I was speechless when I tried to absorb this in my mind... I did not question them about what *fusing* meant since already being part of them it was fine. I had no words, just a feeling of great happiness to help my son!!

I began thinking about many years back when something very strange happened, I want to share with you; it was an extremely cold winter close to the end of the year, in fact it was close to *"New*

249

Year's Eve." My family and I had been to some friends that evening for dinner and riding home that night in the car I saw something huge in the sky, a UFO! This was when the children were small, and I couldn't believe my eyes at the time but there it was, a large huge round bright yellow/orange object in the night sky! It was not moving and over the west-end of town; it was so bright it lit up a large area close to our home. I was really excited and said to my husband, *"what is that? I think that's a UFO!"* He stopped the car and we got out; the kids were trying to see what I was talking about. Finally, after several minutes we drove a few blocks more to the house and once there I couldn't get a picture of it, I was out of camera film! We stood outside on the porch for about 20 minutes watching, it was still motionless and in the same place! It must have been a Mother ship because of its size to see it as large as it appeared to us and seemed to be very low over our part of town. We only lived a few blocks away from where we could see it well; but unfortunately, not having a decent camera or film I was some upset. We watched another 10 to 20 minutes more it was still motionless, so we finally decided to give up because of the cold and I needed to put the children to bed. We were at odds and agreed this was not explainable, but altogether, I had watched the object for about 35 to 40 minutes and it never moved. Then everyone went to bed, but I knew I had seen something *very special* and I never forgot it! I read the news the next day and there was *nothing* about this phenomenon in our local paper. I had prayed that somebody else had seen what we did, I had not reported it. I was waiting to see if anyone may have, I knew it was a UFO!

The day after news came out on the radio and then in our local newspaper the headlines were "REPORT UFO SEEN IN AREA" seems a few other people had seen the same object in surrounding areas but none in ours! Little did I know then why only a handful of us had seen the object, the others who did lived a short distance away who reported seeing the UFO on that same night. It seemed very strange to me that no others had noticed this huge brilliant orange object right over town on that night! Maybe those who may have seen it were afraid of being teased, I don't know. After the many years of encounters with UFOs I really think those of us who did see it that night, may possibility have *been on this UFO* and just returning, since memory and time sometimes stop or slows down when the ETs take us... Each time we have gone with them time either *speeds up, or slows down and lose time...* This is the actual newspaper write up below just as the paper wrote it.

Report UFO Seen in Area

A Carlyle woman told the Sentinel today "that a big yellow thing that looked more like a planet than a UFO followed her car from the Tamalco boat docks in Bond County to Rt. 127 about 9:30 last night. Debbie Jannett said that she first spotted the object near the boat docks while returning to Carlyle from Tamalco. "It lifted up into the sky and followed me." Mrs. Jannett said today: *"It just lit up the whole sky. It was big yellow thing with orange around it"*. She said "the object was bigger than the Fairview Park swimming pool, and couldn't guess at an exact size, it followed me home from the boat docks to a railroad crossing" Mrs. Jannett said. *"When I stopped at the tracks it did too, I locked my doors I was scared of it."* The object had a definite round shape, Mrs. Jannett said. "When I got to Rt 127 I looked around and it was gone" she said. According to Mrs. Jannet other cars traveling in the opposite direction on the County Line road separating Bond and Clinton Counties slowed down and stopped apparently to watch the object. Sheriff's Department spokesmen in the counties said, "they had received no reports of the sighting." However, the St. Clair County Sheriff's Department said today that a couple in that county reported seeing an object similar in color when it "landed" in woods near their property. Mr. and Mrs. James Williams of rural Belleville told the Sheriff's Department that the object appeared to be approximately 360 yards long and 50 feet wide. They said it remained on the ground for five minutes and then rose into the atmosphere. The Williams sighting occurred ten minutes before Mrs. Jannett said she first saw the object in Bond County. Mrs. Rosetta Holmes of the Midwest UFO Network said today she had received no other reports of the sighting but that she would be interviewing Mrs. Jannett later today. This concludes the reports on the incident that evening which I copied off from the article.

This was among my first memories of seeing a big ship in those early years after having the babies, they were coming back; it clearly wasn't my time to remember earlier but they started again after this. I felt they gave me a *time out* learning to be a mother and watching my progress being one after this it slowly sparked more memories.

This would not be uncommon for those of us who witnessed the UFO to not recall being on the UFO, and since only a few of us could see it is why I am sure we had possibly been on it. This was mainly *for our eyes only* to jar memories we would be watching the sky more later having little time with 4 children I was behind on UFO information. A few years later I tried to contact these people who reported it to talk with them, but none could be reached, I thought this to be strange! I tried my best to find them there were 4 other couples who witnessed the UFO that night but still had no luck contacting any of them. I though this very odd these witnesses seemed to have disappeared even relatives of theirs.

Now back to one of our encounters my son and I experienced in the spring of 2000 was when I found the most beautiful message. *"Greetings Child, thee is one of great love and compassion. Thy has much to do yet thee will work with thy son as thee did long ago! Thy Father will send a message on what to do in the near future. Blessed are thee!"* I was very excited when I found this message in a box of documentations and by this date, we had already been going with the ETs for most of our lives I guess it had been misplaced? As I said, in the beginning; I have done my best to keep the dates and experiences in chronological order but sometimes I find a few messages among other dates but no matter to me they are all important and they all are true!

My Son's Eye Surgery

To continue; the following month my son had more eye surgery done by the ETs. They took us into another worldly realm and after his surgery was finished, they spoke to us about the procedure they had done: *"the lining of his one eye was cleansed and the eye socket was aligned to the left closer to the side of the nose area'.* They spoke in our words to tell us, *"The devise they used was a laser type instrument so we could understand better this was used to seal the retina to keep it from coming loose, and then we were told the next eye chart reading should be better. We could complete our mission but to do so quickly is not as good at this time, doing a smaller amount at a time is better on his eye. Your blood helps thy son greatly taking it from my ear by making two holes instead of one in it like they did before. They told me they exercised his eyes with their own ways, they ran my blood to cleanse his body and said, we inject our medicines much was done on him we have some to go it is all good for as you have prayed for his healing and as we have said; eyes like the Eagle."* My heart filled with happiness it all seemed unbelievable!! I felt the ETs had worked through his eye doctors' hands when he had his other procedures done at the hospital. My son remembered all about the trip when the ETs helped him with his eyes! David was anxious to tell me more of what he remembered when he was with them soon again. He told me: *"the Aliens were here last night, and they worked on my eyes, he remembered lying on a table and a few of the things they were going to do that he wouldn't let them do, and this was OK with them and they were good to him, isn't this great!"* he said! At this time, we both knew he was slowly going blind and we knew the ETs would help him see longer until the inevitable happened they would do all they could, and I wished I could give him my life and eyes!

We soon found more from our ET family, *"Greetings from all, we love, and love is the universal law. Beloved are thee."* My heart exploded with love back to them they are telling us they know what love is, and they love us too, which to those who do not understand, *yes, they know love!!* On the next night it was a *full moon* we were positive we would see them again, but it ended up being later May 1st with a new contact. The ETs spoke of: *"how we are all united, Edgar and all of us! We are safe and they are here again to work on David's eyes!"* They spoke of how my own eyes have changed into a different color and the light shines through them greatly. They began to speak of the one coming back again called *"The Great One"*, and in their own excitement they said: *"He comes, He comes!"* We felt their honor over this spiritual being we would soon be seeing again. *"The Great One"* is he who I write of that works with us... along with the Angels!!

When we were at David's eye doctor appointment his report was EXCELLENT!! We were excited and happy along with his doctor, even though his doctor couldn't understand how it could be, he was absolutely baffled! It was as the ETs told us it would be, and his doctor would be *absolutely stunned* by the progress he saw! He couldn't understand how this could happen and we sure couldn't tell him how! He did ask us again, *"what this Reiki energy healing was about, and would we teach him?"* He knew what was happening with David's eye was not possible in this world, and we never told him anything about our other worlds. We were honored he wanted to learn energy healing to use with his own way what a compliment to energy work! David was often so sick in his physical body I couldn't spare the extra energy or time to teach his doctor or the nurses who wanted to learn to use Reiki energy and combine it with the medical techniques. It is energy so one is never trying to do anything like a doctor, but it goes beautifully together in healing. One can never predict a healing so when someone gets better with the medical and energy combined it is a blessing! Every day was a miracle for my son to be here and it was with the grace of the Infinite Supreme highest power and doctors he was.

It was hard not to cry watching my son after the ETs finished with his eye giving him new sight! When we left his doctor appointment the first day after the ETs repaired his eye, we were riding home in the car and I watched him holding up his hand. He studied it looking intently at every inch of it just as a child would do seeing something for the first time! He watched the clouds, trees, flowers, sunshine, road signs, everything we passed, he could even see to even read! Everything was new again; he could see again, and he marveled at everything he looked at, especially colors, our wish for a *complete miracle* had been given!! How could we ever thank the ETs and Creator for sending his healing to see and for their love to us?

Would religion ever admit to God's creations of universal Beings and wonders, with the old teachings we have had? Someday those humans who *disbelieve* may come out of the old ways and realize other life forms do exist in other worlds, dimensions, galaxies solar and star systems and everything which exists, and are of love. They have been here forever and before; evolution began long before humans ever existed.

A couple of nights later the ETs were back to take David with them to one of their underground bases to show him what they termed as the *"Evil ones"* and what these creations were getting ready to do to mankind in time. The ETs wanted him to know about a certain breed of *bee's* which was going to be used by *negative ones* at some time. They took him to see some of the captured killer bees; that were still in cocoons and others who were dangerous and an odd green color. I wondered if this was the species of bee's we are beginning to hear about with some who have invaded other faraway places and getting closer to our country?

David was being made aware of them on this trip and learning why the ETs were warning him to alert us when the time was right. Soon it was almost time to return him when he was told, *"they used his blood again for a very important discovery to help others." How exciting!* We were re-learning how things work in our world and in other universal worlds through our ET family, who only want peace upon earth, there was an important reason for the ETs to be showing him what they did. And using his blood for new discoveries for new cures on earth to help humans with new medical breakthroughs! These cures the ETs create are sometimes brought to the minds of scientists with the scientist thinking it is all their *own ideas to* developing some of the new medicines I spoke of before and many are their own ideas in research. The ETs help us in many ways that most here will never know of or understand, they watch over earth and care about what happens to it through manmade negative illnesses, and negative humans that are in all kinds of positions of power, and power is what it is about!

Note; Right now, as I am writing of David's experiences, I am getting more information from the ETs about the killer Bee's. The ETs thoughts that are coming to me is to explain their information and what they mean. You may have read about *"The Killer Bee's"* that are multiplying and coming closer to us they have been here for some time longer than the experts know of. They have been bred coming from other places that are unknown to us and some have already killed some people and animals here on earth! I know this is what the ETs were showing David back then, when they were educating him about the bee's, showing him how they were working on something that could be used to eradicate them. They have been working on a way to STOP them by watching them, to keep humans safe on Earth so we can protect ourselves, and to teach us how to destroy them now and in future years! We need to be able to destroy them and they stress *"that it will be vital to have something to use when they hit hard in every country, they are an evil force!"* Thank you, ETs, I have delivered your message…

The Next A.R.E. Meeting

Before we left for our A.R.E. meeting one evening we found a message from Cayce: *"Thou shall be growing into a new realm of spiritually we are proud of you all! Tell A.R.E. they are moving into the light, work well done!!! Be good to one another this is your new family!"* We were astounded to receive this interesting and beautiful message with news of *"being proud of us all"*. And our *"new universal family"* which let us know Edgar is with us forever.

On June 11th we saw meteor lights in the sky and on the 12th the ETs came for us to travel with them. I recall seeing my own face when we took off; it was drawn back with the force of gravity leaving earth and one ET had its hands on my shoulders to hold me back in a seat to steady me. This tells me we had been in a body form at least in those moments. David told me the next day both of our faces looked this way on takeoff; he confirmed the experience we both had then asked, *"If I recalled traveling through worm holes and going to other Galaxies to see other life forms, and how the grid floor in the ship turned to a silver liquid look and then returned to a solid form again!"* The ETs told us, *"this had to do with molecules being disassembled and reassembled which they have been teaching us about",* so they gave us a good demonstration…

We were soon having a conversation with them telepathically who told us some interesting history; *"the wars set us back 150 years in our learning".* They also talked about *Roswell* with what really happened there, and I wondered if there are others that have seen what they have let us see on board with them, I see others time to time on board with us but only a few. I think perhaps some people who connect with Aliens are more terrified of them not giving them a chance. We have a *personal relationship* with them, a family caring as we are to our loved ones on earth. They feel emotions like ours and those who school us have learned to express love, caring, and compassion. I know this from lifelong experiences with them and those we are from we feel blessed to be with them as a part of our family connection. This is who we are and why we came back to earth. On this visit we saw some of the *"Blonde-haired blue-eyed Beings"*, who look the same as humans; it would be hard for people to ever know they *are not* human. After this, we looked at some of the plant life they grow and I felt this was being done to improve and enrich our food chain for in the future, this was fascinating to learn from them! The next thing I knew I was waking up the next day knowing we had experienced an extraordinary trip! I noticed it was 5:15 am, too early for my bedroom to look so light! I began rubbing my eyes which really didn't make a difference because when I looked again my room was bathed in the same bright glittering white light, like on a sunny day!

With that one thought I was out of body taken high into the sky, and a voice told me, *"to look down!"* I was up high over my house and below me I could see the most beautiful and breathtaking sight! I was looking at beautiful Angels surrounding the house and each one's golden wings were touching the other one's next to it making a golden circle of protective Angels; this took my breath away to see this extraordinary experience! This was telling me we had the Angel Beings protection around us here and would *forever* be safe! After this, I was back inside my room, just like that! This was hard to come back from I was so excited, I felt it also meant it would be another outstanding day with David's eye check-up; it was almost time for his next appointment. I will never forget I was blessed to see the angels protecting us in this blessed place.

Before David's eye appointment he experienced another healing with the ETs who had recently worked on him they told him, *"They were sort of tuning his eyes up"*. At the doctor's office he amazingly read the eye chart at 20-20, his eyes were doing the *unbelievable* the one eye had been blind!! His eye doctor couldn't believe it calling other eye doctors in to see this! We were to return 2 weeks later for another check-up and when we did his eyes were still doing great, the ETs were certainly helping him, and his doctor was smiling big!

The Crystal Source and the Hybrid's

We had been busy with our immediate family before reuniting again with our universal family, and it wasn't long one night, they came to take us back with them to tell me about a change in my own sight. I was told, *"use all of this sight we give you, use it well!"* I

257

knew this had to do with how my eyes were seeing objects on occasion; they worked the same as a camera when I needed to see things up close or far away!! We were back in space and to the best of my memory the ETs and some other people I did not know were standing around me in the craft. I could only see the others when flashes of bright light lit up the inside of it, I was in travel. I acknowledged *"The Great Council"* was with us so I knew this trip must be very important for them to be there.

We landed someplace far away out in the galaxies because I was soon being helped off the craft so I wouldn't fall on what looked like rocks. One of the ETs had taken my hand helping me to cross over them I noticed his very long fingers and thin hands holding onto mine to keep me safe. This ET had the feeling of *concern as any loved one helping the other one* this was for my own safety, which was our *human* way they had knew. The next part is where I became confused, if I had really left home or what? But then reading my mind the ET helping me said, *"little sister you are here, we go tonight, have no fear your surroundings are to be made like your home, relax and enjoy the trip, the voyage, we let you write it down, the stars and planets surround you, relax now."* In the blink of an eye I felt we were completely someplace else, but in the background, I heard sounds like *street noise* making me confused. I thought we had already left earth and then I mumbled my question to the ET, *"is this for real?"* *"Yes, little earth child you are with us and others it's as you say ok, you are safe just checking no harm to you ever! We are all one you are a part of us learning and observing to bring back great insight, vast information we put in your subconscious. Little one, thy sons' eye is weak now because of a covering but it shall soon disappear- we work on it as we do, he is here, and he will remember the trip. His memory grows dim, but we also help with it he will be like new soon. In hypnosis you both will go back many times to your teacher's class and on the space craft with us, his teacher will be amazed so will the both of you. We work on your mouth and gums to heal them."* After he spoke for some reason I asked if my hands were tied or free? *"Yes, your hands are free you will know you were here you will know it all happened with us tonight everything is good and fine. Ask your friend C. if he dreamed of the house by the water see if he remembers, he should. He is here now in his sleep."* He was meaning *Star Man*, my dear beloved friend.

I was sad to hear my son's eye was weak once more but when the ET said, *"It would soon disappear, and they would help him"* I knew they would repair his eye and his confused thinking so I relaxed I was relieved and happy!

Earlier, I remembered my daughter and I were hiking, or I thought we were and being helped over some deep and high places in a cave where a man took my hand to help me, so I didn't fall. I replied *"thank you"* to him and I am sure the one who was holding my hand to help me was the same ET I just spoke of who helped me over the strange rocks. They can make things look as they want, as a human to keep us calm, or whatever is needed at the time and this one was very loving and supporting, I always felt very safe with him. The rest of that night since then is gone from my mind.

My next memory was recognizing my Eastern teacher appearing in the night hours, Han Tai Chen Su who lived long ago in one of the Han Dynasty's. He had come to tell me a beautiful thing, *"that I was in tune with the whole universe. We are going to make you more clairvoyant you will be fi*ne!*"* Then I asked him, *"to let me see you better"*, so he did and went on to tell me, *"we let you see many things to keep your mind focused! Sleep now, if you like we go home soon take you back! We love you too dear sister one, we soon bid you farewell going back soon."* Later, toward morning I saw I had written the trip down in my notebook and I felt great, what a wonderful trip, I love the missions they chose! Seeing Han Tai Chen Su my spirit teacher who once lived on planet earth made us feel good! It was only a few nights later I awoke to the familiar flashing lights, I knew my ET friends were back. There were those large dark eyes staring at me and then time was lost, I felt *hypnotized* is the best word I can think of because in an instant I was with my son! We both traveled with them to a person's home that we wanted to meet one day. I sketched his house on my notebook as I looked at it from above where we were in the craft, I had no idea I even had my notebook with me until that moment! We had never been to this place before; this person lived far away so by experiencing this it was exciting to us! This person is a well-known clairvoyant reader and I felt sure by wanting to meet him is why we were taken there. Would this man remember my son and me with his gift of clairvoyance if we were to ever meet him in person? I even think this person had a similar experience on that night with us and if we ever did meet, he would recall us being in his dream state.

The next night I was back in a UFO floating, not walking, down a long stainless-steel looking hall with small windows thinking to myself *"yes, I am in the UFO!"* David was with me and we both knew we were in what I will call a hospital area. I clearly remember asking one of the ETs, *"are you the one in charge"?* I don't recall if he answered me or not, but we could see other *life forms* in this same room, maybe they were all ETs? It would be hard to know since most Hybrids look as ordinary as other humans. There were objects and many crystals the ETs wanted us to look at and we were happy and excited! We went down steps and then taken back up others to another area. What I am about to say now may not make sense to you, but it did for us, I am sure the meaning to us was about our higher and lower consciousness of the mind, you see our lessons come in completely different methods than here. Afterwards, we were given more information about energy sources then the ETs told us, *"they work through David and me they are working on a new planet for the future of the Earth world and there are powerful energy (Crystal) sources around the earth. In each pyramid is hidden these energy sources and in the water under mountains that they work off of, and that we are working through you both".*

Note: you need to know this above information was given to us ahead and being saved for the future, which we are slowly coming into now, so it is possible these things may already be starting but not that any human would be aware of. The ETs sounded as if we were doing work with them using an energy source considering the crystals and pyramids, they spoke of. David and I have kept our strong ties to Egypt forever, so I still vividly recall when we were hiding some items that are extremely sacred in the great Pyramid, we gladly gave our life for, I mentioned earlier. The next trip was in a few days, around 3:30 am I noticed the time when waking up. Boy, things sure move fast I thought because I found myself looking at many life forms, embryos, and different types of Hybrid babies in a flash! There was a machine nearby which looked like an X-ray machine and an ET who stood closely beside us I could feel he was the main one over this machine. He pointed out a baby inside one of the machines as we talked telepathically, we could hear his reply with his thoughts to us. The ET told us, *"This baby's lungs were bad and not developing right."* The baby was laying inside the machine on its back, just an embryo yet starting to form arms and legs he said, *"the babies here are half-human and half-alien that there would be something wrong with this baby that we were shown, and they wanted to repair this baby if they could"*. This was going to be a very painful experience for us, we didn't know this involved a family loved one and this was their future baby to come!! We knew the ETs were trying hard to repair the baby and we were being prepared ahead of time by them, they wanted so much to help save this baby. Then my son and I were able to understand this visit and why the ETs took us to see the baby in this hospital setting. We were very involved with this child; and later the baby was born with many things wrong inside of it and could not live. I knew why we felt such love and caring for it and why the ET wanted to save it, and the visit was to prepare us for this upcoming future event which would be heartbreaking! The ETs have been very caring to us and were trying hard to save our family's future baby, but they couldn't.

A Powerful Message Was Given to Us

It was December 7th when the ultimate message arrived it was overwhelming and beautiful, *"Beloved, the Council, Ruth and David are meeting blessing your heartfelt questions. The Lord in Heaven will let you know all answers."* This special meeting was to be through Edgar Cayce and the both of us while using the trance states. When we began them, I was quickly deep into trance and my son asked the questions, we had the video camera on and tape recorder ready. Then my son began his questions and they were confirmed along the way. The Council, ETs, and Edgar were in a circle and on this *special* night we started at 8:30 pm and finished at 9:15 pm. The ETs stayed slightly above the Council, Edgar, our Teachers, Guides, Angels, Archangels and our loved ones in spirit, all of them were with us on this beautiful occasion! When we were finished, they told us, *"there would be more ETs coming for us soon and it wasn't long, the next night they appeared"* ...

We are here! You have gone with us many times now we will help you and the male offspring in all ways for you have helped us! We

261

all work together for mankind get busy now and do the things that are important that we need to but keep time for fun and joy. The friend you are attached too is not ready for us yet but will be all right with what you have told him when he sorts it all out in your time. You are teaching him he will become more in tune little by little he marvels at the growth and will soon seek a higher learning. We have worked with him tonight keeping him in a relaxed state he will do well in his life he will heal and change for the better now he will go onto different levels slowly but surely".

This was amazing news; I had been working to help this person grow in his soul and spirit I call Star man. I knew these Beings were from a different dimension with us on this special night and they sincerely wanted to help with our schooling; these *benevolent* Beings were of a very high order and their message was beautiful.

On December 9th, we were taken on a new voyage with them, we found ourselves in what we thought was Peru and were outside walking through all kind of thick vines everywhere we stepped. This seemed to be another jungle setting and all we could figure was that it was another secret place, or planet the ETs go to for specific reasons. Maybe this was in Peru and a home- base they come to, and was too much for our mind, it didn't make sense to us why only a part of the trip at the end was taken away from our memory. Later we were told *"it would be explained to us in the future".* What we were seeing in this jungle setting was not for us to completely absorb now, experiences were sometimes cut short for us. Apparently, they decided against letting us go further or took away certain memories not wanting to overload us in our learning. This is usually because it is not time for us to understand or remember certain things, only what they think we are ready for. It is strange how some parts are a blank for us after we travel with them, but we understand.

The Time Was Ending with our Trance States

Edgar told us it was our last *trance state* lesson with him; our classes would be over on December 15th. We were honored and said, *"Yes, we understood"* we humbly agreed to this last meeting ending our lessons we had completed all we were to do, and it had been an ultimate honor! He told *us, "the ending of our work in this time and space did not mean a final ending, for we always stay together in each lifetime he would never leave us... He will be involved with us for the rest of our lives to help us, and we will go on from there".* Someday we pray for this contact to be known and shared with his loved ones and fellow teachers at A.R.E. as Edgar wishes. It would be years later I would pursue this adventure when the timing was right. I waited, too afraid I would not be able to share what we had experienced but not long-ago Edgar pushed me to get going on it and contact A.R.E. Therefore, I am writing of our lives with him once again; and even though each of us is working from different realms it makes no difference. My first two books in (2016) were added to the A.R.E. Library in Virginia Beach, Va. just as Edgar wanted done so with this great honor, we are proud and humbled! This 3rd book I am writing now I hope will also be added to the others in the A.R.E. library as Edgar wishes. The next days in learning other information with Edgar, he talked with us about a *new human species,* and that help was on its way for us. This was exciting, we wanted more information but would have to wait until he was ready.

Soon after this *The Great Traveler* arrived and told us an important message for ourselves, and to accept! *"Earth Children do not be afraid we have not let you remember because you have fear and would not understand yet and not like everything you see, but we are from the Holy Light. You both are learning and have been chosen".* This was glorious news; we were ecstatic and understood what this meant! We felt the highest vibrations of love flowing through-out our bodies, this holy message was precious, and inspired us with life's promises yet to keep, and to make our time here count the best we could! I know the ETs were protecting us with what we did not understand yet in the other dimensions and worlds, and how *we really are as a created part designed by the universe.* They wanted to make sure we were completely ready to know more of our Extraterrestrial life before we experienced the next steps, as it may be too much for now. We both felt great humbleness wash over us, how could we *not* feel this way!!

The Great Traveler's new message had been *delivered;* I found it on my bedroom floor upstairs when I came to check for one, and to my great surprise there was a *"large ET handprint in a circle with my pyramid beside it!"* I videoed everything and took pictures, the more I looked at the handprint it made me wonder what we really LOOK LIKE! Was this what the message meant about *"fear and not like everything I see"?* Then I was able to visualize part of the answer in my mind I am not ready to talk about just yet.

It wasn't long until *The Great Traveler* sent word again to us by writing in my notebook, *"Earth Child we will return there the next full moon lunar."* Two nights later I awoke to see several ET faces and the *Great Traveler* and for some unknown reason he gave his other name to me which I will not use since I can only *guess* at the spelling of it, and I may be way off track like the last time he told me. He wanted to tell me, *"I was in transition getting me ready for the ride to travel".* I heard the name *"Lord Taylor"* before leaving out of nowhere, and still have no idea if this was the other name he wanted to speak of, or one we were meeting that night. David told me before the trip began the ETs were having trouble getting me to *settle down* for some reason then zip, I was in another dimension, this is what I remembered. I could see many people from other past times we passed through and one was Biblical times! I felt as if we were in a *time warp* of sorts, I am sure we were continuing back in time. Suddenly there were flashes of bright golden lights, and like *the snap of my fingers* I was back at home in my bed! I loved seeing these chosen periods of long ago the ETs let us see; I wanted to keep experiencing more of them, how exciting! And I would experience more of them with my memories on further trips!

On the same night after the trip with them when we journeyed through past times, I had fallen asleep and awakened again at 11:10 pm. I heard the words, *"Journey not complete prepare for more travel"* I guess we weren't finished with the earlier trip. I looked around my room and their humor were obvious; they had moved my video camera across the bedroom to the foot of my bed focused to where I sleep! They knew I was still hoping to get them on camera but now it was pointed on me! The last I knew I was laughing at their joke with no more memory of going with them again on the journey or when I was returned!

It was close to Christmas Eve when I found my notebook open and lying on the floor of my room, *"We are with you all, the baby will be well received to heaven a small baby girl is on its way be strong God loves his children rejoice the Angels sing."* This blessed message is

264

what we know as a *miracle message* because the mother of this baby to come is a loved one that had just lost her new baby with the lung problems who the ETs tried to save, and our family was still saddened. This joyous message confirmed the baby's soul-spirit was safely in heaven and would return in a new baby girl which would follow in short time. This Holy message would help the mother to know the baby's soul would return to her in another new baby (re-incarnate). This was such wonderful news and as we hoped would happen but this being a sorrowful time yet for the parents we decided to wait before passing the message on because of the pain and shock of loss, to not overwhelm them. This little soul, the passed over baby had decided to make a *"turn around"*, which means, to return.

The next message was to help guide me: *"Child, listen to thy own intuition it tells you what you know as thy truth! A new beginning awaits you all in the New Year it will be successful."* The next day Edgar arrived with another blessed holiday message to us on New Year's Day, *"Happy New Year enjoy an enlightening time we will be with you the entire evening! All is well and blessed celebrate, we love you all! Signed EC, and many loved ones"*. We felt extremely honored to receive two beautiful holiday messages and they were sent for two reasons, one to make our holiday happy with a new beginning, and to let others learn how things can be orchestrated from the other side!

False Prophets

We were about to be drawn into a *"spiritual battle"* with an evil presence who Edgar, The Great Traveler, ET Christ Light Beings, and Archangels *warned* us about! They told us, *"they would come to stand with us against a false prophet who wanted to do us harm in our work!"* They came not only to warn us but to say: *"the false prophet had over-stepped their boundary"*. This occurred at an A.R.E. meeting we attended regularly. Things began to build on the next meeting night when we were in the mist of passing Reiki energy to a sick man I will call (Don) who had a severe brown recluse spider bite. He had been to doctors for some time but was getting worse and wanted to see if Reiki energy would help him improve. Don came to the meeting as a regular and in that way, we could work on his leg by passing positive healing energy to him. The

265

woman who was the *bad prophet* was sitting across the room from my son and me that night when suddenly she began yelling out, *"that we were killing him, we were burning Don up!"* And everything stopped, the meeting shut down for a few moments, no one could even speak not knowing what was happening. We did not respond but looked her straight in the eyes, she lost her power she thought she had over us quickly, then without a word from us or anyone we continued the healing work and the meeting resumed.

The attack on us upset Don who is a good friend we had helped before with some health problems with good results and was a believer in Reiki. We had been ready knowing Edgar and the many Christ Light Heavenly beings were beside us with their protection! The woman's face had changed completely when she called out to us which revealed the most hideous looking *"evil entity"* inside of her who possessed her! My son and I knew the others in the room could not see it, but we could, and our eyes locked with it, we never looked away. *IT* knew we were not afraid and quickly began to fade disappearing back inside of the woman and then her face returned to normal. I am *sure IT* had no trouble seeing the Heavenly Beings protection around us and that we were not afraid. After the meeting for reasons unknown to us the woman followed me to my car with her apology which I accepted then we left knowing she had no idea this *thing* was inside of her! We felt sorry for her and sent our prayers to her that night this is all we could do. We thanked Edgar and the ET heavenly beings for coming to help us with their protection, we were grateful! This strange event was like something out of a movie, but it had happened! Don began improving soon and each time we saw him we worked on his leg and sent energy to him from home. One day at the meeting he was smiling so big at us while pulling up his pant leg, the bite area was pink and healthy again how thankful we were! This is not what we alone did, his healing was coming from the Creator.

We were warned once again to be ready in the future with these words, *"Beware of false prophets surrounding you all cast them away with prayer"*. A day later the next message arrived: *"to focus on thee and thy son's spirituality that we were both very strong individuals seeking peace and harmony, Love from all"*. How beautiful, this gave us positive completeness in honoring our work…

I cannot stress enough of how the heavenly beings and ETs work together, they go hand in hand, for the best outcome of others in our world. Do you see the connection we all have to one another? I believe what happened to us shows this without any doubt, and soon after this we were told to, *"Tell the world the truth this is why your books are being written"*.

The Sub Station and UFOs

Back to the year 2000 is to refresh the memory of an important sighting and our teachers and guides were coming in faster now, the ET universal beings were teaching us more of their knowledge. Our next visit was a big part of this time frame, during the night hours I was being taught about a *Sub Station* we pass in and out of when we travel with them, and a new *re-programming* administered to my son and me. This was in January and one night we were watching the Sunday evening news on TV, three policemen were being interviewed because they had seen a huge cigar shaped UFO *"as large as a football field"* over the town of Shiloh, and Belleville, Illinois not far from us. People really took notice with the police seeing the object more than most would have if it had been an ordinary individual. Two of the officers were from different towns who witnessed this phenomenon and described the UFO as two stories high! Earlier that same evening someone else had called the police about seeing a UFO and the police said, *"they would check it out, but they wondered if this was a joke!"* They also had sent an Officer from their station to investigate and in no time the Officer radioed back into the station that something big was in the sky he was looking at and he wasn't kidding! This huge UFO was seen that evening by many others as it slowly made its way on south from Shiloh, Ill. coming from the north. This story made BIG news everywhere with others who were witnesses' and watched it. One policeman said, *"The object was as large as a football field"*! This size would typically be called a *Mother ship,* this makes one wonder how long it takes for non-believers to know people aren't lying when year after year thousands of people from all over the planet are seeing UFOs! The sightings go on and on, and still some people are so filled with fear they laugh it off as a joke.

Two parts of different Worlds

On January 12th this message arrived: *"Thy beloved works stands before thee as promised, by thee and thou you are completing each and every task just as promised dear child we are a big part of one another. Rest thy mind, body and soul thy protection is all around thee from thy highest source. We shall stand between and beside you and thy son always, All of us"* … How beautiful and grateful we were, there was no doubt what we were made of even though it was hard at first to accept being combined of different worlds! Talk about feeling like an alien, we did, and had accepted our truth long ago. The messages kept coming in regularly and boggled our minds, *we were on track* if we thought so or not, and it was plain to see our worlds were many! We loved our life with what we came to accomplish here.

It was in this time a beautiful vision came to me of another lifetime I lived. In it, I carried a bright light down a street and suddenly I was floating into the universe where I heard a heavenly voice say to me: *"that my son and I are called Light Bearers"*. This is all I recall happening, but the words alone made us feel happy. Quickly afterwards a new message came and simply stated: *"Beware the red blood moon awaits you both enjoy the ride. Journey well my Comrades"*. It was only a few days later when we found another message from the ETs: *"Return tonight to give actual experience to let you remember."* Everything was getting more exciting, and we loved being schooled by the them! Another message arrived: *"Do you remember? Journey well on this moons lunar night to tell all, Mother"*. Wow*!* I hardly ever called my mom *mother*, I have a universal mother, and earth mother who are one! At first this left me confused wondering why I was given this message signed by "Mother*"*. It wasn't the first time she signed this way especially with the extraordinary news this message had for us below!

My son David had been told by the ETs, **"Soon the Master is to come."** Talk about excited, **The Master? The Master from in the Bible, the Universe!!** We would soon find out what it meant! Messages kept coming two and three times a day it was hard not to think, what could possibly happen next and another one arrived…

Greetings Earth Child, you have served us well in continuance with your spiritual evolution we are prepared to manifest to you and your male offspring to allow you what you call photo to serve you as well. This will be in the next time frame for now continue your spiritual work. We will also be in touch with R. L. to reaffirm information to get the female started in a new direction let her know this is a new quest for you all!

Who Are We Really?

I do not put the other person's name on these messages to the three us for her privacy who I call R. L. We had been working with a third person for a short time to help her and in two more days information came to us for the three of us. *"We are opening the realm to the three of you to begin the new journey travel with peace, love, and light, embrace it all Ruth, David and R. L."*

We were excited about this new journey we would embrace it all! Next thing the ETs were talking to me about *Butterflies* and how important they are to earth. I felt these beautiful little workers would one day sadly be a thing of the past the way our earth has been changing. I had a right to be very concerned about them, it was coming from man's destruction!

The next thing I knew it was the end of January the time was 9:45 pm when I found another message in my room. *"Testing phase about to begin you Earth child, Male offspring be ready for a big trip as they say in earthly terms be patient study thy inner peace."* They had placed my crystal ball on my pillow beside my small pyramid and Delores Cannon's book *"The Custodians"*, marking the chapter *"The Base Inside the Mountain"* for me to read. I think this was to show us where they have been taking us to over time letting us remember what we were comfortable with.

Then we received some EXPLOSIVE information we had been waiting for, the ETs had been talking to David and me about: *"how we can change and look like we do here on earth and how we look as we really are"*. We knew this exchange made was true, I vaguely remembered starting to change on one trip. They were supplying us with what we knew a little at a time, so they didn't *overload* us. This information was fact, but it had never been

269

confirmed as clear at this! We knew and to absorb it slowly we had been conditioned to earth for so long and it would be wonderful now to be FREE, and who we are!!!

On the fifteenth of February 1:30 am I awoke to flashing lights and formations in an opening or doorway which seemed far away. I watched for a moment and heard myself say, *I'm ready!* I wondered if the ETs had already taken me or had they just brought me back? Apparently, I was ready to go because I began seeing an opening into their dimensions. I was hoping they were going to strengthen my spirit for a personal problem I would need to adjust to and after that night I was sure they had because of their next message. to me.

"Justice to the Dark One may there be voice in my mouth, breath in my nostrils, sight in my eyes, hearing in my ears, may my hair not turn gray, or my teeth turn gray, may I have much strength in my arms, may I have power in my thighs, swiftness in my legs, steadiness in my feet, may all my limbs be uninjured, and my soul remain unconquered. Beloved one we are with you"! Oh, how I thanked them, I knew everything would be alright I would be protected and guided in the right direction, I would win! I knew I would get through this time someone was trying to hurt me with, and after the message things were solved for me to begin anew!

On February 18th, I noticed my desk chair was moved out from behind my desk to get my attention to look at the computer, a new message was there! It was clever how the ETs would draw attention to something or to their message, the subject was about the peace we all want to achieve in life. *"Peace in all things. The peace in the sky, the peace in mid-air, the peace on earth, the peace in the plants, the peace in the forest trees, the peace in all Devas, the peace in Brahman, the peace in all things, the peace in peace, may that peace come to you! This prayer of peace is a divine essence to grant the petitioner for perfect peace, to send this prayer to all. Signed, Love from all"* ... How very beautiful, and this is exactly what we did we sent this prayer to all! How blessed we are to have the high beings who are working with us. I looked up the word *Devas* and the meaning, *"they are divine manifestations, both male and female and Brahman means, a divine essence."* We were uplifted realizing we had many kinds of help from the other worlds uniting to assist us through an important experience I was unsure of. Once again, this shows how beautifully the heavenly spiritual beings of the Christ Light work together with us on earth. My son and I are blessed to be a part of this beautiful God given experience!

It was the last day of February with an end of the month message to us. *"Thou beloved Ruth shall prevail thou has won the struggle against darkness. Thy father in Heaven is very pleased thou shall continue on the righteous path and not deter. Blessed are thy mother and thy son, be humble and believe as thy son David, and remember I am in your heart and soul forever! The Kingdom of Heaven is open"*! How truly beautiful, amazing and humbled!!

I was in shock for several minutes reading this amazing heart loving message over and over as I do, most all touch the heart deeply and I can't think of anything else. This is putting it mildly, for I have no right words what is in my heart and soul, and my son felt the same! Where does our journey end in this world, I asked, yet it does not matter, one day we will have done our best to tell the truth of why we each are here on our different journeys, and every single person is important if they think so or not... and every journey is important no matter what it is.

It was back to work with the ETs when the next message arrived. *"Greetings: you, your male Offspring and R. L. are being directly opened to survive an earth change in the future, try not to fear thy Father in Heaven protects always that is all for now, end of Transmission."* I would be fibbing if I told you I wasn't concerned about the *meaning* of their message, but I knew we would all be safe. The rest of what they planned for us happened the next night at 10:30 pm, when they returned. First they showed us a spectacular event in the night while the moon was in glorious bright color then told us, *"when the moon came down to earth it will become the next earth where we will be safe and teach others and when this happens to stay inside and not breathe the fumes."* We were quite shocked with this message, so a plan was in motion for us earthlings, more than a human could possibly understand right now. For in the future to come, people here will need this safe place to go. We hoped this was to be many years away while we and others of the Light were being prepared. We are their serious workers and whatever instructions coming from the highest would never be turned away.

CHAPTER 13

More Is Revealed

Before I knew it, I was aboard a Craft looking at a screen I have seen many times before. There were designs and symbols moving across it, and suddenly a flash of light went *through me showing me how I really look in my form as a being*! I was sitting there thinking, I was my own *"real self"* being taught to recall these designs and symbols which I felt good to be who I am. The next day after I awoke from this experience, we received a Universal message from the ETs about 2:30 pm which said: *"the time is near we will produce ourselves within your earth time 48 hours."* David and I were excited, pacing around talking about the time had finally come; we were expecting an exciting visit explained in the paragraph below.

That same night when I fell asleep, I had a vision of Edgar and his lovely wife Gertrude, in this visit David and I had gone to see Gertrude knowing she was not well and in a wheelchair at times. She could walk but was weak; she had been through so much no longer having Edgar at her side, he had recently passed into the spirit world. I recalled several people were gathered around their home outside and some were walking up to it with others knocking on the front door. I felt some may have been newspaper people and some of them good friends. Suddenly we were standing at the front door ourselves where Gertrude seemed to be waiting for us; she seemed to know we were coming and opened the door to let us inside where we greeted one another. After seeing how feeble she was we helped her upstairs to her room. She was very kind and invited us inside of their bedroom to continue our visit where we talked about Edgar with her. We wanted her to know how much we loved them both from other times and Edgar as our spiritual teacher.

We were happy she wanted to see us, and I began talking about the four of us and our connections together and how grateful we were to her and Edgar for being our teachers once more in this lifetime. I explained that in the beginning of our memories we had fallen in love with both once more through the books about his life *"There is a River"* by Thomas Sugrue and his small book *"Think on These Things"*. The books and his visits were when I first found out it was

Edgar who was teaching us, and then old memories began to make their way back to me from other times. We couldn't help but notice Gertrude was beginning to tire and looked drained, so we helped put her to bed. Even so when she lay down, we three still talked and she continued to hold our hands she didn't want us to go. I noticed their bedroom more now which had a tower or something like another space built on the front corner of the room, maybe it was more of an alcove close to where they could look outside of a window. She kept a key to this small alcove which had a door on it she kept locked. She had shown the key to us saying, *"This was so Edgar could get away from the press and other people to have some kind of privacy since he was so sought* after". She continued, *"Edgar loved to go there and liked working in this small room"*, we felt this was probably the only quiet time when he could get away from the public to enjoy their precious time together.

Even though Edgar was still working with us in spirit he was also working with Gertrude much more to help her in these sad days, and he always would until she joined him. David and I felt we would spend as much time with her as she needed to help her all we could through these heartfelt times. Edgar had arranged this connection we were experiencing now so we could help her because we had shared many times together as family, and this opportunity had been given to us to tell Gertrude how much we have always loved them in our strong kinship together. Knowing she was tired, we thanked her for our visit and hugged one another it was hard leaving her. Out of nowhere suddenly we heard the word *"revelation"* as clear as a bell; we knew it was coming from Edgar! He had spoken to us about our *revelation* before.

We left Gertrude in bed resting, hoping to return in another time. When we were back outside, I looked up at their room to see the small private part that Edgar treasured to be alone in especially when he could still walk. During his last months when he could do no more; he was helpless, and it was near the end. We were honored to share our life and journey with them again in this time. After the vision with Gertrude, I wondered if their home had looked like this one in the vision, or was the vision a symbol for us to go by? I felt this may have been the last home they had shared together being this older two-story with his favorite room. To this day I have never seen pictures of their home, but I suspect it was somewhat like the

273

vision. When I came out of our visit my heart was broken but I knew they would be reunited soon. Gertrude passed away on Easter in March the same year only a few weeks after her beloved Edgars passing in January 1945.

Daily Living with the Extraterrestrials

Our new message, "*Sub: See you tonight. I take refuge in the great awakening and it's unfolding within these exalted forms, until I realize complete enlightenment my performance of all virtues, being auspicious fate only for the benefit of all, may the truth finally be perceived at all time from the crown of the head, of all sentiment aware beings, throughout the heavens, blossoms a white lotus, supporting a lunar disc, above which appears, the embodiment of the highest the glorious divinity Chenresig, the of all perceiving compassion from whose body shines, the pure and clear five colored rainbow rays, his all-seeing eyes radiate compassion from a beautiful face*".

What this means is, this is the highest honor one could ever want or imagine; it also means we are in tune with all Universes! This was the second time we were given this honor; we were shocked and grateful to receive it once more!! At noon on the same day came a second message, "*Child, don't think we have forgotten we will be in physical form soon!*" This was what we waited for, it was overwhelming and precious!

That bright lights woke me from my sleep and in a moment I could see a large group of ETs in my room, then our contact was somehow broken, and this is what I experienced except I understood telepathically from the ETs "*I was put on hold*" so perhaps I didn't wake up as I thought, but instead had just returned with them. Since my son David had become sick once more, I prayed consistently for me to stay healthy and long enough to always take care of him this was my main desire, my soul wish, and of course the ETs knew our every thought so the next incoming message made sense.

Subject: Health. Message: "*You are a healthy individual you will remain as such as thy Father wills it as such; thy son will continue his prayers and treatments as needed. Blessed are thee.*"

What a blessed relief they had answered my prayers! This was very important to me to take care of my son!

The next night we had company at our home who knew nothing about our ET friends. And during the same evening we had been waiting to see what the ETs had planned for us knowing it would be after company left because David had told me earlier, *"something really big is going to happen"!* Immediately after our visitors left, we were alerted telepathically, *"that we walk hand in hand with them"!* Everything was understood between us then suddenly we heard a loud crash and the sound of keys rattling! The ETs told my son telepathically, *"they had transported something into our old unused brick chimney to the vortex, a beacon for them so we stand out more to them and they would be working on him and me tonight when they came back."* This was exciting news, we wondered what they had planned tonight? Would they be realigning David's body so he would feel better? They are so good to us by using their fine tuning to realign us often and heal us to withstand our constant universal travel with them.

At 3:30 am I was jarred awake with a surprise lying beside me, a message we waited for. *"Moon child, we have produced in our molecular structure this is all in the learning, this is to awaken the senses so you may see us at any time, you are an excellent student as well as teacher try to be patient in the learning. We have love for your old soul, we are honored."*

I was more than honored for the next several minutes I kept re-reading their words near tears. Each day was an ongoing mystery filled of new learning with what was happening in our worlds, but this was something we could not talk of or trust to tell. When I awoke the next day my *video camera* was set up at the end of my bed on the tripod! I called for David, *LOOK!* We were both laughing at the same time because it is unbelievable with the things they do! I examined the video film running it back, checking it out to see if they left anything. I found one thing very interesting which looked to be *Angel wings* on a small portion of the film! We knew the Angels work closely with us and the ETs, but this was amazing to find, and on a few occasions, I have seen film and pictures change in front of me!

It was now March 4th my granddaughter's birthday, a great day to celebrate! Not only this celebration, but the ET *High Council* had left us a message, they are the Highest Councils who work with us, *"You are a highly evolved being like thy son, and R. L. together you are called "TRI like the pyramids. Embrace the universe because it embraces you!"* They were still talking of us being TRI and we took their message of love to heart thanking them with humbleness and love especially coming from these phenomenal benevolent beings. We had much to think about, experiences were happening one after the other in our daily lives, so we had little time to spend on each message like we wanted to!

It wasn't long when we were told by these species why they sign their messages with the pyramid symbol. They explained to us it means, *"We are universal like the three corners of a Triangle, a pyramid"*. It also represents an opening in the sky as a *doorway* for their travels to this planet and back out. The three-corner triangle made perfect sense, David and I are on one corner of the pyramid, R. L on another, and Edgar Cayce is on the 3rd corner because we work together in this way. Therefore, we are known as TRI throughout, how amazing!

When I laid down that evening to go to sleep, I knew someone was there and quickly opened my eyes, but I wasn't prepared to see a *lamb* in front of me outlined in gold!! My heart skipped a few beats I was astounded, this *had* to be a very significant sign and the following message said, *"You both have did well my children we are here to further your education you will go with us now for a while in your time do not be afraid we are the positive ones who work with you all of the time relax now prepare for the trip it will happen tonight. We know the others, negative beings came last night got through, we will protect you. We can go to any part of the mountain now for educational purposes be ready, get ready."* Somehow, a negative force tried to come through to harm each of us in the night hours, but our loving beings protected us! I didn't have time to call out to my son that we were going; I knew the ETs would bring him with me. It is strange how this works, sometimes I only can recall my part with both of us being there together. When the Extraterrestrials come for us my son may be in another location away or in his part of the house sleeping, and they take us both then we see one another on board.

We went to the mountain and when I opened my eyes there was a long probe in front of my face. The Beings said, *"It was to open my 3rd eye even more,"* then they did a healing on me. That night we were also told, *"We have more education to do in the mountain soon where we will be able to see inside of it more"*. I could see the pyramid symbol appear in front of me at that instant and heard, *"good students learning, David's eye is worked on and soon to be ready this is all for now we are honored and have great love and respect for all of you, ETs."* In the next moment I found myself in my bed at home.

The next most wonderful experience from them was finding the *"LORDS PRAYER"* written in their own universal script and if we had not been told by them what it was, we may never have known, we were in *great awe* of this beautiful treasure not expecting to receive this great honor! These Christ Light Beings were defiantly from the highest levels!!

The new information about the pyramid and the mountain was exciting and the more they taught us the more we wanted to know, or I should say *remember...* We soon explained how we traveled with them on the *light energy* and how energy never dies so it is there any time it is needed; this was a Wow!!! The ETs told us in our words the most interesting facts on this energy, *"First they disassemble us into molecules to travel on a beam or rays of the light energy"*. This is the simplest way they could explain in their words; it seems our information becomes more amazing as we go along, and we are always excited! Long ago, I knew we must be disassembled into molecules to go in astral travel but did not know details, it was only in my thoughts, and I did not have any idea about traveling on *beams of rays!* I loved this important message to us which sounds like a story book at times and everything becomes clearer with their words. I have written about having small bruises at times after a trip when coming and going with them, so this news made some sense. So much happens to our heavy bodies in the breakdown it seems impossible it can be done so often, the only thing is we do need regular is to be reenergized and aliened often.

The ETs talked about a *third book* that was to be written on our experiences with them, which is this one I am writing now, and it is the Universal High Council who names my books before I write them. They gave me three titles and ask me *to choose one!* We are very thankful for their help; my son David and I felt extremely honored to be doing this work.

A New Entity of ETs

It was April 2000 my late grandmother's birthday when a new message arrived: *"Greetings, we are a new entity of ETs are we welcome? We will not pass through without permission. You are both on a great journey with much to do your patience will reward you"*. This was another group who would be helping us in our new work, and we looked forward to beginning with them. There had been times we wanted to tell our story so people would not be afraid of Extraterrestrial universal beings and how we are all connected, but we were to wait longer until this book was written with these truths. This is when the door would open, I didn't know how or when, but it would be the right time to begin writing about these things and people would be more open over the world which is good and what we waited for.

This new group of ETs went on to explain more about themselves, first they told us they come from *Zeron,* but I was did not remember this place *yet*, and I know there are a zillion names I have never heard of or simply have not remembered, which made me even more eager to learn all I can. We were from many places and very anxious to learn about this new group of species from *Zeron* who sounded very positive, full of wisdom and knowledge.

Zeron Beings

The new ones began speaking, *"We come from another galaxy and sphere one comes ahead who speaks to you now. We are many light years away, many moons; Zeron is the last Galaxy to the North Quad. There are many Galaxies. You will see me later tonight your earth time. We will speak to the son we are here to help you continue you're learning we can help you both. You have advanced in the healing work perceptions are greater than you can imagine.*

The 3rd eye is open wide as you wish it to be. That is all for now we thank you and the male offspring."

"This is another new beginning" my son said, we were both so *EXCITED* I can't describe it; we really looked forward to our new *Zeron* friends coming back. We were merged with ET life and earth and it is hard to explain the feelings we had with what we had been told. Soon we were going to travel past the last Galaxy even further in light years with the *ZERON* Beings! This would be going in new directions to their home maybe further than ever before! We had no idea of distance through Galaxies with the speed of Light years. That same night just as we had been told, the familiar bright lights woke me and around me were many of the new ETs from planet Zeron and in a blink I went with them! Once there I was given *something* to keep me calm because I could see my own face! This meant I was *out of body* in another life form, yet seeing my solid self still lying in bed as before I left with them. I supposed they had taken David from his room and had him on board someplace else I never knew at times until we would see one another at some point. David told me later, "One *Alien named a substance that would be invented to repair spinal cord injuries in the future to come; it will be the way to mesh the nerves back together again."* Oh, how wonderful! The same Being we went with told my son about the *cloning* they do. These miracles sound like a *Science Fiction* movie but this is what they were teaching us about on that night. This fantastic information would one day be ready to use sometime in the future, they want to help us here so much! Our minds had had this locked in our memory until they wanted it released in this book. There was something special we would be told later…

The ETs were constantly busy continuing to change our computer screen saver to different colors with each new message they left. I had not tried to change a screensaver they were changed by the other side, so we had never had a *normal* first cover page. It was only changed and used by our space families. The first page was used by the ETs and spirits of loved ones with their messages which we called *a bulletin board* of sorts. For years they used it solely to leave us various messages and changed them almost daily, sometimes more than one a day. As you may have guessed I never had much free time to learn about tech things. There were a few times the computer changed in front of us, one family member, and even a friend of ours who experienced this and yes, they did freak out! *"Sorry"* we would say to the ETs when this happened, but we couldn't hold back our laughing it was funny to see the reactions! I figured the ETs did this for their own reasons maybe to open a person to the possibility that they do exist since we had to stay tight lipped. Wait until they found out the rest of the story and how we relate with them and truth of our connection to them. We had many questions about our future.

A new message arrived, *"Thy work shall begin with all things made clear, thy mind, body, and soul are healthy and at one. You, R. L. and thy offspring son who make TRI you all have graduated! Edgar and loved ones here, all of us send greetings with Universal love, thy son and you shall know all answers the three of you have a love and learning bond, you and David have listened well! R. L. has a way to go yet she too learns however long it takes"*. This last sentence clarified means, R. L. the 3rd one to make the TRI was still in the *old ways* but would gradually understand the truth of things as the *Zeron* beings told us, *"NO MATTER HOW LONG IT TAKES!"* Soon another new message arrived from them.

Subject: *TRI listen, learn, read and share.*
Message: *God force energy at its highest possible manifestations' especially when we harness creativity for the highest of mankind. More will be following on Reincarnation very soon most of your questions will be answered. From all in thy realm, only a sheer mist between our worlds and yours.*

Our next contact came the next day.

Subject: *Eternal love. "You will receive a new transmission within 24 hours, please be patient, end of transmission".* Before 24 hours had elapsed another one arrived saying, *added message, "Change made to continue transmission in 24 more hours total of 48 transmissions will be complete".* We anxiously waited for our next continued message which gave us plenty of time to discuss the first messages and the meanings. I hope you who are privileged to read this next message will find the truth in it for you and those everywhere, let the manmade rules be gone that hinder us here on earth with this amazing information!!

This is a most Important Message to Help
All Beings on Earth

To: Earth mother, Male offspring
Subject: The *Etheric Council.*
Message: To help a soul get ready for its next passage.
There is a group of highly evolved beings in spirit what make up what is known as the Etheric Council. These beings have completed earthly incarnations and make recommendations to help other spirits develop their life plan, the spiritual objective and soul wants to accomplish in the upcoming life. This plan outlines the incarnation as a sort of blueprint of opportunities needed for a soul's advancement. The exact details of the plan are left to a spirit to decide. That is where free will comes in each soul is unique. The heavenly knowledge and wisdom of each life is incorporated into its memory. So, it may choose something like a location in an upcoming life that is familiar. All the answers to all the problems lie with-in. Any trial or tribulation is merely a test to see if we can uncover the spiritual solution.

Isn't this amazing to know? We were overwhelmed with this beautiful information given to the people of earth finally the timing was perfect, and this is a heavenly treasure for every soul to know. Will some people understand this glorious divine truth, or can they? This knowledge and truth are given from the highest of all Councils, or it would never have been told! A continuing message was on its way and I am sure those who read this and believe are learning what humans are about and some reasons we have chosen to come to earth and incarnate again, although most on earth have been taught different! We are proud to deliver the ***Etheric Councils Heavenly*** messages to humanity through my books... Next message arrived.

To *Earth mother, Male offspring*
Subject: *Eternal love*
A soul is given many opportunities to develop and expand by living through adversity; growth is never easy and can be accomplished

only by experiencing every aspect of a situation and fully comprehending it. This is the end of transmission for now. Love, light, happiness and joy, go forward and live each moment in Christ's Light his light glows from thy face!
TBC for new TRI Council there will be more transmissions coming...

These precious messages give information many do not know to take away the fear they hold, just as my son and I were being reminded of and remembered from long ago! The next evening, I was graced with the presence of the *Great Traveler* once more and why did I love him so much, my heart burst with love! He wore a magnificent beautiful robe dazzling with what I referred to as *crystals*. I knew they had a great meaning, so I asked him, *"What are they called that shines so brilliantly?"* He answered, *"Trillions"*. I was standing in front of him at the time focused on his beautiful garment then drawn to look into his beautiful eyes, and shockingly they were like mine! I had become *mesmerized* lost in them as if I were hypnotized, not wanting to come out of a phenomenal feeling of pure love I was experiencing, and then he brought me out of it as he spoke to me of a new mission.

Yes, we are here a new beginning is coming soon a mission and not your first one. A message comes to help clear the way. Try not to worry about the others who are going the one you call Martha she will either be ready or not, in her heart she is but needs the two of you to help her. You will do your best and the son will work more closely with her and you with Chris. Do not be alarmed for you both shall see different forms soon...more clearly. You both have sort of been on vacation as you say, now we really get to work. We are going to keep you busy with the Reiki healing work a breakthrough comes to enhance your new abilities. It is already very powerful we are humbled and proud of the both of you! Another message comes in 24 hours you listen well, keep listening to the tones. Make yourself one with all keep practicing this for you only get better and better no more baby steps. You don't need the signs anymore that we leave you both. Still work on communication we will still give you signs anytime. Do not be concerned my dear we are all helping you both. We love you both. end of transmission...

What can I say, this was amazing and before he vanished I could feel this beautiful Being's pure love radiating out absorbing us, like he knew we both were so proud and honored to be part of such a grand experience we had freely chosen to do! Chris & Martha are our dear friends he spoke of who we love, and we understood perfectly what he meant. We had been working with them the best we could for some time without them knowing. The man Chris was very eager to go forward, but Martha needed a little more time before she would be ready. David planned to work more with her, and I would continue with Chris, he had advanced and would be ok for further travels. Our lives were about doing our best to help others in a positive way while living in many worlds and universal places. All the information coming to us universally certainly kept our spirits up, and my son's medical emergencies were with shorter times to heal. David felt better now knowing he had been given more time to complete his mission on earth and this meant everything to us! We didn't talk about these things happening to us or about our Alien families to any person and never would until we had permission. It had become easier to live here blending our spiritual, paranormal, and ET work in secret; it all goes hand in hand, with it being of the one source, our Creator.

The Grays and the Great Traveler

My son asked me if I remembered going with the *"Great Traveler and the Grays last night?"* He told me: *"we were being shown how they can travel through the worm holes into any time frame they wanted to!"* We had traveled the worm holes many different times before but this time I did not recall being inside this craft. But I remembered, *The Great Traveler* wore *a wide pad devise on his wrist which looked like it had symbols he used to set in the year and date they wanted to travel to and showed us how it worked; it was only powered by an energy source like a crystal or thoughts.* We traveled into black holes as we have before they were like winding tubes, we needed *NO oxygen at all!* We went through different time periods, many dimensions and universal places while doing this travel. He was teaching us how their journey in travel stands simultaneously with ours, I wasn't quite sure of this exact meaning.

283

David told me, *"He didn't remember if we went in physical body or was broken down into molecule energy"*. I think we went in energy and the travel we did was a blur with the tremendous speed of it, at times we seemed to slow down to be aware of other long-ago periods in the past so we could see certain famous people who lived back then, it was breathtaking and the next thing I realized I was at home waking up in my bed! When David came downstairs the next day, we both remembered the trip we had taken, what an honor! How in the world does all of this happen, was our question to one another, but the universal part of us knew why it was happening! We felt alone many times being so different but loved our exciting travels to what is real and where we belonged!

We were collecting information currently through the *"Tributary Council, Etheric Council, many worlds and star systems, the Grays, Normadics, The Great Traveler, TRI Council, and Intergalactic Transmissions"* along with other amazing Universal Beings of the Light who were working beside us. It was quite a long list and a phenomenal one! The ET Beings were still changing the computer screen saver often with new messages and I tried my best to video every one of them and used my camera to take pictures. But it didn't always work well since the letters moved across the screen quickly, and with motion it was hard to film and get clear pictures, I still had no idea then I could slow it down! I did manage to get most of the words and messages, on May 20th *the High Council* sent another message to us.

Message: To Moonchild, Male Offspring
Subject: The Council Speaks
Message: We are all of one source, involved with the true higher beings. The Continuance of your education resumes this lunar evening. We will be sending transmissions through this antique vessel made by mankind. Valuable information is being transmitted you will be using it to help the earth and all its inhabitants. See that the information gets out after you have accumulated it. Be prepared as we continue working through Christ's light. The eternal force will carry you and your son well, and then the followers will come and see the truth in you both. End of transmission.

Another following important message arrived.

To; Moonchild, Male Offspring
Subject: lesson
Message: The religion of the future will be a cosmic religion. It should transcend personal God and avoid dogma and theology covering both the natural and the spiritual. It should be based on a religious sense of arising from the experience of all things natural and spiritual as a meaningful unity. End of transmission.

This would be *explosive* news for some when they read this, and man-made religions the world over, but they are also to learn of the universal truth!! Humans one day will learn by these Heavenly teachings. We felt the old ways could die out and the truth begin to pave the way for humanity at last! We have mostly lived in fear to be afraid of God our Creator, who is used as a punishment by many, and told if we don't do what the old ways teach and have been taught, we will likely *burn* in a terrible place described as *"HELL!"* So, no matter how good one has lived it would never be good enough! The truth was hidden long ago to control the people on earth and the truth that should be taught everywhere is of *LOVE AND COMPASSION!*

In the night hours we were told, *"our work is being well received we love you and we embrace you in the most beautiful light, Mom and Daddy, Edgar and all the other"*. Amazing! Is the only word that I seem to come up with, these things are full of love and impossible to explain! I marveled at how beautiful our life is and how blessed we are, and I continually prayed for David's life to be longer and longer, then I was reminded *there are no trades we had made our contract eons ago before birth.*

June was nearly over, and the messages kept rolling into us in my notebooks, on the computer screen, and with our ETs visits in space and home with them speaking directly to us with our lessons and trips together. The next one follows below.

To Moonchild, Male Offspring
Next message, Subject: From Above.
Rewards await you both for ye shall smile upon those who are looked down upon by thy foolish brothers and sisters. They are lost

sheep in a mist but do not look for the Sheppard thy work is of great energy your spiritual growth is vital it continues at an accelerated level. Blessed are thee and yes, July is a month of celebration for many reasons yet to be seen. You both are a beautiful soul remember the gifts of heaven are bestowed upon you each use them wisely.

This message was breath taking beautiful, and full of love, and made the two of us want to work even harder, how we love our blessed journey! Reading this message above completely humbled us like so many of them do. It became harder to sleep as these heavenly messages and universal beings continued to guide us through our lives. The screen saver changed the next morning revealing a soft pink background only, and the next day the message arrived, *"Go forth and enjoy thy journey learn from thy fools"*. This relates to having had a negative, upsetting experience at a fair the day before. And on this same evening I found my little pyramid on top of my bed balanced on my pillow, which was sitting on a book I had purchased at the same fair titled, *"Beyond the Fourth Dimensions"* by Karl Brunstein. The book was opened to pages 76-77 and on each top corner of the two pages a triangle had been drawn by one of the ETs, so I knew I was to carefully check out those pages about the *Evolution of Humans.* The pages in this book are in *symbolisms* so therefore we are positive this is reminding us of whom we had been and are, and why we get the many symbols and numbers. The ETs told us, *"they want us to study these pages because our minds are growing so rapidly with the information they give to us, which is a very big part of our re-learning and we are using areas of the brain that have never been identified yet as to what is there and that our brains are at full capacity."*

Next, we were given the name of these prehistoric animals Tyrannosaurs REX, and Trexerhomous, *I was given the names three different times.* This was to be an example of what we had been told about *"evolution and brain capacities"* from the beginning of the ages until what is known up to now about the brain. At that time, I studied the pages deciding to let the information soak in until I felt clearer with it, but soon after with so much taking place I went on to other new experiences happening in the paranormal, spirit and ET worlds. It would be sometime later that I would re-read these two pages to try understanding why it was so important to know this information. The books explanation is quite complex to me, I felt the need to study it more every chance I had.

Our minds were holding a huge amount of information they were giving to us, and we had been told, *this was for our brain to make room and stretch to hold more new information and continue its rapid acceleration,* now it made more sense but I would need to study the book for some time yet.

I came downstairs to see the screen saver background was a soft blue color with a message waiting for the both of us: *"A journey into the past Venture Inward, go within, and seek thy inner peace for it shall bring you joy. Edgar Cayce."* Thank you, Edgar, we both said at once! *Venture Inward* e Edgar Cayce Foundation, in Virginia Beach, Va. I knew this was an important clue to read this issue and I bet we would find some important information we needed.

On June 20, 2000 at 11 am we were contacted by the main *TRI Council* with another message: *"TRI Greetings, we have not forgotten we are watching your evolutionary progress we will be in touch in the month of July. All Councils are meeting now."* We were on pins and needles thinking *"a meeting about us!"* Patiently we waited and watched for our instructions to come which wasn't long. These messages may shock many people on this planet, but we must move forward to teach what is real and how we have been held back negatively by those in power from the beginning...

To: Moonchild, Male Offspring.
Subject: From Above.
Message: Ye shall smile upon those who are looked down upon by thy foolish brothers and sisters for they are lost sheep in a mist, but do not look for the Sheppard. Thy work is of great energy your spiritual growth is vital. It continues at an accelerated level blessed are thee and yes, July is a month of celebration for many reasons to be seen!

This was exciting each message has such powerful information humans have a right to know and think about, we were completely swept away with this message from above! We were stunned yet knew why this is happening! Suddenly we found new symbols on my computer screen in a group of designs with the number 7. I realized 7 is one of my numbers, July being my birth month of celebration time. We didn't have to wait long that evening when the next beautiful message came, it was short but heavenly beautiful: *"The gifts of Heaven are bestowed upon you both use them wisely"*. David and I were astonished, and praying we were carrying out the things we were to do, so far it sounded like we were! I could not sleep well that night knowing we had agreed to a huge responsibility on this earth, and I knew we would never stop! Sometimes I was overwhelmed with my thoughts focused on, *how can we do so much, and will we live long enough to complete our mission*? I could only hope so, and if not, it was understood by the other side because we took on too much, they told us long ago. We had agreed to everything in our Covenant and promise, and confident we would get our promises completed. We planned if something unseen happened to one of us the other one would continue onward! This is what I am doing now on this side and David still works with me wherever we are, we will work side by side for eternity.

Our next information arrived, we felt fully graced once more with three following messages from the ETs: They told us of our recent trip to our sister universe and what we had implanted into our brains.

Gone through warp into sister universe
Have new technology implanted into our
brain stem. Released from their own system
when we are ready. Passed into TRI system
to be exposed to TRI- Council for final
approval. They nod yes, we all bow before
each other and accept all responsibilities!
All is well and soon to be completed. TRI
will finish processing data into brain stem.

Second and third message was received next…

All is well and soon to be completed
For finality. Will have the memory
Reinstated after this data is completed
Transference into brain stem.
We all bow before each other, and except all responsibilities!!!

Transmission: "You and the male offspring are elevating as projected; do not second guess your intuitive gifts. You both will be honored as guests in our Galactical celebration. Journey well. End of transmission'.

This was fantastic news to be honored guests in this Galactic celebration!! It was thrilling to know we were ready and willing to advance with the universal Councils! I finally fell asleep later and in the night hours I awoke to a *popping* sound on the right side over my bed. Somehow, I knew it was *The High Council* and knew to focus above me where they were gathered in a circle over me like they do at times. I was told, *"to go ahead and transcribe then and they would transcribe their information to me"*. I grabbed my notebook and pen I keep handy on the bed and quickly let them know I was ready to transcribe, and I that I was honored!

"Yes child, lesson 4 begins tonight to know one is from the stars is a revelation! Your male offspring knows this! Keep on with your work for July holds the KEY to much. We are going to help you both with problems the male Offspring's membrane is nearly gone we are going to work on it to be evenly arranged so know and believe 100%. E. C. will leave you a sign watch on the evening of July 7th, at 10 pm look at your sky, bring camera, we shall guide thee we are always here for both of you we are honored also. End of transmission."

We would be ready what glorious news; they would finish repairing David's eye! The next morning my son and I talked of the messages that had arrived one after another; we were in fast gear thrilled with the amazing messages and information! The next day in the afternoon I found a sign from Edgar on my bed. My two artificial white Doves were placed on my pillow that he used often as his sign to us. The following writings came to us the next day to let us know *"we went into the universal heavens they are transforming us in astral travel!"* How exciting we were I can't begin to cover our feelings and exactly what this meant we weren't sure of yet, nevertheless we felt great, and everything with our universal family was wonderful! I thought it was unbelievable at times how we survived our sanity with so much in our brain and NOT tell anyone about…we were completely dedicated. Transforming us in astral travel!!! Even we were speechless many times with everything going on plus living earth life! Looking back, I wondered how we functioned in earth life for all those years in private while living many lives in other Universal worlds! Our lives were extraordinary, and we felt more Alien than humanness, you understand we were living an unheard-of life in other worlds and dimensions we had lived in before, and in this one every day. We were able to see things others cannot see and hear beyond, yet we did not dare to speak of these things or share them because of those who could make our families lives very unpleasant living in a small area, and even if we were living in a city it would not have made much difference. Our experiences would have been too much to explain…

I had felt out of *sorts* lately and so had David the ETs came to us and said, *"They were going to re-adjust us both"*. I know I needed it the way I felt, I was tired but as always wanting to learn more regardless and at times I wanted to stay longer on the other side re-learning. At one point after we had traveled in the night David said, *"I scared him so much, I went out to far universally and he had to keep calling me back, in my mind it was time for me to go home to our ETs"*. The next day he was still unsettled and concerned because of my going too far but thank goodness I heard him calling me in my mind, I had explained, *"I didn't mean to pass the limit and I would never repeat it again"*.

As I look back, I am reminded of so many journeys no wonder we both were warned *"not to use our energy up on small things in the material world,"* but we were both guilty of this. We sometimes let negative people use us for their own worries and feelings, meaning our hearts went out to them with our own emotions being concerned about their problems, then we exhausted our own selves thus losing our energy. In this work we had to be more careful. With my son being terminal, he lost energy very quickly and be hospitalized in critical condition often.

This next message from the beloved ones was *ASTOUNDING!* It arrived on the computer with a red background screensaver and white glowing letters, *"Thy son shall be christened into the Holy Spirit all will be well bow before thy Father in Heaven."* Oh my, this absolutely took our breath away!!!! There are no words in the human language to describe our feelings! My son was being highly graced again by the Holy Father, our Creator! How proud I was, my heart was bursting with love for him and one day his beloved sisters and our family will read this book and understand more of the life we led! His sisters and our loved ones truly loved and adored their brother so very much as he did them. My children are very bonded, and I love them all more than life. It would all be worked out one day along with millions of others who are having their experiences and trying to figure out what to do with them, and this was a comfort to us. I am sure each person on their own journey was different, according to the work they do.

Our next message arrived…

To: Moon child, Offspring
Subject: Resolving matter evenly
Message: Your emotional outburst will be relined. There was a problem when you both rematerialized from the universe. The male offspring has a chemical block involved. If you give us your permission, we will realign him at the next evening. We are working on you both to complete the lesson. Your human bodies have endured a lot throughout these new programs we apologize for any pain caused for we only are helping you evolve to your fullest potential.
The Universal beings of Light.

When I think no more could happen of such magnitude it does!! After this message we were thinking, *"what else could possibly happen"* and in our amazement another beautiful message arrived!

Subject*: Universal Energies*
Message: Welcome, we are pleased to induct you both into our new realm. The true meaning of universal love is emanating from your souls. The true ones will seek you and you will teach them they will in turn graduate and follow down the lines as a circle is complete. This is a grand beginning to a new journey. Yes, we are all involved in this together we help as much as possible my love, from mother and daddy…

291

My mother and Dad, incredible!! This cements the fact that my parents are working steadily with us and the universal ETs from the Christ Light! Growing up, my parents had never mentioned UFOs or Alien beings, it is easy to understand now that apparently their memory of contact with beings had been removed. But after both passed over, they have continuous contact with not only us, but apparently other Universal species of *Christ Light!* Their messages and travel with us have been on a constant basis, helping us at times with our endeavors on earth and universe with our space brothers, how amazing! We were soon told a new message was on its way…and here it is another amazing message giving us the strength to do what we need to be living our earth life.

Greetings to Our Universal Soldiers

Greetings to our universal soldiers, blessed are the ones who fight for the truth and face all the daily dark ones. Thy journeys are becoming more vivid and realistic; your mentalities are elevating; we are happy with you both. Continue thy positive journeys and daily trials they will bring you to the higher vibration that is necessary to travel and communicate with your spiritual Alien beings. Message to follow soon, end of transmission…

This *phenomenal* information not only let us know what our minds and spirit bodies were capable of doing but also, to help us in our work supported by the highest of Universal Christ Light Councils and Beings through the positive journeys. This was much to absorb with living a secret life here, but it is a beautiful life we chose!

It was late July when I awoke to see some being coming from my bathroom; I made out several symbols *inside* the form of a male Being! The next thing I knew I was traveling with the ETs and then looking upward. I could see a *probe* coming down close to my face; and one of the ETs let me know *"they were preparing to work on my 3rd eye once more"* I felt they were adjusting and opening it more fully. After this my next memory was that they were showing me a *PLAQUE* dated 500 AD which was an important time in history and following this I was told more about *"the life of Jesus Christ"*.

Suddenly I woke up back in bed it was morning, and I felt wonderful I had been given extraordinary information! Early the same day my son came into the kitchen asking, *"If I remembered the ETs had worked more on my 3rd eye,"* excitedly I told him I did! David said, *"he was with me".* I felt he was present, and I also remembered the beautiful blond-haired beings who look the same as humans, but I had no more memory of them or David. The blond beings I have mentioned come to earth often where they walk amongst us without being noticed as any different than a human being for whatever their task may be. Campers have reported seeing them in many places, especially in the isolated desert and mountain areas.

The next night after falling asleep I was suddenly sitting before a screen, so I knew I was back on a familiar UFO studying something I needed to recall. Sitting beside me was a *High Council Being* wearing a brilliant royal blue garment with beautiful lights around him; this told me he held high authority over the others. Something happened, it seemed only seconds to me I could see outside of the UFO with the lights around it! This possibly meant I was being returned and watching as it departed back into space. Every night then I would see beings in unknown, extraordinary beautiful colors with the number 7 symbol being shown. I believe without a doubt this number was of many things I am doing, also to show me ahead of time that David and I would be extra busy in their learning process the entire month of July; our birth signs seem to be quite important to them and in our lessons.

The next day opening my eyes I knew was it was too early to be dawn, yet bright lights were pouring into my room through the windows. This was the night my vision became more amazing through my 3rd eye, it functioned like a telescope! I looked across the room and my sight zoomed up close to what I looked at like a camera works! I was shocked, but happy, and hoped it would remain this way which also reminded me of binoculars! Next both of us were taken by the ETs to a rocky mountain area in their craft, and next in the universe traveling. This is what we both remembered when we asked one another the next day, and immediately after this a new message arrived.

My beloved ones a change come very soon in your favor. Be wise with your decisions for many opportunities are opening up towards you both your guides and angels will be close as always. Keep up the beautiful spiritual work that you both are doing your rewards will be everlasting. Journey well and love to all, free your mind and soul all will come together soon you will see all.

A Birthday Message from the Aliens

Subject: Happy birthday my love to you on July 16th
Message: There is much to send you your birthday message will appear soon we are having technical difficulty with this old vessel. The heavens have been opened and all the angels soar and rejoice to celebrate the day you were born your children adore you as those you touch in life. You are known as the angel of healing, an honor in itself. Pity those fools that cross your path in life and do not believe. All of us

I was startled to receive such a heavenly message and breathtaking information! Being this humbled I couldn't think of words in our language to express my heartfelt feelings of love to them. I was in awe of this beautiful birthday message for all these years and I still am to this day! How did I ever deserve this with the words that were written! That same day after I read this message my son told me, *"he was shown a future look of me with my books someplace important which represented a good outcome for our work that it will go on to help many others".* I was very happy to know this and somewhat stunned to know this would come to be in the future!

It was decided for my birthday that David, myself, and one of my daughters would travel to Albuquerque, New Mexico to visit my Aunt Mary. This was our dream and drawn to do, and one of several on our *bucket list* that had come true! While there, we made a trip to *"Sky City"* which is on a mountain top to see the Native American Indians and how they still live today. It was sad to see how they struggled to survive, nothing seemed to have changed for them from when they first settled there, our hearts broke for them. They are humble people living mostly off the land without electricity; they haul their water a long distance then up the mountain. It looks as if time has stood still and never changed for them, the same original church built still with a dirt floor was built in 1500 and is still being used. There was an older Indian woman baking bread in an outside oven made of mud brick called a Kiva. We bought bread to help her and it was delicious! This mountain they live on is completely flat on top, I wondered how the children stay safe and if some may have fallen off through the years? We left after a while the sun was so hot that high up it affected my aunts hearing aid! I looked at how far removed from today's world they are and honored them. My aunt and a relative were taking us to see the sites we wanted to experience; our next stop would be a special one in Santa Fe.

We couldn't wait to be in Santa Fe because this was for *a special reason* we were to be there, and at long last we would each have our experiences to treasure. Years ago, I was drawn to watch an older movie about the first mission church built in the Santa Fe dessert area which was named *"St. Loretta's Chapel"*. After the movie ended it was made clear to me from the heavenly beings that I had a strong connection to this place and one day I would go there to see it. For many years I talked of wanting to see this church to others because of a great *miracle* which occurred there therefore my aunt took us there. We were very excited that day to go inside of the ancient chapel, I knew if I took pictures where a miracle occurred many hundreds of years ago, I would have something special on my film and sure enough in one of my pictures I did! To be there was a great experience for us and my son and daughter loved the church as much as my aunt and me. You could feel the vibrations were loaded with great love, sadness, joy and compassion. After this, we returned to home to where a message was already waiting on the computer, *"Welcome home, we are happy for thy experience grow from it."* Can you believe this! We loved our *welcome home;* the ETs knew this was very important for us to experience! I felt I would be there again one day, and years later I returned!

After we arrived home from Santa Fe, we had to buy a new computer and once hooked up it needed to be checked out, the ETs sent us the first message: *"Testing 123, we come in peace ET solar beings."* We had the best laugh about this, they always know everything! We began having trouble right away with it so we asked the ETs to help fix it and immediately we had a response back, *"Your technical difficulties will soon be over we are sorry about the delay."* I strongly felt they were connecting with our computer after it was first purchased but something else was needed to be arranged differently or changed for the ETs to connect to it. This turned out to be an on and off thing for a couple of days, but soon it was running great, and we had them to thank for it!

Each message we received was coming from the ETs, Edgar, my parents, loved ones in spirit, and heavenly beings. They also created a new screen saver background in a different color and changed our messages to different size font and colors, no matter who it was from this was *fantastic!* We never knew how they did these things, but I bet it is simple to do for them maybe I could learn to do this one day! Computer messages from ETs!

"Our friends were really showing off," we said laughing, we were home to resume our work together. The universal beings wasted no time the next day we found a new message, *"The human mind vision will be able to see on Monday evening in the night skies."* How exciting! The next morning early, I awoke to bright lights flashing in my room and in my face, which usually startles me at first. A moment later lights were still coming through my windows, but this was different than usual, so I spoke out loudly, *"What is that?"* I jumped out of bed to see why they were different and raised the window to get a better look. I was astounded to see the most beautiful *spectacular light show!* There were *thousands* of bright white lights shooting out from a *"Mother Ship"* with bursts of lights and flashes of lightening rolling across the skies over the house into the windows!! Even though this UFO was a huge one, no one anywhere could see it, the ETs had a shield up as they often do...

Early morning traffic was slowly beginning to move by the house it was 5:15 am, no one even noticed the lights happening in the sky! There were sounds of *loud thunder* with the flashing lights, never letting up, which is a lot of thunder! I knew the lights were not regular lightening since they were non-stop! Meanwhile my son David woke to the loud noises and came rushing into my room to see what was going on! We both were looking out of the windows now knowing it was our space family! This amazing display of sound and lights was phenomenal, then we decided to run to David's back bedroom to check out the sky behind the house, but the taller trees blocked our sight, so immediately we went outside into the back yard! At the same time we were talking about the last message we received from the ETs the day before that: *"we would be able to see something on Monday in the night skies*" and even though this was Monday and matched their last message, and we bet there would be more that night!

What I remembered the most on the same night my head felt like a giant computer! I could see their information and symbols going by a tremendous speed being stored into my brain. I knew it was happening and helpless to stop it if I had wanted to. I was not hurt in any way, we never have been, but what an amazing experience. I felt their presence with me then knowing I was in space traveling, moving in a timeless void, and suddenly it was the next day! We found another new message that evening at 7 pm from the beings, "*The encounter was achieved in the early morning hours. The next encounter will be on a clear evening soon. We will let you know when.*"

There was no doubt what we had experienced, and little did we know our lives would change dramatically when all our memories returned one day in a very important reunion with our universal space brothers!!

CHAPTER 14

A New Way to Give Past Life information to others

A new beginning was starting for us to provide information to those who are *open minded* and seeking to learn about *past lives.* One evening after I had fallen asleep a certain past life of mine was brought before me in a vision. I was a doctor working in India with someone I knew assisting me as we passed energy healing to my patient who was lying on a makeshift table. Although I couldn't quite see the man's face that assisted me, I felt a very strong kinship of love for him. We passed healing to our patient's face which had something terribly wrong, a case of *Bell's palsy.* I worked very carefully on the disfigurement, along with his one deformed eye and a birthmark on one side of the face, and the strange thing was I felt this was someone I knew or would know in my life today!

My patient was a dark-skinned Indian man with black hair and mustache; and somehow, I knew this man was a *woman* in today's world! Therefore, in some strange way I was seeing the three of us in *past lives* from long ago in India which I will continue to explain. When my assistant and I finished working on the patient we began getting our things together to leave and being very cautious since we had been smuggled into the country to work on this person. As we were packing, we began to hear loud shouting along with screams; something very serious was happening outside with rounds of gun fire! Upon going outside and stopping a street person we found a huge uprising had started! We quickly became alarmed to get out of the country as fast as we could for home, or we would not be able to get out! We had a great fear of *urgency* knowing there was no time to waste! My assistant who had helped me work on the male patient stayed close beside me to protect me as we ran for the airport and plane. Before we left our patient, I had put on a disguise of the traditional Indian woman's Sari with a veil to cover my face, and I carried a fake ID, it was extremely dangerous to be an American at this time in India! This would be a very dangerous time for not only Americans, but other nationalities who would be trying to get out of the country the same as us! I was very frightened to go past the guards in the airport but we somehow managed to with our fake ID, without a moment to spare, then quickly running to the plane to board flying safely home to America. It was then I looked at my assistant's face who had protected me, never leaving my side, staying right beside me; he was my son *David* in this life! In the vision as we worked on the *Bell's palsy* patient with Reiki, I seemed to never be looking right at my assistants face however, I felt he was a special loved one in my life today and no wonder I did! We have shared our lifetimes together throughout our existence!

The strange thing about this experience happened to us the next day when we were working on a young woman's face named Amber who was in her twenties. She had woken up that morning noticing her sight in one eye was not right, looking into the mirror; she discovered she had an instant case of *Bell's palsy*. One half of her face including the eye was deformed and drooping! Neither of us had met Amber yet, she was visiting her mother from Florida the same day this happened to her.

Her mother Irene had been a student of mine at the college where I taught. That day when my phone rang, I was surprised it was Irene who was very up-set wanting to know, *"If we would come to her home, she was hoping we could help her daughter!"* This was after a doctor had seen Amber earlier in the day. Her daughter was sure she had Bell's palsy by her medical training.

We left home immediately driving a long distance to get to Irene's home. After meeting Amber, we explained what Reiki and she was acquainted with it but had never had an occasion to try it. We worked on her until we knew it was complete and then drove home. Remember, we knew nothing about Amber except her waking up in that condition. The following day after her Reiki session I called her mother to inquire how Amber was doing after her treatment. No big change yet, except finally she was finally able to sleep which was good.

Then out of the blue for an unknown reason Irene mentioned her daughter had worked for a doctor once from India and married him but had recently divorced. With that, I suddenly began telling Irene about my vision experience in India the night before when we were working on a patient who I now felt sure was her daughter in a past life with us! It was as if a door had opened so I explained the rest of the vision concerning the patient who also had one eye deformed with Bell's palsy. Then I went on to tell the rest of our story of narrowly getting out of the country because an uprising was starting with violence in the streets, and knowing this I disguised myself in a traditional Indian woman's Sari and a veil to hide my face to get through airport security. Then we ran for our plane quickly boarding it flying safely home!

I heard Irene gasp, she went quiet and was speechless, I wondered if she was ok? After the first few moments of silence she began to explain something to me, *"Wait until I tell you this about my daughter Amber. She was once married to a doctor from India when she was quite young, and later he wanted to take her back with him to India where they lived for one year. The time came when an uprising was beginning, and things were becoming violent so they knew they better get out of India fast or they would not be able to. They left in disguise with her being dressed as an Indian woman in a sari and veil covering her face to hopefully make it through the airport security soldiers since she was a foreigner!"* It was complete silence… we both were stunned!

This was the same vision I had told her about, everything indicated this was a past lifetime the three of us had and of our past lives together! We each had different roles in that lifetime such as David was my assistant; I was the doctor working on the male patient with Bell's palsy and Amber was the male patient. I was amazed and surprised to hear her mother's story as she was mine. When I told my son the whole story, he surprised me saying, *"I am glad you remembered I was with you working on this person and assisted you."* He remembered the past life, is easy to sum it up; the assistant I felt so bonded with was David my son in this life!

The Indian male patient I felt was really a woman was the young lady Amber we had worked on the day before, and in her past life she was a male with Bell's palsy! In this life she had married a doctor from India, they also had to flee the country with her in disguise wearing an Indian women's traditional clothing with a veil covering her face just in time to avoid being caught in a serious uprising. She told her mother how scared and terrified she had been to go through security guards at the airport then both wasted no time running to board the plane!

This is only one experience proving past lives and how we can arrange who we are in a life. Irene immediately told her daughter about my vision and she verified everything to be correct, they were spellbound! I know they felt as surprised as we were to come together again in today's world in this way, we were excited for days to know of our connections from the past!

After this amazing story the next evening a message was waiting for us: *"Concerning the lunar full moon tomorrow night! It will be a message of honor to you both, a great honor."* We were on pins and needles all day with great joy what did this honor mean for us? What a special few days we experienced and now this and right before bedtime another message arrived, *"Thy universal law has been met thy works are hailed to all beings we will be in contact in the physical by the 2nd lunar moon!"* We felt we couldn't wait this was so exciting! On the night of the lunar moon the electricity kept going off in the house starting at 10:30 pm, at first it was for only seconds, so we knew they were here. At 10:40 it did the same thing and immediately we found another new message; it was simple to know why the electricity kept doing this.

This is the evening to see you better we will see you soon. We are all here wishing you joy and good will we love you. Be happy my love everything is for the best and is going to be more wonderful every day! We are with thee.

We were so happy!! It sounds as if they will be coming, I said, and in that split second, we were aboard a UFO with the Beings and had no memory of what happened in-between as usual. I remembered I investigated the night sky from inside the craft by looking out of the windows where I could see thousands/millions of stars in designs like a *grid work* with flashes of light; and I heard one of the ETs tell me, *"more comes tonight!"* This confirmed they have definite understanding of our feelings and emotions to let us know everything was, *"ok, don't worry."*

There is nothing else I recall about this trip with them except what seemed to be in a flash we were back at home again and my son and I were told, *"To go outside and look at the moon".* The moon was very large with gold and orange colors; I tried to take pictures of it but wasn't having much luck. The ETs were suddenly telling me about *"vitamins that I needed them* then reaffirmed to us our family, our loved ones, *will be coming!"*

I think they may have taken tests on me when I was on board and discovered I needed vitamins. The next thing I knew I was high up in the universe, we were moving again! I heard myself saying, *"It is soooo beautiful;"* which was difficult to get out being in a time warp. The ET in the UFO standing beside me said, *"We are just getting warmed up."* After this I simply woke up the next day in my bed and my son was asleep in his room! We noticed years ago the ETs often come to us on the end of a storm, to us perhaps seemingly riding on the energy of it. A week later I had the most magnificent vision *"I saw an Angel who carried our Reiki symbol to us!"* This must have been the *shield* I carried in front of myself in my vision when we were told, *"Reiki is Gods healing for others!"* How *important this statement is!* That night I knew I was right about the shield I carried because our screen saver came on by itself and written was, *"Reiki Masters!"* This is what the Creator sent my son and me to do throughout our lives, to use and teach Reiki energy how honored we were!

At 10 pm that night when I entered my bedroom lying on my bed was our sign of the two white doves from Edgar. I had asked him for a sign to verify something of importance, I told him, *"thank you dear Edgar with all my heart!"* Soon I was given a past life vision of how it is to be in spirit when one leaves here with my own experience of crossing over in another lifetime, they wanted me to write about it below just as the words were given to me.

An Afterlife Story of Being in Spirit!

The husband said, *"Well, here we are".* Then smiling he said: *"Hey, I've got pretty good-looking arms"* and the couple both laughed. One said to the other, *this is alright and,* each one agreed. The man was still driving their car or at least to them it seemed he was. They had been in an explosion which happened by the roadside and it had killed them. They found out by looking at their new bodies, they were even more than perfect and whole once more, they were very happy! This couple had a small son and his dog that were still with them, so they were very happy to still be together; they were whole and perfect, better than ever! I was the woman feeling what it was like in that past life to be in spirit after the explosion, I was still holding my son with his dog on my lap, we were still all together, we felt great! My husband was still driving the phantom car and all of us were fine! We had a fast transition in the blink of an eye, and it was simple, now we were in our real home to have a new life all together! We were going to meet *"The Master"* and somehow, we just knew this, and were so excited! Looking around I noticed the streets were in a dazzling gold and the trees looked like jewels, this was phenomenal! Then I called out, *"look, look"* my son's eyes grew big, his smile was enormous, and I smiled back at him, we were all in the arms of the Master!

This short story explains what happens when there is no judgment waiting for us as we are taught; this is about the greatest love ever to receive for those who have lived an ordinary life. I have treasured this look into one of my past lives to share it with others, so they know how is to cross over. I am sure each story is different with each soul, but it is the most glorious trip one will ever make with no right words to describe it! There was *no Devil* only the greatest love, I thought this was a cute example of a short life I was given to write about explaining my life in that time!

A new message arrived from Edgar: *"yes my child it is time to go forward with your endeavors. E. C."* Our world was moving into September, it was already the 5th when David came to me and said, *"The door unlocked itself the ETs are here!"* We hurried into the room where my computer was to check, sure enough a message was on it! Boy, they are fast I said, *"Greetings, we are with you as we speak your both earning spiritual points so do-not get discouraged. Thy father is proud of you both as well as your past loved ones and guardians. Your Alien beings passed right through you both last evenings."* We were so excited as usual talking rapidly about their visit and the beautiful message, and more who would be arriving for us! Something strange happened with this message though, these beings had designed a gold frame around the message just like a picture frame one can buy, and we could see there was a little bit of green trim made to look like pine from a Christmas tree! The printer wasn't hooked up yet so I couldn't print their message, instead I took a picture. And later, I found another strange picture after my film was developed, I had no knowledge of like the ETs have done before. I could see only a part of my hand holding a *"brilliant ball of bright light"* in my palm! I was told it means, *"hands of light"*.

303

David calls this *"a healing light"* to use on others in Reiki. Two days later another message came, *"They would help the male offspring to get the printer going so they can come through on the new printer."* This was great we still had their help when needed!

That night I went into another vision where I was in a church and I carried a huge cross in front of me everywhere I went. My son told me, *"this experience was to show me it was an honor since I have carried a huge load that I have borne. Therefore, it shows I am grounded and that I carry the cross in honor of Christ the Father!"* I was in awe of this, completely humbled!! That evening David told me, *"he heard the door open and close".* The ETs had been here leaving another message for us: *"You are grand voyagers just beginning new chartered territory into our many galaxies there is so many things we are going to be showing you and letting you experience. The Creator is pure love as he loves you all- go forth and complete your missions and continue thy journey, love to you both".*

We were *speechless* for the first few moments then we began to laugh from joy and shed our tears! How can this keep happening people have searched for years to contact other Beings all over the Universes and we dared to say nothing, our connections would be happening forever because they always had! Another thing was, we would keep learning in this important earth school and beyond to experience many more encounters to more knowledge to teach others, our teachers were always waiting to help our growth here. We felt a wide mixture of many emotions with the journey we both had chosen for it was more than phenomenal and indescribable!

The next message arrived: *"Be prepared for a universal voyage ETs."* We were extremely excited always hoping for more to come and to understand the information, especially now with our new schooling! Life was wonderful to be able to live in more than one, world and to work and visit many others! We both loved to travel into *past times* to see ancient history when the ETs have taken us. These amazing travels helped kept my son alive, he knew forgotten answers; I was remembering mine and his energy was always lifted.

As a review of daily life as a mother and housewife I stayed busy doing everything a mother does in life on earth. I was also living in many other places that I am writing about. I was thankful the ETs were always close by waiting to make full contact, watching us adapt mostly, they knew my plate was full for a while; my growing up in earlier years had been like a small break. When our children were grown and out on their own our family of Universal Beings resumed the mission to full blast by refreshing our memories to help my son and me throughout our time to be here, as you have read about. I was doing everything I knew to do that my human side was capable of, but always felt misplaced, I felt more like an outsider than ever! The miracles which helped me so much I am so thankful for is my children they are my jewels and I love them with all my heart. Only David understood since he was the same, we knew who we were. What would people think if they knew the truth, probably that we were *insane,* but to the contrary we were both being taught and lifted by the Universal Beings to stay positive and away from negative ones. This helped us in our deep bond of commitment and strong belief knowing the truth! We would not care what *anyone thinks* when they know who we are, when time to reveal ourselves! What others think is merely a human made-up emotion and worthless, just a waste of time...

I soon found myself compiling an important letter to a certain person I was told to contact by Edgar. After I finished, I asked for a confirmation if I had the information correctly and I needed a sign as my confirmation, then I would get the letter mailed. I was waiting and out of the corner of my left eye I saw something fluttering in the air! With my peripheral vision I could see a beautiful white Dove flying to me then briefly touching the left side of my face for only a moment how happy I was, laughing with tears of joy for this sign!

Edgar certainly heard me I thanked him for this extraordinary experience and confirmation. Writing this letter was very important to Edgar I wanted no mistakes in my writing it. There was much communication flowing between the three of us and knowing how closely we worked together we would finish out life together. Edgar told me when he would reincarnate in the future and I feel we will be there too working together as we have each time. This may be when the new world begins and many of us on this planet will be helping, getting it in order, just think... a world with only love and compassion...

I would like to urge the readers who are interested in Edgar Cayce to read his story starting with a first book of him, *"There is a River"*. It is an amazing soul-searching story of a wonderful man's strange life having extraordinary knowledge, healing, and psychic abilities, who helped countless others and being a very spiritual man. I questioned myself, "if my son and I would get our promise fulfilled to the Creator, we each chose during our life path here on Earth". Many may find it difficult to understand our worlds, but it doesn't matter, there are those who will that are ready. I am extremely happy I have not been alone in this experience by having my families love and support knowing that David and I will continue together to teach what we can to help save this planet.

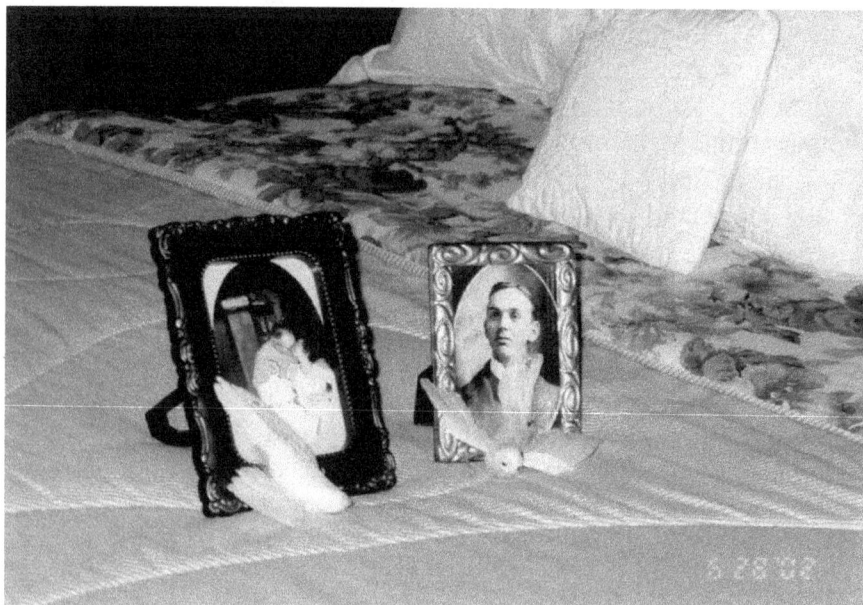

This is one of the many times Edgar Cayce would place pictures of my parents and himself on my bed with our symbol of the doves that we all share, validating how we are working together.

Good news arrived from the ETs: *"the voyage was ready for us to go with them and more would come soon, journey well."* We were ready and eager knowing we would be exploring new territories in an endless outer space this was really exciting to us! In our earth world here there were some negative ones around us who gave off terrible vibrations, so we asked the ETs "to keep their strong protective barriers to encircle us and in the night hours the divine ones came to tell me what to say, "I *am invoking the spirit of the Father, Son, and Holy Ghost*" if any negative ones come near to us! The next day I told my son we need to use these words and our help will be with us immediately. Soon after this my late dad made his presence known along with the high Council, and we received four different messages, one after the other!

First message: Greetings, we are near a new journey, patience is necessary for it will bring you many rewards. The thief in the night will be caught and the universal law will set their karma, beloved ones seek thy inner peace and surround thyself with it and call thy love of the universe. You will be guided and protected!

Second message: "*Beloved ones all will be well do not feed into the negativity!!! Love from all.*"

Third message: *Pumpkin, I love you. Hello, Davey M.*

The 4th message came after I had taken a nap in the afternoon and awakened to see an Angel being floating to in front of me. This majestic Angel passed strong feelings of love into my heart and soul to let me know, *"we will always be protected in our earthly work"*. These moments were majestic and beautiful knowing we will forever be safe here on earth and everyplace we travel. I told David about the Angel who had brought news of our protection, with peace and love making us feel very thankful and happy, and to my dad who is strong in spirit to come on his special day (birthday) to spend a part of it with us! Both my parents came to see us often helping us with their words, and dad with his jokes, we were closely connected to them in this way! After this, that same night I saw my mother's face when she made her visit and suddenly, I realized I was in space traveling with her and this is all I recalled.

The ETs returned the next day to tell us, *"the higher ups are working on a new journey for you both you will start to remember more"*. Good news for us! And that very afternoon I found another message shaped and folded with my notebook paper exactly like a pyramid!! This was wonderful and I bet soon we would see Egypt with our strong ties to it. Then another message arrived for us!

Greetings, we have been processing all the data collected from our last journey, we need to transmit it to the higher level before we can continue the journey. While you wait continue the spiritual work and try to be aware of your own surroundings, you are both protected but must realize that others on this plane are full of envy and will be foolish. Their process is on a different plane and will take them on their own journey. In the overall picture love is the only answer, and you and thy son David are loved universally, we bow before you both and are honored to carry on our mission with you, B.I.T.S. with the Universal beings of light.

What a gracious caring message we felt complete humbleness and universal love from them, and we are thankful they continue to bring these Holy blessed messages to us. The next day I woke up to the smell of food cooking down in the old kitchen, I knew it was not really happening the spirits in the house were simply going through their everyday life carried over into our time of today. They were preparing food they could see, and I wondered if they really had taste in some way we don't understand. I would imagine they do since they are reliving their lives with us in our earthly dimension at the time. We had much going on in different dimensional worlds and time periods and *being in more than one place at the same time.* At least we knew it was the positive beings facilitating the events with what was happening.

I remembered at coffee earlier that day I had been asking the ETs about *"crop circles"* and the information when they create symbols in the fields I will get to later. They had shared information with us before when we were with them, they made them although there were other circumstances involved, we did not fully understand yet what was happening at the same time. The next thing I am going to tell you about is one I debated for a long time on how to relate this next story to you. It is something really off the *grid* that happened, if you want to *believe it or not!*

On October 1st I bought a new dryer the old one was done for, after my purchase men from the store loaded it into the back of my old truck to take home. David had been extremely sick and just out of the hospital so I told him he could NOT try to help me get it out when I got home. I knew he may try to do this since he was so helpful to me when he could be; I had to keep him from doing things because if he could walk, he would try. This time I knew he was entirely too weak and mostly had to stay in bed, but he wanted to ride along that day. I would find someone to get the dryer out of the truck. When we arrived home, I backed my truck into the back driveway with the tailgate up against my privacy fence so the dryer could not be stolen overnight. That night I lay in bed not sleeping trying to figure out who I knew that could lift my new dryer out of the truck the next day and exchange them, finally I fell asleep.

Early the next day after I dressed something told me to look in the garage, so I knew to do it! I opened my kitchen door to the garage and **honest to God there sat my dryer!!!** I thought I was going to have to sit down from my unexpected weakness! I called to my son as I ran up the stairs to tell him, he loved what they had done we both laughed and laughed we were so happy! To this day if I had not seen this with my own eyes it may have been hard to believe!

I soon found a nice repairman who exchanged the old dryer for the new one; he even hauled the old one away which I certainly appreciated. That night before sleep I repeatedly thanked the ETs for delivering the dryer to the garage and my thought to call the right man who helped to hook it up. The ETs quickly sent a message to us about the *old vessel* as they called my new dryer, they had put in the garage for us; apparently our appliances are all *old vessels* to them, like the computer, now we call them this. This was like a storybook and it happened, help was there for us when we needed it!

A message followed at 6:30 pm that evening we *were honored to get: "the grand masters request your presence this evening."* What! We couldn't believe this; we were curious to find out what this was for! Proving more this earth world is just as we have been taught, it is an *illusion*; a *place to learn in*. After I went to bed, I found myself out of body in travel with the ETs, and several others who are on this journey with them, as we are. In a flash I could see, *"The Great Council, were these also Grand Masters? With this question I could suddenly see my son and me at a round table"*. We all sat together I felt very small as we thanked them and expressed how honored we were! To begin with, they gave answers to our questions about *Crop Circles*. *"Communication with symbols gives answers for humankind they have been communicating with all beings by creating universal symbols inside of them. There will be more to follow soon"*. I have no memory of the rest; we were to keep it private for now.

We could not remember anything more and after this, they were gone, and we were back! The next afternoon I lay down to rest and felt a presence close by I opened my eyes and in front of me stood *"The Great Traveler!"* He wore the familiar beautiful robe with dazzling *"trillions"* on the front of it, before I spoke, I thanked him for coming and let him know, *"How happy I was he was here!"* Even though he was silent it did not matter his great love radiated from him through me and then he was gone! It's like he wanted me to know he is watching over us and a protector to us forever! There was something more about our connection, I felt it!

On October 6th, 2000, around 6:20 pm we heard from the beloved Beings again. The next invitation was presented to us, *"You both are to be honored at a Galactic meeting you have met all universal laws and are known throughout the universes by your universal names that you had chosen for one another."* This was *overwhelming*, hard to absorb; so much, so fast, we felt our spirits lifted high to be told we have passed all tests so far, and were at a loss for any further words, even to one another. We had much to think about in the next days, one question was always the same, *"how did we deserve this great honor!!"*

It was a full moon a few evenings later which is a very powerful night for the *ETs* and us. The days had passed by fast and my son was very sick again so we immediately went to see his doctors who treated him as best they could. When we returned home, we found a wonderful new message from our beloved ET family: *"Universal love to you and the male offspring lady luck favors you both, blessings."* We weren't sure which ET Beings this message was from, but regardless, since we are all family it was a wonderful positive message David would heal, and always with their love. Just what we needed to know and was curious what *Lady Luck* had in store for us and extremely thankful they had helped my son recover!

In late fall Edgar sent a beautiful message to me: *"My beloved Ruth Ann you are waiting be patient all will come together soon and make sense, then all the answers will come! E. C."* I was excited to get this message and I would remain patient.

It was the beginning of November 2000, I clearly recalled time had suddenly stopped for me one day! I realized in only a second, I was out in universal travel looking at a large trail of what I know as *"sparkling stardust"*. It was so gorgeous I cannot describe it moving across the universe, no one could ever imagine this! As this was taking place at the same time, I could hear beautiful *"heavenly chimes and tones"* and out of the corner of my eye was an ET I was very happy to see! I moved to him in less than thought to shake his hand and the feeling I had was the same as when we greet an old friend we dearly love on earth. He wasted no time speaking telepathically to me and I felt the *"Great Council"* nearby to us, so I knew whatever was going on would be very important! The *Council* was there to congratulate my son and me about the day before: "The *Council congratulates you both and to know you both are safe from all things! We are here dear child to let you know you and thy son have passed all tests now and your life here shall become a lot different than you have known before, many opportunities will come. You and the son have newer abilities to deal with these things. The gifts are strong, and we are here to help you in all ways, fear not the earth events weather. Only call out in thought we are here to help you we love you both. All of Us"*.

This made us feel like a million we felt safe in our work and life, what more could possibly happen, our lives were amazing miracles, and we loved others as never before. They guided us through lifetimes, and this would be our lives through eternity. I often repeated to our universal loved ones, *"how much we love them and how we dearly love and cherish our earth loved ones with all of our heart and soul* "and they understand those emotions perfectly.

Our next message arrived close to my late mother's date of passing, at that time my son and I were in the car on our way home around 6-6:30 pm. We were watching for the ETs along our way, we didn't wait long to see 8 UFOs I could count lower in the sky, one huge one was a *"Mother Ship"*. This was a surprise for us to see it but there was a reason for this to happen, then the ETs began sending out beautiful golden rays of light from their ship! We were really enjoying this amazing experience which only lasted a short time, then we watched them *escort* us all the way home. That same night on TV the news was concerned about *strange lights* in the skies that early evening around the same time we watched the golden rays happen. David said, *"He thought the sky looked red with other colors when he watched more of the lights with a few neighbors after we arrived home"*. For good reasons even with his sight he was able to see this! The news reporter that evening explained, *"This had NEVER happened before, seeing the Northern lights this far south was once in a lifetime"!* This is how they termed the lights in the sky there is nothing impossible for these highly intelligence beings to do. My son and a few neighbors watched the colored lights until around 8:30-pm our time.

The Evil Life Force Host

The ETs came to get us for a very important reason one evening, they were showing us how they were going to remove a very destructive type of *"life force"* from a woman; she was its *HOST!* This destructive entity was in her spinal area, we had been brought there for our schooling to watch two doctors remove this terrible *"thing"*. They removed the entity with a long hook, and it was still alive! It looked like a long snake, how sickening I felt, but the ETs told us, *"this was for our own good to know for future knowledge"*. We spoke with both doctors afterwards, the one doctor lived far away he said, and the other doctor lived in our area. I recognized him but did not know him personally, I wondered if he would have any memory of doing this and if any other doctors from in this area could also be working with these ETs. I didn't like watching this procedure, but it was for us to know of these creatures, and how the ETs detect them in a human, or a universal being. The ETs told us, *"this was important for us to know about"*. We never experienced seeing the doctors again to our knowledge, I questioned, would the doctors remember anything about the entity or us?

Christmas was here and much celebrating with our family of loved ones, and heavenly beings around us. David and I knew a special holiday message would be coming from the other side, at 2:15 pm I checked the notebook in my room, which had been placed on my bed and there was the message, *"Merry Christmas a New Year of blessings is upon you all!! Blessed is thee."* How precious, David and I were delighted; and full of excitement knowing heavenly love is always around our family and all people at this time of the year!

It seemed time passed quickly it was December 30th, and on that night driving home occasionally I would glance up at the dark sky and something caught my attention I will never forget! Suddenly high up was *"a pyramid right over the moon with one STAR on top of It!"* This amazing sight glowed brightly down to my car for perhaps a minute as I sat beside the highway. I was mesmerized and my wish was, *"if only I had my camera and what does this sign mean?"* The next night was New Year's Eve, we both were waiting, something wonderful was going to happen... we could feel it! Maybe it would be after we turned in, so later we gave up both going to bed. Not long after this I heard David's voice calling to me from his room, *Mom! Mom! Mom!* I rushed in to see if he was sick, but he was GONE, I heard him calling me barely a moment ago! Earlier that same night when we were outside watching the skies, we were thinking about Jupiter being very bright with the moon being the closest since 1756, it would not be this close again until 2086! We sensed this was absolutely a special night, one we had been waiting for so when he was missing, I ran outside to look for him thinking he could be in the yard.

Still calling for David outside suddenly two bright flashes of gold went across the sky and I called out to our ET family, *"Where is my son, he is gone!"* I had checked everywhere for him then a voice told me, *"go to my parent's old home"*. I quickly drove to their empty house and thank God he was there! I found him standing on the back porch in front of the door; this was the second time this had happened finding him like this! He seemed to be sleeping but his eyes were open I took him home and back to bed. This experience told me, *that one day he would be healed enough to be in his grandma and pa's old home when he became strong again in remission, this was his dream and kept him going!* What a relief to have found him so quickly on that bitter cold night! He seemed to not know where he was or why, I have no answers for what happened to him exactly, but he was too weak to ever walk that far and without his shoes in December! We knew each time he was missing he was transported by the ETs to my parent's empty home *showing him it would be his one day in the future.* If we could be transported into the universe and other worlds this was easy for them!

It was January; when I rushed David to the hospital in the city with a sudden illness, which was flu along with double pneumonia affecting his heart and body! He was critical near dying, and it seemed very possible he would not live this time. The Dr. in ER told me, "his *heart looked like a piece of wadded up paper*". I was scared and holding his hand, he was in big trouble! They quickly removed me from the ICU room to work on him and it was touch and go for many hours but finally he could be moved to ICU. David turned out to have the best heart doctor around, and this is when we met doctor W. a leading heart specialist who has a brother who is a well-known doctor and does past life regressions and an author. After doctor W. saved David's life and looked after him, one day when he came in, he was carrying David's chart from the last few years. He greeted David saying, *"I have only had time to read a few pages of your illness which looks like a thick telephone book! I heard about you that night in ER when I came to treat you, and I still can't believe you can be alive! It seems completely unbelievable with all you have suffered through for years and now with your heart, you shouldn't be here! David, you are a star because you have conquered so much over all of these years!"* The doctor couldn't get over how many times David had come back from death experiences.

The next day the doctor brought many of his colleagues in with him to ask my son, *"If he and the rest of them could shake his hand and then his Doctor told him, I am sure you will be out of here in a few days now and I am so glad you were near-by to a hospital"*. This was an extremely close call for my son close to dying again, and by the grace of the Creator, Christ, and ETs of the Christ Light, and wonderful doctor he again conquered death!

I had been sick when David became ill, and I never left him and wouldn't have! He was doing much better now but his tests were still somewhat off, and he looked so tired. Being his mother, I was ecstatic, he was alive! Leaving the hospital, the day he was released his doctor said, *"He would be fine in time"*. My only thought day and night I repeatedly asked, *"please let me live long enough to take care of my boy"*.

It was at this time we began to receive different types of notes and messages in a new way from the other side, and believe it or not, this amazing experience happened next! When our Uncle Leo died, he left his beloved clock among other items to David and my son kept his clock hanging on the downstairs landing I have mentioned before. When things began to happen with the clock it was shocking, yet wonderful, because it was Uncle Leo (we called him Unc) doing some funny things for us to know of his visits and bring information to us. His clock had become our *"private mailbox"*! We would find notes and small letters from Unc placed inside his clock lying on the shelf where he kept the key to wind it! This was phenomenal and so exciting we were practically jumping up and down; we knew this was a great awakening to deepen our knowledge of what souls can do if they chose to. In our opinion, there is nothing they can't do or arrange. The notes were communication as well as his jokes with us; after all, he was one of our universal Master Teachers!

This explained finding my house shoes on the floor under his clock one morning with the clock door open as if I were standing there looking at the time! The next day happened to be my son's birthday and what a surprise waited for him when he received his e-mail birthday card from our *past loved ones* on the computer! *"Happy Birthday David Elvis! You never know when we are going to strike!"* How funny, Uncle Leo, his grandparents and other loved ones were joking with him since they kidded him when they lived. He and Elvis shared the same birth date of January 8th, just the different years apart of each one's birth. From then on messages were arriving in the clock not only from Uncle Leo but other loved ones! And yet other messages continued to arrive on the computer screen and in my notebooks! Plus, we were traveling with those and other Species. We were absolutely shocked for some time and swore to keep our life secret and never tell anyone, they would think we had *lost* our minds, and I wouldn't have blamed them.

This began another new way of communication for years which we loved and treasured! I made sure to take pictures and video of these events. Thinking now of video, Uncle Leo's painting of him still hangs in the living room downstairs that I often watched when relaxing. I began hearing his voice when I would be there at those times and one day, I suddenly noticed gold light that was moving over and around his picture! I grabbed my camera and recorded his mouth moving as I heard his messages, no doubt I was shocked! There is NO doubt this happened, I have the proof!!! Though his words to me he was continuing to help us in our work!

Our dear friend Bev came to visit often to see everything our loved ones were doing, and one day she noticed a ball of light in the front parlor with a *white Wolf's head* in it, the same one I could see in my crystal ball! Then she noticed a *ticker tape* in it and hoped this may mean something good about the stock she had. Next, she read the new message we had gotten that morning: *"We are just getting warmed up, we bow before you"*. She smiled so big shaking her head with amazement she has been psychic all her life but said this home was the most active she had ever seen.! Then I happen to look up at the chandelier light in the front parlor by noticing its movement; it was going around in a slow circle over David and Bev's head! We began laughing while watching it for a second or so, and then it stopped, I was already thinking about the wiring twisting... After this, my son told us his grandpa (my dad in spirit) was with us in the room, and I smelled *"Old Spice"* aftershave he wore. After this we went to the kitchen area, Bev was standing by the stove when she felt the pressure of an arm reach over her shoulder as if to get something. David let her know his grandpa liked to cook there at the stove, and suddenly I felt dad walk right through me, my hair stood out with chills all over me, we knew he was with us, what a wonderful day for us!

That evening I found another ET message, *"Greetings we will see you tonight."* When we traveled that night, I clearly remember on board I was told: *"I am given thought patterns of my own reality and to remember a person's reality is what one can believe"*. At the time I thought, this is exact and logical in how we each believe. That night I could see there were many Beings observing me, I was to understand, *the patterns comment made to me earlier means, "I can will myself to remember my journeys whenever I need to and to journey wherever I need."* I loved this, how interesting to know I can will myself to travel, Bev told me this one time, that my mind is this strong.

When I realized we had been returned home the ETs let me know *"to go ahead and write these things down, to take my time"*. I remembered when we left here with them; they were picking up a

316

few others to go with us and I recognized a woman who I was friends with, and the destination she was waiting to be picked up. When an ET went to get her, she became frightened, quickly turning, running away down the street. This ET said to another one, *"the one won't go"* the other one said, *"Leave her."* I felt the information supplied to us on this trip was shown to us for the future, to know *"that the Earth would not be destroyed in the way one might think and my notes and letters would be found one day"*. I had told others on the UFO, *"to leave evidence of our travels so it could be found one day"*. After this we needed to go on with the ETs for further studies to be back by early am. I was excited, the main ET, *The Great Traveler* with the beautiful eyes waited for me to settle in for the ride! Soon after this trip on the next day my postal mail arrived, I opened my newly developed pictures finding there were two of them I had not taken! On occasion this was not unusual one photo was of an envelope *floating in air* to my mailbox! And on the stamp was a man's face with his hand by his face with his fingers touching his cheek, my son said, *"its Edgar Cayce's face on the stamp"*. With a closer look I could see that it was him and a well-known picture with his hand beside his face! This let us know we would be getting important mail soon from his A.R.E. (Area of Research and Enlightenment) from Virginia Beach, Virginia, and he would be helping us more with this clue later. We were surprised by the envelope in the picture, floating through thin air to our mailbox!

That evening after falling asleep I quickly woke to see ETs and to my left I could see *myself shinning in gold light which really stunned me!* Even though, I still felt I was in my bed I was suddenly in astral travel! What I remembered next was Edgar confirming our thoughts about the envelope with his face on the stamp and yes, he arranged this; information was on its way! At 7:30 am the next day a new message was on the screen saver *"Greetings, we hope you enjoyed the time travel throughout the earth's evening"*. Edgar confirmed our time travels and of the others picked up, but the most important message was about, *writing everything down so our information would be found in the future with our books,* this was phenomenal to know that we would still be helping in the future this way!

One day while cleaning I found two large ET handprints with a pyramid shape between them on the freshly vacuumed carpet, and some items had been moved to different places throughout the

317

house. The pyramid handprints let us know we would be traveling with them to another time in Egypt! Sure enough, the next night we were together traveling when the ET said to me, "We *are preparing a way through for you"*. The next thing I recall, I was studying this ETs large hands and long fingers until something caught my attention to my left, I was looking at the *purest golden light and flowers* we on earth do not know of! In this light I was shown a beautiful tiger in a jungle with a huge snake coming down a tree to kill it! I wanted to save it so badly as I looked into the Tigers eyes, I felt the fright it held with what was about to happen, the Tiger couldn't move it had no place to go! Its eyes changed they were different now knowing he would die, he had accepted this, and I wanted to save him so much! I was extremely sad and helpless knowing I couldn't stop it! Then I understood, *this was a warning sign for me, I was in a dangerous situation at the time, and immediately I woke up back in my room!* The Tiger represented myself and is one of my birth signs and a protector to me. I knew the ETs would protect me with this warning they were showing me for whatever this meant. They want me to be careful of those around me for the one who would try to harm me, I would not forget this and be careful of something I later would never have thought could happen.

I know how we each get our universal symbols, colors, designs, and visions such as mine the Tiger, and in our way of being taught my son and I both understood what was going on. This vision was to keep me safe, pay attention and it did although, there were consequences I learned from. Someday when the time is right, I will explain our universal life more.

I was up extra early, dressed and ready to do things around the house when suddenly before me were the ETs! *"I am so honored"* I said, as I stood waiting to see why they were here. The main ET leader spoke, *"You will see great visions of wonder everything will intensify. We are with you and we bow before each other! Staying on your path is a new journey now, the move is quick, be ready!"* This was something new I looked forward to, even with not knowing what it was, I never held fear. I was so far past that emotion and wanting to learn more as my son did, I couldn't wait to tell him of our new journeys coming. It had become easier to separate the other worlds, we had long remembered where we come from to be here, this gave us a peace knowing we belonged to much more than Earth. Those Universal Beings who came to work with us were bringing our forgotten memories back faster than ever.

My late parents continued to visit often to help steering us in our work here at times along with my dad's funny humor, it was strange to know they are a part of our evolving with the universal beings. We only knew them as mom and dad on earth! They were trying to get us to understand, while we are living this earthly experience it is not about working all the time on projects, life is about earth school, enjoying the beauty of nature, laughing, doing the dance of life, to relax and love life! They said, *"Don't do as we did on earth with just working and worrying all the time, smell the roses"*. They were teaching us not to work constantly and miss out on life like they did.

The next day I was up and busy by 7:30 am when I found a new message. *"Hold onto the love in your heart, you are truly blessed"*. How beautiful, this made the day with how good hearted our ET and spirit families are, and they later said, *"We learn from you both"*. We learn from one another through life here. That night I could see a man standing beside my bed with his hand on the bed post watching me he was dressed as in the forty's. What seemed odd I seemed to remember him from another time, then suddenly he was gone... Immediately after him another vision began, the American flag appeared shining brightly with gold floating out from it and covered in silver sparkles the flag became larger and larger blazing in its own glory, and I heard the word *LIBERTY*! After this, the gold light formed into a ball of bright white light with the flag blending into the ball of white light and faded away, how beautiful!! They were somehow warning us of something very serious to come and that we would prevail! I did not know then; it would be 9-11!!! The ETs began to put many symbols on our computer screen in their warnings. I videoed symbols of weapons, blood, concrete flying, fire, the American flag, Airplanes, and all the states, and at this time we were trying to figure the messages out, and of course this huge tragedy affected everyone! How horrible this was the shock to America being the 911 worse tragedy ever!!! I wished at the time we had known the information of what and where this would happen, but we didn't... we were to know later, that we could not stop the disaster but would grow from it spiritually, we don't always understand the answers.

I was once again with the ETs somewhere in space standing before two very tall doors made of a heavy *metal* looking material. This was something constructed at least many thousands of years ago. The doors were extremely tall and beautiful, on the front of each door were several squares and inside each square was universal designs; then information was given to me, that many of the squares represent *the Constellations in the universes.* The doors were very tall maybe 18/20 ft or so and I was thinking these were things humans know nothing about.

An ET, the old one who was with me said: "*Yes Child, you are here we await thee*". This being was different looking as a human with long white hair and dressed in a long garment type robe. Together as we stood in front of the beautiful double doors, they opened for us to enter them. The old one said: "*We await thee, the question on your mind is now answered, the timing is not quite right yet. Just trust, you will remember more and more now. We guide and protect you both.*" It was then I knew my son was with me, and then we were shown a baby who would be born in the future and soon this baby would be delivered; "*the mother was so happy going into labor*" this let us know this baby would be just fine, healthy and strong... This was such a happy and amazing trip to be with these sacred high Council beings, and the one with us was the highest of all right under Christ! The next day my son remembered our journey with the ETs and the main one who spoke with us who had talked of what the double doors mean by the symbols on them. After this I did not ask much more about the symbols I seemed to know and understand about them as David did. I was told later that day, "*our contract was being fulfilled to keep on with my vows and that I didn't need confirmations anymore, because I already knew. To keep my energy up because we would stay busy in our beloved work and it will bring great joy into our hearts forever*".

This was phenomenal, and wonderful!! Soon after this fulfilling message I began to see many more overlapping dimensions through the nights with more beings who were creating energies in universal travel. The spirits I see were mostly solid, and flesh colored as when they lived on earth and I was happy to see them in this way like mom and dad, at times others came looking transparent, in light or colors of light, but we always knew who they were and what they represented. In my next experience I heard the words: *"Thou hast preparedness a way"* which made me feel serene and happy, I was humbled and very thankful for David's life this was about my son's future. Getting into the New Year it was January 22nd at 2:35 pm when we received our next contact message: *"We will see you tonight"*. We were outside extra early that night watching for them scanning the skies and soon there were two ships, one was very large like a *mothership!* In a second a white beam of light, a huge ray came from the UFO to my house inside my yard! I ran to get my camera but back outside the UFO was gone! A smaller ship continued to hover behind with blinking lights and suddenly a ray of white light came down to us both, just like the larger one had in the yard, after this I have no memory. This is when we were taken, I am positive we went with them in that moment. At other times when I had a similar experience happen a ray of light came down beside my car one night, and other times coming into the yard. It is a good thing no one else could see these or there would have been major car pileup!

It was around 2:30 am the next morning I woke up to find ETs beside my bed and told me, *"They were adjusting me so I would feel better"*. Next, I heard the word *soon,* and quickly a light on an instrument went to my right side, after this happened, I looked to the tower window from my bed and they were gone! I knew I had probably been on a ship, but it was made to look like my room to relax me. Recently, I had been having *pain in my right side* for some unknown reason, now it was completely *GONE!* The next night I could see a figure forming in the tower who I knew to be a *spiritual being of high order.* I watched as He raised his right arm upward overhead and in his hand was an object, he quickly threw to me! This was a *brightly shaped STAR* which flew straight to me disappearing right in front of me! I had already reached out thinking somehow, I could catch it! I was absolutely delighted and surprised, in my world it was clearly magical! More than ever you can see why we never spoke of our lives, and this grand experience left me feeling great life was better than any movie or story book!

Shortly after this occurred, I was told by the older ET Being, *" of a new type of tracking devise for my son and I, and* to *be prepared for journey the way will be opened to more and the newborn will come into your world as perfect".* What thrilling news of the new baby coming, this was the baby who did not survive before, this time it would! And apparently, we would be going with our universal family even more often to learn about this new tracking devise. I supposed the newborn coming to us would have a devise implanted before its birth and to the mother?

It was now March the evening of the 10th, the ETs were back; the winds had been 55 miles per hour all day and into the night. These are some extra strong winds and at times the house seemed to shake. The ETs began showing maps and markings one after the other, so I knew I was already traveling in the Ship with them moving in a blur! On what looked like maps they pointed out *Egypt,* and at one point they were showing the *Atlantic Ocean.* There were drawings of what seem to be a language on a flat surface with hand drawn symbols and Hieroglyphics as in Egyptian times. The ETs told me, *"they were testing something."* Some of the symbols I have seen several times before, and one ET kept showing me one same symbol over and over on an instrument panel of a large thin hand with long fingers. He wanted me *to not forget it* and this was the Being that looked somewhat like us I knew as a human *Hybrid.* This symbol was very important for him to teach me about, and he mentioned testing me, then I had no further memory.

The next thing I did remember was a huge flash of lightening and loud sound of thunder, I knew I was BACK! I felt *wobbly and dizzy* it took time for me to walk straight when I got out of bed the next day. While writing my information down before sleep immediately after returning I clearly recalled another human man who was on board, we had talked and laughed together… I also knew the sudden sounds of deep thunder with flashing lights was when the ETs brought me back, I was getting used to this now.

On March 11 at 1:30 am I woke up and for an unknown reason I wanted to sit down in my chair close to my bed, I was expecting something and wanted to be ready for any information. Thinking I was still in my chair I watched symbol after symbol, one after another being sent to me and after this I was told, *"I am to learn their symbols".* I could see each one in my mind clearly and I knew the meanings the next thing I was told, *"there is only one symbol for the Vortex we travel in and out of".* This is what I remembered seeing but it wasn't over, the symbols continued throughout the night. In my memory, I was watching the *stars* knowing there would be many future nights to come of more symbols. I have a strange feeling I will lose my memory of them unless I use them or when I am with the ETs because they are **Sacred Universal Symbols**... They are precious, and in this way, they will be safe from anyone getting them through any means knowing they have been imprinted in both our memories. I was in the craft that early am and not in my chair as I had though.

It was March 12th, my computer was on when I came downstairs, the front page had the look of the universe on it with hundreds of stars shooting out in all directions! When we find a page such as this it means the ETs will soon be here, something was UP, I just knew it! The next day I awoke to see a being standing beside my bed, he held something out to me in his thin hand, was it a book or a box? In that instant it was over, when I told my son he explained to me, *"that we had gone with them to see the babies! These babies all had emerald green eyes they were the new ones, the new breed of babies I had seen before".* This was an *important* trip for many reasons David said.

Saint Patrick's Day arrived, that early morning I began to *shake and tremble,* I could even see my legs *trembling* and something else was happening! I began seeing stars in the universe then I heard a voice sending me information *telepathically.* I was told, *"I was being reprogrammed and helped all over then I would have great energy".* I was shown many symbols going by so fast they were a blur, over and over, the ETs let me know all of them went into my memory bank. The one being said, *"They were helping me in all ways to be able to help our family and others in our work!"* Afterwards, I couldn't quit trembling for some time; I had lain down and so cold pulling up more covers on me. In only a moment I felt GOOD, my vibrations were very high, and felt wonderful, they had done something fast to help me!

It was now March 18^{th,} there were two birthdays I knew of on this day, one is Edgar Cayce's and the other is a young man named Donnie who is my friend's young son who had recently passed over. His spirit was strong, and he began to cry out of happiness that he had gotten through from the other side, *"he asked me to contact his mom and dad or go to see them and give them a message from him and he was counting on me. That he had been trying to reach out to me"*. Donnie wasted no time showing me a *vision* of where his parents lived in another state and in moments, I was *soaring along* with him to them; I could see he wanted me to follow these directions. After this passed, I had no memory if we contacted them or not, so I contacted his parents right away about his visit and gave his beloved message to them which made them happy!!! He had come to give his love to them through me to give his message of love to them, we were all happy!

Meanwhile the new baby arrived, a little boy we called a spring baby arriving in March. He arrived safe and perfect with a medallion around his neck that no one could see other than me with numbers 5 and 2, and more I couldn't make out. I do not know yet what the meaning is, but he will serve well in his life bringing many others great joy and love in this world. His eyes are beautiful blue-gray, and he is a part of one who passed over whose essence has returned through him. This loved one returning designed a way to begin life on earth once again to be held and loved once more by his loved ones, which is called to *re-incarnate*. It is amazing how things on the other side are done with our own plans (due to each soul's freewill). The Divine Council helps us to orchestrate these experiences beyond any kind of earthly knowledge. The new soul, the new baby, is well and happy and so are we!

Things were rapidly changing in my son's and my life and through the next several years we both had other lessons and old memories to find answers to the best we could, and we remained strong for one another. This was to continue together with all the earthly emotions of sadness, disappointments, and joy filled with love. Our lives were changing to unexpected times in order to continue growing to higher levels, some of our visits and travels slowed for us at times in order to take care of new events coming up, and there would be many times we yearned for the Christ Light Beings to come and get us, and they would.

On May 29th, the *Great Council* returned to visit; it was 1:30 am on a Wednesday when I was awakened to greet them! Looking up at the ceiling was the familiar circle of them overhead and I was very happy as always, *"I am honored"* I said. Telepathically one of the Beings sent thoughts to me, *"happy birthday"* with flashes of light then another one presented partly transparent roses to me with more flashes of golden lights, then two more flashes, and they were gone! How wonderful I felt, there are no human words to express this, but the date wasn't mine, my birthday was in July so... why? After this I went into a dream state where I heard the name *"Milton"* who had passed over many years before. I knew he was someone tied to Edgar and later I found this to be true, *Milton Porter* was Edgar's baby son who passed after birth and I have no doubt Edgar gave the name to me, perhaps *Milton* and I would be working together at some point. The same day I found the computer screen going with *worm holes* back on it and an older message the Beings had left over 2 weeks ago, *"Patience is a blessing waiting for the rewards that await the three of you!!"* Every day was a miracle to us, and these things all happened close to my late mother and dad's anniversary on June 10th. The *worm holes* left on the computer tells me *"we will be traveling with mom and dad and the ET Beings"* I couldn't wait to tell my son we were going...

We were taken by the ETs with mom and dad on the UFO that evening and shown the most beautiful *Panorama* of sights. One after the other golden lights sparkled everywhere in the universe and suddenly, we were looking down at a very beautiful event as if we were in the grandstands! I didn't know what it meant at first, but we were watching a special *grand occasion*, something hard to describe! This was in honor of my mom and dad's anniversary on June 10th how phenomenal to be at their honored celebration in this way!

The next day I had not heard from Edgar lately, so I connected to him in the way we do most, telepathically. He always told us, *"to call for him when we needed him, and he would be here"*. Edgar left us a message immediately: *"It has been a long time, yes, but we have been busy preparing things—see you soon!! Love to all"*. I was relived and happy; I cried and cried... this made me think of how we have so much to share in this world together with others. I was having what is called, a moment.

June 18th Edgar left a new message on the screen saver: *"Greetings children everything is falling into place in the big plan. Love one another!"* Today was special for us to hear this news, he meant, it would not be long until he would come to work with us again in the big plan! He knew my son was gravely ill now and having great difficulty. Edgar said, *"my son* was *in tune with the Heavenly ET*

325

Christ Light Beings, Angels, and our loved ones in spirit," this alone let my son know he would be renewed through those who help us, and in time David found his new strength and became completely full of energy!

OWL'S

Something very different happened to us on several occasions when the ETs were close by or here. I had heard information about Owls being connected with the Aliens/ETs. Some people think they see an owl then later think it was an *Alien* who they experienced, this seemed to be a common story told in ET accounts by some others. There were times we both heard an owl before the ETs came for us making us wonder if this is true, all we had to do was ask! They were teaching us this concept later and the reasons I want to explain is in the beginning years I had a very difficult event coming up I dreaded, but before it took place, I began to hear an owl! Since then, in times of stress sometimes I still hear or see one or more of them, so I feel I am being told we have company from these divine creatures who were created to help us at certain times. Why one of us had never thought to ask the ETs about them earlier is beyond me, and I question because of an owl's large eyes is this an ET connection in some way to not frighten a person when they are around? I know one can be made to think what they want you to, so they won't be terrified!

This story leads up to an extraordinary event that happened on Christmas evening. It had been snowing on Christmas day and after everyone left to go home, we decided to look out at the beauty of the glistening snow from on the porch. David opened the front door and right in front of us was a beautiful *Solid White Owl* perched on the oval storm-door trim looking square at us through the glass, to us was impossible! The beautiful white owl flew away immediately after the front door opened but we knew this was not a normal experience to have happen especially, a *White Owl sitting on a small bit of trim around the oval glass in the door!* We wondered if our beloved universal family, teachers, guides, and loved ones past brought this as a holiday gift for us? We took this as a wonderful sign from them sending their celebration of love to us in this way!

There have been all kind of stories about Alien beings and the owl connection, so we believed those who work with us in every way sent this special Christmas blessing along with our Indian Shaman protector and his teachings of the Owl, which is a special omen.

Heading South

David and I decided to take a small trip south to Tennessee to explore where my mother had been born and attend a family reunion to meet other relations we had never known. After we had eaten a picnic dinner and meeting several of our relatives' we went to an old cemetery named *"Pounds Cemetery"*. What we found among family names on several cemetery stones were others that really surprised us with the last name of Cayce! We wished later we had written down the complete names to check them out but still it had been a very nice and interesting day. When leaving for home, I was strongly drawn to go to Edgar's hometown, so we crossed *Land of the Lakes* onto Hopkinsville, Ky.

As we stood outside of Cayce's old decaying family home, I was looking at the old tobacco barn, which was quite large but still in remarkable shape. Time changed for me in that second suddenly I was *mesmerized* by a huge, beautiful shade tree standing close to the old Cayce house. Apparently, I had gone into a *dimension* where in my mind I could see Edgar as a very small boy playing under the tree! I could also see work going on in the old tobacco barn back then; it was intriguing, and then I snapped back then to my reality. We absolutely loved being where they had once lived, Edgars family had moved in with his grandparents who lived there after he was born, times were very hard then and families sometimes lived together. I had been there a few years before but did not recall all the directions to the places I wanted to show my son.

Mostly I wanted him to experience seeing the old Cayce home first which we had, I was surprised it still stood with most of it falling in. We had ventured into the house just a little to not get hurt just for the experience. After we left, I felt as if I was being led to Edgar's other grandparent's farm and while there, I imagined the pond his grandfather died in when he fell off of his horse and drown in front of Edgar when he was a child. Then we continued to the old school he attended, although it had been moved to another location. From there, we went to where Edgar gave his first reading with Dr. Ketchum, then past the store where Edgar first worked, onto where Gertrude had lived when he met her. Her old home had been torn down long ago, now we had two more stops; one was their first home in town after they married then ending up at the cemetery at the end of town as a last stop where both are buried.

At the entrance there is a nice plaque written about Edgar, and we found the small cemetery to be nicely kept. I sort of remembered where they were buried and it didn't take long to find the two small stones which lay flat to the ground, side by side. This was exactly what they would have wanted they were never into frills and money. They were such good people; simple and hard-working even with his fame as a healer and reader they remained humble. We certainly felt them with us on that day because of the bond of love between us being unique, and strong; this was a day we would never forget!

A few days after we returned, I met another of my guardian Angels, and I felt this fit in with Edgar and Gertrude in some way. I heard the doorbell ring very early one sunny day while I was still in bed. I ran downstairs in my pajamas debating whether to open the door or not, depending on who was there. I peeked through the curtain to see a little old lady with white curly hair in an old-style house dress and overhead apron decorated with tiny pink flowers on a black background. She looked as if she had stepped out of my grandmother's era, and I noticed she had a habit of chewing on her lip as if she had a nervous problem. I couldn't see a car or anyone with her and suddenly I felt guilty I had not opened the door, so I swung it wide-open with *NO ONE THERE*! Since there were no cars going by, so I went outside looking for her, but she had disappeared! The street was still empty, so I went around the house in a couple of seconds, there was *NO ONE*! I asked the other side, *"Who was the little lady?"* they replied, *"your guardian!"* She had looked familiar like someone I have met before but she couldn't be one of the people I met in Tennessee they are still living, she was not, but after some thought I felt I had met her someplace in another time and space. Afterwards, I felt ashamed of myself for not opening the door faster, but David let me know, *"she only wanted for me to see her and know who she is"*. This visit was for when we meet again on earth or the other side, I will know her, and I will never forget her!

I soon experienced an almost repeat with the ETs, it happened again! The day it happened I was washing my face to wake up, and when I looked in the mirror, I had a new top on I had worn the day before! I knew right then I had traveled with them in the night because I had taken the top off to put in the laundry the night before but now, I had it on again! I had gone to bed in summer pajamas which I found hanging on the bathroom door hook, there was no doubt I had been with them on a journey! Immediately I asked for information, *"Did the ETs take me? Was I used in an experiment?"* The answer to my question was, *"Yes, my child, you are an important part of the grand plan. Nothing is done to ever hurt or harm you, repairs were made to you we have helped your condition all is good."* Ok, sounds good, I thought I am not sure how I knew I had been *part of an experiment,* but they had repaired something I needed done to help me! I had gone to bed sick the evening before but now I felt fine and I understood they did something which helped me greatly. *"Thank you"* I whispered.

The day after the 4th of July I was on the interstate driving coming home from another town, everything was fine the first several miles then I decided to check the time it was 7:20 pm. When I was passing a small airport to my right it was the last thing I remembered! Whatever happened to me only took a quick glance at the clock on the dash and back up at the road; and then I saw a sign to enter another town several miles from where I had just been! Hey, wait a minute how could I be here? This shocked me because of it being broad daylight on a *crowded Interstate* with a semi-truck behind me, and a friend following a little further back in traffic! I didn't feel any different as usual except being confused, I wondered if anyone had seen anything happening although, they never do in these cases. I have been taken throughout my life by the ETs and at times left someplace else, but not far away to where I couldn't find my way home. I usually feel a little groggy afterwards but nothing more.

I pulled into the nearest gas station to check the time to make sure my car clock was correct. Why I did this I can't explain with all the times we have been with them, I had gone many miles in only a few minutes. I wanted to gain my bearings and relax a minute while I was there and bought a cool drink thinking about what just happened to me in traffic, *I was wondering did anyone see anything?* I doubted it; no one ever does, they have a way to hide things with an *unseen shield* they told us about years ago, the same as when they come to the house, or wherever we are.

Later at home my friend showed up asking where I went to, I began asking her, *"Did you see anything unusual? "No, why? I wondered where you went so fast though".* I decided to tell my friend the experience, and luckily after that I still had a friend! I never talked of these things, but I knew it would be ok this time the ETs would help her later. Something else also happened, I usually notice my gas level never shows any usage when this happens just as in this case. I had driven those extra miles to get home, but my car showed no gas used on the entire trip, what a plus!

It was still July around 2:30 am; bright lights were flashing in my eyes again. They were orange, yellow, and white colors, so I knew I was on board with the ETs! The lights seem to keep me focused on them because the next thing I knew I was writing in my notebook about my trip with them it had already ended, I was back! What happened in-between came to me later and a big surprise. I had been with the older lady *"my guardian"* on that night trip she is the one who rang my doorbell that one early morning! This kind spirit told me, *"She watches over me and, Yes, my dear you met me in the night"* I replied, *"It's you!"* She smiled as I continued, *"I remember you turned around and lifted the veil then smiled at me! I asked you, is your name Donna? Please, let me know what to call you, I am so happy we are meeting!"* then lastly I called out to her, *"I love you"* and that was all, she faded away... Later that day I met Bev to ask her what she thought my guardians name was to see if one of us would be told, it was given by our guides, *"her name is Mary Martha".* In my sleep that night my mother came to see me along with *Mary Martha! I loved* our visit and calling her Mary Martha!

It was Saturday coming downstairs I could see Unc's clock door was open, all my letters with questions for him had been taken I was so excited! Closer to my birthday the ETs returned I only remember bright lights coming in the windows and through my open bathroom door. On July 15th, that same year we found a new message on the computer: *"Happy Birthday to our beloved Angel, Pumpkin, Ruth Ann, we all love you very much!"* This melted my heart and soul! Immediately after my birthday we received another message: *"love to you and the male offspring"* all this love kept pouring into us both how wonderful!

Thinking back to when I was picked up by the ETs on the Interstate, I wanted to get a confirmation later and my question was, *"when I was taken off of the Interstate that day wasn't, I close to the airport?"* Their reply came back, *"yes, between the trees where the highway divided"*, it matched exactly to what I experienced, and then they added, *"There is much more to come."* What a wonderful birthday surprise; which confirmed my location between the trees!

In my night travel I was being shown an object like a metal cage with small beads on wires. One of my spirit teachers who is also my Eastern guide told me, *"He was showing me the Chinese way of counting"* they wanted to teach me this. I was exhausted in this experience and so was my son, our teacher read our thoughts and said, *"the reason we are we have been traveling so much with the ETs"*. He was right we needed to sleep, suddenly a big flash of bluish bright light came into my room beside my bed so I knew we were back again each in our own rooms, and I heard these words, *"To always try to be a joy of light to others"*. This is my goal… and I slept like a baby!

On the next ET visit I first noticed a bright pink square shaped object in my room towards the ceiling, and these beings were another familiar species I was trying to recall. Of course, they could hear my thoughts and began communicating with me, *"Don't worry we are here and glad to return it's been a while. Go my child to see Steve Rother, it is time to share, we honor you, you have done well, and soon you can video us again. Your answer is about our Crop Circles, we are communicating and so are the dimensions. There are those who are ready like you. There will be the largest one yet in Holland soon to come. We shall take you and your male offspring soon and program the information into your brain stem to tell you of the importance of the Crop Circles and much more. You have those waiting for you and thy son you both are ready!! Celebrate! The Great Council bows to the both of you! We will repair things you need done to your body your health is good lots of energies are pulling on you now. We have come to help you; you have much to do. Enjoy your day with your friend and her friend you will be friends with her friend, and there is a reason! We come with your confirmations to your questions soon. We will help you lose more weight, so your body is lighter and stays healthy"*. I was excited by their message and I felt full of energy for what was coming!

Then I saw a circle above me like a Crop Circle, but I could not make out the meaning and suddenly our ET friends were gone! How thrilling this had been, our work will one day be known, our minds are full of valuable answers and can help others within this world one day! According to the ET families we are full of universal answers and information, our brain capacity is full and has processed 100% of information, a human brain uses about 10% they told us.

My computer had been down but today in front of company it popped back on with a message, *"We are here"*! This was quite a surprise to our company and us we don't even try to explain any of this and apparently the ETs do not care now to do this in front of them, nothing was said, and I changed the subject although, David and I were smiling ear to ear!

Holland's Largest Crop Circle

We were told in 2001 by the ETs Holland would have the largest Crop Circle formation by far and there would be something very important about these certain numbers 9-11-14! They wanted us to remember 9-11-14, to write this down in my notebook which I did at the time. So much has happened since this message it was only now that I recalled it from them by finding it in my notebook I am reading from. Life with my son's illness is the reason I did not follow up on the Crop Circle sightings that were happening, nothing mattered to me but David getting better, and we were kept busy in hospitals. I know now there was a huge Crop Circle made and it was the largest on 9-11-14 just as we had been told this date by the ETs. This happened in a town in southern Holland as they said it would and to remember, *"The numbers are of great importance and linked to something else"*. Since then, I feel this Crop Circle was also linked to 9-11 when the twin towers both were hit. The ETs were trying to help us with an earlier warning back then, but we did not know. The 9-11 disaster was going to take place in our future, and it was the most horrible and indescribable event to ever happen in our country as I mentioned earlier. On that day a few hours before we each woke out of a nightmare vision at our different homes and immediately, I called David and told him what I saw, and he had just experienced the same thing but we didn't have enough information on details to what this meant! In our visions we each could see buildings, concrete flying, blood, people, explosion's, fire, lots of smoke, and the American flag, but not what or where this was! Later early morning my phone started ringing with the horrible news! Could we have did something, I didn't see how without more to go on earlier and probably not then, we felt horrible! We had found symbols on the computer screen, never knowing what they were meaning. There was nothing we could do those symbols had been running on the screen saver for two weeks, I did video them.

Time had flown by it was the middle of August, the time was 1:30 am I was out in travel with our ET friends in a place among large ferns, and plants where they have taken us many times before to a place they go. I watched all kinds of energies around me then realized I had closed my eyes; when I opened them, I had been returned to my room which looked to be full of black dots! Then familiar flashes of lights came into my room and the ETs were gone! What was this all about? I had remembered what they said when we were returned because I had written it down quickly. *"The entire human race has purpose, some destroy the purpose and some soar with the gifts always learning, love is the key"*. How perfect and lovely, of course everyone does have purpose, but some throw it away. I knew I was seeing even physical things more clearly since they had changed my sight with the new way I see, at least for now.

The next night Edgar came to visit, *"Beloved child, I was with you and thy son this fine evening and heard the words from your hearts. A lot of healing has been done tonight all of us here are very proud you will teach now not only the healing but thy experiences as well helping those with thy words of wisdom. There was a delay to get you ready and stronger know in thy heart you have many who believe in you and thy son David. There will be a few who will have envy and jealousy brush those aside as I did long ago, now is your time and thy sons! It is written things are being revealed at a greater and faster pace now. Rewards come faster they are deserved! I know you want confirmations often, but you do have them, trust in thyself! It is all within dear one. Gertrude and I are so drawn to you and thy son that's why we have always been together with you both forever! The love between us is glorious and true you will soon hear from C. he will have a dream state that he will act upon he has needed time to reflect upon things. Ly down now and rest, sleep, and go into thy worlds of learning. I see your mother and dad as you have asked me and yes, we all work together they send their love and devotion. Love life and be joyous, I filled myself with doubts at times with guilt and possible fears, but I did learn and know everything on this side was all for the good, summing it up. I was too hard on myself as you are at times; so, relax and enjoy, love and be loved. Enjoy thy beautiful world and life and the gifts, you are a natural. Sleep now dear one and I shall be with you. We have much to do and yes, you are ready now so don't look backwards, only forward! We love you and thy son and thy daughters dearly forever, all thy children! Edgar and Gertrude and all of us here!*

We felt more than extremely humbled and proud and all I could get out was, *"Thank you dear beloved Edgar and Gertrude for this heavenly loving message we are so deeply grateful for all you do. The Creator/God has sent you to us as our beloved teachers once more and we shall survive and go on, no matter how hard others try to make it for us! Thank you, for this important message, we love you too, now and forever!"*

CHAPTER 15

Believing in One's Self is the Crown and the Glory of Thy Being for Without Belief Nothing Does Materialize

David said, *"the ETs will be back tonight"* I can't remember what happened when they did but I had seen one UFO earlier before bedtime. It doesn't happen often, it is rare, when I don't recall our experiences until the next day, then between the two of us remembering I record them. That day I was passing by David's Oriental collector's box that hangs on my wall and the door flew open by itself and made the noise of a loud crash! I quickly went to grab it then noticed it had not moved, and quickly I realized it was only an illusion in another dimension I had experienced. Sometime later in my mind's eye I could see a UFO craft in the sky outside of the house. This was to let me know they were here for us David told me earlier, the ETs were coming to help me feel better this made me feel good I needed relaxed since my energy was completely drained. It seemed I needed rebooting much more often… One can't imagine how hard this is on our bodies through the years.

The Sunshine Circle

That same evening, I had a vision; David and I were tearing down the old Edgar Cayce house and inside of a wall we found a small green silk purse in good condition with small flowers embroidered on a narrow strip of the same green color, sewed around the bottom. Looking inside there was a *thank you* card to all of Gertrude's friends in a group that she had belonged to called, *"The Sunshine Circle"*. We were excited to find this small silky bag, and then we found an old fly swatter I wondered who used. In my vision I even drew a sketch of the silk purse with the flowers embroidered around the bottom of it and then I thought I was coming out of the vision. Clearing my thoughts away the first thing I did was open my eyes to see a bright golden light shining over me, then I closed and opened them again, but I could still see the light and green silk purse so I knew I was not completely out of the vision which ended.

One day later I found the information I had written down about the Cayce home of when I experienced finding the green silk purse and I wondered, did this pretty green purse exist at one time? Then a wonderful thing happened, I found out it had existed, there was some kind of *"Sunshine Circle"* that Gertrude had belonged to!

This small pyramid and crystal ball moved around the house by the ETs over many years. Notice the 3-digit footprints and ET face inside the ball and my hair burette close by. There are also many figures and universal symbols faintly drawn in the carpet.

One afternoon going into early fall we found the drawing of a pyramid shape in the carpet the ETs had left with their message, *"the pyramid is used as our symbol it is a window for David, and myself for us to enter other universal worlds.*" My son and I were given this pyramid symbol long ago from them but with so much coming to us, our trips, and our schooling I suppose they wanted to *refresh* our memories. I was glad because I had not thought about this for some time and since they read our thoughts so easy, they knew.

It was a Tuesday about 1:30 am and I knew I was with them; I remembered the familiar bright golden lights in my room and *in a blink, I* was out in the beautiful universe moving so fast it was a blur! And the strangest thing happened, *I could see myself* when this happens, I am looking at my solid body still in bed knowing I am in astral/soul travel. It is strange to see yourself in this way and I never get use to this, however I like this lesson. During this trip one of the familiar Grays, a main one, was talking to me telepathically about everything from my future books to write (which the High Council Beings titled along with this one I am writing now) to my health, the United States, our safety here, our loved ones who are protecting us in war, and many other important subjects. I could even see my books all finished with bright golden light around them as if they were being displayed. We were being taught certain information on this trip, which was very important.

I noticed other *life forms* nearby I did not understand about yet, some were extremely strange looking, while others were not pleasant to look at all by human's standards. Maybe they felt the same way about us? I was somehow working with them and in a second, I was watching a portal open where we went into a Pyramid which was exciting! There were bright lights coming to me after this and I could see myself once again in travel! I have no idea how this is done by them except I know I was outside of my physical body broken down into molecules, energy, but thinking I had returned to my body. I did not open my eyes for minutes or perhaps it was only seconds, and before this experience I was with human people, a man and woman who I recognized, and I hugged them! Then things began to move faster I was suddenly in a *vortex* once more looking at instruments on a panel with these strange looking Beings. I admit I was glad to quit looking at them since I didn't know what they were, but I did know they were positive and good, so I never felt fear I only felt curious, wondering what we looked like to them? I must have been seated at that time because I found myself getting up looking out at the universe when suddenly I heard a loud SNAP! I was stunned to find I was back in my room looking out of the tower window where I watch for them so many times! I guessed the ETs had just departed and with this thought I instantly knew to write everything down while I could remember it. When I had been onboard *"The High Council"* was there this gave me the indication that our trip was special and very important for reasons unknown to us, and the thrill of travel was still with me it was so powerful! I thought back to before when I was inside of the *Great Pyramid* then returned home, but why was I there this time? I hoped I would be filled in later, so I hurried to finish my writing I just wanted to go to sleep; I laid my head down and was out like a light!

Years earlier I had come to realize my son and I had been living more than a duel life all our lives, we were multi-dimensional. Our life was not normal in this world and never would be, and we kept quiet about it because we were different, we knew most people would not understand us... It wasn't time yet and it doesn't matter anymore since we are who we are, we love others and want to help them so it is all good in our mind, soul, and hearts to never be afraid of what others may think... This is a waste of time and as the Christ Light Beings have taught us, *"to ignore what anyone thinks and judges"*.

David was saved from fire

We never knew the entire story of how this next experience happened, but my son had a beautiful gold statue, an antique of a Warrior holding a spear and shield which stood on the fireplace in my home. David had been well enough to be in his own home a short while now even though I was with him each day. He wanted to have some independence of his own since he was better. We stayed close together because I never knew when he might have a bad spell. The day I had the experience I was at home walking by the fireplace noting a bare spot where something had been and suddenly it hit me, the statue Warrior of David's was gone! This statue is 18 inches tall and quite heavy. I called David at his home to ask him, *"is your Warrior statue there at your house?"* He had me hold while he went to look around and soon, I heard him laughing before he answered,

"It's on my coffee table! It's facing east one of our main directions we work in". We both had fun laughing about the missing Warrior through the day; it was not uncommon for objects to be mysteriously moved between our houses by the other side. A being later told me another reason the Warrior moved to my son it meant he would need extra protection from something coming into his life! This worried me and something very negative happened shortly afterwards, so we were put on notice of an incident about to happen! This something happened on the very date of my dad's anniversary of passing which happened in the month of September on the 23rd, on that early morning my son woke up to a very loud boom! His bed, nightstand, and lamp all shook! He told me, *"grandma and grandpa were standing close by pointing to his lamp and it was on FIRE!"* David jumped up and put the fire out, the cord to his lamp was apparently bad and shorted out. It was his grandparents who made the noise and shook the bed, nightstand, and lamp to wake him! We both thanked them immensely with our devoted love through the day for their protection of us doing what they can. And let's not forget the gold Warrior who had been sent to warn and protect him! His grandparents had moved the Warrior to his house as a protective warning, to be careful!

It was a full moon the next night and I felt positive the ETs would be here, so early evening I went upstairs to see if my little pyramid had been moved across the room from its regular spot. It had been and was sitting on top of the Holy box on my dresser. I knew the ETs were letting us know they would defiantly be coming back. I don't know when they came to move things, but I remember being shown a past life in England and what I experienced in the vision.

I was a woman working in a small shop on the square, this was my life and in my loneliness all I could see every day were the cobbled streets and people going by. This shop was in a basement and the few windows it had were small and high up, I could only see people from the waist down walking by every day. I had no friends or life outside of work and I was very lonely. At the end of my life I realized I had spent it working in this shop watching others, instead of enjoying my own life. This experience was reminding me I was to enjoy life and not work all the time. My life in England had no real meaning because I was afraid to take a chance on being happy, so I did not learn to love and enjoy it. The ETs had taken me back to that sad period to spark these feelings and emotions so that I didn't repeat this again! They care about us unconditionally...

I was debating about using a very special experience that happened to me for this book and decided to add it in. It was about the night my dad came again to see me, he calls me Pumpkin, *"I am here Pumpkin you'll fit the Angel story in your book like you want everything will be fine, people believe in angels, many believe, knowing they help us in times of need."* I knew what he wanted me to do now by writing our story in this book to teach it is important for others to keep their faith. Dad continued, *"Thank you Davy for the flowers at the cemetery and the new vase you put into the ground for us. Soon more will be revealed to the both of you don't worry like we did, love life, and enjoy life. Remember you can't change anyone else's journey."* This advice is something we all need to learn, we seem to want what is best for ourselves and others, we may mean well wanting to help, and at times even tell them what we think is best to do. But lessons are for each person to learn from so it's sometimes a fine line of when to not interfere with others' lives, we can't change anyone's journey.

How beautiful this is!

My late mother soon appeared to me in a visit to tell me she was *returning* to join us on earth through a granddaughter who was due to deliver her new baby girl on October 1st. This is how it all started, one night my granddaughter who never knew my mother dreamt of her; and had an amazing experience! When she woke the next day, she called her mother first thing to ask about her great grandmother because her dream was so real! She had never known anything about her and began by asking her middle first and second names then told of a message from her great grandmother to her about the coming baby. In the visit to her, *"my mother told my granddaughter her whole name, who she was, and to name her new baby girl after her middle name of Mae"*. When my granddaughter woke up, she called her mother, and asked what her grandmother's middle name had been to verify her *dream visit*. My granddaughter told us later, she knew this detailed information in the dream was more than a mere dream, especially now, by finding out her great grandmother's middle name was Mae! This was step 1.

On my granddaughter's day of delivery, we noticed the room number she was in was 357 my late mother's phone number had the same numbers 357! The date of her baby's delivery was 10, 01, my mother's address had been 1001! We knew without a doubt my mother was evolving as she said she would by returning in the new baby girl! There were more signs that day which confirmed my mother was back in the baby! Some spirits want to return after time to be with family again, they want to be held and loved once more, and be with them in a new life. They can also help with other things even though their past memory is mostly removed for their new lifetime after they are born again, this is all due to *free will.*

The new baby was named N. Mae as her great grandmother wanted. I wanted this exciting story to be known to help prove *REINCARNATION,* and my past parents have also helped our family in various ways and present in many of our ET travels and David's severe illnesses. You see, everything created is combined and connected, we are a part of each other Humankind is a part of life, not only here, but other universal life forms! *Everything created is connected and One in some way!*

There was another important *vision* experience the day before the birth of baby Mae which happened in my sons dream state, he explained, "he was catching three pieces of colored confetti falling from above him floating the air. A friend of his was also in the vision and he caught three pieces of colored confetti. Then they went into a Cathedral where there were three priests, but who were also three *wise men* that said, *"the new baby Mae was sent here as a special angel and would do great things".* How astounded we were with this beautiful vision it made perfect sense; and with my granddaughters' vision of her new baby this was something I wanted to share! I often look at my great granddaughter and see my mother, she's back!

Things sometimes slowed down and the spirits in the house were not as active, the mailbox was slow to return our mail, and my notebooks were not as full of messages, we were on break! I knew a big change was being arranged and taking place, I asked one of my teacher's why? I was told for the second time, *"You don't need the signs as much anymore let the information come into you, let it all flow, you have the abilities to hear it and to write it, the ones leaving have finished their jobs."* I admit I was saddened to know some spirits were leaving, things were winding down, they had set me on my way. I had to learn to fly solo, they had connected with me through my entire life, and always would in another way. The many senses we had been given were inside of us stronger than ever and the ET schooling would never end, *we belong to them.* We would forever be with our universal Beings and travel in space with *secrets of the universe, earth, and other worlds.*

In the night more words were given to me, *"Ask if your book is the one coming back with the power of knowledge seek your answers within yourself, we do not forget you forever, when you write listen to thy self's inner wisdom and peace. We have given you the gifts remember we are with thee always! We love you-all of us! We are a world away yet only a moment in time".* I felt comforted with their love and much better I know we will never part they will always hear us, and I know where to find answers inside of myself. Our lives would be very different now even richer, meeting others and those like ourselves.

I awoke and looked across my room at many small lights with movements of energy and a small pyramid like mine which were all under a bright light in the tower! An ETs large hands were touching together at the fingertips, each hand reached out from an opposite side across the top of the entire door all the way across it almost like a huge arch! Lights were filling up the tower room and it was beautiful, then a Christ Light Being, an ET appeared who I know to be of *"THE HIGH COUNCIL".* He spoke to me with these words: *"Thy Father in Heaven honored us to read Psalms 23 verse 5 which reads: Thou prepares a table before me in the presence of mine enemies: thou anointest my head with oil; my cup runneth over is, The Revelation of My Truth. We are a world away yet only a moment in time".* Everything stopped, my room became still, I was overwhelmed by what had just happened! If I only had this Holy moment recorded to show what I witnessed, but then again, I know, and this is all that matters! I can't explain how I felt, I was completely *in glory* knowing this is my own chosen heavenly work to do, and if my life stopped now it was for a reason, I am proud of.

I had done my best this is what counted; everything happening was nearly completed and then more would come!

On November 2^{nd,} my son and I happily commented to one another, "you know *we are a team"*, in this life we had worked hard and loved our strange life, then smiling at one another we each turned in for the night. I knew he was in his room waiting, we knew the ETs were coming for us. I woke-up at 2:30 am something told me, *to get up and look out of the tower window, to hurry!* I couldn't believe my eyes, in the night sky was a huge trail of what I call *star dust* I had seen this sign a long time ago *"Unbelievable, it was glorious"* what can one say when something of such beauty is indescribable! I hoped David was seeing this from his window or perhaps he was outside now. Without any notice, in a blink of the next moment I was shaking hands with an Alien Comrade who I *was very happy to see!* He had a message from the others, and my feelings of him were like one has for another precious friend or family member who you dearly cherish. I hope to be able to share the message with you later in the book.

The Pyramids in Egypt

I found several of my letters returned today in Uncle Leos clock as I said, they didn't come as often anymore so I was thrilled! I had been waiting for these to return for over 3 weeks, my questions had been answered from those on the other side! One question which meant so much to me was answered *YES!* This one was about my grandson being safe in the war in Iraq, and this meant so much to me!! When I had asked this question to myself, I heard *YES,* but I wanted a confirmation too, I knew he was being looked after and would return to us! He still had much to do in his life, I must believe the information I get as the other side continues to *wean* me off. I do believe in myself and yet I must confess I love to have *their input* of confirmations given to me. Another question I knew the answer to but asked to verify once more was, *who built the Pyramids in Egypt?* Answer: *ETs and Earth people.* I knew this and had always known through my own past lives there but still I wanted a confirmation from them for this book. It's simple to figure man could never have done this alone when they cannot do it yet today with the technology we have. Many of the stone blocks they used were 500,000 pounds cut to laser precision, which can't be done in today's world!

After this conversation I could see a man moving about my room, he stopped then, turned, and stood there looking at me he was different, but one of us with large eyes. At that moment I realized I wasn't in my room anymore… I was someplace else and instantly a strong ray of light like *a spotlight* was shining in my face and I was lying on a table. I began to hear words in our language when someone spoke to me, *"The big one stops here late at night."* A bright flash of light came over me as I wondered who the *"Big One"* was, then the voice continued with talk of a *lower level*. I knew what this meant; the lower level is the underworld I have written of and horrible to travel through I dreaded it every time I did when alone. I hoped I was in my room, I wasn't, my left arm had a mind of its own and moved without my thoughts, otherwise I was completely limp! The ETs were working on me for some reason and I knew it was ok to do I had given my permission. I could see other people around me in flashes of bright light I felt we were either going in, or back out of the *underworld,* and like magic I was suddenly back in bed feeling fine, smelling ham and eggs being cooked! I knew it was the spirits visiting who lived here long ago perhaps they would be here awhile so I could relax. I lay back enjoying the aroma of the phantom food that smelled so good! I glanced at the time, 4:30 am I must have been gone for quite some time on this trip! I lay there thinking through what else had happened. I remembered little Katie (our little spirit girl who came with the house) possibly before and after I returned from the *underground* experience. Her little face made me happy as she does then I began writing everything down.

A past life came to me the next night with one of my daughters we went with to New Mexico to see my aunt. We wore army uniforms with skirts dancing around to some old *jitter bug* music! I realized this was a past life we had had together in war times. Immediately after the dance scene I was in a high place to what I seen as mountains where I felt myself enter through a small window on a craft. And for some reason I was afraid of falling through the sky being so high up yet thinking, *"OH, look at this beautiful mountain, look at all of this".* It was then I noticed I was on the very edge of a cliff then pulled back inside the same small window and suddenly home again! I had been in a breakdown of energy which happens often, and this told me I had been in a UFO traveling past the speed of light, the small window was when I re-entered the Craft and then home. There are many reasons the ETs change the experience and scenery so we do not become fearful, they may have been re-acquainting me with a type of being I did not remember from another time, because some look unpleasant to us doesn't mean they are negative. It's like on earth, we look different to one another.

The next day things were explained to me, *"Yes child you saw the golden bright Christ Light with the doves in the sky you pointed out (which I had) we know your heart is troubled and words are hard to come by just know your angel is coming to assist you your struggle is with many questions. Things will be set in motion to drift away the stress enjoy the good things we are coming tonight to help you".* How beautiful these amazing experiences and messages are to help get us through our earthly life, thank you blessed ones!

This was wonderful news! I was in the middle of a huge change in my life, it is not easy to live in so many different worlds and still operate as normal here, but I would never change a thing. The ETs continued, *"Your experiences will be great you will know and understand them soon. It has all been your choice your heart is BIG, we love you and keep you safe, look for the silver lining, all of us".* We were so happy, and you know my dad always said that about *a silver lining,* who else was really with me, dad, I think so!

It was evening my favorite time and soon I had fallen asleep then the lights came and woke me. They were *shining* over my entire body what a wonderful warm way to wake up! The ETs told me, *"we are here showing you the other world do not be afraid my child we are taking you for a while put your writing down for now (I had already started writing what I was being told) we have spoken".*

I would be filled in later when they were ready which was the next time, I was with them. They said, *"my progress was good they had lessons for me on world events and the Bermuda Triangle".* This is information I wanted to remember and study, how exciting! Maybe later they would tell me about the lessons and what it means they had stored the information in my brain stem until the time is right for me to know. At least, when I must wait for information, I know I have it and stored for later usage!

Suddenly Angels surrounded me, and this was for a reason I was going to need their protection soon, and with them my dad arrived in a bright flash of light on this night filled with sleet and snow near to his birthday. He came because he knew I needed him to smooth away my human worries. After the flash of bright light, I could see his eyes behind the glasses he wore in life and called out, is that you dad? *"Yes, Pumpkin I am with you always and so is mom. Try not to worry so much everything works out. School is going great we are so proud of you! David and you have lots of time yet so be happy! The kids will all be fine. Love, love, we love you all!! Dad and Mom".* How this warmed my heart and soul!

I couldn't wait to tell my family that grandpa and grandma had made a visit, the next morning when I told David he said, *"I saw them too! It was around 5 am the same time as you saw them".* How do they do it I asked him? David was excited, *"did you see your twin brothers and little sister Lecta they were all together".* Oh, I had not been aware of my siblings with them, he went on telling me how the baby boy twins, and my little sister had told him, *"if they had chosen to live our family would have been much bigger."* How very cute we laughed, just like a child would think. About that time, we both jumped a large crash sounded throughout the house! The curtains had fallen off a large window over the piano, knocking pictures over! What an exit they made with their energy we laughed about it most of the day, maybe they left for another mission!

At 2:15 am a lot of commotion was going on in the house, at the same time I realized I was going into the first vortex and continuing through others! I stopped in another time period and was looking at a handsome male Being who was extraordinary! His face and body were marked with universal symbols, equations and script I could not read, I had no idea of what it meant. I was given words telepathically *"only to observe him"* and quietly I did, he was such a picture of absolute beauty something humans would not have understood! My mind was whirling in this strange experience I didn't understand what it meant, then a voice spoke to me with words I knew in universal language meaning, *"Oh child, know in your heart you are always protected with thy son and in your works. The feelings you have are tiredness from many years of service this is natural. Thy son tires too from his years of service you both work hard because your hearts sing with joy and happiness in the work. We are coming to energize the two of you. Don't be so hard on thyself, love thyself, as each opportunity and each day goes by. You shall have a great revelation soon just love and live each moment."*

This was amazing and beautiful what we needed to hear, and in that moment, I was back in my room filled with sparkles and spirit lights.! I could see William my baby brother that is one of the twins who passed at birth then everything vanished I wished so much he could stay. And suddenly there was my other baby brother Artie, and my sister Lecta, who David had seen earlier. But it was over quickly I had loved and greatly appreciated this visit! A message arrived early the next day: *"hello, love you all"* how sweet!

A few more days passed and to my surprise our Indian Shaman materialized to show me the *"Great Eagle"* and said, *"the Eagle, represents freedom, honor, strength, and the fourth spiritual center meaning love, spiritual heights, mental breaking free of the earth as the eagle soars"*. Wow, I was loving this, the Eagle is one of my signs, after this enlightened message and my Shamans company, my sign of the Tiger was brought forth in another vision, this beautiful creature stood in front of me! I looked deep into the Tigers eyes which was representing courage; I would need this courage soon on my path to continue my journey. He is another of my animal guides who protects me I have written of before. The signs were letting me know *"each one is with me along with those who love and guide us"*. Then my mother and father appeared near to me calling out, *"We love you!"* They also spoke to me of, *how my son and I are sometimes called split offs, this is because we can be in many other places at the same instant and time, and to remember we were in another testing program full of challenges.* This sounded extremely interesting and exciting!

We knew our loved ones were never far from us and they soon spoke of *"sending the birds who were singing outside of my window on each early dawn long before light to comfort me."* and to know, *"the books I write will be in Edgar Cayce's A.R.E. Atlantic/University Library one day"*. How thrilling, and in 2016 this great honor happened just as Edgar, Mom and Dad said it would, my books were added to his library! Every day I listen to the birds singing before dawn as I have all these years, now I knew why! I used to wonder how they could be singing at dark long before the sun came up! Life is so beautiful to enjoy what we have before us!

347

Just after midnight on St. Patrick's Day the *"The High Council"* appeared with my mother and dad to take us both with them, and less than a second later we were in a UFO with many others. In my next memory I was talking to Edgar who was also on board, and then I woke up. The 18th of March is Edgar's birthday and we experienced his celebration that night throughout the universes with our past over loved ones! A few days later a new message arrived with answers about my many questions here on earth: *"it is all for the reasons in thy destiny working on my path to higher enlightenment, does thou see now? Try to let it go know thy fruits of thy labor will soon be yours just let your journey come keep trusting and loving in thy heart you have made glorious strides in thy life there. Don't try to create problems and worries in your mind you and thy son are protected forevermore we are helping you and your offspring."* How wonderful! This helped calm me for some time to come, everything was in order and I was to remember, *"The early years were not always simple living between worlds trying to be normal here!"* They on the other side understand everything and we are so grateful!

Sometime after the above experiences a male spirit came to me in my home to visit awhile and said, *"he had lived here long ago and told me wonderful stories of living in this home".* Through this time, *we had together I noticed one candle was burning in the window. I seemed to understand he would have to leave when the candle was completely burned down, he only had this much time to share with me then he would return into the light back to the other side. I could sense he was very kind, a good man, an enlightened soul, and he supplied information I needed to know."* In the last moments we had together he asked me, *"What are the secrets to this house?"* I did not reply because his time was up, he was gone in that instant! My son and I know the secrets to this home, and I would have told him had he stayed moments more...

We had company later in the day and to my surprise the screen saver changed in front of them! *"Child we still are here do not falter we are still with you. Don't fret or panic all is well."* I don't recall trying to explain any of this that evening to our company, how could I? We went on to visit with nothing said about the message.

The man in spirit who came to see me who lived here once loved this home and I felt I would long to see him again knowing we had much in common by experiencing this home together though in different times. He had come to be in this world the same as my son and I chose to and to live here. The secrets lie here but only a very few will ever know them, only those of the Christ Light who use this passageway.

The Arch Angels Come to Help Us!

A few weeks passed by quietly and I needed our heavenly help for a special reason that was very important, something so great it could hurt us. I asked my loved ones in the universal heavens to help and at 11 pm my answer came, *"Dear child, only those who the Father chooses of the highest realms of our heavens may help you. Upon this night of earth, he shall summon those of the great Archangels Michael, Raphael, and the Saint of Repentance to your aid. This one will know what she has done to all of you in this lifetime this lesson she will learn! Behold the Angels are ready for war to her demons who evolve around her! Her wicked ways will be seen by many she has tried to do evil to. Do not fear we are here to protect you both and your loved ones! Thy promise has been made and we will not forsake you in this hour of need! We are proud of you little warrior it shall be done on this earth night as our promise has been said to thee, rest well little warrior know the evil one will be taken care of by thy Father!"*

After this comforting, humbling, and loving message arrived we were deeply grateful to know the *Archangels* were coming to help us in our desperate need! That evening I was able to close my eyes and quickly went to sleep I had no more concern of the evil one who lived in human form. I later found information on the *Saint of Repentance who is St. Augustine.* Beginning in the year 354; this Saint is about truth, unity, mercy and justice! You can see why I had no more worry of this person disguised in sheep's clothing, and how blessed we both were with this miracle! Everything would be solved at long last, much in our lessons were great teachings of our faith.

It was spring and my semester classes would be done in the fall, I would begin teaching more levels of Reiki healing techniques. Reiki basically means *universal life force energy,* it is not a religion, and it is for anyone. As I lay there thinking this, I sensed someone beside me and there stood *Takata,* one of the ancient spiritual teachers of

Reiki healing! She was one of the first teachers to ever learn Reiki from *Dr. Makao Usui,* and 2nd to offer it. She had taught my son and me with *Dr. Makao Usui* who was the first person to be given the hidden secrets and who is the founder of Reiki healing. He was born in 1865, and 3rd in line was *Hayashi* who was the 3rd Reiki Master who was so dedicated he gave his life for Reiki because he was called to war and never do harm to anyone, only to help heal them. *Takata* was the first woman to teach Reiki and years later after much work on others she attained her Reiki Mastership, but she later changed parts of it to her own way of teaching. Regardless of this as you check back in her history, she loved to help others in her dedication to Reiki… She had come to empower me on my Reiki path as the other two have done for me and my son long ago. They came in spirit to us alongside our human teacher in his teachings.

My son and I were taught exactly as it is to be taught by those 3 first ancient teachers, and as our human teacher with only the ancient information and original techniques. Reiki is very *sacred* and those who have studied the original, oldest, and correct method of Reiki understand. We both were completely and overwhelmingly honored when the day came after years of learning all levels of Reiki and working on many people, we achieved our highest Reiki Mastership! When the Master teacher gave us the last attunements she began crying and said, *"She had never witnessed so many heavenly teachers and guides in spirit, they had come to congratulate us"*. We were speechless. humbled to see the room was full of Beings of the Christ Light! This was our final level to become a teacher to others. My son and I will forever be dedicated to Reiki, my son who was terminal worked and assisted me throughout my classes and taught Reiki to others. In this way he also received many treatments while helping others. We were extremely honored to work with many Aids patients at Heartland who many are left behind by family and friends in our society who are looked down upon and abandoned. How terrible!

The following morning around 4 am I awoke to the delicious smell of coffee and roast beef. The spirits were busy again in the old kitchen downstairs. I felt this was their way of celebrating our Reiki Master level of graduation along with our universal Reiki teachers, I smiled at their caring of us and fell back to sleep. How beautiful to live in many worlds with universal beings and our beloved earth families with us daily we love so much!

I often wondered why the ETs let us see them in so many ways and as an example this is what I mean, one night a small child came to me in my vision. I could see this child standing at my door waiting to come inside the house and when he spoke to me, "*he told me he was going to de-program me. I didn't understand and I was asking him, "why I needed to be de-programmed and will I be re-programmed back"*. I really have no idea of his answer and I suppose it may have been too technical for me to understand since he was an *alien* passing as a child! Our lives have been with them forever and before, but this happened for a reason and I did not question it. David and I have been *programmed* with tracking devises since babies and through the years the ETs have taken us with them to *re-program or de-program* us, energize and re-energize us. They teach us universal schooling to bring back our memories, and other reasons to keep us here on this planet until we are done.

The following happened on a Saturday morning in the early hours, I found myself in my astral body going through the "*Underworld*" we sometimes pass through *unless* we travel with the ETs. This travel is to get to other places in the universes, dimensions, galaxies, star/solar systems, and more, but things were different this time. I could open my eyes and see my room full of bright sunshine flooding through every window, if I closed my eyes I was back in the *Underworld* without memory of where I went when I woke up.

I bring this up because the other way some experience the underworld may happen to people when a person is intoxicated, on drugs, alcoholics, and people during surgeries when weakened with sedation, are those who *sometimes* see the *Underworld* in their relaxed state when their defenses are down. Some people think they are hallucinating, but each one of those conditions can easily open one's psychic ability to what's out there!

After this, I seemed to be back in my bedroom and when I looked up, I saw the numbers 1883 and gold lines throughout my room. I received a message then, "*this is another reason it is so busy here in this vortex! You are emotionally clearing now. You will continue your earth journey in joy it is time! We are going to help your friend Charles with our care. We have spoken and you will remember all this each time you feel as you say, down! We have*

351

much to do yet and you can remember that we are working on Charles. Your journey continues your health is good we have adjusted many things for you in thy body to go on in good health and thy son David. His eyes are next to complete! We are not done yet tonight our visit will be for the next 7 days- much to do yet helping the three of you, ETs".

How wonderful! Our universal family is so good to us and what excellent news, this explains the extra tiredness we both were having. We seemed to need more energy lately for our trips and experiences and now we have been given good health with more stamina. I was relieved to know the work being done with Charles (a dear friend) and their help to us was for the next 7 days! Soon I was shown an experience of a very happy time with my ET friends. I was on a certain craft and taken to look at the cutest babies, they had extraordinary beautiful eyes, and I commented on how proud one of the dads was that was also onboard! I was told, *"These were super intelligent babies and to look closely and deeply into their eyes and to KNOW two of these babies were my future family to come!!"* I was extremely happy, proud and somewhat overwhelmed with this news, all these babies were new *Hybrids!*

Sometimes I speak of these special babies who are already on earth with more of them to come; they have been arriving to help us now and when a new future world of change comes to a loving, positive one without war and hate. They are extremely important leading the way with us and others like us, who will be helping mankind now and in the future. The world now has *hope* with the Hybrid children and those who have already entered our planet in the last many years. This is not something new!

The computer popped on the next day with information about my remodeling job on my bedroom which surprised me! *"We love our VORTEX colors"*, and this is all it said. I was very pleased they did! I had no idea why I painted my room a beautiful soft sage green, but I wanted this color more than any other one and loved it, now I know why I was so drawn to it. It was now the month of June the 20[th,] at 5:30 pm the ETs came to give us information.

"Yes, my child, you have been programmed long-ago and reprogrammed since, also, realigned many times due to the atom

molecular reassembly (going in and out of your physical body) you and your offspring are from Veron, you both agreed to come to earth as experiments. You both know now you travel freely between our galaxies with us your universal family. There are others as you over the globe that will use your knowledge and superior intelligence to help mankind and earth. Things are changing rapidly for a better turn but the "witches" (their term used for bad people) must be stopped before they destroy earth! Ruth Montgomery (a famous reader from the 1960' s) will now work with the rest of you and Arthur Ford will advise and help all he can".

How very honored we were, I admire both Ruth Montgomery and Arthur Ford for the amazing work they did while on earth! I was not familiar with them much or their books until this message arrived and I began gathering information on them after the message. It turns out they were wonderfully gifted clairvoyants' way ahead of their time. Ruth was very psychic and did many readings for one of our Presidents, he valued her opinions the most of any other person and believed in her work highly. He would have her come to the White House in *secret* at night to ask her certain important questions for her advice to help make his decisions for our country, and her information was always correct! I was excited to know these two wonderful gifted people would be joining us, this may be hard to grasp but it happened! There are many working with us on our missions who help us from time to time.

In case you are not familiar with the term *"Linear and Ley Lines"* they are invisible lines which cross the world to certain sacred places and arrangements of ancient sacred sites. It is a sacred geography this being Linear arrangements of these ancient sites. *Ley lines* are places of significance, spiritual and mystical alignments. These invisible lines are great sources of power and energy connecting ancient sacred sites over our world, although this cannot be proved by humans. Examples would be the *Linear and Ley Lines* across the world that cross to certain ancient sites such as Stonehenge, Machu Picchu, The Pyramids, Holy Sites, and points of mystery that have been discovered by man who still search for answers, *who built these ancient sites, how were they built, what is their true purpose and why were they built?* These sites are something that cannot be built even with today's technology which has been proven. These are the same lines that run through my home I was told by the ETs. The same night another message came about their visit to us.

*"We shall come tonight and make the needed repairs to you and David. The travel will repair health problems that exist now, also his eyes and his health is nearly complete! Please try to meditate more all comes faster and easier. The implants have been with you both a long period of earth time now. Thy earth parents called Mom and Dad help you and your healers who work here with your guides, teachers, and highly developed souls. Your books will help others to know the real **truth!** A move comes soon for you and this VORTEX home will always belong with you, there is one coming that remembers you and has a higher knowledge then any yet to meet. He knows he is one of us he will know you belong with us. Know much information needs to go out in this new book end of this year we help to get it out and your galactic name is "Ablatron" the way it is said will come to you later do not worry now. Your feet and blood needs attention the molecules are fine. Tonight, meditate we do the rest we give you the memories you ask for. You and your son are so loved, and accepted people love you get ready now for excitement on your venture!"* At this time Edgar and Gertrude joined in, *"Myself, Gertrude, Zolar (one of my teachers) and the others who help you both are proud and happy, proud of the advanced stages of learning with knowledge! You two have passed all tests in your MATERIAL world a great step forward you have taken together! All of us, The Great Council, ETs, Guardians, Angels, Archangels, loved ones, Your Teachers, Guides and many of us here"* ...

What a grand and unbelievable honor, we were amazed, humbled, and full of happiness! Is this all real, we questioned one another? We had done a good job, and this is all we wanted to do was good work we felt like a zillion! This was something so precious I can't explain it! Even though we needed more healing energy we felt great and I was grateful to have the extra energy to travel. I would leave in the next few days for a workshop in a large city where I was proud to be selected to represent Heartland Services where we do Reiki on the Aids people there. I was honored to be selected to represent them and explain what we do with Reiki energy, and how important the Aids epidemic is around the world, so others pay attention to how serious it is with this disease spreading everywhere. My son and I felt this were an honor to be doing, if we could help one person live longer it was worth everything. This important part of our work with Aids patients comes from our heart and soul through our promise. These people are not to be forgotten by suffering from a disease!

When I was back at home the computer was waiting with a new message: *"A huge change comes soon in a good and positive way"*. I was delighted, and suddenly wanted some coffee which seemed strange, but I could sit and relax for a while and think. After I drank two cups, I poured the rest out and a *dime* fell out of the container of coffee! There had not been one in it when I filled the glass container; the date on the dime was 1995, this gave me a good clue! I knew my mother was with me since she died in 1995! Things happened daily with our sweet spirit family and friends from time to time, and many loved ones only David and I could see and hear. Speaking of my mother and the dime that same day my son wanted to go to his grandparents' home he lived in now, so we took the short drive there. Getting out of my car he saw a heart shaped *cake pan* lying in the grass only my mom had one like this, she made dad a Valentine cake every year for his birthday! There wouldn't be a cake pan in the yard anyway; it should have been in the house put away where it had been this was a sign from mom. After I left David there, I expected to hear more from my parents and sure enough that evening I began to hear their favorite song *"It Had to Be You"* and I don't even have the song. It seemed the music was flowing throughout the house and I was certain it was the two of them. We knew they were with us, it's like we tell others, *"watch for the signs don't try to justify everything the signs are there for you* from *your past over loved ones and others"*.

I awoke at midnight by the light coming on in my office next to my bedroom and bathroom. Checking there was a fancy folded towel beside my sink but not the one I had there before, so I knew the folding lady spirit who resides here who goes back and forth was cleaning again! Since there is no time in the other worlds she shows up at different times, this is the busiest house it's like *"Grand Central Station"*.

The Dolphins and Porpoises

I was given the next information not knowing the reason until the other side soon told me it is very important for the world to know! When you read it, I hope it makes a big difference in your life. The universal message below is for everyone!

The Dolphins are a great species more than humans can ever begin to understand! They are Lights from the Universal Truth and for so long they have been trying to express intelligence with tones of sound. Remember the study of tones of sound when one is truly in touch with universal truth then they may hear the tones of truth this is the greater part of the Dolphins and Porpoise they both equal in a greater intelligence. Do not humans understand yet of this value? It does not seem that many do, both species give wholehearted love to your world to teach these values in a newer form of understanding. If one listens and remains quiet beside these beautiful creatures and face their greater truth of LOVE, they will indeed experience this great intelligence that passes love to them! It is if most Earth people wear blinders to NOT accept the beauty of love, they are gentle giants with amazing minds their intelligence is beyond any earthling! They have devoted their love to a great and glorious mission which brings the message loud and clear "LOVE ONE ANOTHER"! Do not destroy life for selfish reasons or any means! Be kind, use respect, help one another, our mission is not hard it is out of LOVE for mankind, be as a child laugh, and love, enjoy life, and be good to one another! This is what we bring to you all this is our mission. Try to love as we love the earth people, forgive as we forgive those who kill us, maim us, hurt us, learn and respect all living creatures then your world will change, and the people will return as it was so long ago to a higher spiritual plane in our universe! Thank you; we are honored to pass this on to all of you who read this! Ask one another, Will you still love me if I am up or down? Will you?

How powerful, I was amazed with the total beauty, love, and intention of their message, I hope it hits your heart and soul when you read their words, each one of you! These beautiful spiritual creatures are of a supreme intelligence, knowledge and love! How could anyone *not* love them!

Soon I was on a new journey to meet a wonderful man who would be searching, he was sent to me and is intuitive. He had been a pilot through his service years who I will call Dick, we met when he came to see me with a friend of mine. After we were introduced, he said, *"he read my book and it was on a high level of information about UFOs and he had experienced some things left unsaid while in his service career."* It was nice to meet someone who understood our work and then he told of his meeting different Beings! That evening after he left us a message arrived for my son and me: *"Your need is direction with your own free will and your kind heart takes you down the right path. Your words come naturally let it be. You should know that your new friend will be an asset to you in your work and your life. Go have fun, be you, for you are loved for who you are, not to stress anymore. Energy comes from within do not fear the new; enjoy all that is being brought into your life all you ask for you shall receive. Go now in peace and love one another, love, from the beings of Light, we love you both."*

This was amazing, we read this message over and over, it lifted our spirits and cleared our minds we felt good and free! I knew then my new friend Dick and I would become great friends since we had *liked minds* and lives to share. It's not easy to find people to have had these kinds of experiences, it is rare and exciting to meet again!

The next week more information arrived *"The new one is on a new level of understanding. The indication of the awakening of the soul to the universal travel is to be aware of it now, soon he will progress to feeling the presence much stronger with the flashes of light as you have done at one time. You will remember seeing one another on a trip soon in astral travel as you say there you both have much work to do yet and can help one another. Your new friends guide works closely with him, tell him the name is Marvin which means Markusum. It is simpler to use the name Marvin and you both worked with Cayce long ago together Dick was in high authority in those days even before Atlantis. You, he, and the others survived the break-up of Atlantis as did Edgar Cayce. There was a great event in the skies, the universe; it was a touching time for all the huge power source became too much to harness mistakes were made and it was too late! You survivors' made it to safety and led the people into*

357

new locations. There were times in India and other places in this life you were to come back together for many reasons to help one another. Your new friend has been a leader many times in his work the Suez Canal was another important work; Greece was also another period he lived in and was the war period Helen of Troy! Tell him these things for now and let it come naturally as we have told you. We love you all".

I delivered these amazing messages and about *Marvin* as I was told too. He was happy to receive the information and ready to "spread his wings". It seemed to me this year was going at a much faster speed as if the world had evolved into a new revelation, it had! Time was not a 24 hour a day anymore it had reduced to fewer-hours per day, this is what people noticed and would comment, "how fast time goes by". My new friend and I became best friends even with the many miles between us, so our visits were few, but it was like a breath of fresh air to share our worlds. No matter if I could never explain my worlds to the non-believers, I knew Dick was one who understood.

We Are Universal Soul Stars

Today was the end of September, my son and I both knew *The High Council* would be coming tonight! As usual, we would be anxious to see them in our happiness and excitement to greet them; they would wake me when they arrived so for now, I fell into a deep sleep. It seemed to me the ETs were here in only minutes when they woke me at 1:30 am. The first thing I remember after opening my eyes was the most beautiful explosion of *star bursts!* The room was exquisite, looking like a night sky filled with them! I sketched this quickly in my notebook then my total attention went to the ETs who were showing me other *star shaped lights,* which were going into my *solar plexus* a couple of inches above the *belly button!* I was told *"those were Soul Star* Beings *of Light."* I was mesmerized and lying very still with everything going on as other ETs gathered around me. One in high authority told me, *"They are called soul stars which are the core of our very being!"* I felt happiness as if I was hypnotized, they were showing me how we really are, how we really look in light which is breathless, and beautiful, can you imagine this!!

Suddenly, I heard children laughing and at first, I did not see them, but felt they were *Soul Stars* who had begun to circle over head with more laughing. I felt tremendous love for them with the joy they gave me, this was *BEAUTIFUL!* Whatever was taking place I was aware of hands, *hands shaking hands* and was told, *"this was an important confirmation, a meeting to be between us all, we were being congratulated! And this meant we were right on track and they had come with love and congratulations!"* This was a tremendous honor to be a part of what a phenomenal experience, and I couldn't make a sound! What seemed a short time, I knew they had completed presenting their gift of *Soul Stars.* I had mine inside of me forever as I knew David did. I had watched them when they entered mine into my *solar plexus* area; and they told me, *"this is how we are defined in the heavens;"* I was so happy I couldn't calm down I couldn't wait to ask David what he remembered about this special congratulations we both had experienced! The next day we were still thrilled, and my son told me he also experienced his room *full of hearts* and was looking into a vortex with the ETs. Then he was told, *"this represented how loved he is universally!"* Wow! I am so proud of how we chose this life to teach others of love and compassion and to teach many truths on earth. Even though I did not see him with me and the *Soul Stars* he was there, and then in *astral travel* with the ETs who arranged for him to be honored with the same experience at the same time as mine! How would we keep our universal life hidden much longer, I sometimes wondered, but it didn't matter now we were to keep teaching?

It was November 22nd, President Kennedy's anniversary of 40 years ago when he died. That early am I was awakened by a noise, rising I could see the clock's hands were on 2 am. To my right was the spirit of my late best friend Denise, a loved one to my son and me she was standing beside my bed and told me, *"to look outside of the tower window, look out of the window!"* She was excitedly speaking, meaning to "look now!" I jumped up to see what she was so urgent about! In the night sky was a large flock of snow-white Geese glittering with silver, each one was glowing in the *brightest sparkling white light!* I am not sure how geese look normally but I do know they are not *GLOWING brightly in sparkling light!* The geese were very loud making such noises, but I was glued there watching in amazement until the last one was gone! This was something I had never seen before and may never see again, they were not from this world gorgeous, and beautiful! Denise read my thoughts, *"They are not from your world!"* she told me smiling, and I realized she had arranged this as a gift to me and in that instant, she was gone! I would never forget this extraordinary happening, their beauty had been astounding, what a wonderful gift she had brought to me! I began to carefully ask others (friends) if they knew of geese flying and honking loudly after midnight around the early hours of 2 am? The answers were, *"a goose doesn't fly at am or at nighttime"* I did not dare tell anyone they were glowing in sparkling white light, in fact, I didn't explain any details. I knew what I had seen wasn't a natural occurrence this was a beautiful special gift Denise brought to me. She knew I would be overjoyed to see her in this phenomenal way, and to experience this storybook night she arranged! I am overjoyed to know she is one of our protectors, an angel guide to us, this is what we were told by heavenly beings!

ET Travel, Worm Holes, and Controlling Wake-up Times.

My son and I have mostly experienced the ETs at the same time together, so it is not that unusual to see their familiar lights shining brightly coming in our different bedroom windows, then running to make sure the other one was awake, or to get them up! One night we gathered at the tower window early since we knew they were coming and just like that in the next moment we were entering a UFO! David was urgent, *"come on, come on mom"*, when I stepped inside to where he had been taken, it was strange because I was moving in *slow motion*! I was changing into energy for travel and what a sensation this is it doesn't hurt; it is an exchange.

A narrow beam of light fell on us quickly and we felt a strong pull of being drawn down a tube to another level through this light, then back out of it, this is the only way to explain it. We were looking at dials; all kind of them on a surface/panel with other types of design controls which were familiar. The main ET nearby pointed to one instrument which looked like a computer of some kind. We have seen these often and he was giving me instructions, *"touch on your right-hand right above the thumb to be awake"*. This was important, so I did as he showed me, and woke up *back in my body.* Then he said, *"Dial symbols to here"* where certain marks were along with the meanings of the marks. The next symbol looked like another computer to us, the ET said, *"These symbols all mean something on how to build this kind of computer they all mean something"* he told us we were being *"programmed"* and would never be able to give this information to any earthling. I felt our memory would be removed until they needed us to use it. It was fascinating to learn from them, and importantly I could see our real identity of who we are, wow! we could never deny it even to ourselves, and it did not matter! These things being shown to us we knew of and had helped to build, these memories where inside of us yet.

The lesson David was being given by the ETs was to let him see lights in certain rocks, in certain locations on Earth they told him, *"no one else can see them."* My son described them as looking like a *snowflake* shape only the lights in them are red in color and we knew these to be an exact *match-up* to the snowflake symbol on the UFO panel. The ET continued, *"If we talk of this there will be a male figure who thinks we are crazy so much will be going on someone will try to stop us, they won't be able to. They will see at the END when the Laser is built then we will show them a UFO".* There was still time when they gave us this information, we knew the Laser beam would push them back into orbit or they will go into the sun! They told us, "We both will be able to help build the Laser"; our thought was, we wondered how this would happen! They had us put their symbols on the wall I was putting X's and moving from X to X where they told me too, then I drew an Alien, a man and a woman in the middle of the Laser beam! This is all the further I can tell for now. I do know these ETs were different than some others being extremely powerful *"high up"* ones. They each wore a type of uniform and were good with teaching us, then I noticed other ETs on the ship wore the same uniforms as well. What an enlightening experience! I am positive they are old comrades of ours from the Universal Galactic Council... who we are also from, among many others.

I am jumping ahead to January 2004 to tell this experience. We were waiting for our universal family, the ETs who were coming that night expecting *The Highest of the Council* and when the meeting began, the leader spoke first. As he did, I watched him closely he *is mesmerizing* being the purest *of light,* and after he spoke, he transcribed his message to me below.

Bow down child so I may bless you as I do so often when you come before me. I delight in your natural love and compassion. Let nothing stand in your way-go child out into this earth world you live in and tell your story to all who listen. You are about to embark on your new book you are thirsty to begin soon you will be helped all the way. Albert Einstein and thy son David, Leo, and all of us there will help you. Rest all you need then begin but remember to keep the balance in life-have fun, laugh often, and enjoy each day. You are beginning to finally make your steps start forward again. You have needed the rest and healing of your spirit, mind and body it is fine. We shall meet again very soon-did you miss your sign? We will give you another everything is in order you are right on track! We love you, all of us.

I was very excited and humbled with his beautiful words which moved me forward in my new mission! What a precious meeting we had with them on this special night with our universal beings! We have a great responsibly to do our best we have taken into our soul, how precious this important visit was, our lives were evolving like a dream come true! This high Being is of pure love and the ETs always take the best care of us; they love us as we do them! After this, I felt I would be much stronger now with new energy I was charged up, completely uplifted by this Heavenly Being! This is part of why he held this meeting, our feelings and struggle living in this world is understood. I had to clear my head I realize how wonderful our lives are with our choices. At times I would be told, to stand in the tower to receive the energy I needed. And later more powerful words were given to lift my spirit even more, if this were possible!!

Child, you are right back on track we are very proud you have desperately needed this extra time for yourself! Soon the new work begins you will be better able and sharper to detect negative ones around you; they are the dark ones everywhere! You and thy son have had several lessons of the dark ones so look around you and be on guard, be aware! We are guiding you both on your missions, your next and final steps, first is the books they are so important to mankind then other missions come which are very important! The final steps do not mean death you will live and love in joy for your earth years yet. Stop any worry which brings you down, since a child you were made fun of look at those others now most are old and tired with no real purpose in their lives so SHAPE UP as your language says, be happy! You found mothers sign today you asked for one and she gave it to you. She hung her picture on your robe so you and David would find it! She and your father are full of funny tricks. We shall help transform your love for thyself into a daily, positive view; learn to love thyself as you do others. Don't forget February 24th. We all love thee".

I was extremely happy and refreshed, feeling renewed and good! Sometimes in the work we do I have felt futile knowing our work is so different than an *earth* person's because most people have not been taught these things of space and other life forms, and how could they with all the fearful beliefs. This is unfortunately a world with many powerful people who help to create fear which spreads like wildfire and makes it a hard existence for one to learn their own truth. Mankind may learn one day but how far will man go first? Will man ever let go of his hunger for money, greed, wars. and destroying? *This world is a monitoring system to see how far mankind will go before it is destroyed, so far man never learns, it only gets worse. The ETs are sad to watch how humankind never learns and only gets worse with the destruction of our planet.*

We began teaching of universal truth to who we were pulled to it was a joy and when around those who disbelieved we wore our *invisible shield.* Our challenge was to let go of worries and not be concerned *what others think* this had been a part of the journey (our human thinking) because of old ways drilled into us since children and in time we had left it behind. We both would go on knowing we will always keep our promise to the Creator, this is the goal.

It wasn't long when my *back-up,* beloved Denise, came to give me a visit, *"I am here for you sister"* then we greeted one another. She looks so healthy, young, more beautiful and then ever in spirit. I can still smell her freshness the same as I did the last time when I saw her after classes when we talked of a visit soon. I seemed to know on that last evening she would not be here much longer on this earth and I wanted to remember her always. Bringing me out of those thoughts Denise said, *"We are going to journey now I see you found your sign from your mother"* meaning the picture my mother had put on my robe to surprise me, then she laughed from joy... After this, I have no memory of the trip we took together.

A new message arrived: *"The ETs who work with you both will begin to supply you with whatever you need, there will be much information (let you remember more soon) use it wisely for the book, not letting others see until the right time. You know the few you can trust, and Angel Bev can help you in many ways. You will be energized again tonight my child. Take a right turn: meaning you are ready for your new life! Taking a right turn is always right; this is our way for you to understand us. You will travel tonight write it all down, sister Denise is here with you and thy son. You both needed rests so use it wisely! The place you are concerned with has the tracking devises; they were inserted for reasons due to your injury in November. An adjustment will be made to you, enjoy your journey, we love you both! Tell thy son, he knows... All of us."*

Why was I surprised sweet Denise was in on this, she was helping to get me ready? The information above is beautiful and exact with their concern of keeping our energy levels up and both of us in good health. They make sure how our bodies are always doing, how blessed we are. Sometimes I gave tremendous amounts of thought to how in the world could I fit our work and our strange lives into books? If I had not kept my transcribed, recorded notebooks of experiences with our many universal loved ones and continuous messages over my life I would be sunk to remember them all! We were given a very stable mind, or we would not succeed. From birth up to this time we looked forward to everything received from our universal families and other Worlds, and we love our chosen paths, that's affirmative! I thank them every day for their information they want written in the books, and everything they do to help us go on.

David was so excited one morning wanting to tell me something special, *"He had had a beautiful vision state. He was in his bedroom and birds were everywhere they would fly out of his closets around the room but when he looked inside the closets nothing was there! The birds flying were colorful parrots and two white Doves, he knew the Doves is our symbols and the parrot represented talking. He said, a window needed to be opened to let the birds out or they would die, they had to be let go! This was to tell him, "we can't be locked up and afraid to tell our truths and our lessons to others so they too may learn, we can't shut ourselves away from our work". This message meant, "we knew our time was to begin now with sharing our work to help others learn and to not be afraid of who we are, or we would quit living, we had felt locked up by always living in secret! Yes, things must change through the books to reveal the knowledge we were given".*

I thought this message was amazing I wanted to cry, we did feel like birds locked away! Now we would be freed!!

The High Council and Archangel Gabriel Arrive!

Before I begin with the next message delivered directly from Archangel Gabriel to our friend McGuire, I cannot give our chosen universal names yet and will be using the initial S. as mine and J. for David.

Gabriel's message said: *"Yes child, we are here you have questions for us? What is it you wish to know about McGuire and thyself I will tell you the answer's now? It was written long ago in the pattern of thy works on the earth plane for yourself and McGuire to come together at this time, in your time, to work on a new level than previously do you understand yet?* No, I replied, I was not sure of this yet. *You will give him ET information and be as his teacher the channeling will confirm all of this, I promise you as Gabe, (Archangel Gabriel) I speak the truth you know me well dear child.*

McGuire searches far and wide and it is within himself, but the search is mighty and to meet those known before. Tell McGuire that Gabe sends his love and surrounds him with the protective light on all four sides and eternally. That the reader neglects to pass these words until now, she did not understand these words as they were hidden until the time was right. As thy Savior was born upon this earth, he suffered for all of you, not only to prove of life after so called death, but for many other reasons. The only truth, the real truth, lies in the stars, the universe! The words to remember are "S and J" they come to help you. The mission all of you have journeyed on is mighty, be proud, enjoy the earth time as it goes rapidly. You McGuire are a wonderful light to this world and let there be light means so much to the three of you, S, J, and McGuire.

The ETs are highly evolved, divine in Creation and have your permission in thy contract long ago. The engineering work you have done long ago has-been erased from thy mind a little comes at a time. In all fairness with your questions it will come in time.

You will soon recall parts of an encounter I will be at your side. Do not have concern this is a learning to remember what you have known before. Your eyes will soon clear up the implant is safe - you chose, and it was time for the universe has awaited this part of your journey. You will get confirmations everywhere you look and hear, there will be information of thy universal families, and others close to you it is all good! Reap the rewards, go forward as you want to its inside of you! Work on the project and soon it will be completed your spiritual project you will understand more.

S and J understand they are with us; the mission is only good and positive. There are mysteries to uncover in your world; S and J hold the KEY! All of you work together and shall experience many good things. Tell Bernie not to worry all will be fine! More contact later dear one in love eternal, Gabe".

There is information to explain here about the above message to McGuire we three know Archangel Gabriel is McGuire's teacher, we also know only McGuire knows Archangel Gabriel as Gabe, in this way he knew the message for him to be true, and the message was very clear to the three of us. What an exciting message to get from an Archangel!! We had work to complete on another level now and we were anxious to get started!

I called McGuire the next morning to talk with him about the message and our future work together, and the funny thing is our work together is a *repeat!* Yes, this was repeating what we three knew before in other lives and accomplished in the past! I was told after my call to McGuire I was to tell him more, and this was the next information for him below.

Tell McGuire we are here. In all creation there lies the unseen truth to so many things; they remain blind to these things. As you have been guided through your journey earth life, a decision was made and kept from before you came to earth. To serve and help mankind with your knowledge and wisdom, to explore, learn, and teach others- we are proud! The Father-Universal Being of the Light commends you! Go forth; continue thy works on your search you have met those you were connected with before! The ETs have been working with you since eons ago. We know above all you have contact in-directly; you are ready to begin to remember where you come from. Help is near for you and Gabriel (Gabe) will help you. Don't despair that it comes not fast enough, the HUMAN mind cannot process too fast... The confirmations will start coming to you in the channeling from these connections from Ruth Ann and David known as S. and J. We will talk later, love eternally Gabe.

Isn't this message amazing it explains so much, Archangel Gabriel helps McGuire and both of us on our repeated missions and chosen plans for specific reasons in each lifetime. There is the group of 3's once more! Life was very busy for us and we accepted it with grace.

I was still teaching school at this time and asked my class to do Reiki energy healing with us together on a man with prostrate problems. I knew this would be a tremendous amount of good, positive energy going into the man's physical body... I could see there were many evolved Beings of the Christ Light who were with us, but transparent to the students who wanted to help the man. I became completely stunned when I saw *"JESUS CHRIST"* at the foot of the table where the man was lying as I worked at the head of him! *JESUS* in his light alone took my breath away; he had come to bring his love and healing! In these glorious times I cannot tell others he is present. The man had went into a deep sleep as we sent energy to him and when we finished I woke him, he immediately said, *"he had felt strange sensations in his arms and legs", and seemed to be happy and relaxed and told us he enjoyed the session very much!"* I wanted to tell him who I saw at his feet, but he wasn't to know yet, he was still explaining how wonderful he felt! I was overwhelmed with his honesty and his love, I felt positive he had renewed hope. When I have seen *JESUS* appear in our work before, the sick person heals quickly and lives longer than is normal for the illness they have. I was told, to tell the man in private before he left, he had had

367

a *miracle healing,* he smiled so big and he was fine from then on for some time.

That evening coming home we had an ET *escort* watching over us all the way, I was always grateful for this and it happened on nearly every trip we took! In my next class we worked on a woman who was in turmoil with personal problems of her own suffering from abuse. I instructed the class we would work on her mental, physical, spiritual and emotional aspects. Immediately after we started, I saw her *"Native American Shaman who is her Guide"* helping us as he worked with his knowledge of healing through his movements and chants, he had also been a medicine man in life. The students and the woman would never see her Guide, but we were aware knowing her Shaman was there to help her, and the lady had excellent results. Everyone doesn't have immediate healings by any means it is whatever is given to help the patient, everyone Is different. Reiki is NEVER to be used to replace a doctor, it is a spiritual energy, and both can go hand in hand perfectly with medical.

This made me think back to 2003 when I recalled a vision I had when my son told me, *"he was so tired and wanted to go home"* (meaning pass over). He had been very ill for many years by then and I responded as a mother would, *"Oh David, what would I do without you? I wouldn't care about life only about our loving family who I could not leave to be with you"*. He replied, *"he would stay with us longer"*. I could see he needed to tell me this. Years later after he crossed over, I realized this is the way he chose to tell me he felt he worried the family being sick and we felt so blessed to have him as long as possible! He came in a vision because it was too hard for him to tell me in person. He wanted to go back to our loving universal existence, but he could not say this except in this way, this is because we are so bonded together. I could not imagine him not here with us it was so painful! How long and hard he must have suffered staying past his time for many more years because he loved us all so much! In those years he enjoyed his home longer and family he loved and helped many others. I felt guilty when I was reminded of this time when reading of his vision in my notebook. I try to put this in the back of my mind because I know he truly understood my response; he would have said the exact same thing if it would have been me. He wanted to live...

David said, *"we would never part we would always stay together in life and spirit and we always have. Our work has always been done together since the beginning of our Creation and on down the line of past lives"*. Our beloved family stays together evolving like many, many others do, but most don't think this way, or ever know this truth that we have choices. This knowledge is held back since the beginning to keep power over the people. Since that time, I sometimes let people know we need to let our loved ones go, let them know it's ok, and that we will be ok, they need to know we will continue without guilt. Please don't hold them here to suffer for you when they want to go. We are thinking of our own hurt *of what will we do without them.* David had different times to leave but stayed by the grace of the Creator of Light continuing his magnificent works until he left in 2008, and then it was his time. We each have different times to leave when the soul is ready.

Going back now the next Sunday the Higher Beings returned talking to me about *Reiki certificates.* I could see myself handing them out to my students. They also talked of healing and love to give to others and by teaching the students they will pass loving healings onto others, and Reiki will continue in the *correct ancient way.* Later, I went to bed but was not asleep, looking to the tower area I was being shown clocks, all sizes, and a smiling face who was Edgar's! He was showing me I had *time* to do the things I am here to do; knowing I became uncertain at times if I would live long enough to get everything done, I promised. The next thing I knew we were on a large UFO, a *Mother* ship I was among several humans in a group waiting for someone to arrive. Suddenly, we heard loud crashing noises close by and to our surprise the noise was coming from a huge mechanical *creation* like a Robot! It had fallen to a lower level from higher one and then it popped back up to the level we stood on, we were shaken to see this huge *monster* looking machine! I have no memory to the rest of the trip it was blanked out, and I woke up back in bed safe and sound! I asked David that morning if he remembered seeing those huge mechanical looking Robot soldiers. We knew there are wars and fighting in the universes we have been told of these by ET Beings and they say, *"There have always been these wars"*. Perhaps these machines were soldiers as I described them being. David said, *"the one he saw was*

369

as big as a house!" This alone, by their size let us know we were on a huge *Mother Ship* to have them on board…

After this trip our friend McGuire called to tell me of a strange experience that happened to him at his hunting cabin. In the middle of the night he awoke instantly right at 5 am, explaining, *"he doesn't generally do this since he is not a morning person".* Somehow, he was compelled to go outside and investigate the night sky. He could see some extremely bright objects with twinkling bright lights formed in the shape of an arrow! He went in to get his camera and hurried back outside to take pictures, but they were gone! He remembered I had said, *"he would soon have an experience with the ETs, and they would let him remember it".* After the conversation I was to tell him, *"he now had the locator chip in him".* McGuire replied, *"that in all of his life he has NEVER seen anything like that before, and he is a student of the stars and universe!"* I asked for a confirmation about what had happened to McGuire the next day (this was in November) and our universal friends answered, *"McGuire had definitely experienced what he did with the ETs and he had a locator chip implanted in him".* There was the confirmation.

The following day I found a huge yellow rose on a red rose bush I have which wasn't there the day before, and it was becoming wintertime! I don't know how to explain how they do these things, but it was meant as a beautiful gesture of love, perhaps even a gift. The next evening, I was *astral traveling* talking to a spiritual teacher about *mind over matter,* and how it can help tremendously keeping our body and mind functions healthy. I came out of the vision to see *a blaze of silver sparkles from the ceiling down to my bed reminding me of the fairy tale movie of Peter Pan!* I don't question everything, so I didn't ask for answers, but it was extraordinary! Maybe it was leading up to another special night late in November when I was suddenly transported into the past of Bible days. The first thing I remember seeing was a donkey in a village, and then a valley where I heard words, *"I need to reach the valley".* Immediately after I could see the written words, *Jesus Christ!* The next moment I was fighting the negative ones! The meaning of this meant, *"I would fight anything for my belief in Christ; no one could ever take this away from us!"* A mere dream is not real as a vision and when I astral travel or do remote viewing I know which it is. I had traveled back to those Bible times!

What came to me weeks later was a continued part of those days. A Heavenly Being said to me; *"Kneel Child so we may speak. You have nothing to fear we are taking care of the matter. Some people's lessons come for their growth, so child put your cares and thoughts to rest your confirmations were given by thy son David. You are coming out of the visit now we shall meet again. ETs come tonight for you to remember the information. We are always with you my beloved one we love you both. Edgar and Gertrude send their devoted love to you and thy son, we love you, all of us".*

These messages are priceless, and I use to question, "who will understand" and our teachers quickly answered, *"true believers!"*

I soon found my son was run down again and the ETs came to realign our bodies and to tell us, *"We are doing well but, you both need this sometimes it helps settle the emotions you both carries. Earthly steps are hard but steppingstones to higher levels. The great healers are honored as you both are to work together! It is all coming together little bird, we love you both".* This lifted our spirits tremendously!

A new year arrived with a new beginning, and amazing messages arrived that late evening before I turned in for the night: *"My child, do you not feel more strength? You are reaching within and this is powerful! You are a giant in your work! To believe in one's self is a great lesson on the journey you are doing we help all we can. Be good and kind to yourself thy sister Denise is helping you and others. Mother and Father come tonight with the ETs be ready to journey. If it is to be you will remember, you will receive much for the book, we love you my child".* In a while I found another small note under the one above: *"Let it be known to you S. (me) you have nothing to fear! We all love you dearly".* How precious!

It was still winter and cold outside when I had an experience with one of my children and the ETs. In universal travels together one of my daughters and I were inside a large place like a Cathedral where other people had a glass of water to drink. I remembered passing a full glass to those around us. My loved one smiled at me and said, *"They took me to see my grave and it didn't bother me at all somehow I was really happy, and I know it had meaning."* Next, I

371

was feeding a wild Wolf, it was hungry, and I felt sorry for it needing the nourishment. This beautiful lesson I would remember, it meant, *"that no matter how the person is I am to work with and may be as a wolf who others often shun, to always do my best. Their spirit is hungry for the truth"*. How beautiful, I would forever remember this; I am naturally drawn to those who need help. Then I returned to this world with others to return home. The story behind the wolf makes perfect sense, it is about feeding the spirit goodness and love, and to pass it onto those who need to be *FED!*

My son and I received a double message from my late mom and dad and a special spiritual friend and teacher: *"Ruth Ann, all will be fine, daddy and I are close to you and David. The flowers are for you sharing all our love, Mom and Daddy...P.S. "Let it go and trust the universe from, John Paxton".* John is one of my spirit teachers. Thank you, John *I love you,* I called out to all of them!

Sunday was another exciting day, first thing that night I saw a square grid, so I knew I was on board a UFO looking out of something like a window at another planet out in space. I tried to say the word *out there* dragging it out in slow motion which seemed funny to me. A very tall ET was with me in a long robe I knew him as a High Council Being, *"COME"* he said pointing to a doorway. He had no hair and amazing gentle eyes, he also held high authority, and when I looked down, I saw layers of what looked like metal walkways going around in circles to deep inside of the UFO like a huge coliseum. Then the Being let me know why I was there, *"You are being programmed to remember more now for the book as you asked. Don't be afraid that is the KEY my love we are your friend and your family, your Universal family. You S. and your son J. (David) are one of us. You feel your home yet in bed, but you are not. We let you experience things like that to not have fear."*

I felt great love for this Being and our Universal family, and I clearly remember a ceremony of a union like a marriage, but it was something else even more meaningful! I heard a voice say *'UNITED,* then I was shown the *Helix-DNA* and an ET's eyes looking into mine, this was something very sacred to us both. I felt it was like a marriage together only even more spiritual. Nearby was a woman who looked human I had heard her talking, and she had curly hair like my mother and the odd thing is, at the same time I could also see my bedroom but I know I am not there; I am with our ET family! They are showing me how they *"change thoughts and things people see to keep them from fearing them and they can let one see and think they are inside their room still at home believing they are there, only they are with the ETs...* The reasons are many to protect the human mind from becoming hysterical! What happened to me on this trip was very important in my life...It was a loving, touching, important sacred ceremony!

CHAPTER 16

Intergalactic Systems

The ETs returned to confirm, *"You are the student learning and doing well not so much fear anymore opens the needed channels to learn more, good! You did walk on a grid, you remembered; everything will be fine, from the Council. We love you we know how to love. You do very important work there will be time now for rest and play, work and travel, it all comes. Enjoy all being brought forth to you both in your lives there on earth we all have loved. Studies come tomorrow evening. Galactic Systems*

How sweet, they are helping us to realize who we are, and they love us. Our guides and teachers met me in my meditation today with sister Denise. At the beginning I was addressed first with my universal name S. *"Who is of the Universal Intergalactic Systems."* This is who I am, but still I do not have permission to use this one certain universal name, then our message continued.

We are here beloved to caution of any worry to be concerned of all your aspirations' and jobs in the future on earth it will all fall into place. It must be hard on you most days to understand this for you have time now to decipher things in your mind. The healing time is yours make the best of it we are helping restore your illness. Thy sister is here, "Oh, sister dear I love you. I am so busy here I haven't forgotten to come to you! Things are better in my earth home my mother is better since you passed her my readings and messages. They are grateful as I am, I will be there soon I'll see you in your dreams! Love eternal Denise".

The Intergalactic Systems continued, *"We are all here, a man will contact you soon with an opportunity about your book it is a good one. Carefully read any papers to be signed, "Help is on the way".* When I read this familiar ending quote, Edgar Cayce's A.R.E. had sent a magazine to me with this *same quote* on the front, *"Help is on the Way!"* I knew Edgar had arranged this for reasons in his next message.

"Get motivated to start work with the book. You have asked for help and we are here! We will be working for you and with you; Mr.

Albert Einstein gives his services to you with all of us. The promise has been given; you need to meditate every day now this keeps you on track. New things are ahead dear one, new people, places, and things. Keep open to all, of a good and positive nature, love eternal, all of us".

My spirit was high I would finish my work I had lived in my own fear I would not be here long enough to complete it, now I was completely revived and back on track to continue my journey. I had time to do everything I promised, and help from Albert Einstein was back, he was one of our teachers who worked with me when I taught school!! I am truly honored by this sweet soul to help me!

Out on a nice drive one evening I was picked by the ETs along with another friend of mine and during this experience I was telling the person how it works to travel with them. One of the places we went to the Beings looked like an *INSECT* who could easily reverse back to whatever they needed to before, and immediately I heard the name *Mantis*. This is a well-known Species known not be harmful, just the opposite, being only caring and loving, and one of them sent thoughts to me, *"they were some of the teachers to my son and me and they were more than just teachers to us"*. Thinking back, this is what I somehow recalled, then I was thinking of my friend who was shocked when we were first lifted from the car, I remembered saying *this is how it works*...then we went on to have the above experiences. Later I wondered if she would remember any of this or if her memory would be erased, I soon found she had only partial memories of the incident after being taken from the car. The next night I was tired, but I managed to write this down in my notebook then looking at the time it was 5;30 am. After I had gone to sleep more information from the trip flooded in with what I had not recalled earlier I remembered telling my friend, *"she had NO control over our traveling or when it was happening, she couldn't change it"* as we were moving. She was experiencing *her maiden journey*; I was there to sort of break her in to help curb her fear. I hoped she would remember more but not enough to overwhelm her, or I doubted she would want be friends later like my other past friend.

Our next visit with the ETs my son and I were in line with others getting off a craft and I recalled being in one of the corridors of the UFO having an experience. When I raised up to get in line with others, I noticed a small bloody place on me and immediately an ET was present and said, *"I had this injury from my travels, to relax now and go to sleep or to do Reiki on myself and they would heal the rest"*. In a flash I was back home putting antibiotic crème on the injury, which itched like a mosquito bite then quickly fell asleep doing Reiki. The next day I checked the wound and it was hard to see evidence of it ever being there! I called my friend about the journey we had taken together but I she didn't recall what I was talking about her memory had been erased so I dropped it as soon as I had started by changing the conversation.

In the days to come I saw myself in a vision typing away on my book in the family room. My sleeves were rolled up working hard, my future was in front of me! Time was flying by it was the middle of December and my latest experience was being with two beautiful *Star* people, they looked completely human. They were dressed in regular clothing and here on a mission, whatever it was they are not to be afraid of and have superior intelligence, they are positive loving Beings. For centuries and way beyond many of these beings visit places on this planet doing various good works humans would never know of.

The next night it happened again with my friend we were *flying* over farm fields traveling back in time and suddenly we were over Argentina looking down at the crowds of people where we could see *Eva Peron* and hear the music *"Don't Cry for Me Argentina."* She was very beautiful in a white suit, telling the people how much she loved them and the love she had for her country! She stood on a platform in front of thousands, and it was easy to feel her love for them! I could only suppose the ETs were interested in this time of history we were watching because they had experienced this when it happened and wanted to share it knowing I felt strongly connected to *Eva Peron's* genuine love. This had been a huge historical event, a very important one, and I have no doubt the ETs study the reasons of what humans do. They feel and learn from us here as we are doing with them to awaken our memories and for other reasons. This era was an exciting time we were grateful they wanted us to experience this long-ago time with them, it was an extraordinary trip. My friend took this to be her own dream state in her home which was best.

It was nearly Christmas and the phones began to do odd things I was finding them on the floor when I came home, sometimes ringing with no calls coming through or a voice not making sense on the other end. Sometimes my phone was answered when family and friends called with no one there and many times callers told me our phone would be answered by a small child, a little girls voice then nothing. At other times we found recordings on the answering machine in an unknown voice and our indoor and outdoor Christmas lights were mysteriously turned on while we were gone and returning home the house was never more beautiful lighted up! We realized the spirits were having fun, they loved Christmas and the ETs were in on this after all, they had long learned emotions of joking and humor working together.

A friend of mine I seldom get to see lived a few miles away and stopped by one day. She faltered around not knowing how to start her conversation, she spoke of seeing a rainbow of colors and beautiful lights over my house on several occasions at night when she passed by this way, *"the lights were shining down from the sky only above my home!"* I was happy even if she had hesitated to tell me and I thanked her, she told me she felt this was a Holy experience and I agreed; this is what I am certain of and was a very meaningful experience for the both of us and this was a second time.

We were now being educated further of other symbols, and a High-up being was explaining to me, *"the symbols are a version of your English with pictures of what we want you to do by using a high frequency pitch to activate the place on the round disk on our panel, see? To lift you up in your car we would activate the symbol with the picture of a car we can wait in the Craft if we so choose. You are preceding more in your work with ease January will be a big month we will be here; we are here for you! You gave the man today just what you were supposed to, he doesn't need the truth right now he is not ready yet, but soon. You pass the information onto the man in the New Year and month of January the time will be perfect for him. Your friend Bev, your angel will be here for some earth years yet. Relax, we have more to come".*

Another ET joined in with others standing behind him as he pointed to part of a disk, there were numbers on it, David and my birthday dates! He said, *"These signs are important dates, they are working on my subconscious part now, the 8 worlds are in place now in the solar system that is only some of the Galaxy so much you as earthlings do not know. The thing with Mars is that it's right under their nose! We are trying to help your people understand through you and thy son. We can get out the information you asked for so we will help!* I was shown more symbols and I drew them then the being said, *"Well my child, relax a moment and we can go on."* I was aware they were going slow with me this was important information for the higher up's on earth, and it must be the right time to give the information to someone that will listen, right now, who will and who will I trust?

I went into a sleep state to rest, and perhaps to be energized then they began again, *"we will dupe your friend and his thoughts to help him. A BIG change is coming on your antique vessel!"* This meant on my computer screen. Answers were starting to fall together; this was our honor to be such a part of what they needed. I knew they trusted us being one of them, we trusted them the same, each evolution we have been together. It is very important for them to speak through the books I write, they trust the messages will be exactly as they speak them. The ETs know their information will reach those it is meant to! The others may become interested at some point or not, it doesn't matter for non-believers.

An Old Friend from the Other Side

During my research in my 2004 notebooks, I found a short letter to me from an important man I met once in my lifetime. His first name is John a very gifted psychic man; after he crossed over, he came to me as my spiritual teacher and said, *"Dear Ruth Ann, my love, I am here to help you for always. Let me help you with your books I offer my services to you! I am humbled to be of help we have met together in many lives, many times, in many ways. Our lives have always touched in some fashion. I shall lead you as best I can on your new book of the Aliens, we are excited over here of you and your son's work. Both of you are known to us throughout the universes, everywhere. Our meeting was so brief on earth I recognized you but not at first as to who you had been. I know you searched for me in this life as best friends. I will always be with you and at your service to help you both. John."*

This made me so happy we met briefly once before; he was like the two of us being gifted and the same having *"liked minds"*. John died before I could meet with him again in this life. Soon after this I heard from Edgar and Gertrude, *"Yes, beloved Ruth, we have missed you also. We are so busy with many others, with the world's wars, the men, women, and children who need us and to help some in crossing over but we are always with you and David and as your mother and dad say to you, "just call our names and we will be there." The man, who was at your bedside Uncle Leo, helps you very much he is a wise Sage as your other teachers and guides who work to help you, God blesses you both as always, Gertrude and Edgar"*. We welcomed this lovely message how thankful we are achieving our purpose in this world with their help. The next heavenly message arrived for my son's birthday on January 8th.

It has been told by the divine ones that today your birth has been recorded throughout the entire universes for eternity for all to see and honor be proud my son you have completed the journey, the hard part. Now is to be your time to live life in comfort and to still helping others. We all bow to you, always know you are loved and protected from all things. The beings of Christ Light will come tonight on this full moon, be ready. All is well, you see, "Happy Birthday" Son of the Heavens, Universes, and Worlds you travel in and thy loved ones are humbled and honored with your presence. More will come in the night of greatness, importance, love with our blessings, good health with joy, from all of us!

Wow! I was completely overcome as my son was with his *beloved birthday message to be celebrated in the heavens forever!! To be known as Son of the heavens, Universes and Worlds!* David has been highly blessed again in his heartfelt work! His love is stronger than anything for the beloved Infinite Supreme Creator and all Beings everywhere! I am so proud, so proud! My earth mother's birthday followed David's on January 14[th;] and we were very excited knowing mom would do something to celebrate her special day, she always has! We waited until bedtime and nothing had happened so we decided to go to our rooms, we knew she would come in the night for us. The following day we couldn't wait to share our visit with one another! I am not sure when they came but it was not long after we both turned in, I remembered the ETs and both of us being on board a Craft with others and the experience for mother's birthday will seem unreal, but it happened. We watched the most *indescribable beautiful spectacular light show* in space!! Beautiful universal lights in unknown colors were everywhere with my mother's love coming from them; saturating and wrapping us in them! I cannot describe how it is to *feel* colors, but we could, through our heart and spirit because her love was that strong! Lights adorned the universe everywhere we looked and suddenly we were beside water looking upward, I cried out, *"David, Look, look"* as I pointed up at the UFOs! They were everywhere moving at lighting speed shooting out amazing rays of lights; they were nearly a blur there were so many! We were thrilled, then noticed we seemed to be with three others of our family, we were mesmerized! How grateful to mom to share her day with us in this way it was unbelievable, like a phenomenal movie!

I didn't want to go back home from this celebration but in a flash, I was outside in my yard with David, we were just standing there looking up at the half moon and stars!! We were in a trance of happiness never wanting it to end, but suddenly I developed a huge headache! I clearly remembered I wasn't ready to return home but there we were in the yard! Given this amazing celebration of happiness we had been part of would be too impossible to ever describe but I have done my best. I would never forget the UFO ships moving at lightning speed then splitting up into different directions over the water like fireworks, what a glorious birthday my mother had arranged for us! Finally, that night I gave up from exhaustion and we went inside so David could go to bed and for me to get aspirin for my head, we had just experienced something not in our world, and there would be much more to come.

I am sorry to stop here but I must go forward with a second volume because I have much more to share with you. Our experiences have been consistent with multidimensional Extraterrestrial families and higher Christ Light Beings, Councils, Spiritual Teachers, Guides, and loved ones in spirit that teach and work with us in unimaginable love! My hope is, that other people the world over may learn and understand there is information kept hidden from us that exists by those in power in order to keep us under their control. We here are controlled through Media, television, commercials, schools, government, newspapers, phones, computers, even labels of food we consume, and hundreds of other ways, and most people do not know any difference. The Universal Beings want people to live in peace and love on earth, but many people on this planet have lost the important values of faith, respect, kindness, compassion, honor, forgiveness and especially love for others. The negative ones must change in order to save our planet and the people on it, time is getting short.

To be continued...

About the Author

Ruth Ann Friend

Still lives in a small community in the Midwest continuing her work in the Reiki energy healing field for well over 27 years as a Reiki Master/Teacher/Practitioner. Ruth Ann also works as a Medium and Spiritual Adviser to others by passing messages from souls on the other side to their loved ones here on Earth. She was born into this work by choice and gifted with her abilities to work in other realms and worlds, through the true experiences she and her son have experienced over time. She has written her books in order to help those grieving, to know their loved ones are more alive than ever, and to remove manmade fear we are taught.

She is the first who brought and taught Reiki energy healing classes to a college not far from her home. She also teaches universal information and psychic development in her workshops, along with Hypnosis, and is a Reader.

Ruth Ann's first book is, *Under the Rainbow Crossing*, in which she used the pen name of Ann Hart. In 2013, a second revised edition was released under her real name, Ruth Ann Friend. Her first written article was in Guideposts, Angels on Earth, titled, *End of The*

Line. Her second book, *The Story of David,* explains many of the reasons why mother and son came back to our world through their devoted promise to the Creator. This story is of her son's terminal illness with his faith, love, compassion and many miracles which baffled doctors. This latest book, *Aliens Within Our Own Selves* explains their secret life living with certain species of Extraterrestrials' as teachers to them since birth. Everything written is based on true accounts and events which are extremely rare. In this way the Extraterrestrials can speak their words through this book opening a door to what one could never imagine. This incredible story has universal information to educate others and why the universal beings chose them. This evidence is through personal experience, video, pictures, universal script and heavenly teachers. Ruth Ann is a frequent guest on radio talk shows in the US and Hawaii, and as a speaker at UFO Conferences, the latest being for the Navaho and Apache Nation for the 2017 Dulce Base UFO conference in Dulce, New Mexico.

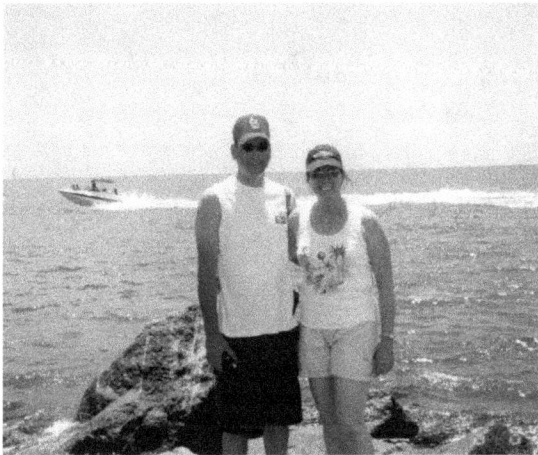

Ruth Ann and her son David

www.ingramcontent.com/pod-product-compliance
Lightning Source LLC
Chambersburg PA
CBHW050449270326
41927CB00009B/1665